Commercial Application Development Using

ORACLE DEVELOPER 2000 FORMS 5.0

To RAYMOND FERNANDES

Commercial Application Development Using

ORACLE
DEVELOPER 2000
FORMS 5.0

IVAN BAYROSS

BPB PUBLICATIONS
B-14, CONNAUGHT PLACE, NEW DELHI - 110 001

FIRST EDITION 1999
Distributors:
MICRO BOOK CENTRE
2, City Centre, CG Road,
AHMEDABAD-380009 Phone: 6421611

COMPUTER BOOK CENTRE
12, Shrungar Complex, M. G. Road,
BANGALORE-560001 Phone: 5587923, 5584641

MICRO BOOKS
Shanti Niketan Building, 8, Camac Street,
CALCUTTA-700017
Phone: 2426518, 2426519

BUSINESS PROMOTION BUREAU
8/1, Ritchie Street, Mount Road,
CHENNAI-600002 Phone: 834796, 8550491

BPB BOOK CENTRE
376, Old Lajpat Rai Market,
DELHI-110006 Phone: 2961747

DECCAN AGENCIES
4-3-329, Bank Street,
HYDERABAD-500195 Phone: 512280, 593826

MICRO MEDIA
Shop No. 5, Mahendra Chambers,
150 D.N. Road, FORT, MUMBAI-400001
Phone: 2078296, 2078297, 2002732

INFO TECH
G-2, Sidhartha Building, 96 Nehru Place,
NEW DELHI-110019 Phone: 643825, 6415092, 6234208

INFO TECH
Shop No. 2, F-38, South Extension-1,
NEW DELHI-110049 Phone: 4691288, 4641941

INFO TECH
B-11, Vardhman Plaza, Sector-16, Electronics Nagar,
NOIDA-201301 Phone: 91-512329

COMPUTER BOOK CENTRE
SCF No.-65, Sector-6, PANCHKULA-134109,
CHANDIGARH Phone: 561613, 567538

ISBN 81-7656-068-5

Published by Manish Jain for BPB Publications, B-14, Connaught Place,
New Delhi-110001 and Printed by him at Pressworks, Delhi.

Foreword

The need of today's software development is competence in a G.U.I based front-end tool, which can connect to Relational Database engines. This gives the programmer the opportunity to develop client / server based commercial applications.

These applications give users the power and ease of use of a G.U.I with the multi-user capabilities of NT based RDBMS engines such as Oracle.

From the array of G.U.I based front-end tools Oracle Developer 2000 stands out. Many clients are looking for people with Oracle Developer coding capability today. Oracle Developer 2000 offers a host of technical advantage over Oracle Forms 4.5, which was an excellent tool in itself. This book focuses on the new feature available in Oracle Developer 2000 2.0 (Forms 5.0) and has many applications that explain the commercial application development techniques used with Oracle Developer 2000.

All the important coding techniques used by programmers; in OOPS based coding is brought out in full and in great detail. This is coupled with material on how to use the carious tool sub sets available in Oracle Developer 2000. The examples given in this book also focus on standards that have to be maintained in a software project and how a programmer can maintain these standards whilst coding in Oracle Developer 2000.

The book pre-supposes that the person reading it has a DBMS background and that the basic concepts of DBMS commercial application development are already in place. The combination of a sharp drop in hardware prices and quantum jump upward in software technology makes working in Client/Server very much within the financial budgets of most organization. This release's to users, the power of working with a G.U.I based front end to manipulate data in any RDBMS back end. Programmers capable of writing fine tuned code are really invaluable today.

I have found DBMS/RDBMS to be the most exciting environments to work with. With the availability of powerful, easy to use G.U.I based, Client/Server TOOLS; commercial application have really

I have tried to use my extensive commercial application development experience in Oracle using Developer 2000 a book that has answers to most of the questions that seem to puzzle programmers in developing a commercial application.

Every single programming question has not been answered, indeed if I tried to actually do that I would fail since I believe that I myself have not encountered every single programming problem. However, I've chosen several key areas in commercial applications and tried to address a set of issues that most commercial application developers require.

Concepts are built using simple language. Examples have easily understood logic. Once this is grasped, the skill gained, must allow any commercial application developer to develop programs in Oracle Developer 2000 very very quickly.

This foreword would not be complete without my thanking the many people who encouraged me and put up with my many revisions and updations of the material with patience and tolerance.

My sincere "THANKS" goes to:

1. My publisher Mr. Manish Jain who has criticized me and made me redo my work sometimes, each time I've improved. Thanks Manish, I'm getting better each day.

2. Ms. Mita Engineer who tested each example in this book, then formatted this book to complete my satisfaction. Mita, honestly, this book would have NEVER made it without you and the "TLC" you gave it.

3. The many graduate engineers who study Oracle Developer 2000 at SCT. Each time you found a mistake and suggested a correction you helped me towards perfection. A very big "Thank You".

4. The many programmers who read this book I would welcome your brickbats or bouquets. Without you I would not be an author. You can contact me via my publisher Mr. Manish Jain at BpB New Delhi.

5. Finally to my wife Cynthia who always encouraged me whenever I thought that I'd never get this manuscript ready for publishing. You've always helped keep my feet planted firmly on the ground, with you I am truly blessed.

Ivan N. Bayross.

TABLE OF CONTENTS

CHAPTER ONE

Working with Forms

IN THIS CHAPTER

> Oracle Forms Tools

> Application Development using Form.

> Objects Included in the Forms Module

> Using the Forms Builder Tool

> Form Wizards Available in Forms Builder

> Creating, Generating and Running a Form

1. WORKING WITH FORMS

BASIC CONCEPTS

As commercial application developers, our primary task is to design data-entry forms that look as close to the printed sheets of paper that the data entry operators use in the current manual system of data collection.

Hence when the data entry operators switch from paper / pen to keyboard / VDU what they see on the VDU will look familiar to them.

Oracle Forms:

Oracle Forms Builder provides a powerful 'Graphical User Interface' to design such forms. All objects, properties, triggers can be selected by simply clicking on an appropriate icon. A Forms wizard can be used to quickly create forms. This tool allows commercial application developers to design forms that will capture, validate and store data with the very minimum of coding.

Forms Builder, Oracle's GUI based forms creation tool comprises of the following components:

- Forms Builder
- Forms Compiler
- Forms Runtime

Forms Builder is what is used create a form. The design and layout of data entry screens, the creation of event driven PL/SQL code used for data validation and navigation can be done via Forms Builder.

Forms Compiler is required to compile the file created in *Forms Builder* and create a binary file, which can be executed by *Forms Runtime*.

Forms Runtime is used to run the compiled code created by Forms Compiler. To run an Oracle form only the Forms Runtime module is required. At the time of software deployment only the Forms Runtime module needs to be installed on machines on which forms created by Forms Builder are deployed.

To create, add program code, test / debug an Oracle form, a complete installation of Oracle Forms Builder is required.

APPLICATION DEVELOPMENT IN FORMS 5.0

Applications built using Oracle Forms Builder will contain the following components:
1. Form Module
2. Menus
3. PL/SQL Libraries
4. Object Libraries
5. Database Objects

Form Module:

The primary object created using *Form Builder* is a form. The Form module is nothing but a collection of objects such as blocks, canvas, frames, items and event based PL/SQL code blocks called triggers housed in an MS Windows '*Command*' Window.

Menus:

The menu module is a collection of objects such as menu items, sub menus, sub menu items and PL/SQL code blocks.

PL/SQL Libraries:

The library module is a collection of PL/SQL functions and procedures stored in a single library file. This library file is then attached to a form / menu module. All other objects in the form or menu can now access and share the collection of PL/SQL functions and procedures.

Object Libraries:

In a development environment, standards need to be set and maintained. Standards can be maintained by developing common objects, which can be reused throughout a commercial application as well as across applications.

Object Libraries provides an easy method of creating and storing reusable objects and enforcing standards.

An Object Library can be created to:
- Create, store, maintain, and distribute standard and reusable objects.
- Rapidly create applications by dragging and dropping predefined objects on to form.

Database Objects:

Oracle's interactive tool i.e. *SQL*Plus* allows the creation of Database objects like Stored Procedures, Stored Functions and Database Triggers using appropriate SQL and PL/SQL syntax.

FORM MODULE

A Form module consists of the following components:
- Blocks
- Items
- Frames
- Canvas Views
- Window
- PL/SQL Code blocks

Blocks:

A form contains one or more blocks. Blocks are logical containers and have no physical representation. Only the items contained in a block are visible in the form interface.

A block can be conceptualized as a parent container object that holds a related group of child objects such as text items, lists, and push buttons, etc for storing, displaying, and manipulating table data. Each block has a set of properties that determine the behavior of the block.

A block connected to a database object is called a '**Data Aware**' block. A block not connected to any database object is called '**Control Block**'.

A block can be connected to a database object like a table, view or synonym. A block can also be connected to 'Stored Procedures'.

Each Data Block can be directly related to a (*single) database table, view or synonym*. A table, view or synonym connected to a block is known as the '**Base Table**'. Each column of the base table may have an associated block item bound to it. The association or binding of block items with table columns is done by giving the item on the block the *same name* as the table column. This direct relationship allows the data in a base table to be manipulated at will.

Blocks have several characteristics that can be defined. Some of these are the attributes that determine how to sort information retrieved into a block from the base table, the number of records that can be displayed in the block, etc.

Blocks can be related to each other by specifying a master-detail relationship. A master-detail relationship corresponds to a primary-foreign key relationship between the base tables of the blocks. Whenever a row is retrieved in the master block from the master table, the master detail relationship automatically displays the corresponding set of rows from the detail table in the detail block, without any special processing code being required.

Items:

Items are objects contained in blocks. At the most basic level, items serve as containers for data. The user can manipulate values in an item. A procedure or a trigger can also be used to manipulate item values. An item is always associated with a block. Each block normally has one or more items.

The items in a block are usually bound to columns in a base table. Entering data into such items will determine the values entered in associated columns of the base table. Alternatively, items can be filled with data from the base table by performing an SQL query on the base table.

Items need not always be bound to the columns of a base table. They can also hold calculated values, display related information from associated tables or accept operator input for processing later. Items not connected to a base table are called **'Control Items'**.

Items have attributes that can be set via the item's property palette. These attributes may be set dynamically at runtime via suitable code as well. These attributes determine an item's behavior at form run time.

Oracle Forms Builder supports several types of items that can be used to build a form. The items supported by Oracle Forms Builder are described below:

Text Item

 Text item displays data values, and can be edited.

Display Item

 The display item shows information that must be fetched or assigned programmatically. These items are not navigable to and their contents cannot be directly edited.

List Item

 A list item displays a list of choices from which only one value can be selected at a time.

Button

 A button is a rectangle with text label or an icon graphic. These items are normally used to initiate some action.

Check Box

 A check box is a text label with an indicator that displays the current value as checked or unchecked. It is normally used as an item, which takes in a yes/no or true/false like value. This item is normally bound to a table column, which must hold a single character value or a boolean value.

Radio Group

 A radio group is a group of two or more radio buttons, from which only one radio button can be active. This item is used on a form to hold several radio buttons which are bound to a single table column. A technique commonly used when multiple options are available, with only a single value being stored in a table column.

Chart Item

 A chart item is a bordered rectangle of any size that displays a chart generated by the Oracle Graphics Tool.

Image Item

 An image item is a bordered rectangle of any size that displays images stored in a database or in a file. Image items are dynamic and can change with the image being displayed when required.

OLE Container

 An OLE container is an area that stores and displays an OLE object. OLE objects are created for OLE server applications. OLE objects can be embedded or linked in an OLE container.

This feature is available for O/s that supports Object Linking and Embedding. Object Linking and Embedding is currently available on Microsoft Windows and Macintosh platforms.

OCX Control

 An OCX control is a custom control that simplifies the building and enhancing of user interfaces. *OCX Controls are available for forms running on Microsoft Windows, as Microsoft Windows is the only O/s that supports OCX controls.*

Frames:

A frame is a graphic object that appears on a canvas. Frames are used to arrange items within a block.

- A frame is an object with properties
- Each frame can be associated with a block
- When a frame is associated with a block, the items in the block are automatically arranged within the frame.
- Frames can be sub-classed or included within an Object Library to enforce visual standards.

Canvas View:

The canvas-view is the '*background*' on which Items, Text and Graphics or Frames are placed. The items in a block can be placed on different canvas-views. Each canvas-view can be displayed in different windows.

The Oracle Forms, Block wizard allows items to be placed on different types of Canvas like '**Content**' and '**Tab**'.

Window:

Every new form is automatically held in a default window named WINDOW1. Additional windows can be created as needed by inserting them in the Object Navigator under the '*Windows*' node.

For each window created, at least one *canvas-view* must be created. The canvas-view is the background on which *items* are placed. The canvas-view is linked to a window by setting the 'Window' canvas-view property appropriately.

Window properties can be set at design or runtime, which determine the appearance and functionality of the window at runtime.

PL/SQL Code Blocks:

Data manipulation can be done using the default form created by the Oracle Forms wizard. Forms created by the Forms Wizard can be customized to suit a commercial application or to map to the standard set for the application.

The Oracle Forms tool provides suitable facilities to attach PL/SQL code blocks to 'Events' built into all Form objects. This allows the form to map to the object oriented standard of 'Event driven' form processing. 'Events' can be conceptualized as PL/SQL code holders that automatically execute the PL/SQL code when a specific event occurs.

Based on the needs of the application, an appropriate event must be selected and PL/SQL code in its rigid format must be written in the selected event. For example if data needs to be validated to ensure input / output or business rules, PL/SQL code must be written in the WHEN-VALIDATE-ITEM event. PL/SQL code written in this event gets executed when item navigation occurs after data entry.

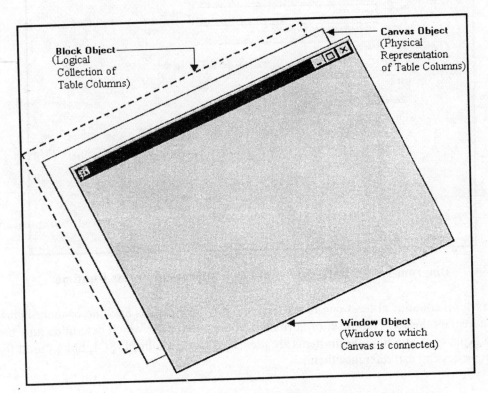

Diagram 1.1 : The Sectional View of the objects on the Form

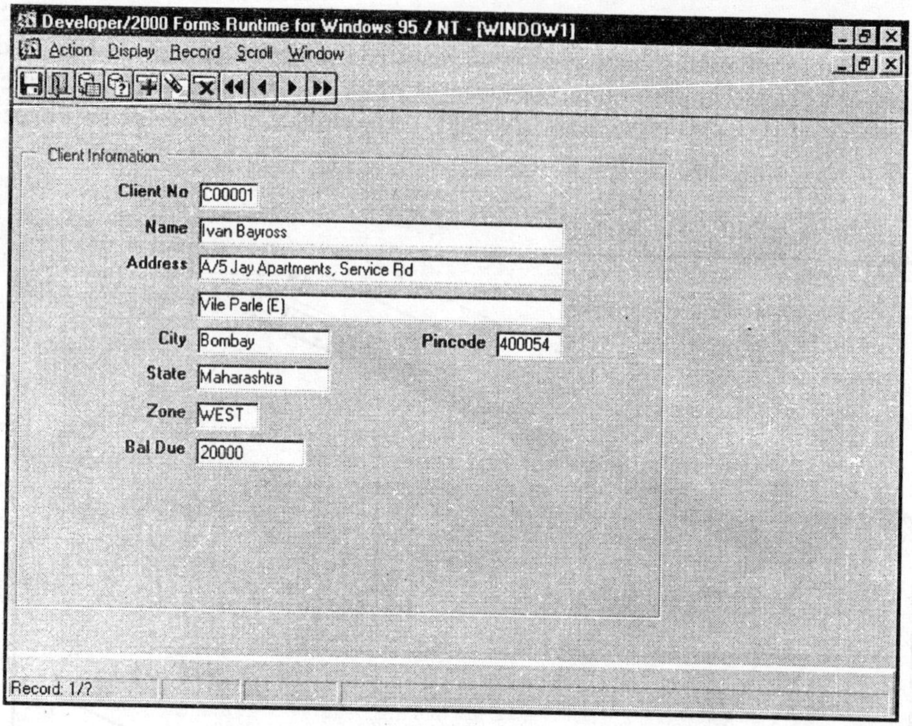

Diagram 1.2 : A Data-entry form as it appears in Forms Runtime

Every form contains at least one block, one window, one canvas and one or more items. Each item on the form has a set of attributes or characteristics, which determine how the item behaves at, run time. Form items are *named* so that code in PL/SQL blocks used for form processing can reference them.

USING FORMS BUILDER

Parts of the Forms Builder Window:

The tools available in the Forms Builder window are:

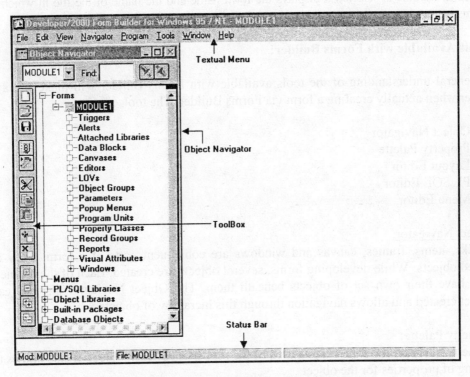

Diagram 1.3 : Layout of Forms Builder Window

Textual Menu:
Forms Builder comes with a built-in textual menu, which allows access to all the tools of *Forms Builder*.

Object Navigator:
Blocks, items, frames, canvas and windows are some of the constituent parts of a form. Each is an object. While developing forms several objects are created and each of these may have a set of objects beneath them. The Object Navigator allows navigation through this hierarchy of objects.

Status Bar:
The status bar at the bottom of the screen is an area, which displays Oracle Forms messages. Information about a selected object is also displayed in the status bar.

Toolbox:
Forms Builder comes with a built-in iconic toolbar menu. The iconic toolbar menu allows the access of different tools of Forms Builder.

For Example:
If a form module is selected it displays the form name and the name of the file in which the Forms is stored.

Tools Available with Forms Builder:

A general understanding of the tools available with Forms Builder will make life a lot easier when actually creating a form via Forms Builder. The tools are:

1. Object Navigator
2. Property Palette
3. Layout Editor
4. PL/SQL Editor
5. Menu Editor

Object Navigator:
Blocks, items, frames, canvas and windows are constituent parts of a form. They are called objects. While developing forms, several objects are created. Each of these objects may have their own set of objects beneath them. The Object Navigator displays each object created and allows navigation through this hierarchy of objects.

Property Palette:
Property Palette allows the examination of the properties of each object. It also allows the setting of properties for the object.

Layout Editor:
Forms developed will have different objects like text items, check boxes, radio buttons, labels, graphic objects to name a few. The Layout editor allows the sizing, positioning and alignment of these objects. Font characteristics can also be set through the layout editor.

PL/SQL Editor:
In Commercial Applications, application specific tasks need to be performed. To achieve this appropriate PL/SQL code must be written and attached an event, belonging to a Form object. The PL/SQL editor provides the interface via which this is done.

Menu Editor:

This tool is used to create user-defined menus. Forms Builder automatically provides a default menu with default functionality like querying, inserting, deleting records and navigating through different records. However for system specific functionality a user-defined menu which overrides the default Oracle Menu needs to be created. This is done via the Menu Editor.

FORM WIZARDS

Forms builder provides a number of wizards for creating different objects on a form. Some of these wizards are:

Data Block Wizard:

The Data Block wizard allows the creation of data blocks. The data block wizard displays a welcome dialog box and then asks for additional information to create the data block. The information required to create a data block will be *Data Source i.e. Table or Stored Procedure.*

If *Table* is selected as a data source, the *Table Name* and the *Field Names* must be specified. If a *Stored Procedure* is selected as a data source, the *Procedure Name* must be specified.

The Data Block wizard then leads to a Layout wizard.

Layout Wizard:

The Layout Wizard works in conjunction with the Data Block wizard. The Layout Wizard allows the layout of the data block objects to be designed.

The Layout Wizard displays a welcome dialog box and then asks for information about the canvas that must be used in the layout. The canvas information required is *canvas name* and *canvas type*. A list of data blocks and the columns included in the block are displayed. A specific canvas item must be bound to each table column selected.

Each item associated with a table column and displayed on the form generally includes a prompt / label that gives information on the type of data to be loaded into the item. A label or prompt along with its height and width can be specified for each table column.

The layout style i.e. *Form* or *Tabular* is then specified. The Layout style determines how items will be arranged on the form.

Items are grouped inside a frame. The frame title, number of records to be displayed and the distance between the records needs to be given to the layout wizard.

The form layout is then created based on the information specified in the Layout wizard. The form so created is a *default form*. This form can be run to perform data manipulation operations such as View, Insert, Update and Delete.

CREATING A FORM

1. Click on **Start..Programs..Developer 2000 R2.0..Forms Builder** to invoke *Forms Builder* as displayed in diagram 1.4.

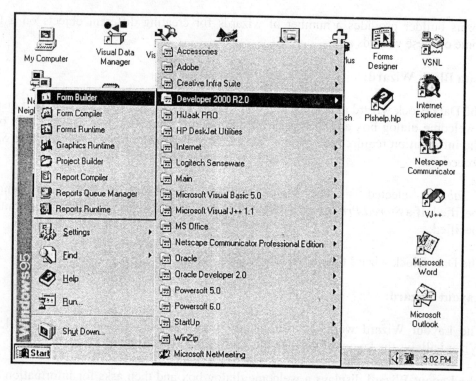

Diagram 1.4 : Invoking Forms Builder

2. The 'Welcome to the Form Builder' opening screen is shown in diagram 1.5. The opening screen allows the use of wizards to
   - Create new forms
   - Open existing forms
   - Build a form from a *template* or
   - Learn more about Forms Builder.

   - If the Data Block creation option is selected, an appropriate wizard is displayed.

   - If manual form creation is specified, a new form will be created.

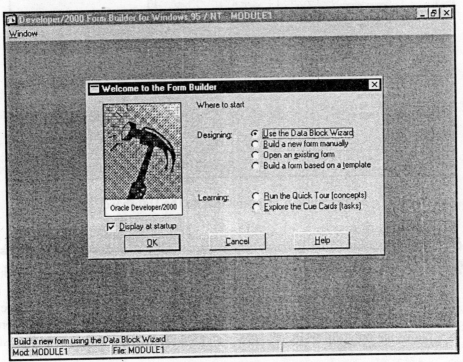

Diagram 1.5 : Forms Builder Welcome Screen

3. To create a form, first connect to the Oracle Database. Click on **File** and select menu item **Connect**. Specify User Name, Password and the Database Connect String. Click on the '**Connect**' PushButton as shown in diagram 1.6.

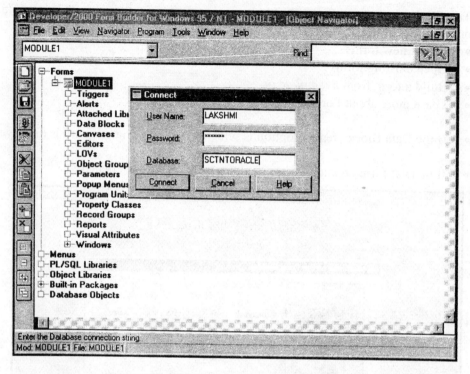

Diagram 1.6 : Connecting to the Database

Note

The Company's DBA may have configured a Client machine so that it automatically connects to a default database. In that case, connect string need not be specified. A connection will be automatically made to the default database, allowing the commencement of form building. Automatic connect information is generally passed via an Oracle entry in the Windows Registry.

4. Since the '*Use the Data Block Wizard*' option has been selected, a new form can be created using the wizard. When created the new (default) form module name is 'MODULE1'.

Note

If an existing form is to be opened, *Forms Builder* asks for the name of the form file and then opens it.

5. Right Click on the form. It displays a pop up menu. Click on *'Property Palette'* to display the properties of the form. Change the name of the form to *'CLIENT'* as shown in diagram 1.7.

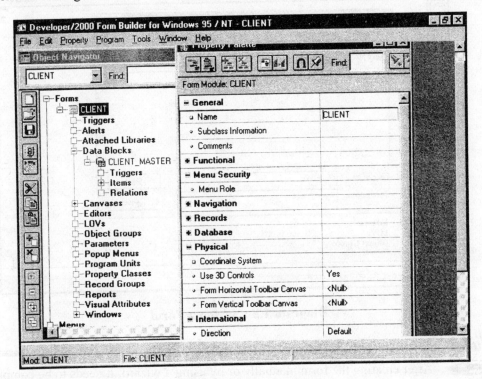

Diagram 1.7 : Setting the Form Name property

6. Save the form by clicking on **File..Save** menu option. In either case, it displays the *Save* dialog box as shown in diagram 1.8.

Tip

The current form is being saved in a directory named *'Student'* in Drive 'C'. Please choose a sub-directory and / or path to save the file appropriate to the computer being worked on.

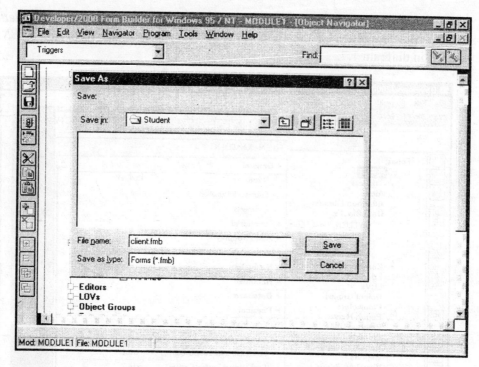

Diagram 1.8 : Saving a Form

Note

After creating the form manually or by using a wizard, it needs to be compiled and then executed.

GENERATING AND RUNNING A FORM

Compiling a Form:

Oracle Forms Builder allows three types of Compilation. These are:
- Full Compilation
- Incremental Compilation
- Selective Compilation

Full Compilation:

Before a form runs an executable (.FMX file) must be created from the (.FMB file) module created by Forms Builder. *Forms compiler* compiles a form and generates a .FMX file from the .FMB file of the form module. Click on **File**, **Administration** and **Compile File** menu option to compile a form module.

A form module can also be compiled by selecting **Program..Compile..All** menu option.

'Incremental' or 'Selective' compilation:

Forms Builder also supports incremental compilation. If changes are made to a form file, instead of compiling the entire form module, incremental compilation can be used to selectively compile changes made in the form module.

Incremental compilation can be done by selecting **Program..Compile..Incremental** menu option.

Selective compilation can be done by selecting the object that needs compilation and then clicking on **Program..Selective Compilation** menu option.

Running a Form:

Once the form module is saved and compiled, its **.FMX** file can be executed. The **.FMX** file can be executed by selecting the **Run Form** menu item under the **Program** menu item. The current form is executed in the Run Forms environment.

Forms Runtime, with default form created by the forms wizard is displayed in diagram 1.9.

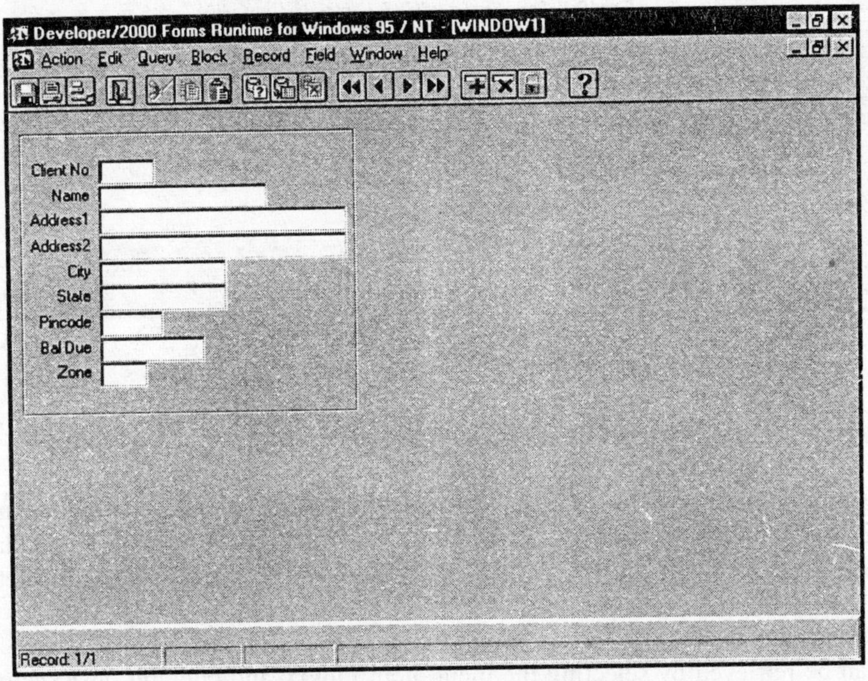

Diagram 1.9 : Forms Runtime

Setting the Default Environment:

A default form environment setting can be done to ensure that Forms Builder generates a form before executing it. This can be done, by selecting **Tools..Preferences** from the textual menu. The Preferences screen has four tab pages. These are *General*, *Access*, *Wizards* and *Runtime*. Click on the *General* tab page and set the *Build Before Running* option to *true* as shown in diagram 1.10. Similarly to save before compiling the *Save Before Building* attribute must be set to *true*.

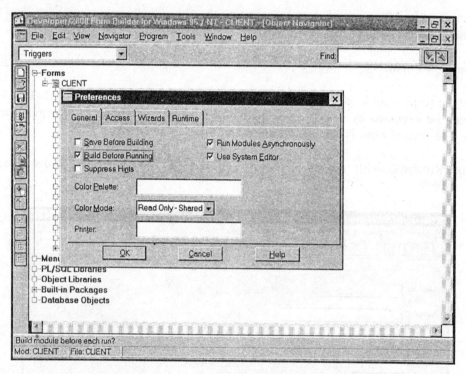

Diagram 1.10 : Setting Forms Builder Preferences

Data Retrieval and Manipulation Operations:

During runtime the form comes with a default Menu and toolbar. The default menu as well as the toolbar provides all the options for *Navigating* through table data and performing standard data *Manipulation* such as Retrieval, Insert, Update and Delete.

Data Retrieval:

Data can be retrieved by selecting the menu item **Query** and clicking on **Execute**. This would retrieve all records from a table. *The status line at the bottom of the screen will indicate the number of records retrieved.*

For a conditional query to be performed, select **Query** and click on **Enter**. This clears the block and allows the user to enter a query value in item or combination of items.

Once desired values are entered, Oracle Forms Runtime automatically creates a where clause by using the item name for which the value is entered and the value entered by the user. The default operator used is '='.

Execute the query by Clicking on **Execute** from **Query** Menu item. Oracle runtime executes the query and applies the appropriate the where clause. An appropriate record set then is retrieved from the table, rather than all records.

Note

> To generate a where clause that uses operators other than '=', enter a '&' in any item and then click on **Query.. Execute** Menu item. Oracle runtime will display a dialog box that allows users to specify a where clause. A condition for the WHERE clause is shown in diagram 1.11.

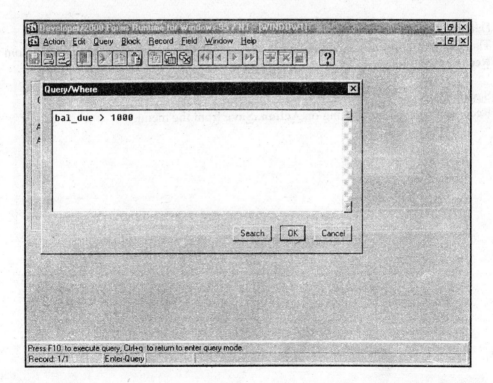

Diagram 1.11 : Specifying Where clause in Enter Query Mode

After entering the desired where clause, click on OK to retrieve appropriate records.

Navigation:

If several records are retrieved, click on **Record** and select **Previous** or **Next** to move to the previous or the next record.

If a form displays more than one record, the *number of records* displayed on the form is treated as a record set. The **Scroll Up** and **Scroll Down** menu options under **Record** can be used to move from one record set to other in ascending or descending order.

Inserting Data:

To insert a record in the table, a blank record must first be inserted in the form. The values can then be entered in the blank record and saved. When the records are saved, Oracle Runtime generates an insert statement and inserts the newly created record into the table. Click on **Record..Insert** to insert a blank record in the form. Enter values in the different items as required. After entering all the values click on **Action..Save** to generate an appropriate number of Insert statements and execute each insert statement automatically.

Deleting Data:

The Current Form Record displayed can be deleted by clicking on **Delete** from the **Record** menu item.

Saving Data:

Records are saved by clicking on **Action..Save** from the menu.

SELF REVIEW QUESTIONS

TRUE OR FALSE

1. Blocks are logical containers that have no physical representation.

    A) True   B) False

2. A single block can be connected to multiple database objects like a table, view or synonym.

    A) True   B) False

3. When a frame is associated with a block, the items in the block are automatically arranged within the frame.

    A) True   B) False

4. Scroll bar for a block can be attached to a block only at the time of block creation.

    A) True   B) False

5. A Window is connected to a block.

    A) True   B) False

6. Every form contains at least one block, one window, one canvas and one or more items.

    A) True   B) False

FILL IN THE BLANKS

1. GUI stands for _____.

2. The _____ item can be used only to show information that must be fetched or assigned programmatically.

3. Forms Builder provides the user with the _____ Editor to write appropriate code blocks.

4. The _____ at the bottom of the screen displays Oracle messages to the user.

5. Oracle Forms Builder allows three types of Compilation. These are:

- _____

- _____

- _____

PICK THE RIGHT OPTION

1. If an item is connected to the base table column, the name of the item and the name of the base table column must be
   A) the same.
   B) can be different.

2. When a new form is created, Forms Builder creates _____ by default.
   A) a window named window0.
   B) a canvas named canvas0.
   C) a block named block0

A Quick Review

An Introduction to Forms

Components used to Create an Application

Objects that make a Form
- Blocks
- Items
- Frames
- Canvas View
- Window
- PL/SQL Code

Using Forms Builder Tool

Forms Wizard available in Forms Builder

Creating a Form Using Forms Builder
- Invoking Forms Builder
- Connecting to the Oracle Database using Forms Builder
- Saving a Form

Generating and Running a Form
- Setting Forms Environment
- Data Retrieval and Manipulation Operations

CHAPTER TWO

Master Form

IN THIS CHAPTER

➢ Default Form Creation

➢ Customizing Form Layout

➢ Creating a Control Block for Data Manipulation and Navigation

➢ Triggers

➢ User-Defined Procedures

➢ Form Data Validation

➢ Displaying Context Sensitive Help

2. MASTER FORM

PRODUCT MASTER DATA ENTRY SCREEN

Focus:

To create a Product Master Form via which the data of the **product_master** table can be manipulated. This is a single table, which is a part of a Sales Order System.

- Provide complete data manipulation operations (Add, View, Modify, and Delete).

- In the view mode, allow table data browsing, one record at a time using push buttons First, Next, Previous, Last.

- Include a search operation that retrieves a record, which matches a *product_no* entered.

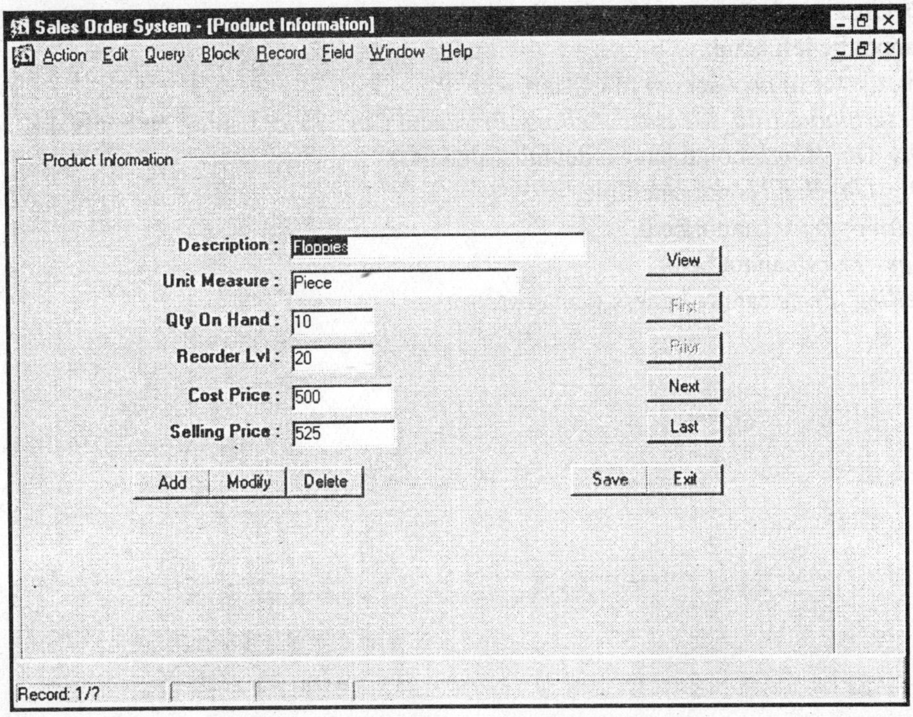

Diagram 2.1 : Product Master Data Entry Screen

Table Name: product_master
Description: Used to store information about products supplied by a company.

Column Name	Data Type	Size	Column Description
product_no	varchar2	6	Primary Key
Description	varchar2	25	Description of a product
unit_measure	varchar2	10	Unit in which a product is measured.
qty_on_hand	number	8	Quantity which is available in stock
reorder_lvl	number	8	Quantity when stock should be re-ordered.
cost_price	number	8,2	Cost price of the product.
selling_price	number	8,2	Selling price of the product.

Integrity Constraints:

• *PK_Product_no* Primary Key constraint applied to *Product_Master. Product_No.*

Validations in the product master data entry screen are as follows:

• *Product_No* is Primary Key i.e. duplicate values are not allowed in *Product_No*. It cannot be left blank.
• First letter of *product_no* must start with 'P'.
• *Description, Unit_Measure, Selling_Price* and *Cost_Price* cannot be left blank.
• *Qty_On_Hand* should have a default value of 0.
• *Qty_On_Hand* is not enterable.
• *Selling_Price* cannot be 0.
• *Cost_Price* cannot be 0
• *Selling_Price* cannot be less than *cost_price*.

THE SOLUTION

The approach to create such a form is:
* Create a default form
* Arrange the layout of the form.
* Create a button palette block.
* Write PL/SQL code that permits data navigation and data validation.

Default Form Creation:

1. Click on **Start..Programs..Developer 2000 R2.0..Forms Builder** to invoke *Forms Builder* as displayed in diagram 2.2.

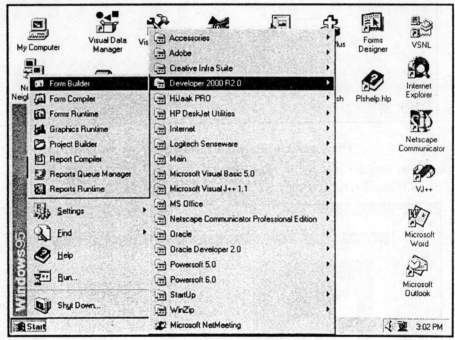

Diagram 2.2 : Invoking Forms Builder

2. The 'Welcome to the Form Builder' opening screen is shown in diagram 2.3. From the '**Designing**' option select '*Use the Data Block Wizard*' to create a new block. Click on 'OK'.

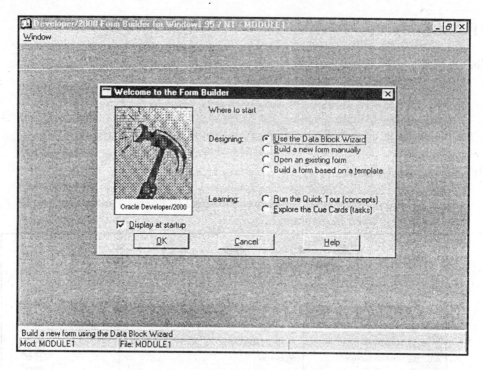

Diagram 2.3 : Forms Builder Welcome Screen

Oracle Forms Builder invokes the Data Block wizard which displays a *'Welcome to the Data Block Wizard'* screen as shown in diagram 2.4. Click on Next.

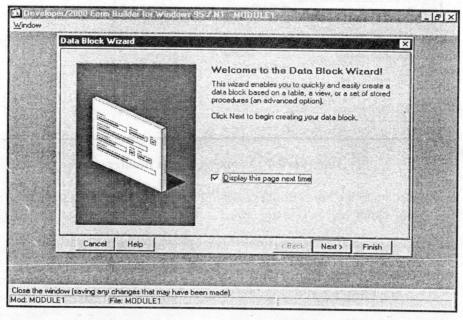

Diagram 2.4 : Data Block Wizard Welcome Screen

3. Indicate the data source as shown in diagram 2.5.

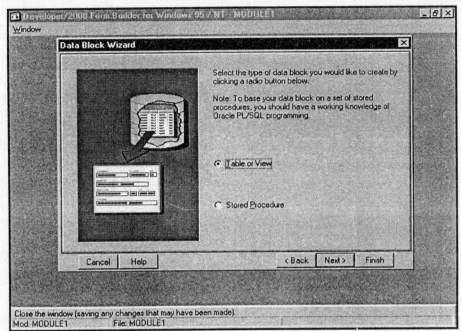

Diagram 2.5: Data Source Selection

The available options are:
- Table or View
- Stored Procedure

Radio button labeled 'Table or View' is selected by default. Click on Next.

5. A screen that allows table and column identification is displayed. Click on the **Browse** push button as shown in diagram 2.6 to select a table from a list of tables.

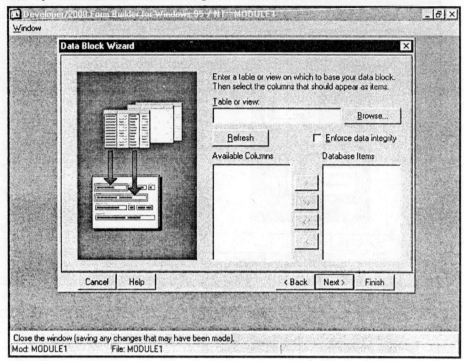

Diagram 2.6 : A screen showing table and column selection

Note

To display a list of tables, the Forms Builder tool must first connect to the database. Thus Forms Builder opens a dialog box that accepts user name, password and connect string as shown in diagram 2.7

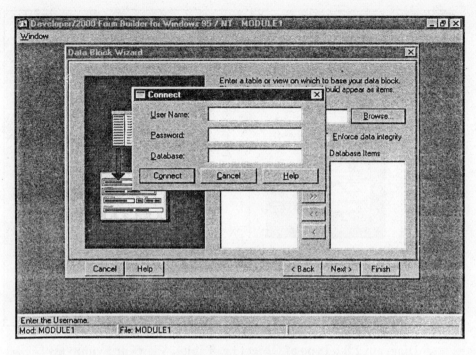

Diagram 2.7: Connecting to the Database

6. A Data aware block can be created by connecting the block to tables, views and synonyms. Hence the next step is to select one of these.

Note

A form can be created by using a database object, which is owned, or to which access 'rights' have been granted. Based on access/ ownership rights on an object an appropriate list of names of table, views or synonyms will be displayed.

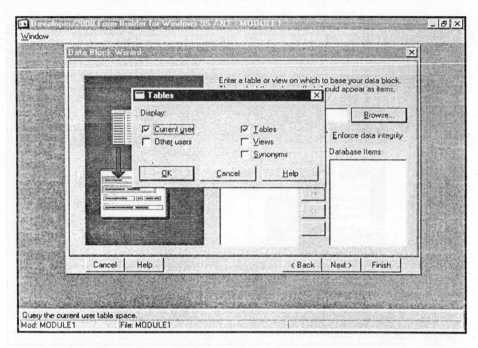

Diagram 2.8 : Type of Object i.e. Tables, Views or Synonyms

7. If the 'Tables' check box is activated. A list of tables will be displayed as shown in diagram 2.9.

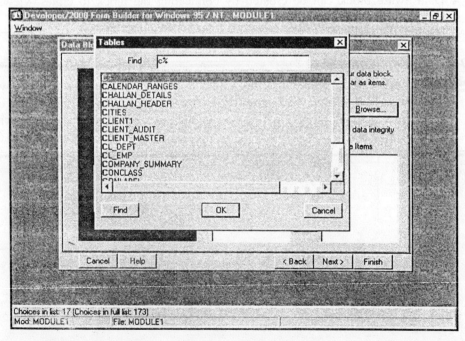

Diagram 2.9 : List of tables Displayed by the Data Block Wizard

8. When a table is selected from the list, a list of table columns to select from is displayed as shown in diagram 2.10.

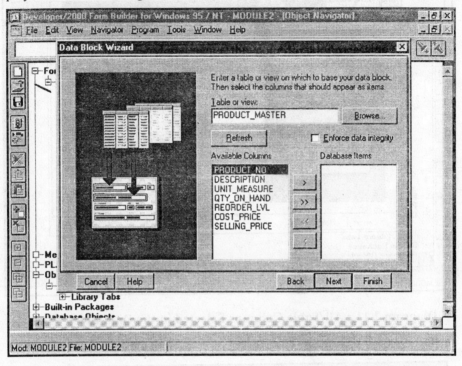

Diagram 2.10 : Table Columns Displayed by Data Block Wizard

9. The columns of the table to be included in the form must be specified. This can be done by selecting and by placing the column in the 'Database Items' list. Four icons to select or deselect the columns are provided.

Icons	Description
>	Include the Selected column
>>	Include all the columns in the table
<	Exclude a selected columns
<<	Exclude all the columns in the table

10. If all columns of the table *Product_Master* are to be included in the form, click on >> icon. The completed screen will be displayed as shown in diagram 2.11.

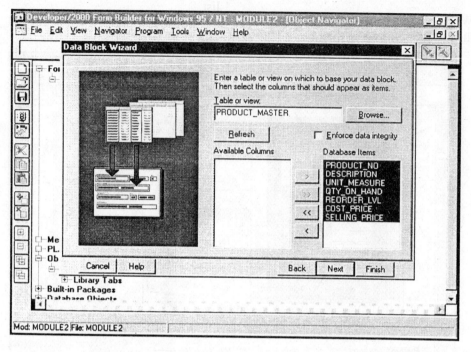

Diagram 2.11 : All Table Columns Selected in the Data Block Wizard

11. The Data Block Wizard asks for confirmation to invoke the Layout Wizard.

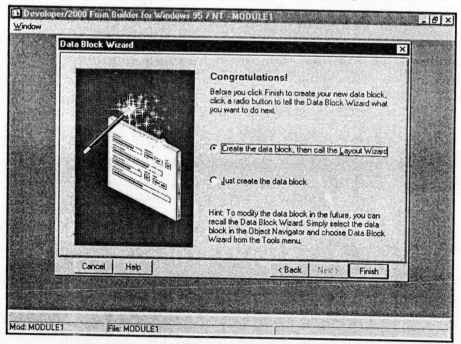

Diagram 2.12 : Confirmation to Invoke Layout wizard

12. The option selected is '*Create Data Block, and then call Layout Wizard*', the welcome screen of the layout editor is displayed as shown in diagram 2.13.

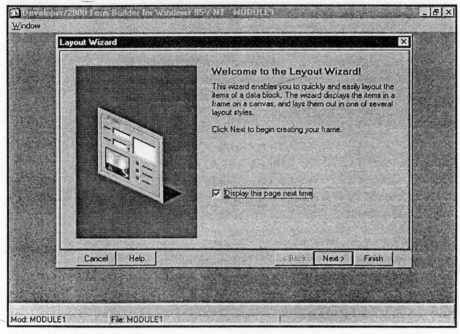

Diagram 2.13 : Layout Wizard Welcome screen

13. Click on Next. The layout wizard prompts for a Canvas *Name* and *Type* as shown in diagram 2.14.

   By default, the type of canvas is '**Content**' *i.e. the canvas expands vertically as well as horizontally to fit the size of the command window*.

Note

To create a tab notepad, the type of canvas must be set to '**Tab**' and the tab page name must be specified. If 'New Tab Page' is selected a canvas of type 'Tab' is created with one tab page.

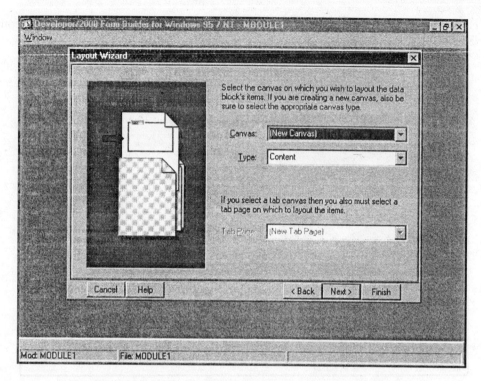

Diagram 2.14 : Specifying Canvas Name and Type

14. The next screen displays items that have been included in the block. Select items that must be displayed on the canvas from the list provided. Click on [>>] to select all the columns from the block.

After selecting the items to be displayed on the canvas, the item type of individual items can be specified. The default item type is *'Text Item'*.

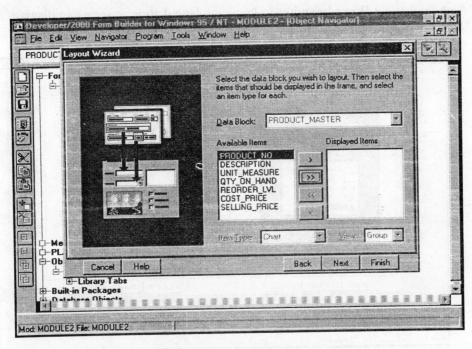

Diagram 2.15 : Items displayed on the Canvas

15. The Label / Prompt for each canvas item along with its height and width is displayed as shown in diagram 2.16. If required change the prompt, its width or height and click on Next.

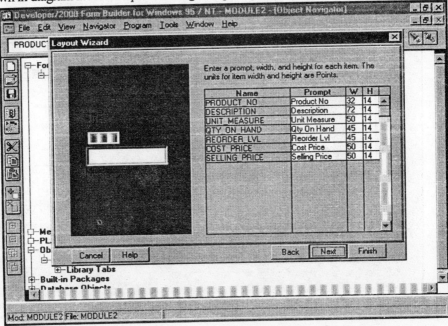

Diagram 2.16 : Setting Item Prompt, Width and Height

16. Next the Layout Wizard requires to know the layout style as shown in diagram 2.17. The layout style can be 'Form' or 'Tabular'. *Form Layout is selected by default.* Click on Next.

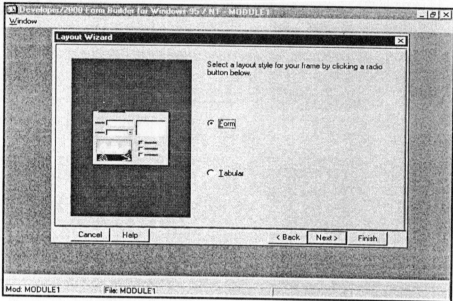

Diagram 2.17 : Setting Layout Style

17. Selected table columns items are grouped within a frame bound to canvas. The frame title, number of records to be displayed and the distance between the records must be entered. Confirmation to display a scrollbar is also asked for.

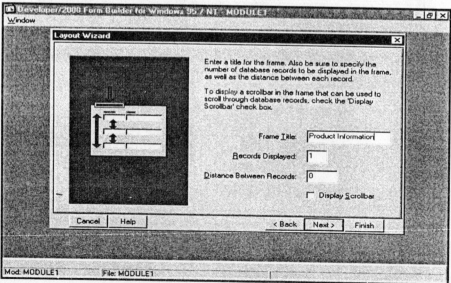

Diagram 2.18 : Setting Frame Properties

18. Finally a congratulation screen is displayed. Click on Finish.

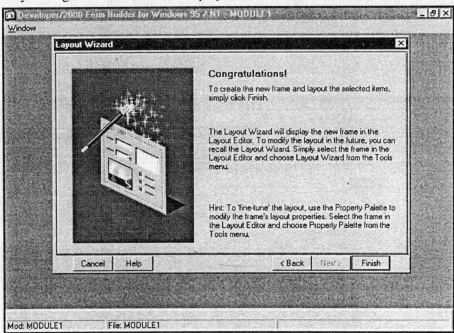

Diagram 2.19 : Congratulation screen

19. All the objects described to the wizards will be created and displayed in the object navigator as shown in diagram 2.20.

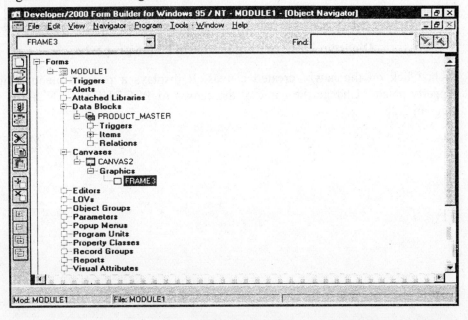

Diagram 2.20: Object Navigator Displaying Block, Canvas and Frame Object

Once all the objects required by the form have been created individual properties of each object need to be set to control the form behavior.

21. In the Object Navigator, right click on Module1 (the Default Form Module). A pop up menu is displayed. Click on property palette. Change the name of the form to 'PRODUCT' as shown in diagram 2.21.

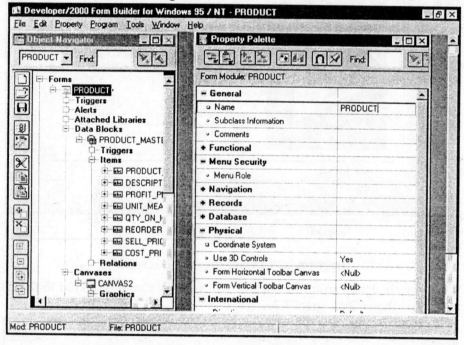

Diagram 2.21 : Setting the Form Name property

22. Right Click on the newly created canvas. It displays a pop up menu. Click on property palette. Change the name of the canvas to 'PRODUCT_CAN' as shown in diagram 2.22.

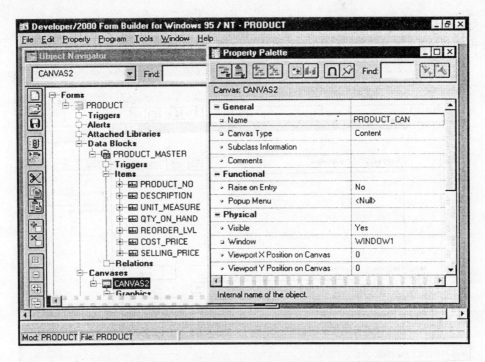

Diagram 2.22 : Setting the Canvas Name property

23. Double click on the **Windows** node in the *Object Navigator*. *Window1* is displayed. Right Click on Window1. A pop up menu is displayed. Click on property palette. Change the **Name** of the window to *'PRODUCT_WIN'* and **title** to 'Product Information' as shown in diagram 2.23.

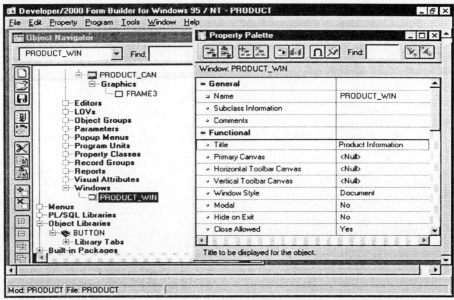

Diagram 2.23 : Setting the Windows Name and Title Property

24. Save the form created by clicking on **File..Save** menu option. A Save dialog box as shown in diagram 2.24 is displayed.

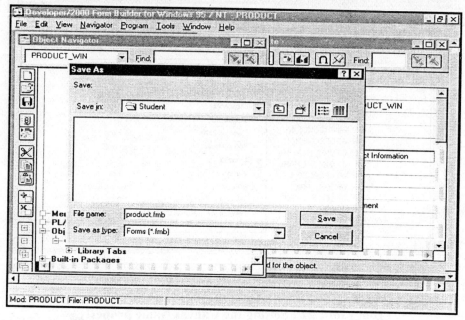

Diagram 2.24: Saving a Form

Tip

The current form is being saved in a directory named '*Student*' in Drive 'C'. Please choose a sub-directory and / or path to save the file appropriate to the computer being worked on.

20. After creating the form, run the form. To run the form, click on **Program..Run Form**. The Forms runtime screen will be as shown in diagram 2.25.

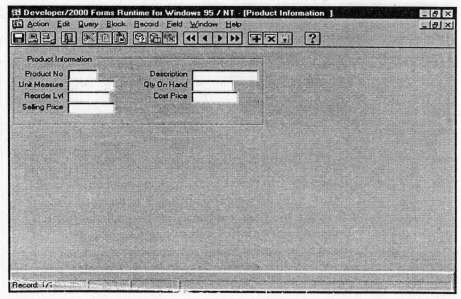

Diagram 2.25 : Product Master Form runtime

Note

Oracle Forms Builder automatically adds a textual menu and a toolbar menu to the current form and thus allows default data manipulation and navigation when the form is executed.

Laying out the objects on the form:

As seen in diagram 2.25, the items of the *Product_Master* block are placed in the top leftmost position on the canvas.

To arrange items on the canvas as required, Forms Builder provides a toolbar in the layout editor that allows alignment and sizing of items. The toolbar also allows other formatting features like font setting, bring to front, send to back etc. It also includes icons for zoom facility.

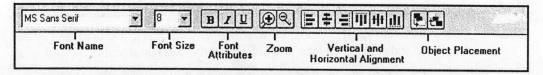

Diagram 2.26 : Formatting Toolbar in Layout Editor

Arrange the items of the *Product_Master* block as shown in diagram 2.27 using 'drag and drop' technique and appropriate formatting toolbar.

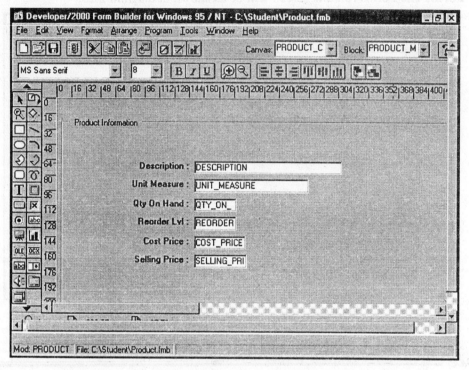

Diagram 2.27 : Arranged Items of the Product_Master block

CREATING A CONTROL BLOCK

If *user-defined* data manipulation is required the default toolbar menu provided by Forms Runtime must be *disabled*. The technique commonly used for creating user defined data navigation and manipulation is the creation of a 'Control Block' on the form and placing push buttons on the control block. Once the push buttons are in place suitable PL/SQL code attached to the trigger WHEN-BUTTON-PRESSED provides for data manipulation.

A new block called *button_palette* must be created.

1. To create a new block, select the *Data Blocks* Node in the *Object Navigator* and click on **N**avigator..**Cr**eate menu option.

Note

A new block can also be created by selecting the *Data Blocks* Node in the *Object Navigator* and clicking on icon in the [⬚] Object Navigator toolbar.

A dialog box is presented that asks for confirmation to use a wizard for new block creation as shown in diagram 2.28.

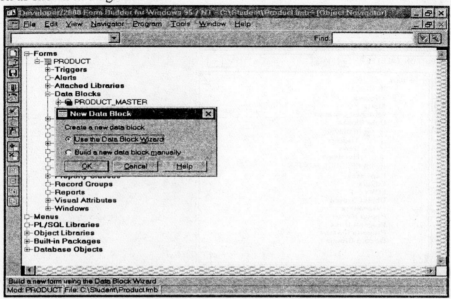

Diagram 2.28 : Confirmation to use Wizard for New Block Creation

2. The block wizard given by Oracle Forms Builder can be used only to create a data aware block. Therefore the Block Wizard cannot be used to create a *'Control Block'*.

3. A new block with default name (block with some default number) is created and displayed in the *Object Navigator* as shown in diagram 2.30.

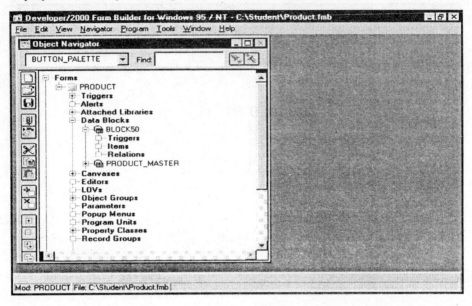

Diagram 2.30 : New Block created with Default Name

4. Right click on the block name and select *Property Palette* from the popup menu. Change the block's name to **Button_Palette** as shown in diagram 2.31.

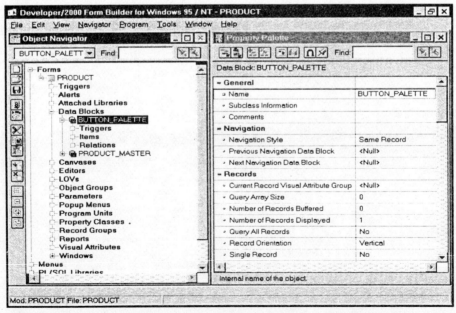

Diagram 2.31 : Changing the Block Name to Button_Palette

5. Right click on *Button_palette* block in the *Object Navigator* and Select Layout Editor from the popup menu. From the item palette on the left of the layout editor select the push button item and place it on the layout. Change the Name and the Label property of the push button to *pb_view* and *View* respectively.

Similarly place the required number of push buttons as shown in the table below and set the *Name* and the *label* property of each pushbutton.

Push Button Name	Label	Push Button Name	Label
pb_add	Add	pb_exit	Exit
pb_view	View	pb_first	First
pb_modify	Modify	pb_prior	Prior
pb_delete	Delete	pb_next	Next
pb_save	Save	pb_last	Last

The completed layout for the *Product* form will be as shown in diagram 2.32.

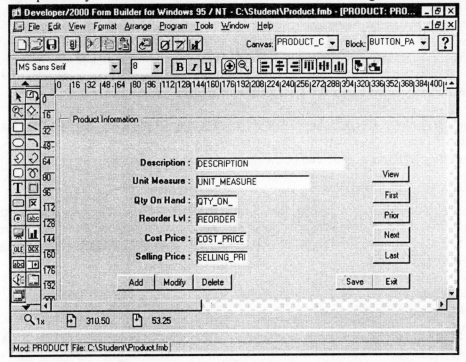

Diagram 2.32 : Layout after placing all the buttons

TRIGGERS

Event Driven PL/SQL code has to be written to add functionality to each push button placed on the form. The code is executed based on a specific event occurring with respect to the push buttons, generally when the push buttons are pressed.

Event Driven Programming:

An 'Event' that gets executed at a specific moment in time is a 'Trigger'. Triggers are named and built-into form items. PL/SQL code blocks when attached to these events are executed when the event (trigger) occurs.

If no PL/SQL code is attached to a trigger, the trigger will fire but no processing of any kind will take place. If PL/SQL code is attached to an event (trigger) when the event occurs the PL/SQL code executes and whatever processing is specified in the code block is carried out.

An Oracle Form Item and its appropriate trigger name must be selected. For example, when push button *pb_view* is clicked, a trigger named '*When-button-pressed*' is fired. PL/SQL code i.e. *execute_query* is written in this trigger using which a call to the underlying base table is made and the records of the base table are displayed on the form.

Type of Triggers based on the User action or programmatic control:

When selecting triggers, it is important to understand precisely when triggers fire, both in relation to other triggers, and in relation to form processing. It is necessary to identify the type of trigger. Form triggers can be categorized into the following basic types:

Interface Triggers:
Triggers associated with user interface objects are called *Interface* triggers. Some of these triggers fire only in response to operator input or manipulation. Others can fire in response to both operator input and programmatic control. Interface triggers can be further classified into:

- Key Triggers
- Action Triggers associated with User objects
- Mouse Triggers

Key Triggers:

Example:

Trigger Name	Key
Key-Next-Item	Tab or Enter
Key-ExeQry	F8
Key-NxtBlk	Shift F5
Key-Commit	F10

Action Triggers associated with user objects:

Triggers that get executed due to user interaction are called Action Triggers. Action triggers are associated with specific objects. The examples of action triggers are:

Example:

Trigger Name	Action
When-Button-Pressed	Pressing a button
When-CheckBox-Changed	Clicking a check box
When-Image-Pressed	Clicking the image
When-List-Changed	A List Item is selected
When-Radio-Changed	Clicking On a Radio Button.
When-Window-Activated	When focus is on a specific Windows
When-Window-Closed	When a window is closed.

Mouse Triggers:

The triggers associated with the Mouse Action are called Mouse Triggers. The Examples of Mouse Triggers are as follows:

Example:

Trigger Name	Mouse Action
When-Mouse-Click	Left Click with the Mouse button.
When-Mouse-DoubleClick	Double Click with Left Mouse button.
When-Mouse-Enter	When Mouse Cursor Enters in a user Object.
When-Mouse-Leave	When Mouse Cursor is moved out of a user Object.
When-Mouse-Move	When the Mouse Cursor is Moved within an Object.

Navigational Triggers:
Navigational triggers fire in response to navigational events. When the operator clicks on a text item in another block, navigational events occur as Oracle Forms Builder moves its focus from the current item to the target item.

For example when **the cursor navigates** out of a text item to another text item the *Post-Text-Item* trigger for the current text item and *Pre-Text-Item* trigger for the next text item it moves to will both fire in sequence.

Navigational events occur at different levels in the Oracle Forms Builder object hierarchy (Form, Block, Record and Item). Navigational triggers can be further sub-divided into two categories:

- **Pre-** and **Post-** triggers
- **When-New-Instance** triggers

Pre- and Post- Triggers:
Pre- and Post- triggers fire as Oracle Forms Builder cursor navigates internally through different levels of the object hierarchy. These triggers fire in response to:
- Cursor Navigation initiated by an operator, such as pressing <Tab>, <Shift><Tab> or a mouse click.
- Cursor Navigation initiated programmatically by using Oracle's built-in procedures like Go_Item, Go_Block etc.
- Internal navigation that Oracle Forms Builder automatically performs during default processing. Oracle's Internal navigation:
  - from one record to another
  - from one block to another
  - is initiated if records for different blocks in a form are saved using the *commit key sequence* or by programmatic control like *commit_form*.

When-New-Instance-Triggers:
When-New-Instance triggers fires after the form's focus is positioned on a given form, block or item.

To know when these triggers fire, there is a need to understand the Oracle Forms Builder processing model.

Consider a form named '*Product*', with a block named *product_master* with text items associated with the columns of *product_master* table.

As soon as the form is opened in memory, a series of navigational triggers are executed. The sequence of triggers that fire when a form is invoked are as follows:

Sequence	Trigger Name	Remarks
1.	Pre-Form	The first Navigational trigger that gets executed. This trigger gets executed even before the form is displayed to the user.
2.	Pre-Block	This triggers fires while entering the block and also during navigation from one block to another.
3.	Pre-Record	This triggers fires for the first time before entering the first record in the first block on the form. *Subsequently* it fires before navigation to any record in that block.
4.	Pre-Text-Item	This triggers fires for the first time before entering the first enterable item in the first block on the form. *Subsequently* it fires before navigation to any item in that block.
5.	When-New-Form-Instance	This trigger fires when the forms focus is on the first item in the first block after the form is displayed.
6.	When-New-Block-Instance	This triggers fires after the cursor is positioned on the first item of the block and also during navigation from one block to another.
7.	When-new-record-instance	This trigger fires when the forms focus changes from one record to the other.
8.	When-New-Item-Instance	This triggers fires after the cursor is positioned on the any item on the form and also during navigation from one item to another.

The sequence of triggers that fire when a form is closed are as follows:

Sequence	Trigger Name	Remarks
1.	Post-text-item	This triggers fires after leaving the current item.
2.	Post-Record	This triggers fires after leaving the current record.
3.	Post-Block	This triggers fires after leaving the current block.
4.	Post-Form	This triggers fires just before exiting the form.

Smart Triggers:

Each object in the object navigator, has a set of events (triggers) associated with it. Oracle Forms Builder provides a list of pre-defined triggers for the form, block or specific item. Oracle Forms Builder shows a list of triggers attached to a specific object. When Triggers are classified on the basis of the object, they are termed as **Smart Triggers**.

Example of '**Smart Triggers**':
The triggers associated with push button Item are:
- When-New-Item-Instance
- When-Button-Pressed

Writing Trigger PL/SQL code blocks:

The steps for writing PL/SQL code blocks for triggers are as follows:

1. Select the object for which trigger code is to be written in the *Object Navigator* and right click. A popup menu is displayed.

2. Click on *Smart Trigger* in the popup menu. It displays a list of triggers to select from that are connected to the selected object as shown in diagram 2.33.

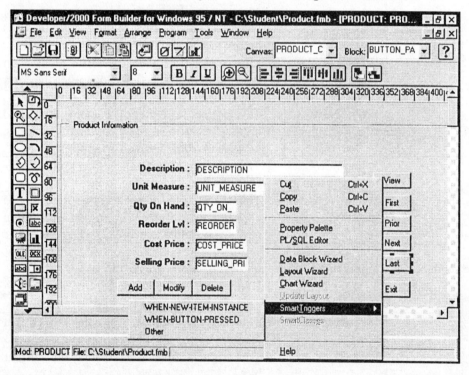

Diagram 2.33 : List of Smart Triggers that can be connected to the selected object

3. Select a trigger from the list provided. Oracle Forms Builder displays the PL/SQL Editor where PL/SQL code blocks can be written as shown in diagram 2.34. In the current example the PL/SQL block of code that makes the 'View' button functional must be written.

Right click on push button *pb_view* to see a list of triggers associated with the push button item. From the list displayed select the 'When-Button-Pressed' trigger. The PL/SQL Editor will display the following details and allow creation of suitable PL/SQL blocks.

Type   : Trigger
Object   : pb_view in block Button_Palette
Name   : **When-button-pressed**

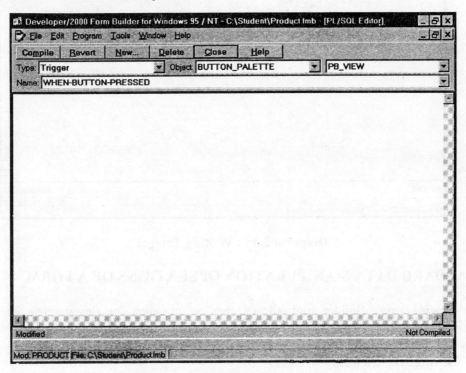

Diagram 2.34 : List of Trigger Names

4. Type in appropriate PL/SQL code in the text area of the PL/SQL Editor tool. The Completed *When-Button-Pressed* trigger code attached to *button_palette* and the item *pb_view* is displayed in diagram 2.35.

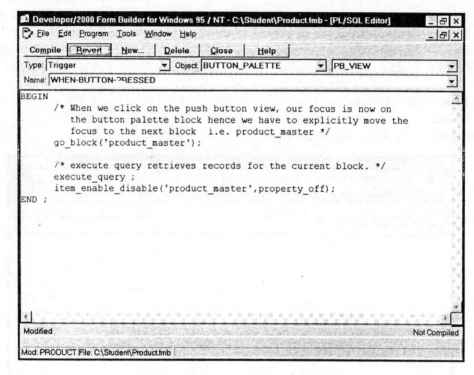

Diagram 2.35 : Writing Trigger

STANDARD DATA MANIPULATION OPERATIONS OF A FORM

The Oracle Forms Builder tool allows creation of form for the purpose of data manipulation and validation. Conceptually in a commercial application, the very same Oracle form will be used for:

- Viewing data in a table
  - Scrolling from one record to another
  - Searching and retrieving specific data from a table.

- Inserting new data into a table
- Updating data that exists in a table
- Deleting data that exists in a table.

The Forms Mode of Operation:

There are **two** types of the operations that can be performed on a table:

- A table '*Write*' operation
  This operation will be include Insert, Update and Delete.

- A table '*Read*' operation
  The table 'Read' operation includes viewing data in a table.

A read operation must precede a Delete and Update operation. This is because unless the data is displayed on the form the record cannot be really updated or deleted.

A form cannot behave in *exactly the same manner* for Viewing, Inserting, Updating or Deleting data. Each operation is unique and form behavior must change from operation to operation as the very same form is used for all the operations. The form behavior must be as follows:

Form Behavior while Viewing Data:

When the form is being used to 'View' data from the table, none of the items on the form must be updateable. Data navigation i.e. scrolling from one record to the other is allowed. Any form of data manipulation must not be allowed.

Form Behavior while Inserting Data:

When the form is being used to 'Insert' data, every item on the form must be enterable. This form behavior is exactly the opposite to the forms behavior in 'View' mode.

Form Behavior while Deleting Data:

When a form is being used to 'Delete' data, the status of the items placed on the form is really not an issue. *However, it is best if the items on the form are not updateable.*

To delete a record, the record must be visible in the form. Record scrolling can be done to position the cursor on the record that must be deleted. The current record can be deleted by pressing the 'DELETE' push button. Since a 'View' operation precedes a 'Delete' operation, all the items in the form should in any case be non updateable.

Form Behavior while Updating Data: [*Primary Key problems*]

While Updating the contents of a form, the contents of the *Primary Key Item* must be **non-updateable**. This restriction is placed on the primary key item to maintain *Referential Integrity* of data between tables.

Note

If a *change* in a Primary Key value is needed a *Delete* and an *Insert* operation must be carried out.

DATA NAVIGATION VIA AN ORACLE FORM

Multiple Rows being retrieved From the Table:

To navigate through several records via an Oracle form, Push Buttons appropriately labeled as *First, Next, Prior, Last* are placed on the form. Clicking on a push button will cause its *When-Button-Pressed* event to fire. Any code attached to this event will in turn execute. Hence, by clicking on the appropriate push button navigation through the records retrieved is possible.

There is a need to super control the push buttons themselves. When the forms tool is focused on the *first* record the *Prior* and *First* push buttons should be disabled. When the forms tool is focused on the *Last* record the *Next* and *Last* push buttons should be disabled.

Having these push buttons enabled when the forms tool focus is on the *First* or *Last* record will achieve nothing if the user clicks on them. The movement is completely illogical.

Similarly, when the focus of the Forms tool is on any record *other than first* or *last* it is necessary to have all the push buttons enabled. Having them disabled would now be completely illogical.

Every form will behave the same when it comes to navigating through several records.

Hence a procedure, which scans the record buffer and enables or disables navigational push buttons according to the record *'In Focus'* would work very well.

A Single Row being retrieved from the Table:

The enabling or disabling of the scroll control buttons on a data entry form must be dependent on the number of data rows retrieved from the Server as well.

If only one row from the table is retrieved, then the *First, Next, Prior, Last* navigational control push buttons must all be disabled.

Changes in Form Behavior:

To ensure that the form behaves as required in a commercial application, event driven PL/SQL code must be written to ensure:
- Navigational control push buttons are enabled or disabled appropriately.
- The 'Text Items' on the form are 'Updateable' according to the 'Mode' the form is currently in.

The navigational control push buttons themselves can be used to indicate the 'mode' the form is operating in. Hence a call to a user-defined procedure that will enable/disable the Navigational control push buttons appropriately, can be made in the 'WHEN-BUTTON-PRESSED' event of the push buttons.

Trigger Name	: **WHEN-BUTTON-PRESSED**	Form	: product
Block	: button_palette	Item	: pb_view
Trigger Level	: Item Level		
Trigger Focus	: Retrieve all the records and go to the first record in the product_master block.		
Text	: BEGIN		

```
          /* When the push button view is clicked, the focus is on the button
           palette block hence the focus must be moved explicitly to
          product_master block. */
          go_block ('product_master');

          /* Execute_query retrieves records for the current block. */
          execute_query ;

          /* Item_enable_disable is a user-defined procedure that enables
          the fields so that the contents of a field are not updateable in
          'View' mode. This procedure is explained in the section
          PROCEDURE. */
          item_enable_disable (property_off);
     END ;
```

Trigger Name	: **WHEN-BUTTON-PRESSED**	Form	: product
Block	: button_palette	Item	: pb_first
Trigger Level	: Item Level		
Trigger Focus	: Go to the first record in the product_master block.		
Text	: BEGIN		

```
        go_block('product_master');
        /* Position the cursor on the first record of the current block */
        first_record;
    END ;
```

Trigger Name	: **WHEN-BUTTON-PRESSED**	Form	: product
Block	: button_palette	Item	: pb_prior
Trigger Level	: Item Level		
Trigger Focus	: Go to the previous record in the product_master block.		
Text	: BEGIN		

```
        go_block('product_master');

        /* Position the cursor on the prior record of the current block */
        previous_record ;
    END;
```

Trigger Name	: **WHEN-BUTTON-PRESSED**	Form	: product
Block	: button_palette	Item	: pb_next
Trigger Level	: Item Level		
Trigger Focus	: Go to the next record in the product_master block.		
Text	: BEGIN		

```
        go_block('product_master');

        /* Position the cursor on the next record of the current block */
        next_record ;
    END;
```

Trigger Name	: **WHEN-BUTTON-PRESSED**	Form	: product
Block	: button_palette	Item	: pb_last
Trigger Level	: Item Level		
Trigger Focus	: Go to the last record in the product_master block.		
Text	: BEGIN		

```
        go_block('product_master');

        /* Position the cursor on the last record of the current block */
        last_record ;
    END ;
```

Trigger Name	: **WHEN-BUTTON-PRESSED**	Form	: product
Block	: button_palette	Item	: pb_add
Trigger Level	: Item Level		
Trigger Focus	: Insert a blank record in the product_master block.		
Text	: BEGIN		

```
            go_block('product_master');

            /* Insert a new record in the current block and position the
               cursor on the newly inserted  record */
            create_record ;

            /* Item_enable_disable is a user-defined procedure that enables
            the fields so that the contents of a field are updateable in 'Add'
            mode. This procedure is explained in the section PROCEDURE. */
            item_enable_disable (property_on);
    END ;
```

Trigger Name	: **WHEN-BUTTON-PRESSED**	Form	: product
Block	: button_palette	Item	: pb_modify
Trigger Level	: Item Level		
Trigger Focus	: Set the primary key item i.e. product_no as not updateable and set all other items updateable so that the record in the product_master block can be modified.		
Text	: BEGIN		

```
            go_block('product_master');
            item_enable_disable(property_on);
            /* item_enable_disable is a user-defined procedure that enables
            or disables a 'text_item' updateable property depending on a
            parameter passed by the push button. This procedure is
            explained in the section PROCEDURE*/
            set_item_property('product_master.product_no', updateable,
                    property_off)
    END ;
```

Trigger Name	: **WHEN-BUTTON-PRESSED**	Form	: product
Block	: button_palette	Item	: pb_delete
Trigger Level	: Item Level		
Trigger Focus	: Delete the current record in the product_master block.		
Text	: BEGIN		

```
            go_block('product_master');

            /* Delete the current record in the block */
            delete_record ;
    END ;
```

Trigger Name : **WHEN-BUTTON-PRESSED**   Form : product
Block   : button_palette   Item : pb_save
Trigger Level : Item Level
Trigger Focus : Save the changes to product_master table.
Text   : BEGIN

> /* FORM_STATUS, a system variable holds the current status of a form. Form status can take three values. These are:
> CHANGED (at least one record has changed in the form. changes may be in the form of insert, update or delete)
> NEW   (Contains only blank records i.e. the user has inserted new rows but no values are entered for the items. Oracle doesn't post blank records into the database
> QUERY (contains records that have been queried but no changes have been made. If the value in any field is changed them FORM_STATUS will hold the value 'CHANGED'. If the commit is successful FORM_STATUS holds the value 'QUERY'*/

```
        IF :system.form_status = 'CHANGED' THEN
        /* If the FORM_STATUS holds the value 'CHANGED' then
            commit changes */
            commit_form ;
            IF :system.form_status = 'QUERY' THEN
                    item_enable_disable(property_off);
            END IF ;
        END IF;
END ;
```

Tip

Trigger *When-Button-Pressed* on pb_modify, pb_delete, pb_save calls a procedure named *item_enable_disable*. This procedure is explained in the section called PROCEDURES in chapter MASTER FORM on page 66.

Trigger Name : **WHEN-BUTTON-PRESSED**   Form : product
Block   : button_palette   Item : pb_exit
Trigger Level : Item Level
Trigger Focus : Quit product form.
Text   : BEGIN

> /* Close the form. If there are any changes in the form the system asks for confirmation to save changes */

```
        exit_form ;
END ;
```

DISABLING THE DEFAULT FORMS TOOLBAR

The default toolbar provided by Oracle Forms Runtime must not be visible since a set of user-defined pushbuttons have been placed on the form.

An appropriate form property must be set to make the default toolbar invisible. Select the *Product* form in the Object Navigator. Right click and open the property palette of the form. Locate the form property **Menu Module**. Menu Module has a default value of **DEFAULT&SMARTBAR** where DEFAULT displays the default textual menu and SMARTBAR displays the default toolbar.

To make the default iconic toolbar invisible, set the *Menu Module* property to **DEFAULT**. When the form 'Product' is run it will be as shown in diagram 2.36 without the default toolbar.

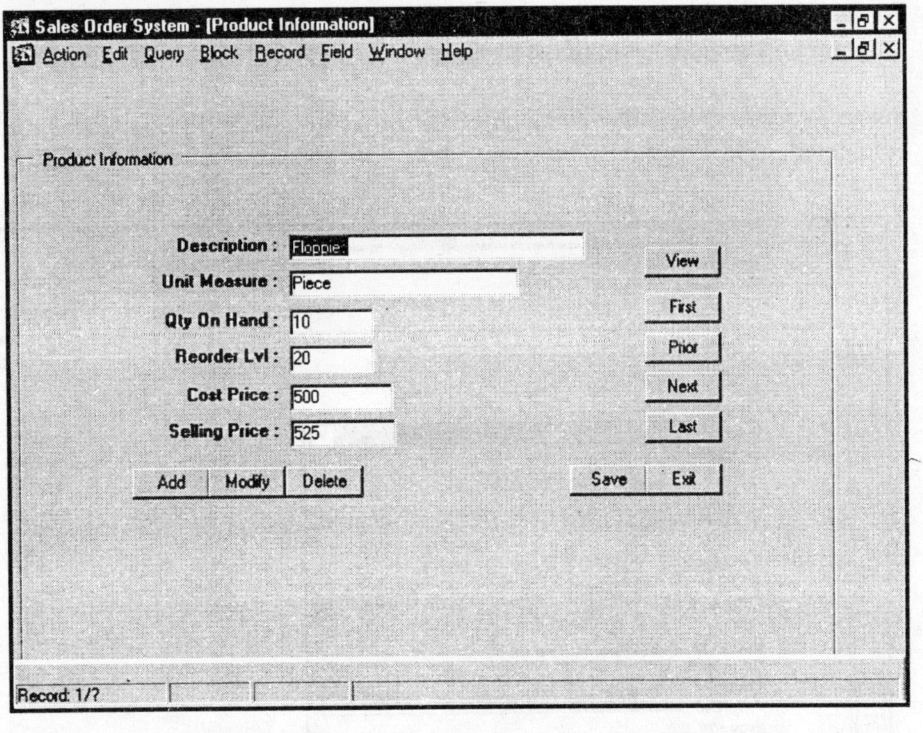

Diagram 2.36 : Product Form Displayed without Default Iconic Toolbar

PROCEDURES

Triggers can be used to call user-defined procedures and functions to control form behavior. User defined *procedures* and *functions* are called **Program Units** in Forms Builder. The steps in creating program units are as follows:

1. Select the *Program Unit* node in the *Object Navigator* and click on **N**avigator..**Cr**eate menu options. The different type of program units that can be created in Forms Builder include.
   - Procedures
   - Functions
   - Package Specification
   - Package Body

   Forms Builder will display the *New Program Unit* dialog box that asks for the type of program unit and the name of the program unit.

2. Select *Procedure*, specify the name of the procedure as SCROLL_CONTROL. The completed *New Program Unit* dialog box will appear as shown in diagram 2.37. Click on OK

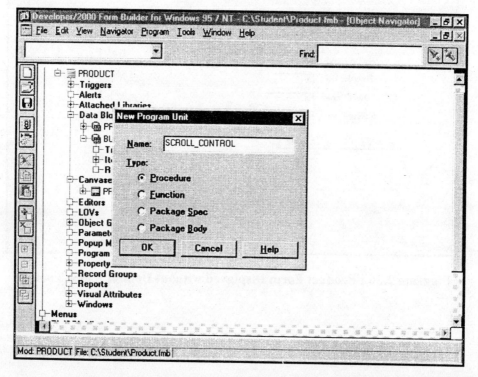

Diagram 2.37 : Completed New Program Unit dialog box

Click on OK. The PL/SQL Editor is displayed as shown in diagram 2.38.

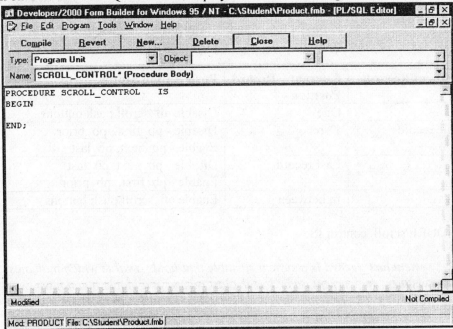

Diagram 2.38 : PL/SQL Editor displayed user-defined procedure

3. Enter the PL/SQL statements for the procedure. The *scroll_control* procedure is displayed in diagram 2.39 and detailed immediately below diagram 2.39.

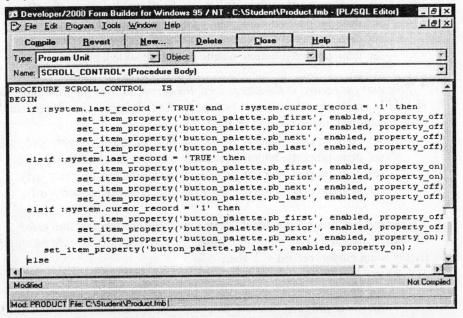

Diagram 2.39 : Writing Procedures

Procedure Name : **SCROLL_CONTROL**
Trigger Focus　　: To enable or disable the push buttons i.e. first, prior, next and last based on the total number of records retrieved by the form focus on the record.

Total No. of Records	Current Record Position	Push Button Status
One	One	Disable all scroll push buttons
Multiple records	1st record	Disable - pb_first, pb_prior Enable - pb_next, pb_last
	Last record	Disable - pb_next, pb_last Enable - pb_first, pb_prior
	In between	Enable all scroll push buttons

PROCEDURE scroll_control IS
BEGIN

　　　　/* **system.last_record** *is a system variable that holds a value which indicates whether the current record is the last record in a block. It can have two values i.e. TRUE: (current record is the last record) and FALSE: (current record is not the last record)*

　　　　cursor_record, *is a system variable that holds the current record number. If the current record number is 1 and system.last_record is 'True', all the scroll buttons should be disabled since there is only one record in the form data buffer* */
　　　　if :system.last_record = 'TRUE' and　:system.cursor_record = '1' then
　　　　　　　set_item_property('button_palette.pb_first', enabled, property_off);
　　　　　　　set_item_property('button_palette.pb_prior', enabled, property_off);
　　　　　　　set_item_property('button_palette.pb_next', enabled, property_off);
　　　　　　　set_item_property('button_palette.pb_last', enabled, property_off);

　　　　/* *If the current record is the last record, the scroll buttons for first and prior should be enabled and the scroll buttons for last and next should be disabled* */
　　　　elsif :system.last_record = 'TRUE' then
　　　　　　　set_item_property('button_palette.pb_first', enabled, property_on);
　　　　　　　set_item_property('button_palette.pb_prior', enabled, property_on);
　　　　　　　set_item_property('button_palette.pb_next', enabled, property_off);
　　　　　　　set_item_property('button_palette.pb_last', enabled, property_off);

　　　　/* *If the current record number is 1, the scroll buttons for first and prior should be disabled and the scroll buttons for last and next should be enabled* */
　　　　elsif :system.cursor_record = '1' then
　　　　　　　set_item_property('button_palette.pb_first', enabled, property_off);
　　　　　　　set_item_property('button_palette.pb_prior', enabled, property_off);
　　　　　　　set_item_property('button_palette.pb_next', enabled, property_on);
　　　　　　　set_item_property('button_palette.pb_last', enabled, property_on);

/ If the current record is the not the last record and the record number is not 1
    then, all the scroll buttons should be enabled */*
else
　　　　　set_item_property('button_palette.pb_first', enabled, property_on);
　　　　　set_item_property('button_palette.pb_prior', enabled, property_on);
　　　　　set_item_property('button_palette.pb_next', enabled, property_on);
　　　　　set_item_property('button_palette.pb_last', enabled, property_on);
　　end if ;
END;

The scroll control procedure must fire when the Oracle forms focus moves from one record to the other.

The change in the record position may be due to the following reasons:
- When a form is loaded in memory i.e. executed, Oracle Forms inserts a blank row in the form buffer and moves the record focus to the inserted record.
- When the *create_record* packaged procedure is executed, Oracle Forms inserts a blank record in the form buffer and moves the focus to the newly inserted row. This packaged procedure is called
  - When push button named *Insert* placed on the form is clicked
  - When the menu items *Record, Insert* included in the default menu provided by Oracle Forms is clicked or
  - When the user presses *F6* i.e. the function key for inserting a record.

- When the *delete_record* packaged procedure is executed, it deletes the current record. This packaged procedure is called
  - When the push button named *Delete* placed on the form is clicked
  - When the menu items *Record, Remove* included in the default menu provided by Oracle is clicked or
  - When the user presses *Shift F6* i.e. the function key for deleting a record

If the deleted record was the last record in the form buffer, the focus moves to the previous row in the form buffer, otherwise the focus will move to the next record relative to the record that was deleted.

- When the *execute_query* packaged procedure is executed, records are retrieved from a table into the form buffer and form focus is moved to the first record (go top) in the form buffer. This packaged procedure is called
  - When push button named *View* placed on the form is clicked
  - When the menu items *Query, Execute* included in the default menu provided by Oracle Forms is clicked or
  - When the user presses *F8* i.e. the function key for retrieving records.

- Each time Oracle packaged procedure *first_record, previous_record, next_record* or *last_record* are executed, the forms record focus will change. These packaged procedures are called
  - By the push buttons on the form named *first, prior, next* and *last* respectively.
  - When the menu items *Record, Previous* or *Record, Next* included in the default menu provided by Oracle is clicked or
  - When the user presses *Up Arrow* or the *Down Arrow keys* i.e. the keys for record navigation.

Thus the *Scroll_Control* procedure must be executed either when the user performs an *explicit navigation* operation or when there is *implicit navigation* due other commands like *create_record, delete_record* or *execute_query*. A common trigger that is always executed when there is *implicit* or *explicit* form navigation is *When-New-Record-Instance*.

A call to a user-defined procedure named *Scroll_Control* must be made in the trigger When-*New-Record-Instance* which fires under all the above conditions.

Trigger Name   : **WHEN-NEW-RECORD-INSTANCE**   Form   : product
Block   : product_master   Item   :
Trigger Level   : Block Level
Trigger Focus   : calls procedure scroll_control that enables or disables the push buttons
                       i.e. first, prior, next and last based on the total number of records
                       in the form buffer and the current record position.
Text   : BEGIN
                      scroll_control ;
             END ;

Enabling and Disabling the Text Items based on the Mode of Operation:

If the form is in view mode, the contents of the Oracle Form items must not be allowed to be modified i.e. *the items should not be updateable.*

Similarly, if the form is in Add mode, data entry must be allowed in all the items on the form i.e. *the text items must be updateable.*

In Update mode, certain items are updateable. Generally the text items associated with the primary key column/s must not be updateable.

The property that controls such behavior of a text item is its '*Updateable*' property. If the *Updateable* property is set to *Property_on* then the user can change the value in a text item. If the *Updateable* property is set to *Property_off* then the user is not allowed to change the value in a text item.

To achieve this objective (i.e. change the behavior of the text items based on the mode of operation), a programmer needs to set the value of this property to *property_on* or *property_off* based on the mode of operation.

The set_item_property (i.e. an Oracle Forms function), is used to set the property of a text item dynamically at runtime.

The syntax of set_item_property is:

Set_Item_Property(Itemname, Property, Value)

For example to set the updateable property of *product_no* to *property_off* the syntax will be:

Set_Item_Property('product_no', updateable, property_off)

In the current example, the value of the updateable property of each text item (i.e. property_on / property_off) is dependent on the mode of form operation. Hence the user-defined procedure needs to know the form mode. This value must be passed by the caller of the procedure as a parameter.

For example if the procedure is called from pb_add the value passed to this procedure must be *property_on*. Similarly, if the procedure is called from pb_view the value passed to this procedure must be *property_off*.

The technique used in the user defined procedure item_enable_disable is described below along with the complete listing of the code that controls all the text items.

Procedure Name : **ITEM_ENABLE_DISABLE**
Trigger Focus   : To enable the fields so that the contents of the field can be modified or new values can be entered in the add or modify mode. To disable fields so that the contents of the field cannot be modified in view mode.

```
PROCEDURE item_enable_disable (item_on_off IN NUMBER) IS
BEGIN
        set_item_property('product_master.product_no', updateable, item_on_off) ;
        set_item_property('product_master.description ', updateable, item_on_off) ;
        set_item_property('product_master.unit_measure', updateable, item_on_off);
        set_item_property('product_master.qty_on_hand', updateable, item_on_off);
        set_item_property('product_master.reorder_lvl', updateable, item_on_off);
        set_item_property('product_master.cost_price ', updateable, item_on_off) ;
        set_item_property('product_master.selling_price', updateable, item_on_off) ;
END;
```

Please refer to page 61 to 64 for an understanding on how the item enable disable procedure is called.

VALIDATIONS

As programmers it is our responsibility to ensure table data integrity. Business managers make business decisions based on table data. If table data is not valid then the business decision being made is going to be erroneous which is likely to cause a company to lose money.

To ensure table data integrity, it is necessary to validate data *prior* it being stored in a table. What this really means is via programming data being stored is checked to ensure that it conforms to a set of pre-defined business rules.

Business rules differ from business system to business system.

Not only must data be validated according to business rules but data also needs to be validated according to database input / output rules as well. This is because programmers are responsible both for table data integrity and the speed of table data extraction.

Using a Database Trigger to ensure table data integrity: [I/O validation techniques]

One or more than one columns of a table can be set aside to uniquely identify a record in the table. This column /s must hold data that is *unique*. No cell in that column/s can be left blank. Such a column/s is referred to as *primary key* column/s.

In the *product_master* table, product_no is a primary key. In a multi-user environment, a data entry operator is generally *not allowed* to enter a primary key value. The primary key value is always generated by the system.

Simple but effective methods that can be used to generate a primary key value is by using a Sequence. The Oracle engine provides an object called a *sequence* that generates numeric values starting with a given value with an increment as required. A sequence must first be created using SQL*Plus.

Once the sequence is created a database trigger can be written such that a value is retained from the sequence and used as a part (*or whole*) of the primary key value.

Syntax for Sequence Creation:
The syntax for creating a sequence for product_no is as follows:

> **CREATE SEQUENCE** *product_seq*
> **INCREMENT BY** *1*
> **START WITH** *1;*

Database trigger Creation:

A Database trigger can be created by invoking SQL*Plus and writing appropriate code. The Oracle Forms Builder Tool also provides an interface for creating, compiling and storing database triggers.

The steps in creating a database trigger using the *Database Object Interface* of Forms Builder are:

1. Select *Database Objects* Node in the *Object Navigator*. Oracle Forms Builder will display a list of users as shown in diagram 2.40.

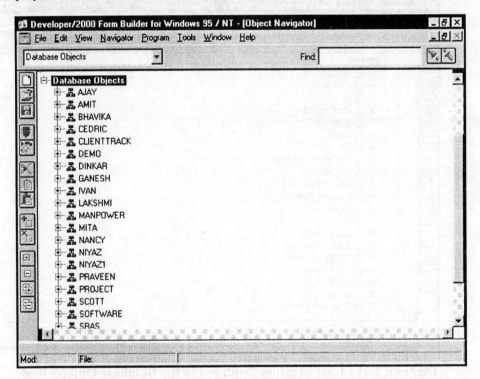

Diagram 2.40 : List of Users displayed in Database Object Node

2. Select the user for which the database trigger must be created. Oracle Forms Builder displays a list of objects that can be created and stored in the database. These include
    - Stored Program Units
    - PL/SQL Libraries
    - Tables
    - Views

Since a database trigger is connected to a table click on the *Tables* Node. A list of tables belonging to a specific user is displayed as shown in diagram 2.41.

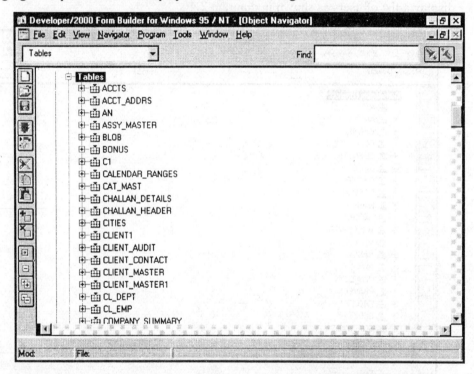

Diagram 2.41 : Lists of tables displayed in the Database Objects Node

3. Each *Table* Node is further subdivided into *Triggers* and *Columns*. The *Triggers* Node will display a list of triggers if any currently exist, attached to the selected table. To create a new trigger, select the table on which the database trigger must be created and click on **Navigator..Create** menu option.

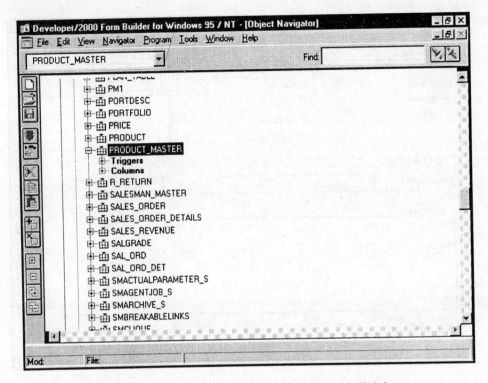

Diagram 2.42 : The Table node with its subdivisions

Oracle Forms Builder displays an interface that allows database trigger creation as shown in diagram 2.43.

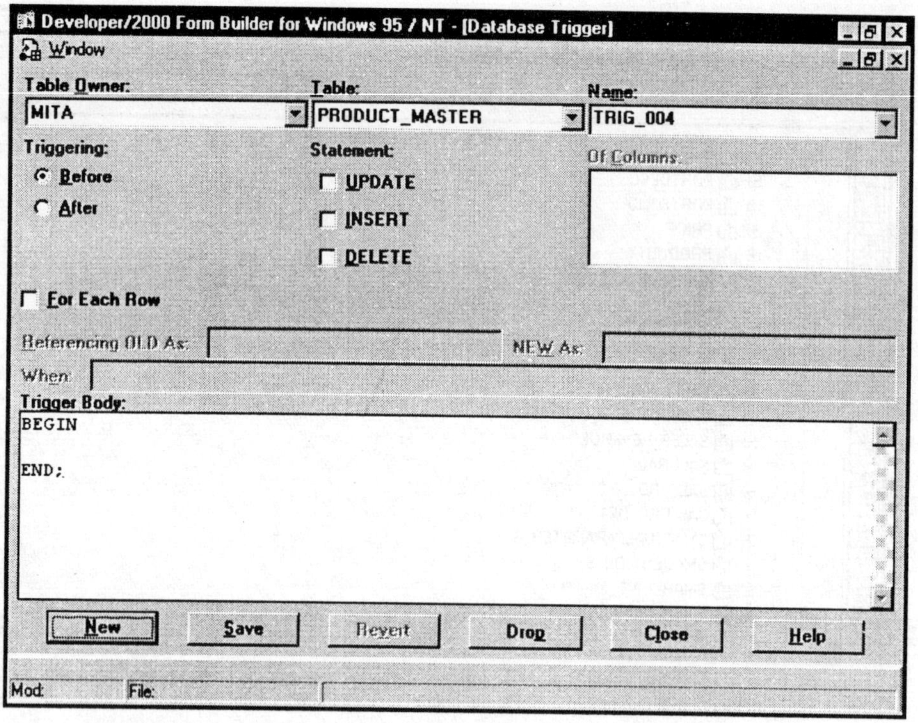

Diagram 2.43 : Interface to create a Database Trigger

4. Click on New. Oracle Forms Builder creates a new trigger with a *default* name. Change the name of the trigger to *product_no_generation* and set the database trigger parameters as follows:

    Triggering Time   : Before
    Statement   : Insert

    Also check the *For Each Row* check box. The equivalent Oracle PL/SQL syntax for the above parameters will be:

    > **CREATE OR REPLACE TRIGGER** *product_no_generation*
    > **BEFORE INSERT**
    > **ON** *product_master*
    > **FOR EACH ROW**

    Oracle Forms Builder allows PL/SQL statements block to be keyed in that is a part of trigger executable code. Enter the code as required.

The PL/SQL block that must be written for automatic generation of primary key is as follows:

```
DECLARE
        primary_key_value varchar2(5);

BEGIN
        SELECT lpad(to_char(product_seq.nextval), 5 , '0')
                INTO primary_key_value FROM dual;
        :new.product_no := 'P' || primary_key_value;
END;
```

The completed database trigger interface will be as shown in diagram 2.44.

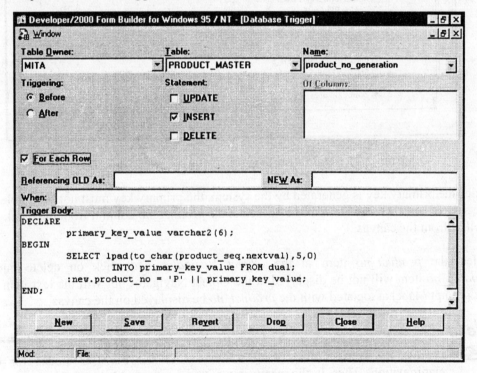

Diagram 2.44 : Completed Database Trigger Interface

5. Click on 'Save'. Forms Builder Interface will convert the text into an appropriate PL/SQL trigger block and pass the same to the Oracle Engine. The Oracle engine will compile the PL/SQL block and create/ store the database triggers. Once created the name of the trigger cannot be modified. The *Object Navigator* displays the newly created trigger as shown in diagram 2.45.

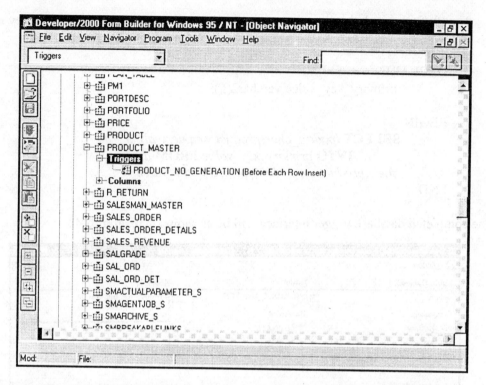

Diagram 2.45 : Database Trigger displayed in Object Navigator

Since the primary key is generated by the system, the primary key must not be visible on the screen. Thus we need to remove / deselect the *product_no* column from the block as well as from the canvas.

Select the *product_no* item in the *Object Navigator* and click on delete button. *product_no* item will not be displayed in the Object Navigator nor will the text item and the prompt / label associated with the *product_no* be displayed on the canvas.

Note

Product_no item is also being referenced in the PL/SQL blocks for data manipulation. Thus if the *product_no* item is removed any references to the *product_no* item must also be removed. Currently the *product_no* item is referenced in:

- When-button-pressed on pb_modify
- Program Unit Item_enable_disable

Product_no item is referenced in the set_item_property function. Delete the statements that reference product_no in the push button modify as well as in the procedure item_enable_disable.

Not Null Check using ON-ERROR Form Trigger:

If a column is defined as a NOT NULL column at the table level, Oracle Forms Builder sets the '*Required*' attribute to '*Yes*'. If the '*Required*' attribute is set to '*Yes*', Oracle Forms Runtime will display an error message if such an item is exited *without* entering any value. I.e. leaving the item *empty*.

Note

If the text item is left blank, Oracle Forms Runtime displays an FRM Error as follows:

FRM-40202 : Field must be entered

This system error message can be *user defined* by writing appropriate code in the ON-ERROR trigger at the form level.

Working of Form Runtime in case of an Error:
In case of an error Oracle Forms Runtime checks if the ON-ERROR trigger is written at form level. If an ON-ERROR trigger is written, Oracle Forms Runtime executes the statements specified in the ON-ERROR trigger.

If the PL/SQL block is not written for the ON-ERROR trigger, Oracle Forms Runtime displays a *Oracle default* Forms Runtime Error along with the error message on the status bar.

To customize the *error message* code must be written in the ON-ERROR trigger at Form level.

Writing PL/SQL code for the ON-ERROR trigger:
To handle an error in the ON-ERROR trigger, first identify the error based on the *error number* or the *error description*.

Standard functions available in Oracle Forms allow identification of error type, error number or error message.

These functions are ERROR_TYPE( ), ERROR_CODE( ), ERROR_TEXT( ) respectively.

For example, Oracle Forms Runtime returns error type - FRM, error code- 40202 if a required field is left blank.

Trigger Name   : **ON-ERROR**   Form   : product

Block   :   Item   :

Trigger Level   : Form Level

Trigger Focus   : NOT NULL check handling.

Text   : DECLARE

/* *Variables that hold the name of the current item and the text*
      displayed in the associated label or prompt */
error_item varchar2(50);
current_item_label varchar2(100);
BEGIN

/* *Check that the error code is 40202 i.e. required validation*
      violated. */
if error_type = 'FRM' and error_code = 40202 then

/* *Identify the name of the item that triggered ON-ERROR* */
error_item := :system.trigger_item;

/* *Get the label prompt associated with the item* */
current_item_label := get_item_property(error_item,
      prompt_text);
/* *Display error message on the status bar as a*
      concatenation of item prompt and a constant string
      'cannot be left blank". */
message(current_item_label || ' cannot be left blank.');
else

message(error_text); /* *Display default error message* */
end if;
END;

Implementing Business Rules using the When-Validate-Item Trigger:

Trigger Name : **WHEN-VALIDATE-ITEM**   Form   : product
Block   : product_master   Item   : cost_price
Trigger Level   : Item Level
Trigger Focus : cost price should not be 0 and cost price should be less than selling price.
Text   : BEGIN

```
        if :product_master.cost_price =  0 then
            message('Cost Price  cannot be 0');
            raise form_trigger_failure;


        /* Any comparison with a null value always evaluates to False. Thus
            if the selling price is null the comparison of selling price and cost
            price will evaluate to false and it will pass the validation test */
        elsif :product_master.cost_price >
                :product_master.selling_price then
            message(' Cost Price cannot be greater than Selling Price');
            raise form_trigger_failure;
        end if;
    END;
```

Trigger Name : **WHEN-VALIDATE-ITEM**   Form   : product
Block   : product_master   Item   : selling_price
Trigger Level   : Item Level
Trigger Focus : selling_price should not be 0 and it should be greater than the cost price.
Text   : BEGIN

```
        If :product_master.selling_price =  0 then
        message('Selling Price  cannot be 0');
        raise form_trigger_failure;


        /* Any comparison with a null value always evaluates to False.
        Thus if the cost price is null the comparison of selling price
        and cost price will evaluate to false and it will pass the validation
        test */
        elsif :product_master.cost_price >
                :product_master.selling_price then
        message(' Selling Price cannot be less than Cost Price');
        raise form_trigger_failure;
        end if;
    END;
```

Setting the default value to 0 for the text_item qty_on_hand bound to the table column:

The *qty_on_hand* column in the *product_master* table always shows· the current stock position. The default value of *qty_on_hand* must be 0.

Open the property sheet of *qty_on_hand* text_item and set the **Initial value** property to *0*. The Property Palette of *qty_on_hand* is as shown in diagram 2.46.

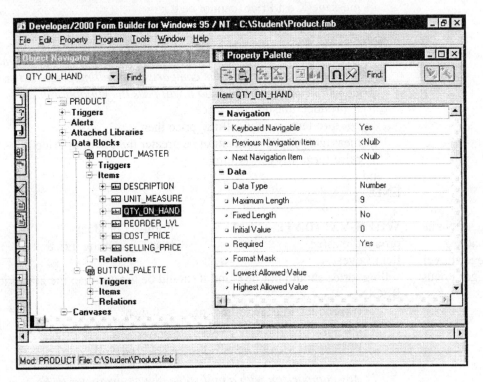

Diagram 2.46 : Setting the Initial Value property of qty_on_hand

Similarly, set the default value of *Reorder_lvl* to 0.

INCLUDING A SEARCH FUNCTION IN A MASTER FORM

Focus:
To modify form functionality to include a search function that retrieves record/s to matched to specific search criteria.

Focus:
To retrieve data based on specific search criteria associated with the table column product_master.description.

1. Check to see that the *Query Allowed* property for the field *description* is *True.*

2. Right click on the *button_palette* block. A popup menu is displayed. Click on *Layout Editor*. The form layout tool is activated. Click on the object palette and select the icon labeled *button* and place it on the form. Set the *Name* and *Label* property as:

    Name   : pb_search
    Label   : Search

3. Write the necessary code.

Trigger Name   : **WHEN-BUTTON-PRESSED**   Form   : product
Block   : button_palette   Item   : pb_search
Trigger Level   : Item Level
Trigger Focus   : To search for a specific record.
Text   : BEGIN
                    go_block('product_master');

                    /* enter query function flushes the current block and puts the
                        form in the query mode. The user can enter the value in any
                        field and execute a query. The query will use the values
                        entered by the user in the where clause */
                    enter_query;
        END;

When Enter_Query is executed, Oracle Forms Runtime clears the block and allows the entry of any value in any text item.

Once the value is entered as desired, Oracle Forms Runtime automatically creates a *where clause* by using the text item name for which the value is entered and the value entered by the user.

After entering the search value in the desired column, execute the query by clicking on **Query..Execute** in the textual menubar. Oracle Forms runtime executes the query after creating the appropriate where clause and attempts to retrieve data appropriately from the table.

Note

 A where clause that uses operators other than '=', can be created by entering '&' in any text item on the form. Click on **Query.. Execute** Menu item. Oracle Forms runtime will display a dialog box that allows users to specify a where clause.

For example user can query the *product_master* table and display all records where the quantity on hand *is less* than reorder level. The completed where clause is shown in diagram 2.47.

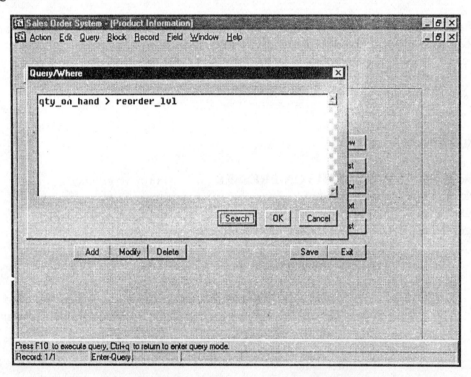

Diagram 2.47 : Specifying Where clause in Enter Query Mode

After entering the desired where clause, click on the OK button to retrieve appropriate records.

DISPLAYING CONTEXT SENSITIVE HELP

The end user for whom a form is designed, does not necessarily have knowledge of Oracle. Hence the form must be made as user-friendly as possible. Hints or help must be available constantly to make the job of data entry simpler.

Oracle Forms can display context sensitive help text (HINT) by using the methods mentioned below:

- Display help on the status bar at runtime
- Display *Balloon Help* when the Oracle Forms cursor enters any object on the data entry form.

Display Context Sensitive Help on the Status Bar at runtime:

Context sensitive help text can be displayed in Oracle forms by setting the *Autohint* and the *Hint* property of the individual items. The values of the properties are as follows:

> Autohint : True
> Hint : *String to be displayed as the 'Hint'.*

Hint text is usually advice to the operator on what to enter into the text_item.

Example:
The hint text for a text_item *client no* might be "Enter a Unique 6 digit Client Identity Number." The values of the properties are as follows:

> Autohint : True
> Hint : Enter a Unique 6 digit Client Identity Number.

Note

 Hint Text can be upto a maximum of 255 characters.

Oracle Form displays the hint message automatically when the Form cursor is on the item which has the Hint string specified and its Auto Hint property set to True.

Displaying Balloon Help using Tooltip:

Since the Hint String is displayed on the message line, the user's attention may not be caught. Hence Oracle Forms provides the user with *Tooltip*. A *tooltip* is a small text box that displays help information about an item when the mouse cursor enters the item.

The text appears in a box centered directly beneath the item. The size of the box is determined by how much space is needed to display the help text. The box is just large enough horizontally and vertically to display the text with a thin border around.

The tooltip remains visible until the mouse cursor is moved outside the item. When the user moves the mouse cursor from one item to another the text changes depending on the item for which the tooltip is being displayed.

The following are the steps involved to create a tooltip:

1. In the Object Navigator, double-click the icon beside the item description for which you want to create a tooltip. This will display the Property Palette.

2. Under the Help node, select the tooltip property

3. Type the desired tooltip text in the tooltip property field. For example, a tooltip can be *'Enter a Product Description'* as shown in diagram 2.48.

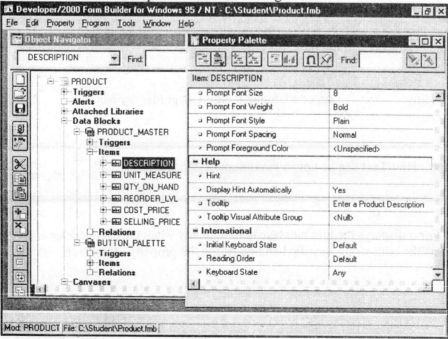

Diagram 2.48 : Setting the Tooltip property in the Property Palette

4. Now when the Product Form is run and the mouse cursor enters the text item *description* the tooltip text will pop up beneath the text item as shown in the diagram 2.49.

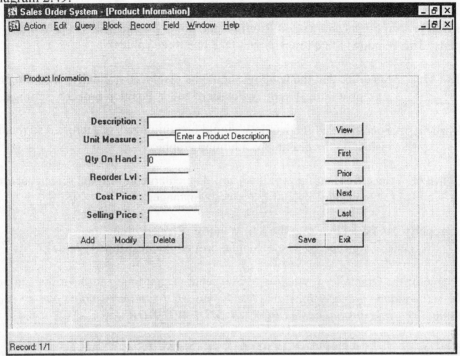

Diagram 2.49 : Tooltip displayed at runtime

5. Similarly the tooltip property can be set for all the items with appropriate text for providing additional help.

SETTING ORACLE'S MDI WINDOW PROPERTIES AT RUNTIME

Oracle runtime window is an MDI window. MDI stands for **M**ultiple **D**ocument **I**nterface window i.e. a special window that will allow other windows to be opened 'within it' and 'stay active' at the same time. This MDI runtime window is owned and controlled by the Oracle Forms runtime environment.

At runtime two windows are visible:
• Forms Window
• An MDI Window within which the Forms Window is displayed.

The user can set some of the properties of the Form Window at design time using the Property Palette provided by Forms Builder.

Unlike this, the properties of the MDI Window cannot be set at design time. Oracle Forms Builder provides the user with certain built in functions through which some of Oracle's runtime window properties can be set at runtime.

One such property that can be set at Runtime and not at Design time is the Window_State Property. The Window_State property can take one three values:

NORMAL   : Specifies that the window should be displayed normally, according to its current Width, Height, X Position, and Y Position property settings.

MINIMIZE   : Specifies that the window should be minimized, or iconified so that it is visible on the desktop as a bitmap graphic.

MAXIMIZE : Specifies that the window should be enlarged to fill the screen according to the display style of the window manager.

This property can be set by using the Set_Window_Property function.
     Set_window_property(windowname, propertyname, propertyvalue);

The name of the Oracle form window can be set at design time and the same can be used in the set_window_property function. *The Forms MDI runtime window can be accessed by using a special constant named **FORMS_MDI_WINDOW**.*

Trigger Name	: **WHEN-NEW-FORM-INSTANCE**	Form	: product
Block	:	Item	:
Trigger Focus	: To maximize the window during runtime.		
Trigger Level	: Form Level		
Trigger Text	: BEGIN		

```
            Set_window_property(forms_mdi_window, window_state, maximize);
            Set_window_property ('product_win', window_state, maximize);
        END;
```

SELF REVIEW QUESTIONS

TRUE OR FALSE

1. The enabled and visible property of an item cannot be disabled at runtime if the cursor is on that item.

    A) True   B) False

2. A Window is connected to a block.

    A) True   B) False

3. The Pre-Form trigger fires before the When-New-Form-Instance trigger.

    A) True   B) False

4. When-Validate-Item cannot have navigational code like next_item, next_block, etc.

    A) True   B) False

5. By default, the type of canvas is 'Content'.

    A) True   B) False

6. A Control Block is created by using a Block Wizard.

    A) True   B) False

7. New_Record procedure creates a New Record at Runtime.

    A) True   B) False

8. Execute_Query retrieves rows from the table and displays first record on the form.

    A) True   B) False

9. MessageBox( ) is used to display messages on the status bar.

    A) True   B) False

10. A where clause that uses operators other than '=', can be created by entering '&' in any text item on the form.

    A) True   B) False

FILL IN THE BLANKS

1. Data Blocks can be created from _____ or
   _____.

2. The two types of layouts allowed in Forms are _____ and
   _____ and the default layout is _____.

3. _____ trigger fires when the row focus changes from one record to
   the other.

4. Context sensitive help can be displayed on the status bar by using _____
   and _____.

5. The hint displayed under the item when the mouse cursor moves from one item to the
   other is called _____ help.

6. If the Not Null constraint is defined, the _____ property is set to true.

7. _____ property is used to set the default value for a text item.

8. _____ is used to stop the default operation of the form cursor
   moving to the next item in case if the item's validation has failed.

9. Window properties can be set at runtime by using _____ function.

10. The Runforms Window in which a user defined forms window is displayed can be
    referenced by using _____ constant.

11. The window can be opened in maximized mode by setting _____
    property of the window.

12. The values returned by System.Form_Status system variable are:

    • _____

    • _____

    • _____

13. The default value of the Menu Module property is set to _____.

14. Oracle Forms allow identification of error type, error number or error message by using:

    • _____

    • _____

    • _____

15. MDI stands for _____.

Default Form Creation

- Using the Data Block Wizard to create a Data Block
- Using the Layout Wizard

Customizing Default Form

- Laying out Objects on a Form
- Creating a Control Block for Data Manipulation and Navigation

Defining Triggers for Data Navigation and Manipulation

- Types Of Triggers
- Smart Triggers
- Steps in Defining a Trigger

Creating User-Defined Procedures

- Enabling / Disabling Navigation Push Buttons
- Enabling / Disabling Text Items based on the form's Mode of Operation

Form Validations

- Implementing I/O Rules Using Database Triggers and a Sequence
- Implementing a Not Null Check Using the On-Error Trigger
- Implementing Business Rules Using the When-Validate-Item Trigger

A QUICK REVIEW

CHAPTER THREE

Property Classes and Visual Attributes

IN THIS CHAPTER

> Form Standardization Requirements

> Working with Property Classes

> Working with Visual Attributes

> Differences Between Property Class and Visual Attributes

3. PROPERTY CLASSES AND VISUAL ATTRIBUTES

MAINTAINING STANDARDS WITHIN A FORM

The Oracle Forms Builder offers excellent facilities to maintain standards across all commercial applications data manipulation forms.

Each form in the same commercial application should look and behave alike irrespective of what data is being manipulated. This approach will help users of the commercial application to get quickly accustomed to how the forms work.

Standards are easy to apply across a commercial application because Oracle Forms Builder in an Object Oriented Programming System. Using any OOPS based system the facilities offered to maintain standards across entire commercial applications are simplified to a very large extent.

Standards in a Commercial Application:

Standardizing all the objects on data entry forms would generally require that all the Aesthetic (Visual) and Data Control properties of each object on each data entry form are loaded with the same values.

A very simple example would be all the *data entry fields*, on the form must have the very same font type, font size, font weight assigned to them in addition to an appropriate background and foreground color.

This sort of standard is normally done by the forms create tool itself. There is a standard default *font type, font size and font weight* along with a default *foreground* and *background* color set by the Forms Builder tool.

Should for any reason, one or more than one of the properties of data entry field require changing all the data entry fields on each and every form need to map to this change as well. Maintaining standards across the commercial application will be incredibly tedious if properties were to be individually set. Tedious jobs generally lead to a drop in standards.

To help overcome this situation, Oracle Forms Builder offers several simple but exceedingly effective methods. The correct use of these methods helps to maintain standards right across the commercial application.

Setting Standards in Oracle Forms:

Each data aware or data control object used in forms has an associated property sheet. This property sheet has a list of properties, which either hold default values or NULL values.

Loading an appropriate value into a specific property on the object's property sheet, will cause the object to visually look different or change the way the object behaves when it handles data.

The simplest approach to apply standards across a commercial application, would be to create a user-defined property sheet and attach it to objects where required. The object would then take its visual and data handling properties from the user-defined property sheet. This feature of Oracle is called **Property Class Inheritance**.

If the user defined property sheet, lists properties less than the default properties of the object, then for all the properties not listed in the user defined property sheet the object would be set to their default values obtained from the default property class.

PROPERTY CLASS

Property class inheritance is a powerful feature that allows quick definition of object properties that confirm to interface and functionality standards.

A **Property Class** is a named object that contains a list of properties and their values.

Once a property class is created, other objects can be based / set on it. An object based on a property class can inherit the setting of any property in the class that makes sense to that object.

Property classes allow global changes to an application's properties quickly. To change the properties globally, change the value of the properties defined in a property class, the changes will be reflected in the properties of all objects that inherit properties from that property class.

There can be any number of properties in a property class, and the properties in a class can apply to different types of objects.

Example:
Separate property classes can be created for enterable items, required Items and read-only items. When the appearance and functionality of all such items in an application needs to be changed, all that is required is to update the properties in the appropriate class.

A property class might contain some properties that are common to all types of items, some that apply only to text items, and some that apply only to check boxes.

When an object is based on a property class, there is complete control over which properties the object should inherit from the class and which should be overridden locally.

A property class can itself be based on a property class, to provide multiple levels of property inheritance.

Example:
A BASE_FIELD class that contains standard property settings for all text items in any application, such as Font Name, Font Size, Height, etc can be created. Similarly, a DATE_FIELD class for text items that display date values can also be created.

The DATE_FIELD class could inherit the properties defined for all items in the BASE_FIELD class, plus properties specific to date fields, such as Data Type and Format Mask.

Property classes are separate objects, and, as such, can be copied between modules as needed. Perhaps more importantly, property classes can be referenced in any number of modules. (Refer to REFERENCING OBJECTS IN OTHER MODULES)

Creating a Property Class Object:

In the *Object Navigator*, property classes appear under the **Property Classes** node in the appropriate module.

There are two ways to create a property class.
Create a new property class in the Object Navigator and then add properties to it.
Create a property class from an existing object's properties.

Creating a Property Class in the Object Navigator:
1. In the Object Navigator, position the cursor on the *Property Classes* node and choose **N̲avigator..C̲reate** menu options. A property class object with a default name is inserted under the node. The property sheet of the new property class will contain two properties i.e. *Name* and *Class*.

2. In the Properties window, add properties to the class as desired.

Creating a property class in the properties window:
1. In the Object Navigator or layout editor, select one or more objects whose properties must be included in the Property Class.

2. In the *Properties* window, click the Property Class button on the toolbar. A messagebox is displayed to confirm the name of the class being created.

3. The new property class includes all of the properties of the selected object. If certain properties of the selected object are not required in the Property Class, they can be deleted from the Property Class.

   Example:
   A property class can be created from definition of an existing text item such that the same font and height characteristics can be applied to other text items. However, the new property class would also contain the X Position and Y Position properties.

   Since these properties define display coordinates that would almost always need to be overridden for each text item that is based on the class. These properties might then be removed from the class definition.

   To view the definition of a property class *i.e., the properties it contains* select the property class in the Object Navigator and see its properties displayed in the Property palette. (If necessary, expand the Property Classes node by clicking on +.)

   To this property sheet we can assign specific properties and assign values for those properties.

Assigning the Property Class to Other Objects on the Form:

All that has to be done now is to assign this property class to an object on a data entry form. This will determine how the object will look visually and / or how it will handle data, if data aware.

Simply by assigning the user defined property class to required objects on all data entry forms, standards will be applied across the commercial application. Should the standards ever require tweaking, making the change in the user defined property class will cause the new standard to be applied across the entire commercial application.

Oracle Forms Tool allows visual attributes of data aware objects to be set independent of the data handling attributes. This goes a long way in making it easy to set standards in aesthetics on the data entry form which really are independent of the setting of data aware attributes.

Focus:

Create a property class object, with properties mentioned below and attach it to all the push buttons in the *product* form.

Name	: PClass_Button
Width	: 23
Height	: 23
Iconic	: Yes
Background Color	: Gray
Canvas	: product_can

Solution:

1. Open the *product* form and connect to the database

2. In the Object Navigator, position the cursor on the *Property Classes* node and choose **Navigator..Create**. A property class object with a default name is inserted under the node.

3. Open the property sheet of the newly created Property Class object and a property sheet will open up. Change the name of the object to *PClass_Button* as shown in the diagram 3.1.

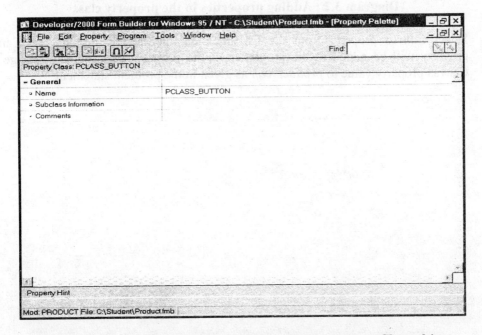

Diagram 3.1 : Property Sheet of newly created Property Class object

1. To add properties to the property class object, click on the **Add Property** 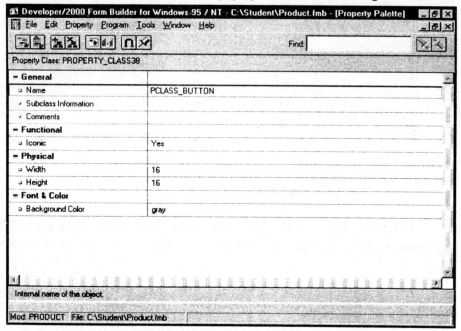 button on the toolbar. A list of properties will pop up as shown in the diagram 3.2.

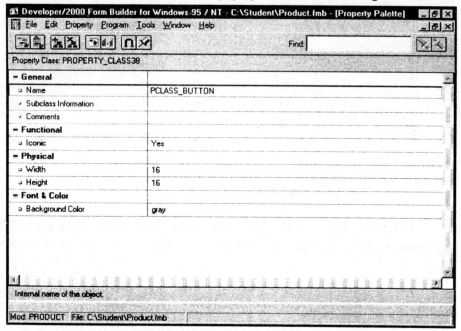

Diagram 3.2 : Adding properties in the property class

2. Select *Canvas* property from the list and click on the OK button. The Canvas property will be added to the properties of the property class object. Change the Canvas property value to *product_can* as given in the problem statement.

3. Similarly go on adding other properties and change each of their values as listed above. The final screen will be displayed as shown in the diagram 3.3.

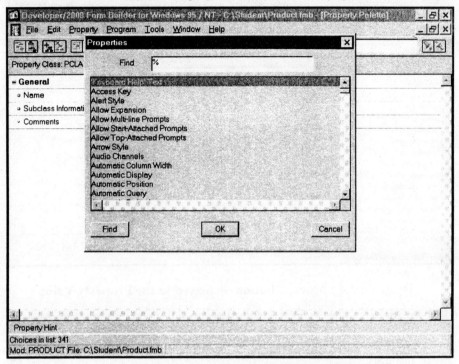

Diagram 3.3 : Property Sheet after adding required properties

4. To attach *PClass_Button* object to the buttons, select the pushbuttons one at a time in the button_palette block button and open their property sheets.

5. Select the *SubClass Information* property. It displays **More...** as the property value as shown in diagram 3.4.

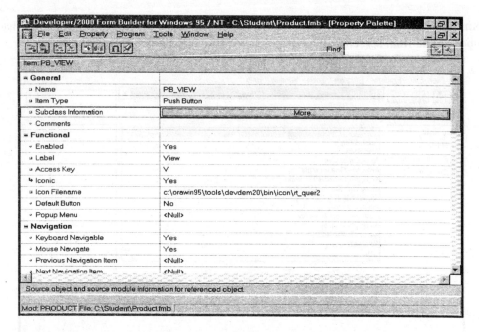

Diagram 3.4 : More... button displayed in the Property Value

6. Click on More... The *SubClass Information* dialog box is displayed as shown in diagram 3.5.

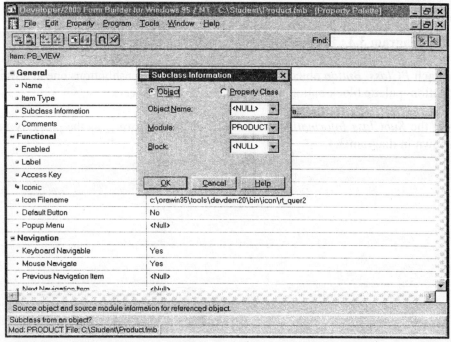

Diagram 3.5 : Subclass Information Dialog Box

7. Select **Property Class** radio button. *SubClass Information* dialog box now displays two properties i.e. *Property Class Name* and *Module Name* as shown in diagram 3.6.

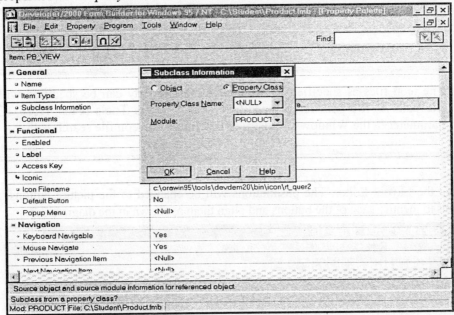

Diagram 3.6 : Subclass Information Dialog Box with Property Class Information

8. Set the property class name to *PClass_Button* using the list available.

Note

The properties of the push buttons that are inherited form the property class ↳ will display an arrow.

9. Close the property sheet. The Object Navigator displays the push button with a referenced 🔁 icon.

10. Setting the *Iconic* property to 'Yes' enables display of pictures on the face of the button. Select each push buttons individually and set the *Icon Name* property as follows:

Button Name	Icon Name
pb_view	c:\orawin95\tools\devdem20\bin\icon\rt_quer2
pb_first	c:\orawin95\tools\devdem20\bin\icon\rt_rec1
pb_prior	c:\orawin95\tools\devdem20\bin\icon\rt_rec2
pb_next	c:\orawin95\tools\devdem20\bin\icon\rt_rec3
pb_last	c:\orawin95\tools\devdem20\bin\icon\rt_rec4
pb_add	c:\orawin95\tools\devdem20\bin\icon\rt_radd
pb_delete	c:\orawin95\tools\devdem20\bin\icon\rt_rdel

pb_modify	c:\orawin95\tools\devdem20\bin\icon\clear
pb_save	c:\orawin95\tools\devdem20\bin\icon\rt_save
pb_search	c:\orawin95\tools\devdem20\bin\icon\rt_quer1
pb_exit	c:\orawin95\tools\devdem20\bin\icon\exit

Tip

The icon files as specified in the *Icon Name* property can be specified without file path. If file path is not specified Oracle Forms Tools reads TK25_ICON parameter in the Windows Registry to determine the icon file search path..

11. Open the Layout Editor. The pushbuttons will be changed to the picture buttons. Add labels to identify each of the buttons and align them as shown in the diagram 3.7.

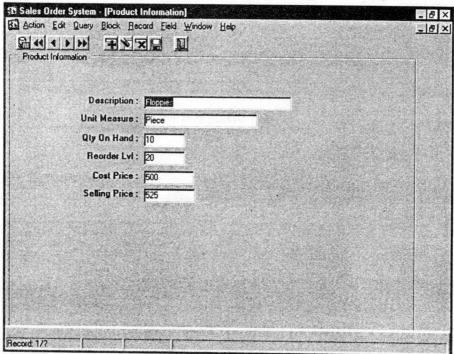

Diagram 3.7 : Final Layout

VISUAL ATTRIBUTES

Visual Attributes are the font, color and pattern properties that can be set for form and menu objects that appear in any commercial application. Visual attributes include the following properties:

Color and pattern properties   : Foreground Color, Background Color, Fill Pattern, White on Black

Font properties   : Font Name, Font Size, Font Style, Font Width, Font Weight

Named Visual Attributes are similar to Property classes, the differences are:
1. Named Visual Attributes define only font, color and pattern attributes whereas property classes can contain these and any other properties.

2. The appearance of objects at runtime can be changed by changing the named visual attribute programmatically.

Note

Property class assignment cannot be changed programmatically.

3. When an object inherits its visual properties from both a *property class* and a named *visual attribute*, the named visual attribute settings take precedence. Any visual attribute properties in the property class are ignored.

Setting the visual attributes of an object:

There are several ways to set the visual attributes of objects in Oracle Forms Builder:
1. In the Properties window, set the Visual Attribute Name property as desired, then set the individual attributes (Font Name, Foreground Color, etc.) to the desired settings.

2. In the Layout Editor, select an item or a canvas and then choose the desired font, color, and pattern attributes from the Font dialog and Fill Color and Text Color palettes.

3. Define a named visual attribute object with the appropriate font, color, and pattern settings and then apply it to one or more objects in the same module. An object's named visual attribute can be programmatically changed by setting the font, color, and pattern of the object at runtime.

4. Create a property class that includes visual attribute properties and then attach the property class to objects so that the properties of the property class are inherited by the object.

Every interface object has a Visual Attribute Name property that determines how the object's individual visual attribute settings (Font Size, Foreground Color, etc.) are derived. The Visual Attribute Name property can be set to Default, Custom, or the name of a named visual attribute defined in the same module.

Default Visual Attributes:

Setting the *Visual Attribute Name* property to *Default* specifies that that the object should be displayed with default color, pattern, and font settings. When the Visual Attribute Name is set to *Default*, the object's individual attribute settings reflect the current system defaults.

Custom Visual Attributes:

Setting the *Visual Attribute Name* property to *Custom* specifies that the object should be displayed with the attribute settings that have been specified for the object explicitly at design time. The attributes can either be set in the Properties window (by setting specific visual attribute properties) or in the Layout Editor (by selecting fonts, colors and patterns from menus and palettes).

Named Visual Attributes:

Setting the *Visual Attribute Name* property to a named visual attribute defined in the same module specifies that the object should use the attribute settings defined in a *Named Visual Attribute*.

A *Named Visual Attribute* is a separate object in a form or menu module that defines a collection of visual attribute properties. Once a named visual attribute is created, it can be applied to any object in the same module. This way standardization can be brought in the way all objects look in an application. To change any visual property, changes need to be made only to the visual attribute object, for the change to be reflected throughout the application.

Creating Named Visual Attributes and applying the same to several objects:

When a named visual attribute is applied to an object, only those attributes that make sense for that object take effect.

Creating a Named Visual Attribute:

1. In the Object Navigator, position the cursor on the *Visual Attributes* node and choose **N**avigator**..Cr**ea**te**. Oracle Forms inserts a new named visual attribute.

2. In the Properties window, set the font, color, and pattern attributes of the named visual attribute as desired.

<u>Applying a Named Visual Attribute to an Object:</u>
1. In the Object Navigator or the Layout editor, select the desired object.

2. In the Properties Palette, set the *Visual Attribute Name* property to the name of the desired visual attribute object.

Note

> When the visual attributes of an object in the Layout Editor or the Properties window is explicitly set, Oracle Forms converts the objects Visual Attribute Name setting to *Custom*, and the association with the named visual attribute is lost.

Focus:

If the data keyed into a text item violates the validation rules defined the *item text* must be displayed in '**Red**'. After making necessary changes in the data if the data entered passes validation the test, the item text must be displayed in '**Black**'.

Solution:

1. Open the '*Product* form and connect to the database.

2. Create two visual attributes, with appropriate properties mentioned below. These Visual Attributes will be attached to the items by using appropriate PL/SQL code in the form triggers.

3. In the Object Navigator, position the cursor on the *Visual Attributes* node and choose **N**avigator..C**r**eate. Oracle Forms inserts a new named visual attribute.

4. In the properties window of each of the visual attribute object, set the following properties:

Name	: VA_ERRORS
Foreground Color	: Red
Name	: VA_NOERRORS
Foreground Color	: Black

5. Change the When-Validate trigger as follows:

Trigger Name : **WHEN-VALIDATE-ITEM**   Form   : product
Block   : product_master   Item   : cost_price
Trigger Level : Item Level
Function   : Cost price should not be 0 and cost price should be less than the selling price.
Text   : BEGIN

```
        if :product_master.cost_price = 0 then
            message('Cost Price  cannot be 0');

            /* Visual Attribute for an item can be set at time using the
               set_item_property function. The property that attaches a
               Visual Attribute to an item is 'current_record_attribute'. In
               case of errors the visual attribute must be set to VA_ERRORS */
            set_item_property('cost_price', current_record_attribute,
                    'VA_ERRORS');
            raise form_trigger_failure;

        elsif :product_master.cost_price >
                  :product_master.selling_price then
            message(' Cost Price cannot be greater than Selling Price');
            set_item_property('cost_price', current_record_attribute,
                    'VA_ERRORS');
            raise form_trigger_failure;
        else

            /* If no errors then visual attribute must be set to VA_NOERRORS */
            set_item_property('cost_price', current_record_attribute,
                    'VA_NOERRORS');
        end if;
    END;
```

Trigger Name	: **WHEN-VALIDATE-ITEM**	Form	: product
Block	: product_master	Item	: selling_price
Trigger Level	: Item Level		
Function	: Selling price should not be 0 and it should be greater than the cost price.		
Text	: BEGIN		

```
BEGIN
        If :product_master.selling_price = 0 then
                message('Selling Price cannot be 0');
                set_item_property('selling_price', current_record_attribute,
                'VA_ERRORS');
                raise form_trigger_failure;
        elsif :product_master.cost_price >
            :product_master.selling_price then
                message(' Selling Price cannot be less than Cost Price');
                set_item_property('selling_price', current_record_attribute,
                'VA_ERRORS');
                raise form_trigger_failure;
        else
                set_item_property('selling_price', current_record_attribute,
                'VA_NOERRORS');
        end if;
END;
```

Note

The technique of visually indicating erroneous data entered is very useful when the data entry operators are not completely comfortable in English.

SELF REVIEW QUESTIONS

TRUE OR FALSE

1. If the user-defined property sheet lists properties greater than the default properties of an object then new properties are added to the object's property sheet.

   A) True   B) False

2. Multiple Level Property inheritance is not allowed in Oracle.

   A) True   B) False

3. A property class can be created from an existing object.

   A) True   B) False

4. There are fixed number of properties defined for a Visual Attribute.

   A) True   B) False

5. The Named Visual Attribute cannot be changed at runtime.

   A) True   B) False

6. Visual Attributes are used to set only aesthetic properties of an object.

   A) True   B) False

7. If the same property is defined in the Property Class and the Visual Attribute then property values defined in the property class takes precedence over the property values defined in a visual attributes.

   A) True   B) False

FILL IN THE BLANKS

1. Properties of the objects placed on the form can be divided into _____ and _____.

2. The method of creating a user-defined property sheet and attaching the same to the objects such that the object takes the property values from the user-defined property sheet is called _____.

3. _____ is a named object that contains a list of properties and their objects.

4. Properties can be added to a property class by selecting _____ button on the toolbar.

5. Property class can be connected to an object by setting _____ property.

6. _____ and _____ property must be set to create an iconic push button.

7. _____ parameter is used to identify the icon file search path if the icon file path is not specified in the icon name property.

8. Visual Attributes are connected to an object by setting _____ property.

9. The three types of Visual Attributes are:

   • _____

   • _____

   • _____

10. Visual Attributes can be changed at runtime by setting the _____ property.

A QUICK REVIEW

CHAPTER FOUR

PL/SQL Libraries and Alerts

IN THIS CHAPTER

> What is a PL/SQL Library

> PL/SQL Library File Formats

> Creating and Attaching a PL/SQL Library

> Working With Alerts

> Setting Alert Properties at Runtime

4. PL/SQL LIBRARIES AND ALERTS

A PL/SQL library is a collection of program units, including user-named procedures, functions and packages. PL/SQL Libraries provide a convenient means of storing client-side program units and sharing them among multiple applications.

Once a PL/SQL library is created, it can be attached it to any form or menu. The program units stored in the PL/SQL library can be called from triggers, menu item commands, and user-named routines written in the form or menu module to which the PL/SQL library attached.

The same PL/SQL library can be attached to multiple forms and menus. Conversely, a single form or menu can have more than one attached PL/SQL library.

PL/SQL libraries can also be attached to other PL/SQL libraries. When a PL/SQL library is attached to another PL/SQL library, program units within the attached PL/SQL library can be referenced in the current library.

PL/SQL libraries support dynamic loading. Program units are loaded into a computer's memory only when an application needs it. This can significantly reduce the runtime memory requirements of an application, but tends to slow an application. The trade off is between speed vs. memory usage.

LIBRARY FILE FORMATS

There are three library file formats, .PLL, .PLX, and .PLD.

1. **.PLL**
   A library .PLL file contains both library source code and the compiled, platform-specific p-code (executable code). The .PLL file is created or updated when it is saved in the library module. When the library module is saved, the changes are reflected in each module to which the library is attached.

2. **.PLX**
   A library .PLX file is a platform-specific executable. When an application is ready to be deployed, there would be a need to generate a version of library files that contain only compiled p-code.

Note

A .PLL version of a library is attached to a form module. Oracle Forms looks at the .PLL file at compile time to ensure that the procedures and functions are referenced correctly. At runtime, Oracle Forms looks for a .PLX file by that name in the default search path.

3. **.PLD**

   The .PLD file is a text format file, and can be used for technical documentation of the library files.

CREATING AND ATTACHING A LIBRARY TO A MODULE

A library is created by opening, defining, compiling, and saving a library module.

One can define the following types of PL/SQL subprograms in a library:
- Procedures
- Functions
- Package Specifications
- Package Bodies

Creating a New Library:

1. In the Navigator, to create a library, choose menu items **File..New..PL/SQL Library** or select the **Libraries node** and then click on **Navigate..Create**.

Note

Library module Name cannot be changed by editing it in the Object Navigator. *Instead, the library name can be changed when it is saved.*

2. To create a program unit, expand the desired library node, select the *Program Units* node, and then click **Navigator..Create**. The *New Program Unit* dialog appears.

3. Specify the *Program Unit Name* and its *Type* (Procedure, Function, Package Spec, or Package Body). Click on OK. The *PL/SQL* Editor is displayed.

4. In the PL/SQL Editor, define appropriate program units and then click on **Compile** to compile and apply modifications. Click on **Close** to close the editor.

Note

Library program units must be compiled because Oracle Forms cannot execute uncompiled program units at runtime.

5. Choose **Program..Compile..Incremental** to compile any uncompiled library program units, or click on **Program..Compile..All** to compile all library program units.

6. Click on **File..Save** to save the library module to a file or to the database.

Note

Developer 2000 objects can either be stored in file format or stored within the database. The **File..Save** Options allows storage both in file and database object format.

If the Developer 2000 objects are stored in File format, then file 'Write' permissions are required on the directory in which the file is saved.

If these objects have to be stored in the Oracle database, appropriate Developer tables that store Developer 2000 objects must be built and then grants must be given to these tables. These grants are given by running SQL scripts using SQL*Plus.

The scripts for building Developer 2000 tables can be directly be executed by clicking on **Start..Programs..Developer 2000 Admin..Developer 2000 Build**.

The scripts for building Developer 2000 tables can be directly be executed by clicking on **Start..Programs..Developer 2000 Admin..Developer 2000 Grant**.

Attaching a Library to Another Module:

After saving a library module to the file system or database, the library module can be attached to a form, menu, or library module.

Note

Attached libraries are read-only. An attached library is not editable in the form or menu module. References to the program units within a library can be made from the form or menu module. To edit a library module, open the library module in the Object Navigator and use the PL/SQL Editor to edit program units.

1. In the Object Navigator, open the desired form, menu, or library module by clicking on **File..Open** and then specify the module type to open.

2. Expand the module and then select the **Attached Libraries** node. Click on **Navigator..Create** to attach a library. The *Attach Library* dialog appears as shown in diagram 4.1.

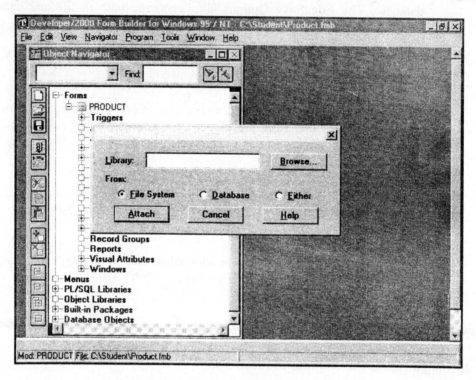

Diagram 4.1 : Attach Library Dialog Box

The *Attach Library* dialog includes the following:

Library:	The name of the library to be attached to the current module.
Order :	Applies only when at least one library is already attached to the current module. Choose *Before* or *After* to specify whether the attached library is to be inserted before or after the other libraries already attached to the module.
	When a program unit i.e. procedure / function is called, Oracle Forms looks for the program unit under the *program unit* node of the current form. If the program unit is not found, it searches in the attached libraries.
	If there are multiple libraries attached to a form, when resolving a procedure call at runtime, Oracle Forms searches the attached libraries in the order in which they are sequenced.
Attach :	Attaches the library named in the Library field to the current module and closes the dialog.

3. Specify the name of the library to attach as shown in diagram 4.2.

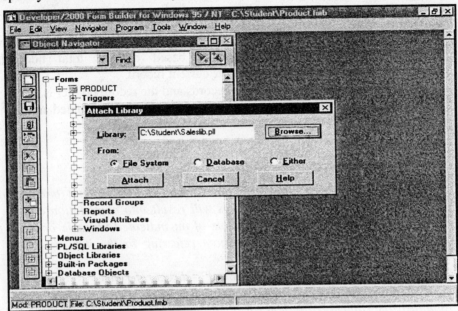

Diagram 4.2 : Specifying the Library Path

 Tip

Saleslib.pll library has been saved in a directory named '*Student*' in Drive 'C'. Please specify a sub-directory and / or path in which the library was saved as a file appropriate to the computer being worked on when attaching the library file.

4. Save the active form or menu module to incorporate the library attachment in the module definition. Generate and run the form to check the library attachment.

Hands on:

Create the *scroll_control* procedure in the new library called *saleslib.pll*. Attach this library to the form **product** and call *scroll_control* in the **product** form.

Solution:

1. Create a new library as explained in step 1 of *Create A New Library* in chapter PL/SQL LIBRARIES AND ALERTS on page 118.

2. In the *Program Unit* dialog box of step2 and step3 select the procedure option and type the name of the procedure as *scroll_control*. In the PL/SQL editor of the procedure *scroll_control* type in the following PL/SQL code.

The Procedures is defined below:

Procedure Name   : **SCROLL**
Function   : To enable or disable the scroll push buttons and scroll menu items i.e. first, prior, next and last based on the total number of records on the form and the current record.
e.g. If there are multiple records and the record pointer is on the first the first and the prior picture button should be disabled and the next and the last picture buttons should be enabled.

```
PROCEDURE scroll IS
BEGIN
        /* Forms system variables or the objects on the form cannot be referenced
        directly in the library. Such references will result into compilation errors. The
        NAME_IN function returns the contents of an indicated variable or item. It is
        used to get the value of an item without referring to the item directly.   The
        following statements are equivalent:
                        :description = 'Keyboard' -- direct reference
                        name_in('description') = ' Keyboard ' -- indirect reference
            Similarly the contents of system variables can be referenced indirectly as follows:
                        name_in('system.last_record') = 'TRUE' */
    /* Setting the enabled property to false for all the buttons if there is only one
    record. */
    if name_in('system.last_record') = 'TRUE' and
                        name_in('system.cursor_record') = '1' then
                set_item_property('button_palette.pb_next', enabled, property_off);
                set_item_property('button_palette.pb_last', enabled, property_off);
                set_item_property('button_palette.pb_first', enabled, property_off);
                set_item_property('button_palette.pb_prior', enabled, property_off);
        /* Setting the enabled property for the buttons last and next to false and first and
        prior to True  if focus is on the last record. */
    elsif name_in( 'system.last_record' ) = 'TRUE' then
                set_item_property('button_palette.pb_next', enabled, property_off);
                set_item_property('button_palette.pb_last', enabled, property_off);
                set_item_property('button_palette.pb_first', enabled, property_on);
                set_item_property('button_palette.pb_prior', enabled, property_on);

        /* Setting the enabled property for the buttons last and next to True and first and
        prior to False  if focus is on the first record. */
    elsif name_in('system.cursor_record') = '1' then
                set_item_property('button_palette.pb_first', enabled, property_off);
                set_item_property('button_palette.pb_prior', enabled, property_off);
                set_item_property('button_palette.pb_last', enabled, property_on);
                set_item_property('button_palette.pb_next', enabled, property_on);
```

```
        else
                /* Setting the enabled property for all the buttons to True if focus is not
                on the first or the last record. */
                set_item_property('button_palette.pb_next', enabled, property_on);
                set_item_property('button_palette.pb_prior', enabled, property_on);
                set_item_property('button_palette.pb_last', enabled, property_on);
                set_item_property('button_palette.pb_first', enabled, property_on);
        end if ;
END;
```

3. Compile the *scroll_control* procedure and save the library with the file name *saleslib.pll*.

4. Attach the library *saleslib.pll* to the **product** form as explained in the topic *Attaching A Library to Another Module* explained in chapter PL/SQL LIBRARIES AND ALERTS on page 119.

5. Call the *scroll_control* procedure in the WHEN-NEW_RECORD-INSTANCE trigger. Generate and run the form to check that the *scroll_control* procedure works correctly.

Note

If the procedure *scroll_control* is already defined in program unit node of the the form please ensure that it is deleted so that the call to is made to the *scroll_control* procedure defined in the library and not in the form.

Oracle Forms tool first searches for the procedure in the program Unit section of the current form module. If the procedure is not found in the form module, then each attached library is scanned for the procedure.

Thus the search path used by Forms is:
- Current Form Module
- Libraries Attached to the Current Form Module

Hands On:

Create the *item_enable_disable* procedure in the *saleslib.pll* library. Call the procedure in the **product** form.

Procedure Name   : **ITEM_ENABLE_DISABLE**
Function   : To enable the fields so that the contents of the field can be modified or new values can be entered. To disable fields so that the contents of the field cannot be modified.

```
PROCEDURE ITEM_ENABLE_DISABLE( blk_name IN char, item_on_off
IN NUMBER) IS
        nxt_itemname varchar2(70);

BEGIN
    /* get_block_property is a function that gets the value of specified block property. The
      First_Item property holds the name of the first enterable item in the block. */
    nxt_itemname := blk_name||'.'|| get_block_property(blk_name, first_item);

    /* set a loop that gets the next navigation item and sets the updateable property to
      true or false. Next Navigation Item holds the name of the next navigational item in
      the block */
    loop
        set_item_property(nxt_itemname, updateable, item_on_off);
        nxt_itemname := blk_name||'.'||get_item_property(nxt_itemname, next_navigation_item);
        /* exit if the Next Navigation Item is rowid. */
        if (nxt_itemname = blk_name||'.ROWID') THEN
                exit;
        end if;
    end loop;
END;
```

Note

Procedure *item_enable_disable* has been generalized so that it can be used in any form. It takes in two parameters i.e. the *Name of the Block* and the *Value for the property*.

ROWID is an invisible item created by Oracle Forms Builder as the last item in the block. Thus when the *Next_Navigation_Item* is ROWID the loop must be exited.

The ROWID item is used by Oracle and its properties cannot be changed either at design time or in runtime mode.

The call to the *item_enable_disable* procedure will change as follows:

> item_enable_disable (block name, property_value)

Note

The call to the item_enable_disable will have to be changed in all the triggers in the *product* form.

Example:

When *item_enable_disable* is called in the When-Button-Pressed event of *push_button_add*, the procedure makes all the fields in the *product_master* block updateable.

The call to this function will be as follows:

> item_enable_disable ('product_master', property_on)

ALERTS

Commercial applications will generally encounter two types of error conditions. Those that are system generated and those that arise out of business rules being violated by the data being captured. In either case the user of the commercial application must be informed of what occurred and if required be given information on how to correct the error condition. *For example, if the user has entered the cost price of a product as 0, then the system must display an error message as '**Cost Price cannot be 0**'.*

Often choices are given on how to actually process an event e.g. if the delete button is clicked the system must ask for a *confirmation to delete the current record.* If the user clicks on the 'Yes' or 'OK' button, the record must be deleted else the delete operation must be aborted.

Oracle Forms Builder allows creation of an object called an 'Alert' that makes displaying an error message and/or offering different processing choices quite simple and elegant.

An alert is a modal window that displays a message. Alerts are used to inform the user of unusual situations or to give a warning for an action that might have undesirable or unexpected consequences.

There are three styles of alerts: **Stop, Caution, and Note**. Each style denotes a different level of message severity. Message severity is represented visually by an icon that is displayed in an alert window.

Oracle Forms Builder uses many built-in alerts that display pre-defined messages. Custom alerts created by a user can also be displayed in response to application-specific events.

When an event occurs that causes an alert to display, the alert must be responded to by selecting one of its predefined *Alert Buttons*. Selecting any button immediately dismisses the alert and passes control back to the program that called it.

When an alert is created, basic information such as the message to be displayed by the alert and the text labels for the alert buttons must be specified.

After creating an alert, an appropriate trigger or user-named routine must be written to display the alert in response to a particular event. In addition, the action that each button initiates is determined by the PL/SQL code written in the trigger or user-named routine.

An Alert can be displayed by the SHOW_ALERT( ) function. The SHOW_ALERT( ) function returns alert_button1, alert_button2 or alert_button3 based on the button clicked by the user. This return value can be used to determine what action that has to be taken.

Creating an Alert:

1. In the Object Navigator, create an alert object by selecting the Alerts node and then choose **Navigator..Create**.

2. In the Properties window, set the **Alert Style** property to the style that corresponds to the severity of the message either *Stop*, *Caution*, or *Note*. At runtime, an icon representing the selected style is displayed next to the message in the alert window.

3. Set the **Message** property by entering the message string that must be displayed at runtime. A maximum of 200 characters can be entered.

4. Define one or more buttons for the alert by entering a text label in the Button 1, Button 2, and Button 3 properties. (The default text labels are "OK" for Button 1 and "Cancel" for Button 2.)

Note

At least one button must have a label. Buttons that do not have labels are not displayed. Buttons are displayed in the alert in the order that they appear in the Properties window. That is, Button 2 is displayed to the right of Button 1, and so on.

5. Choose the Default Alert Button, either Button 1, Button 2, or Button 3. The default button is the button that is selected implicitly. It is denoted by a dotted rectangle on the button's surface when displayed.

Displaying an Alert:

To display an alert, the application must execute the SHOW_ALERT built-in subprogram from a trigger or user-named subprogram. SHOW_ALERT is a function that returns a numeric constant. The general syntax is as shown below.

Memory_variable = Show_Alert('alert_name');

The constant returned by the SHOW_ALERT function indicates which alert button was selected and is one of the following:

- ALERT_BUTTON1
- ALERT_BUTTON2
- ALERT_BUTTON3

The value returned by the SHOW_ALERT function must be assigned to a variable, and then appropriate action can be taken in the trigger depending on the value held by the variable which depends upon which alert button was pressed.

Example:

In every data entry form in *Sales Order System* when a request to delete a record is made the system must display the 'Delete Confirmation' message via an alert.

"You are about to delete this record, are you sure?"

Button 1 is labeled OK and button 2 is labeled Cancel. This **alert_delete** is invoked from the *When-Button-Pressed* trigger of *push_button_delete*.

If the user presses the delete button, an alert displays the above message. The operator can select OK to confirm the deletion or CANCEL to abort the delete operation.

Focus:

Create an alert that displays delete confirmation message with two buttons labeled as **OK** and **Cancel**. If the user clicks on OK, the current record must be deleted.

Solution:

1. Open the product form in the Forms Builder. Locate the node labeled **Alerts** and click on **Navigator..Create**.

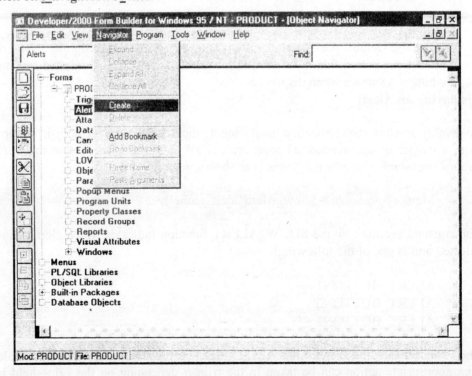

Diagram 4.3 : Creation of a New Alert

2. In the Properties window, set the following properties:

Name	: ALERT_DELETE
Alert Style	: Caution
Message	: You are about to delete this record, are you sure?
Button 1	: OK
Button 2	: Cancel
Default Button	: Button2

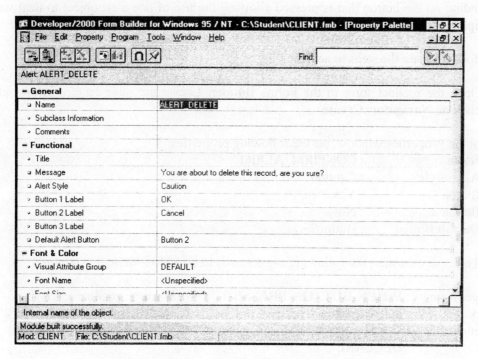

Diagram 4.4 : Setting the Alert Properties

3. To display the alert the following trigger need to be added where it is required.

Trigger Name	: **WHEN-BUTTON-PRESSED**	Form	: product
Block	: product	Item	: pb_delete
Function	: Displays the alert message box before deleting a record.		
Text	: DECLARE		

```
                chk_button number;
            BEGIN
                go_block('product_master');
                chk_button := show_alert('alert_delete');
                if chk_button = alert_button1 then
                        delete_record ;
                end if;
            END;
```

SETTING ALERT PROPERTIES AT RUNTIME

An Alert may have to be displayed when the 'Exit' button on the data entry form is clicked. The functionality of this alert is the same as all other alerts except the *Alert Title* and the *Message* in the alert box must be different.

Instead of having two separate alerts, one for Delete and one for Exit, Oracle Forms allows these properties to be set at runtime. The Title and the message can be changed depending on the button that is pressed allowing the use of one alert object to deal with multiple situations.

The following are the steps to achieve this.

1. Open the product form in the Forms Builder. Locate the node labeled **Alerts** and click on **Navigator..Create**.

2. In the Properties window, set the following properties:

Name	: CONFIRM_ALERT
Alert Style	: Caution
Button 1	: Yes
Button 2	: No
Default Button	: Button2

3. To display the alert the following trigger need to be added where it is required.

Trigger Name	: **WHEN-BUTTON-PRESSED**	Form	: product
Block	: button_palette	Item	: pb_delete
Function	: Displays the alert message box before deleting a record.		
Text	: DECLARE		

```
            chk_button number;
        BEGIN
            go_block('product_master');
            set_alert_property('confirm_alert',title,'Delete Records');
            set_alert_property('confirm_alert', alert_message_text,
                    'Do you really want to delete the record?');
            chk_button := show_alert('alert_delete');
            if chk_button = alert_button1 then
                    delete_record ;
            end if;
        END;
```

Trigger Name	: **WHEN-BUTTON-PRESSED**	Form	: product
Block	: button_palette	Item	: pb_exit
Function	: Quit the product form.		
Text	: DECLARE		

```
                answer number;
            BEGIN
                /* If there are any changes in the form the system must asks for
                    confirmation to save changes */
                If :System.form_status = 'CHANGED' then
                        set_alert_property('confirm_alert',title,'Save Changes');
                        set_alert_property('confirm_alert', alert_message_text,
                                'Would you like to make Changes Permanent?');
                        answer := Show_Alert('confirm_alert');
                        If answer = Alert_Button1 then
                                commit_form;
                        End If;
                End If;

                /* Close the form. */
                exit_form(No_Commit);
            END;
```

SELF REVIEW QUESTIONS

TRUE OR FALSE

1. If a PL/SQL subprogram exists in a library and a PL/SQL subprogram with the same name also resides program unit in the form, only the subprogram in the libraries will get executed.

    A) True   B) False

2. An alert can have a maximum of five buttons.

    A) True   B) False

3. When a library is attached to a form the PL/SQL blocks included in the library are included in the form file.

    A) True   B) False

FILL IN THE BLANKS

1. An alert can be displayed by using _____ function.

2. _____ is a collection of Functions, Procedures, Package Spec and package Body held in a PLL file.

3. A library can be attached to a form by using the _____ node in the object navigator.

4. Form field variables and form system variables can be referenced in the library by using _____ function.

5. The name of the first item in a block can be picked up or referenced by using _____ function with _____ property.

6. The three styles of alerts are:

    - _____

    - _____

    - _____.

PICK THE RIGHT OPTION

1. The constants used as return values for an alert are of the format
    A) Button1, Button2,...
    B) Alert_Button1, Alert_Button2, ...
    C) AlertButton1, AlertButton2, ...

2. If the label for an alert button is not specified, that button
    A) is not included in the alert
    B) displays a button with no label

A QUICK REVIEW

CHAPTER FIVE

Object Libraries

IN THIS CHAPTER

- ➢ Maintaining Standards across Multiple forms

- ➢ Introduction to Object Libraries

- ➢ Creating an Object Library

- ➢ Storing Objects in an Object Library

- ➢ Referencing Objects in an Object Library

5. OBJECT LIBRARIES

MAINTAINING STANDARDS IN FORMS

A commercial application includes a number of forms deployed at client's site for data manipulation and navigation. Forms should be created based on the following minimum standards:

1. Each form must manipulate information in as efficient a manner as possible.
2. Each form must be designed keeping in mind the end-user.
3. Each form must have the same look and feel.
4. The data navigation and manipulation functionality for each form should be the same. e.g. *Text items in each form must be enabled in add mode and disabled in view mode.*
5. Forms must be designed such that they can be changed when required with minimum effort.

Each form includes a number of objects whose behavior is determined by the properties of those objects and the PL/SQL code written in the triggers attached to these objects.

Standards within a form can be maintained by

- Creating Property Classes and Visual Attributes based on pre set standards and attaching these objects to the items placed within a form. e.g. *Every push button placed on the form will then have the same height, width, background color etc.*
- Creating Procedures and Functions as Program Units of a form and calling them in from triggers attached to form items.

As seen earlier, Procedures and Functions common across multiple forms can be created and stored within a PL/SQL library. This library can then be attached to the form module and the procedures and functions defined within the library can be referenced from the form module when required.

Note

PL/SQL Libraries allow creation and storage of only PL/SQL code blocks in the form of Procedures, Functions and Packages.

Oracle Forms Builder allows creation of **Object Libraries** that store **objects** like Property Classes, Visual Attributes and Triggers.

An Object library is a collection of common Oracle objects that can be used in any form where appropriate.

Form modules can then reference objects stored in the Object Library and thus object standards can be maintained across forms.

Example:
Visual Attributes VA_ERRORS and VA_NOERRORS can be used in all forms of a commercial application. Both these objects can be placed in an Object Library. Form modules for a commercial application can then reference and use these objects.

Object Libraries allow global changes to be made to applications very quickly. If the items in a button palette block were inherited from a property class that references an Object Library, a change in any property will immediately be reflected in all forms that reference this property class.

Advantages of Object Library:

The advantages of using an object library are summarized as under:
- Object libraries can be used to store and distribute standard, reusable objects
- Rapidly create applications by dragging and dropping predefined objects onto a form.
- Object libraries are automatically re-opened when the form referencing the object library is opened in Form Builder. Thus reusable objects are immediately accessible.

Example:
If push buttons in a button palette block have identical PL/SQL blocks of code and an identical aesthetic look, the button palette block and its corresponding canvas can be stored in an object library. Once stored in the library, the same block can be referenced in all the forms by simply dragging the block from the object library onto the Block node in the form module.

OBJECTS INCLUDED IN AN OBJECT LIBRARY

Any valid Oracle forms object can be placed inside an object library. The common objects included in an object library are:

- Alerts
- Blocks
- Canvases
- Property Classes
- Visual Attributes
- Windows

CREATING AN OBJECT LIBRARY AND PLACING OBJECTS IN THE OBJECT LIBRARY

Focus:

Create an object Library named *comobj.olb* that stores three objects

- VA_ERRORS — Visual Attribute with properties that indicate an error condition.
- VA_NOERRORS — Visual Attributes with properties that indicate normal conditions.
- PCLASS_BUTTON — Property class referenced by push buttons on a form.

Solution:

1. The objects included in the Object Library must first be created using the appropriate node in a Form module. Once created, the objects can be moved into an Object Library.

Note

An Object Library does not allow creation or alterations of its objects. Objects must be created or altered using an appropriate node in the Forms module. Once created or altered, the objects can be moved to the Object library by using the drag and drop technique.

2. Create a new form module by selecting menu items **File..New..Form** or select the Forms node and then click on **Navigate..Create**. A new form module will be created.

3. Create two Visual Attributes objects named VA_Errors and VA_NoErrors using the Visual Attributes node in the form module. Set their properties as shown below:

Object Type: Visual Attribute
- The first visual attribute as:
  Name : VA_ERRORS
  Foreground Color : Red

- The second visual attribute as:
  Name : VA_NOERRORS
  Foreground Color : Black

4. Create a property class object named PClass_Button in the Property Class node in the form module. Set the properties as shown below:

Object Type: Property Class

Name	: PClass_Button
Width	: 23
Height	: 23
Iconic	: Yes
Background Color	: Gray

The completed Visual Attribute and Property Class objects displayed in the Object Navigator will be as shown in diagram 5.1.

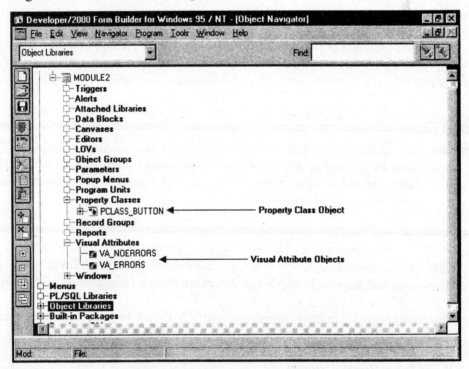

Diagram 5.1 : Objects created in the Forms Module

5. In the Object Navigator, create an Object library module. To do so, choose **File..New..Object Library** or select the Object Libraries node and then click on **Navigate..Create**. A New Object Library with default name i.e. OBJLIB3 is created as shown in diagram 5.2.

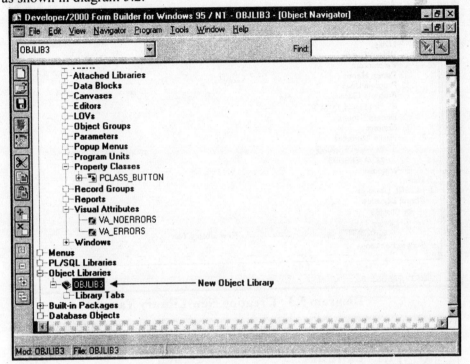

Diagram 5.2 : New Object Library created in Object Navigator

6. An Object Library is a collection of one or more **Library Tabs**. Thus objects of different types can be organized and placed in different Library Tabs. Double click on the *Library Tabs* Node to create a new Library tab in the object library. A new tab with the default name i.e. LIB_TAB0 is created as shown in diagram 5.3

7. Change the name and the Label property of the tab page as follows:

   Name   : LIB_VATTR
   Label   : VATTR

   The completed property sheet for the library tab is as shown in diagram 5.4.

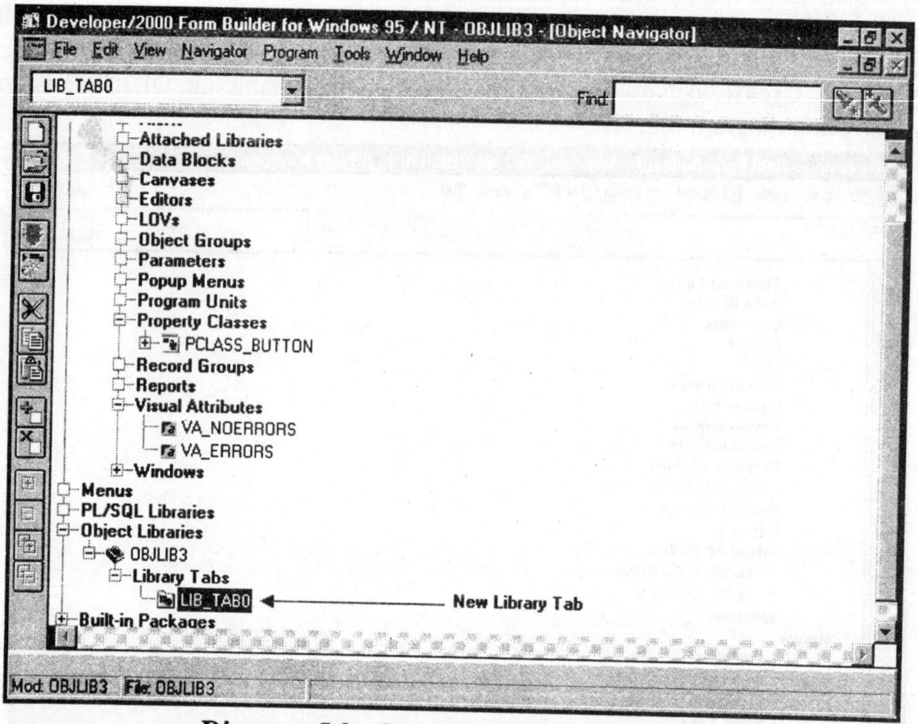

Diagram 5.3 : Creating New Library Tab

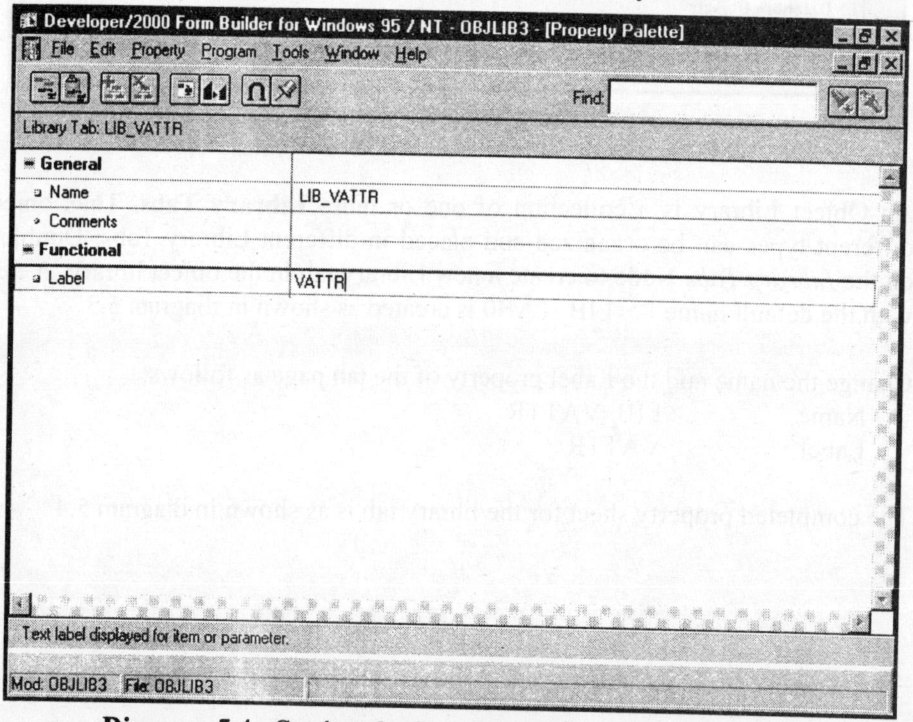

Diagram 5.4 : Setting the Properties of the Library Tab

8. Create another Library tab to store a property class. Set the new library tab properties as follows:

Name	: LIB_PCLASS
Label	: PCLASS

9. These objects created can now be placed in an Object library in appropriate tabs. To place an object the tabs must be opened. Select **Tools..Object Library** menu options of click on 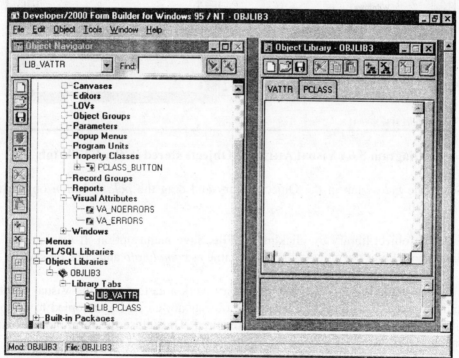 to open a library tab.

    Opened library tabs will be displayed as shown in diagram 5.5. Note that Forms Builder displays both the tabs i.e. VATTR and PCLASS. The library tabs currently does not have any objects.

Diagram 5.5 : Library Tabs opened in Forms Builder

10. Select Visual Attribute objects i.e. VA_ERRORS and VA_NOERRORS in the forms module and drag and drop it on the VTTR tab. The VTTR tab will now display two objects as shown in diagram 5.6.

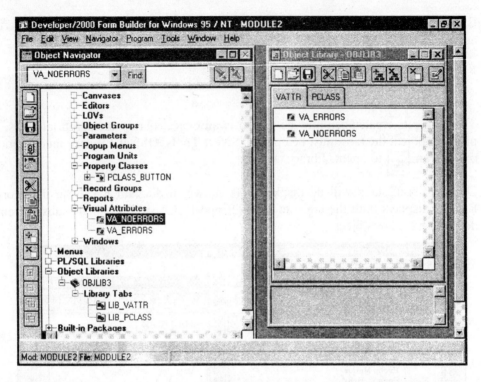

Diagram 5.6 : Visual Attribute Objects stored in the VTTR tab

11. Select the *pclass* tab in the Object library and drag the *pclass_button* object in the *pclass* tab.

12. Save the object library by clicking on **File..Save** menu option. It displays the *Save* dialog box. Enter the object library file name as *comobj.olb* and click on save.

13. The form module was used as a temporary work area to create the Visual Attributes and Property Class objects. Once these objects are created and copied to the object library, the form module is no longer required. Thus close the form module without saving.

14. Once the objects are stored in the object library, they can be referenced in the form module as required. For example every form in the sales order system must reference the property class *pclass_button* and Visual Attributes *va_errors* and *va_noerrors*.

Open the *product* form and delete the property class and visual attributes. Open the library tabs by clicking on the *comobj.olb* library and Selecting **Tools..Object Library** menu options. Select *pclass_button* in the *Pclass* tab and drag the same to the property class node of the *product* form.

Forms Builder displays a dialog box as shown in diagram 5.7 asking for copying or subclassing the dragged object. If 'Copy' option is selected, a copy of the dragged object will be made in the current form module.

If 'SubClass' option is selected, a link is established between the form module and the object library such that the Forms module at runtime or at design time will reference the object in the object library.

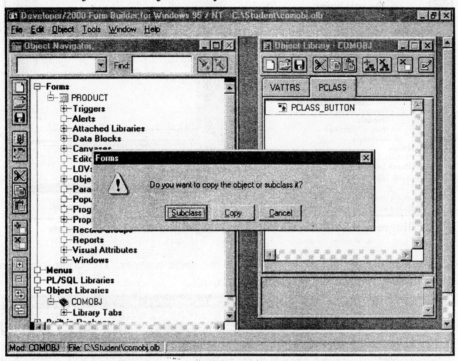

Diagram 5.7 : Confirmation for Copying or Subclassing

15. Click on SubClass. Forms Builder creates a reference to the object in the object library. Referenced objects are shown with a red arrow in the object navigator as shown in diagram 5.8.

Caution

When a property class is attached to an object, the property values of the object are taken from the property class. If no property class is attached the object takes default property values.

To ensure that the property values are taken from the referenced property class, the referenced property class must be reattached to the push buttons.

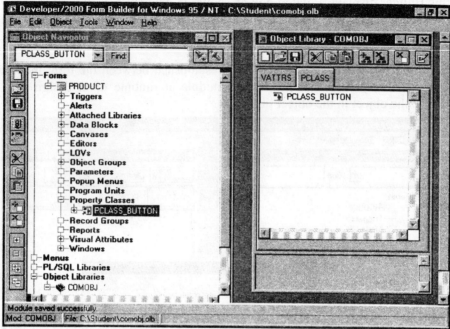

Diagram 5.8 : Referenced object displayed with a Red Arrow

16. Reference the Visual Attribute object in the same manner. The completed product form will be displayed as shown in diagram 5.9.

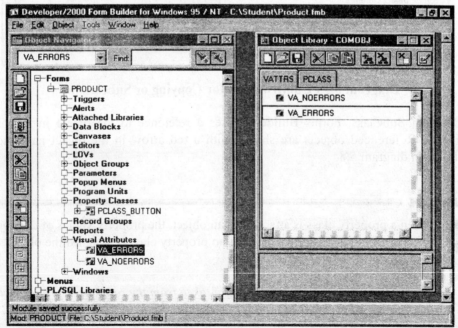

Diagram 5.9 : Completed Product Form with Referenced Objects

Note

When objects in an Object Library are referenced in the form module, the form module stores the name of the object and the name of the object library from which the object is referenced.

*The Object Library path is **not stored** in the form module. Instead, Oracle Forms Builder as well as Forms Runtime refers to the **FORMS50_PATH** parameter defined in the Windows registry to locate Object Library search path.*

Common Triggers included in the Object Library:

The ON-ERROR trigger written in the *product* form includes generalized PL/SQL code to handle the NOT NULL constraint. All forms in a commercial application will require PL/SQL code to handle NOT NULL constraints.

Thus such PL/SQL code blocks can also be moved into an Object library. The steps for moving the ON-ERROR trigger is as follows:

1. Open *comobj.olb* Object library in Forms Builder. Select *Library Tabs* node and click on **Navigator..Create** menu options. A new library tab with a default name is created. Change the *Name* and the *Label* property of the library tab as follows:

    Name   : LIB_TRIGGERS
    Label   : TRIGGERS

The completed Object library will be as shown in diagram 5.10.

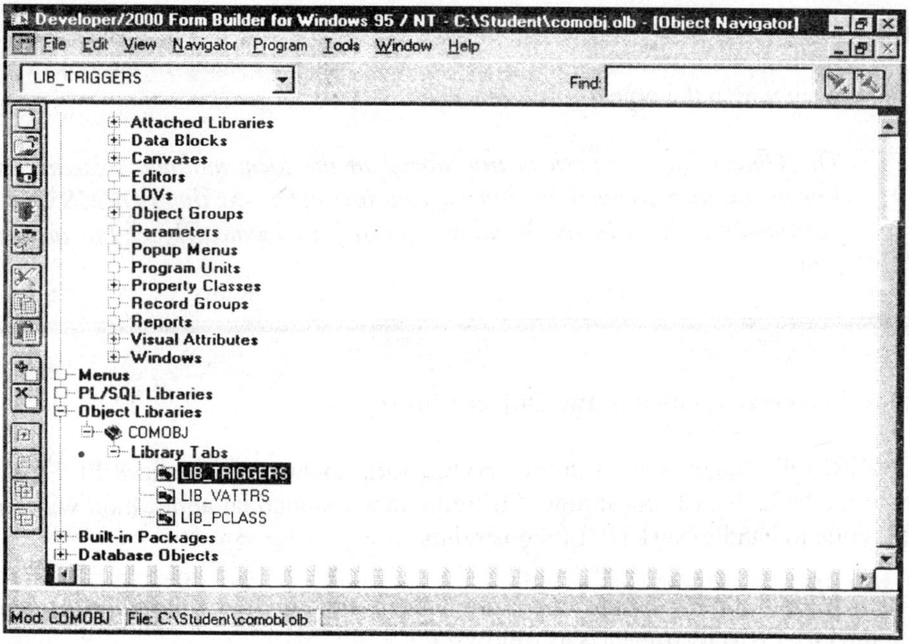

Diagram 5.10 : Completed Library Tab

2. Open the *product* form in Forms Builder.

3. Open the *Triggers* tab by selecting **Tools..Object Library** menu options.

4. Select the ON-ERROR trigger at form level and drag and drop it in the *Triggers* tab. The completed screen will be as shown in diagram 5.11.

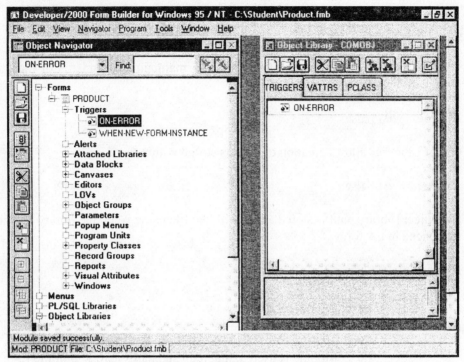

Diagram 5.11 : Triggers Tab with the ON-ERROR Trigger

5. Since the ON-ERROR trigger is included in the Object Library, the ON-ERROR trigger must be deleted from the *product* form. Select the ON-ERROR trigger and press the delete key. Forms Builder will ask for conformation to delete the trigger. Click on 'Yes'.

6. The ON-ERROR trigger must be referenced in the *product* form. Drag the ON-ERROR trigger from the Triggers tab in the Object library. When the trigger is dragged and dropped on the form module, a confirmation to subclass or copy the trigger is asked for. Since the trigger must be referenced in the form module, the **Subclass** push button must be clicked. The ON-ERROR trigger will be displayed in the forms *Triggers* node.

7. Run the form and check if the NOT NULL constraint is being handled as required.

SELF REVIEW QUESTIONS

TRUE OR FALSE

1. Visual Attribute and Property Classes help in maintaining standards of the objects placed within a form.

   A) True   B) False

2. Object Libraries allows creation of objects stored within them.

   A) True   B) False

3. An Object Library path is stored along with the file name when the library objects are referenced in the form.

   A) True   B) False

FILL IN THE BLANKS

1. _____ Module is used to maintain standards across multiple forms.

2. Objects included in the Object Library must first be created using an appropriate node in the _____ module.

3. Object Library is a collection of _____ that help organize objects in an object library.

4. Objects can be stored in the object library by using _____ technique.

5. Objects from an Object library can be _____ or _____ to the form module.

6. Object Library search path is specified in the _____ parameter defined in the Windows registry.

A need to Maintain Standards across multiple forms of any system

Creating an Object Library
- *An Introduction of Object Libraries*
- *Creating an Object Library*
- *Creating Object Library Tabs and Organizing Objects in the Object Library.*
- *Creating Objects in Forms Module and storing them in the Object Library*
- *Referencing Objects from an Object Library.*
- *Common triggers stored in the Objects Library*

CHAPTER SIX

The Master Detail Form

IN THIS CHAPTER

6. THE MASTER DETAIL FORM

A Master Detail form has at least two data aware blocks. These data aware blocks are related to each other. This relationship is called a **Master-Detail** relationship. The relationship between the blocks is modeled upon a primary key-foreign key relation between the tables on which the blocks are based.

Consider the material delivery section of an Inventory System. Material delivered to the client is generally documented using a delivery challan. The delivery challan must include two types of information.

Information specified once on the 'Challan' such as:
- Challan Number
- Challan Date
- Client Name
- Delivery Address, fax, phone etc.

Information for the items that are delivered repeats more than once since several items can be dispatched to a single client using a single delivery challan. Material information included in the challan includes:
- Serial Number
- Item Description
- Quantity Delivered

This is an example of a 1:many relationship between the Challan Header information and the material delivered against this challan. Hence, this information needs to be stored in two tables with a specific (one to many) relationship defined and enforced between the tables.

Challan_Header table is used to store challan and client information and *Challan_Details* table is used to store information about the material delivered to the client. 1:many relationship is enforced between the tables by defining a primary key for the *Challan_Header* table and a foreign key is defined in the *Challan_Details* table that references *Challan_Header*.

Similarly the master and detail blocks on the form connected to the *Challan_Header* and *Challan_Details* tables respectively must also be linked using an appropriate form object. This form object is called a **Relation Object**.

- Thus three form object are involved in defining a master detail relationship at form level:
- The *Challan_Header* block i.e. the master block
- The *Challan_Details* block i.e. the detail block
- A *Relation Object* that joins the master and detail blocks using a common text item between the master / detail blocks.

THE RELATION OBJECT

A Relation object is a logical Oracle Form object, which stores information about the relation between a master block and the corresponding detail block.

In the Object Navigator, the relation object appears in the **Relations** Node under the block defined as a **Master** block.

When defining a master detail relation, minimum of three properties must be specified. These properties are:

- Master Data Block i.e. the name of the master block
- Detail Data Block i.e. the name of the detail block
- Join Condition i.e. a condition that joins the master and the detail block.

These properties of a relation object can be specified at the time of creating the detail block. The above mentioned properties simply indicates an existence of a relation between two blocks. These properties do not specify how these blocks are coordinated based on the form's mode of operation.

The relation object thus includes additional properties that determine the coordination behavior between two related blocks based on the mode of operation. Oracle Forms Builder sets default values for these properties and thus determines the default behavior of a master detail relation. These properties can be set by selecting appropriate values from a defined list of property values.

View Mode:

When records for the master block are retrieved or when the form cursor navigates to another master record, the behavior for the detail block must be specified. The available options are:

- Retrieve associated detail records immediately after retrieving master records
- Retrieve corresponding detail records when the cursor is positioned on the detail block.
- Do not retrieve the detail records automatically.

This behavior of the relation object is determined by two properties that accept a 'Yes' or 'No' as property values.

- Deferred
- Automatic Query

<u>Immediate retrieval of records in the Detail block:</u>
If **Deferred** property is set to '**No**', associated detail records are retrieved immediately after master record retrieval.

<u>Postponing Detail Record Querying:</u>
If **Deferred** property is set to '**Yes**', forms tool reads the **Automatic Query** property to determine whether the detail records must be retrieved for not. If **Deferred** property is set to '**Yes**' and **Automatic Query** is set to '**Yes**', the associated detail records are retrieved when the form cursor is positioned on the detail block.

<u>No Detail Record Querying:</u>
If **Deferred** property is set to '**Yes**', forms tool reads the **Automatic Query** property to determine whether the detail records must be retrieved for not. If **Deferred** property is set to '**Yes**' and **Automatic Query** is set to '**No**', the associated detail records will not be retrieved. An explicit *execute_query* must be executed for retrieve corresponding detail records.

Note
 By default the Deferred property is set to 'No' and Automatic Query property is set to 'Yes'.

Delete Mode:

If end users attempts to delete a master record
- Forms Builder can prevent deletion of master records if detail records exists
- Form Builder can delete the associated detail records also?
- Forms Builder can delete the master record without affecting the detail record

The **Delete Record Behavior** property specifies how the deletion of a record in the master block should affect records in the detail block. The values that can be specified are **Non-Isolated, Cascading** or **Isolated**.

<u>Non-Isolated:</u>
A master record cannot be deleted if associated detail records exist in the database.

<u>*Cascading:*</u>
A master record can be deleted, and any associated detail records are automatically deleted from the database at commit time.

Note

Master Detail relationship can be maintained by defining Foreign Key constraint at the table level. Foreign Key can be defined using the CASCADE option i.e. if master is deleted the Oracle engine will generate SQL Delete statements to delete associated detail records. The syntax is as follows:

FOREIGN KEY (columnname) REFERENCES table (columnname)
ON DELETE CASCADE

If ON DELETE CASCADE is specified, while defining foreign key, then **Cascade Delete** option in Form Builder must not be used.

Isolated:
A master record can be deleted, but the associated detail records are not affected.

When a relation is created between blocks, Oracle Forms Builder generates the triggers and PL/SQL procedures required for enforcing a master detail relationship based on the property values set in the relation object.

Example:
When the current record in the master block is changed, Oracle Forms populates the detail block with a new data set specifically associated with the in the master block since the deferred property is set to 'No' and automatic query is set to 'Yes'.

Thus the relation object on the form set to its default values does the following:
- Ensures that the detail block displays only those records that are linked with the current (master) record in the master block
- Coordinates querying between the two blocks.
- Prevents deleting data from the master block while associated data in the detail block exists.
- Prevents inserting data into the detail block when there is no related data in the master block.

CREATING A MASTER-DETAIL FORM

Focus: Challan Data Entry Screen

Challan details are recorded when the client is supplied with material as specified in the order placed by the client. The Challan form includes information like challan number, challan date that identifies a sales challan, the order identity number that identifies the order against which material is delivered and client information along with the products supplied to the client.

Design a data-entry screen that allows data manipulation in the *Challan_Header* and *Challan_Details* tables. These tables have a master-detail relationship determined by the column *Challan_No*.

A Sales Challan document generated using a manual system generally displays the Challan Number, Challan Date, the Sales Order Number against which the challan is generated, the name of the client, and the details of the material delivered. Thus the data entry challan form must also display the same details.

The challan form must also display the name of the client to whom material is being delivered. Details of each client are stored in the *Client_Master* table. Each client is identified by a unique *Client_No*.

The *Client_No* is used to identify· the client when an order is placed. The *Client_No* is recorded when the client places an order. Client name can be retrieved based on the *Client_No* retrieved based on the order number entered.

The relationship between *Challan_No*, *S_Order_No*, *Client_No* and *Name* can be depicted as follows:

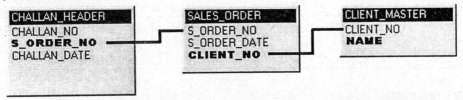

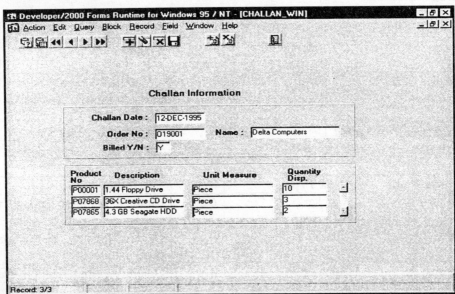

Diagram 6.1 : Challan Data-Entry Screen

Provide complete data manipulation operations (Add, View, Modify and Delete) for the challan data entry screen. In the view mode, allow browsing through table data, one record at a time i.e. First, Last, Previous, Next operations.

Add mode   : All items in the master and detail block must be updateable.
Modify mode   : All items other than the Primary Key can be updateable.
View mode   : items are not updateable in view mode.
Delete mode   : Delete *Cascading* must be 'Activated'.

Include a search operation that searches and retrieves data from the *Challan_Header* table to match a *Challan_No* entered. In the detail section, automatically display the *Description* and *Unit_Measure* from the *Product_Master* table when an appropriate *Product_No* is entered.

Table Name   : Challan_Header (Master)
Description   : Use to store challan information.

Column Name	Data Type	Size	Attributes
Challan_no	Varchar2	6	Unique primary key allotted to each challan.
Challan_date	Date		Date on which challan is generated.
S_order_no	Varchar2	6	Sales Order against which material was delivered.
Billed_YN	Varchar2	1	Is the Challan Billed?

Integrity Constraints:

Constraint Name	Description
PK_challan_no	A primary key based on the column *Challan_No* of the *Challan_Header* table.
FK_sales_order	Foreign Key based on the column *S_Order_No* that References *S_Order_No* from the *Sales_Order* table.

Table Name   : Challan_Details
Description   : Use to store information about challan details.

Column Name	Data Type	Size	Attributes
Challan_no	Varchar2	6	Challan number against which challan details are stored.
Product_no	Varchar2	6	Product identity of the material being delivered.
Qty_disp	Number	8	Quantity of material delivered.

Integrity Constraints:

Constraint Name	Description
PK_challan_details	Composite Primary Key that is based on the *Challan_No* and *Product_No* column of the *Challan_Details* table.
FK_product_details	Foreign Key based on the column *Product_No* that References *Product_No* from the *Product_Master* table.
FK_challan	Foreign Key based on the column *Challan_No* that References *Challan_No* from the *Challan_Header* table.

I/O and Business Rules to be enforced in the Challan Form:

- *Challan_No* is a Primary Key column i.e. *Challan_No* cannot be left blank and duplicate values are not allowed in *Challan_No*.
  Implement this by generating Primary key value using a database trigger.

- *Challan_Date* cannot be greater than system date.
  Implement this by writing appropriate validation code.

- *S_Order_No* must be present in the *Sales_Order* table. Only the sales orders that are not fully processed must be included.
  Implement this by using an LOV.

- *Product_No* must be present in the *Sales_Order_Details* table.
  Each Sales Challan is generated against an Order placed by the client. The Order information like Order_No, Order_Date, Client_No is stored in the Sales_Order table and the Product_No and quantity ordered is stored in the Sales_Order_Table.

  The s_order_no entered in the challan_header block can be used to retrieve product_no from the sales_order_details table i.e. an L.O.V. with a list of product_no for the selected s_order_no can be created and used to validate product_no.

- *Quantity_Disp* must not be left empty and cannot be 0.
  Implement this by writing appropriate validation code.

Setting Default Values:

- Set the default value of *Challan_Date* to system date.

Displaying Additional Information on the Form in View , Add and Modify Mode:

- *Client Name* must be displayed using a display item when a valid value for *S_Order_No* is entered or when a global query is fired.
- The data entry form must display the *Description, Unit_Measure* in the detail block using display items when the *Product_No* is entered or when the detail records are retrieved.

Cross Table Updations:

Whenever a record is inserted, updated, deleted in the *Challan_Detail* table the *Quantity_On_Hand* in the *Product_Master* table must reflect a change in the stock level. The quantity delivered against a challan would change the *Qty_On_Hand* of *Product_Master* as follows:

- Whenever an *insert* is performed decrease the *Qty_on_Hand*.
- Whenever a *delete* is performed increase the *Qty_on_Hand*.
- Whenever an *update* is done the *Qty_on_Hand* is adjusted appropriately.

Order status flags i.e. not processed (NP), in process (IP) or fully processed (FP) is maintained in the *Sales_Order* table. The order status will be updated from the challan data entry form. If the *Qty_Ordered* and *Qty_Disp* of all the products is the same the status is set to 'FP' i.e. fully processed and if the *Qty_Disp* is greater than 0 for any item in the order then the status is set to 'IP' i.e. In Process. If *Qty_Disp* is 0 for all the items included in the order, the status is set to 'NP'.

The Lookup Master Tables used with Challan Data Entry are:

Table Name   : Client_Master
Description   : Stores information about clients.

Column Name	Data Type	Size	Column Description
Client_No	Varchar2	6	Unique primary key for each client.
Name	Varchar2	20	Client's name
Address1	Varchar2	30	First, line in the client's address.
Address2	Varchar2	30	Second, line in the client's address.
City	Varchar2	15	City in which client's is located.
State	Varchar2	15	State in which client's is located.
Pincode	Number	6	Pin code
Bal_Due	Number	10,2	Balance amount receivable from the Client.

Table Name : Product_Master
Description : Stores information about products supplied by the company.

Column Name	Data Type	Size	Column Description
Product_No	Varchar2	6	Unique primary key for each product.
Description	Varchar2	25	Description of the product
Unit_Measure	Varchar2	10	Unit by which the product is measured
Qty_On_Hand	Number	8	Quantity which is available in the stock.
Reorder_Lvl	Number	8	Quantity level when the stock should be re-ordered.
Cost_Price	Number	8,2	Cost price of the product
Selling_Price	Number	8,2	Selling price of the product

Creating the Master Block:

1. Invoke the *Forms Builder Tool*.

2. The 'Welcome to the Form Builder' opening screen is shown. From the **'Designing'** option select '*Use the Data Block Wizard*' to create a new block.

3. Oracle Forms Builder invokes the Data Block wizard and displays a '*Welcome to Data Block Wizard*' screen. Click on Next.

4. Next enter details for the data source. The available options are:
   - Tables or View
   - Stored Procedure

   Select *Table or View* data source.

5. In the next step enter the name of the table and the columns that must be included in the form. Click on the **Browse** push button to select the table from the list. If not connected to the database a *Connect* dialog box is displayed. Enter the *Username*, *Password* and *Connect String*.

6. Data block can be created using tables, views and synonyms. 'Table' object is selected by default. Click on OK.

7. The list of tables is displayed. Select *Challan_Header* table.

8. After selecting the table from the list, a list of columns is displayed. Select all columns from the column list.

9. Confirm to invoke the Layout Wizard. Click on Finish. Since the option selected is '*Create Data Block, and then call Layout Wizard*', the welcome screen of the layout editor is displayed

10. Click on Next. The layout wizard asks for the canvas name and the type of canvas. If the canvas name is set to (New Canvas) the Layout wizard creates a new canvas.

11. The next screen displays the items to be included in the block. Select items that must be displayed on the canvas from the list provided. Click on [»] to select all the columns from the block.

12. The Label / Prompt is displayed for each item along with the height and width. If required change the prompt, width or height and click on Next.

13. The next step is to choose the Layout style. Set the layout style for the Master Block to 'Form'. Click on Next.

14. The selected items are grouped within a frame. In the next screen enter the frame title, the number of records to be displayed and the distance between the records. Confirm the need to display a scrollbar.

15. Finally a congratulation screen is displayed. Click on Finish. The required objects will be created and the object navigator will be displayed.

Creating the Detail Block:

1. Create a new block for the detail section. Click on **Tools** and select **New Block**. Oracle Forms Builder invokes the *New Data Block* dialog box asking for confirmation to start the data block wizard or create a data block manually as shown in diagram 6.2.

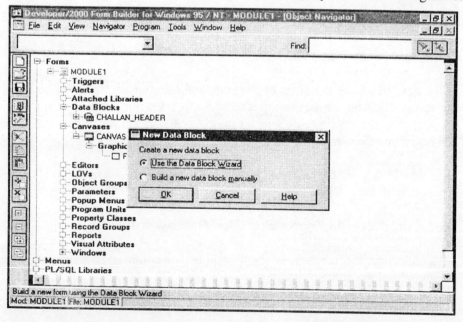

Diagram 6.2 : New Data Block Confirmation dialog box

2. Ensure that *'Use Data Block Wizard'* is selected and click on OK. A *'Welcome to Data Block Wizard'* screen is displayed. Click on Next.

3. Next select the data source. Select *Table* data source. Click on Next.

4. Next, specify the name of the table and its columns that must be included in the form. Click on the **Browse** push button to select the table from the list. Data block can be created using tables, views and synonyms. 'Table' is selected by default. Click on OK.

5. The list of tables is shown. Select *Challan_Details* table as shown in diagram 6.3.

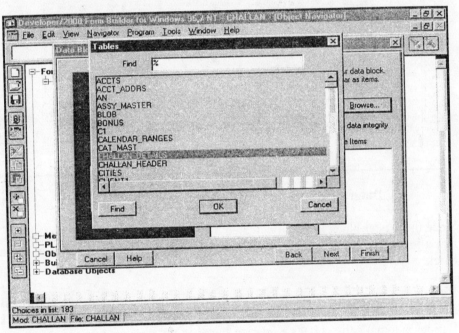

Diagram 6.3 : Selecting Challan_Details Table

6. After selecting the table from the list, a list of columns is displayed to select from. Select all columns from the column list as shown in diagram 6.4.

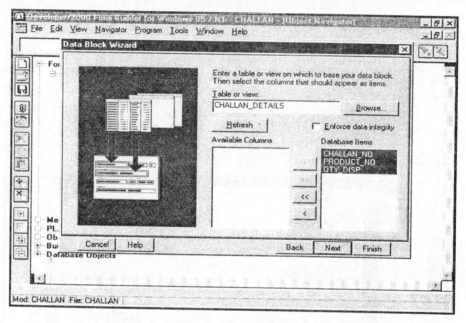

Diagram 6.4 : Selecting Columns in the Detail Table

7. Since the master block is already created, Oracle Forms Builder displays a dialog box that allows creation of a relation object that connects the detail block to the master block.

If Foreign Key constraint is defined in the detail table, the **Auto Join Data Blocks** checkbox can be checked. When the *Create Relation* push button is clicked, Forms Builder automatically creates a relation between the primary key and the foreign key of the master and details tables.

If the foreign key constraint is not defined, the **Auto Join Data Blocks** checkbox must be unchecked. When the *Create Relation* push button is clicked, Forms Builder automatically displays a list of blocks in the current form. *challan_header* is the only block created in this form and thus the *challan_header* block will be displayed as shown in diagram 6.5.

Caution

If the foreign key constraint is not defined, the **Auto Join Data Blocks** checkbox must be unchecked else it displays the following error message:

FRM-10757: No Master blocks are available.

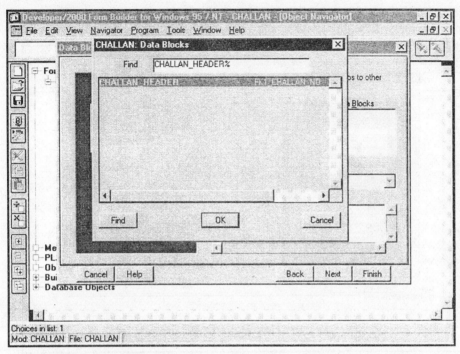

Diagram 6.5 : Challan_Header Block to which relation can be set.

8. Select *Challan_Header* and click on OK. The selected block is displayed in the *Master Data Block* list box and *Master Item* is set to *(No Join)* as shown in diagram 6.6.

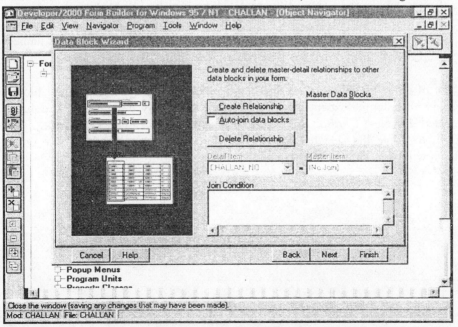

Diagram 6.6 : Master Data Block Selected

8. Select *Challan_No* from the list of columns from the master block. The completed join condition will be displayed as shown in diagram 6.7.

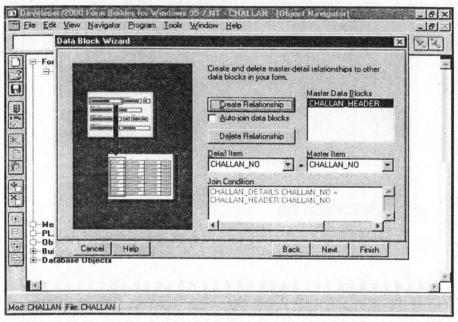

Diagram 6.7 : Join Condition set between the Master and Detail Blocks

9. Confirm to invoke the Layout Wizard. Click on Finish.

10. The *Welcome* dialog box of the Layout Wizard appears. Enter the canvas name in the next screen. The master canvas is selected by default. Click on Next.

11. A list of columns belonging to the detail block is displayed. The detail block must display all columns except the foreign key column. By default all the columns are selected. Deselect *Challan_No* column by using <CTRL> + <Left Click>. Click on ⟩ to move the selected columns to *Displayed Items* list box. The completed screen will be as shown in diagram 6.8.

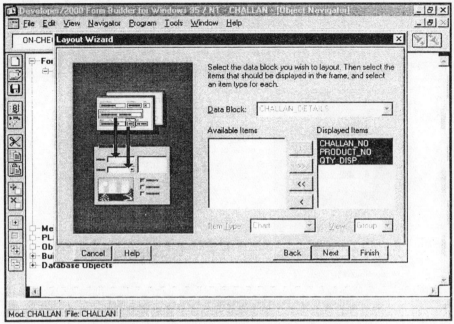

Diagram 6.8 : Displayed Items in the Detail Block

12. The list of selected items with the *Prompt*, *Width* and *Height* properties is displayed. Accept default values by clicking on Next. Choose the *Presentation Type*. Select *Tabular*.

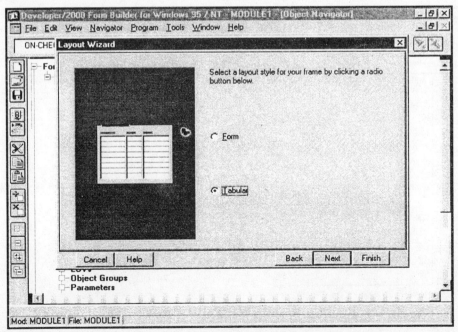

Diagram 6.9 : Presentation Style Selection

13. Enter the *Frame Title, Records Displayed, Distance Between Records.* Set *Records Displayed* to 3 as shown in diagram 6.10.

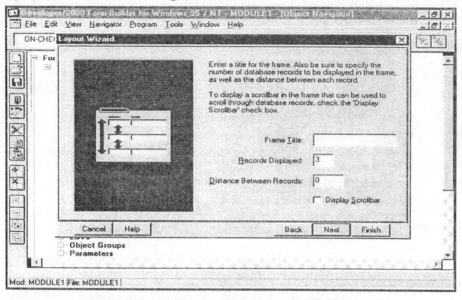

Diagram 6.10 : Number of Displayed Records

14. Click on Finish. A detail block with the master detail relation will be created and displayed in the Layout Editor as shown in diagram 6.11.

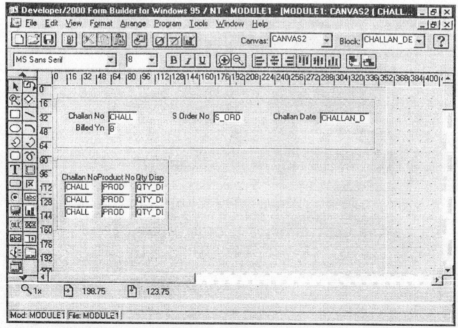

Diagram 6.11 : Detail Block displayed in the Layout Editor

15. The master-detail form is ready. Save the form by selecting **File..Save** menu items.

16. Arrange the items as shown in diagram 6.12.

17. Place a label object and enter the text as 'Challan Information' as shown in diagram 6.12.

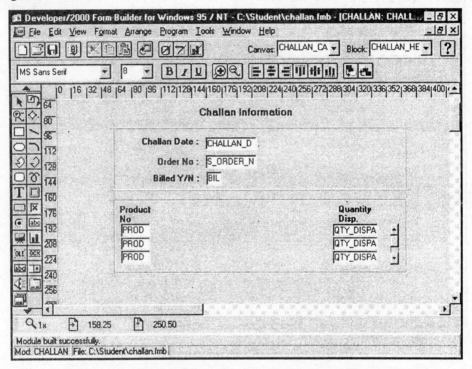

Diagram 6.12 : Item placement in the Layout Editor

 Note

 Space is left between the items in the detail block to insert additional objects to display 'Description' and 'Unit_Measure'.

RUNNING A MASTER DETAIL FORM

Run the Form by selecting the **Program..Run Form** menu option. The completed master detail data entry screen is displayed as shown in diagram 6.13.

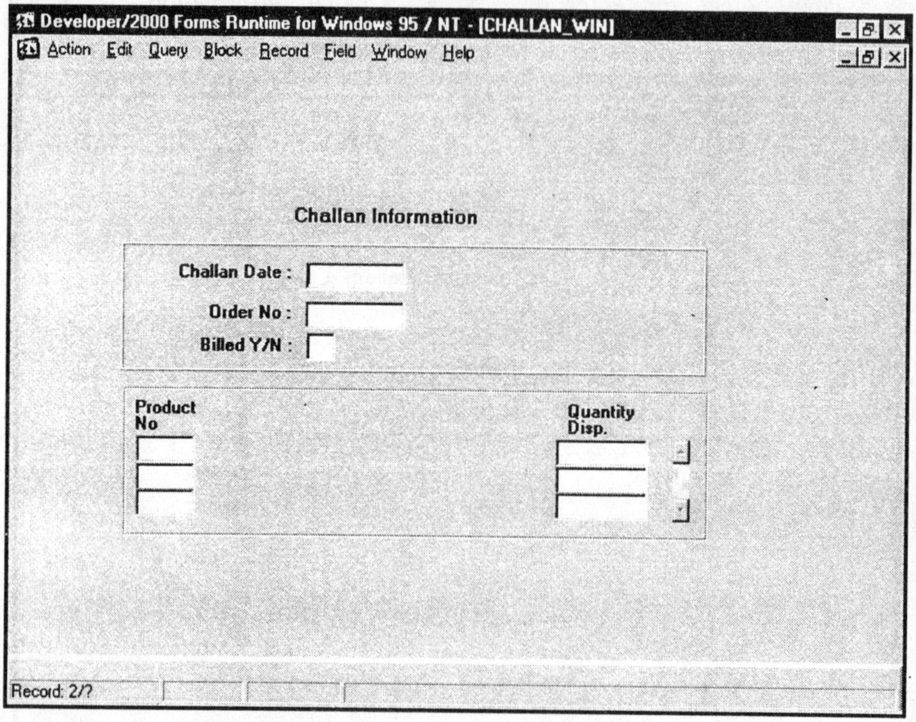

Diagram 6.13 : Runtime Challan Form

Data Retrieval and Manipulation Operations:

At runtime the form comes with default Menu system. The default menu system provides all options for Navigating within the form and performing data manipulation tasks such as First, Last, Previous, Next, Insert, Delete, Update, Save and Exit.

Data Retrieval:

Data can be retrieved by selecting the menu item **Query..Execute**. This would retrieve all the records from the master table. As soon as all the records of the master table are retrieved, Oracle Forms Runtime will display the first record in the master block. The Primary Key of this record is then used to retrieve the records for the detail block.

This controlled data retrieval of records in the detail block is taken care of by the **Relational Object**.

If a conditional query must be performed then select **Query..Enter**. The data block is cleared and a search value can be entered into for any item of the data block. Type in a value in the appropriate item. By doing so, a condition is automatically defined at the block level.

Any condition must have a column name, an operator, and a value. Thus the condition will include the name of the column in which the search value is entered, the equal to '=' operator is used by default and the value is also included in the condition.

Example:
If the value 'CH0001' is entered in the *Challan_No* item then the condition will be

      challan_no = 'CH0001'

Execute the query by Clicking on **Execute..Query**.

To generate a where clause that uses operators other than '=', enter the character '&' in an appropriate item then click on **Query..Execute**. Oracle runtime will display a dialog box that allows users to specify a where clause. After entering the desired where clause, the OK button can be clicked to retrieve records that satisfy the 'where' clause specified.

Please refer to DATA RETRIEVAL in chapter WORKING WITH FORMS on page 20 for details on the generating a where clause using other operators.

Navigation:
If several records are retrieved by a query, click on **Records** and select **Previous** or **Next** to navigate through the record set.

When the current record changes in the master block, Oracle Forms runtime updates the detail block to display only those records associated with the record in the master block.

Inserting Data:
To insert a row click on **Records..Insert**. Enter appropriate values in the text items. In this manner several records can be inserted.

Inserting a new master and detail record:
If the form cursor is on the master block and the insert instruction is given, a new record is inserted in the master block, the detail block is cleared, and blank records are inserted in the detail block.

Inserting a Detail record only:
If the form cursor is on the detail block and an insert instruction is given, a new record is inserted in the detail block for the current master record.

Deleting Data:
Records can be deleted by clicking on **Records..Delete**.

Deleting the master records:
By default, when an attempt is made to delete the master record that is related to the detail records, an error message is displayed.

The error message indicates that the master record cannot be deleted since the child record for the master record exists.

Note

By default the following error message is displayed when a master record is deleted and the detail records are existing.

Cannot delete master record when matching detail records exists.

The master record will not be deleted unless all the corresponding detail records are deleted.

The **Delete record Behavior** property determines the behavior when a master record is deleted. Please refer to **Delete Record Behavior** in chapter The MASTER DETAIL FORM on page 177 to override the default delete behavior.

Deleting a Detail record:
If the form cursor is on the detail block and a delete instruction is given, the current record on which the form cursor is on will be deleted leaving the other detail records and the master record intact.

Saving Data:
Records are saved by clicking on **File..Save** menu item.

WORKING OF A MASTER DETAIL FORM

Oracle Forms Builder sets up a relationship between the master and the detail blocks on the form by using an object called the '*Relation Object*'. When a 'Join' is created using the block creation tool, Oracle Forms Builder generates triggers, PL/SQL procedures and sets the properties required for enforcing the special relationship between the master and detail blocks.

The actual code that Oracle Forms Builder generates depends on how the properties of the relation are set. Refer to The Relation Object in chapter The MASTER DETAIL FORM on page 156 for explanation on properties of the relation object.

The Master Detail Triggers can be categorized as:
* Form Level Triggers
* Block Level Triggers
* Item Level Triggers

The Master Detail triggers and procedures can further be categorized based on the functionality of the trigger or procedure.
* Trigger that Populates the detail block when the master block is populated.
* Trigger that clear the details when a new record is added to the master.
* Triggers that perform appropriate delete operations in the detail block when the master record is deleted.

The *triggers* created by Oracle Forms Builder to ensure the master detail relationship between the master and the detail blocks on the form are as follows:
* ON-CLEAR-DETAILS
* ON-POPULATE-DETAILS
* ON-CHECK-DELETE-MASTER
* PRE-DELETE

The *procedures* created by Oracle Forms Builder to ensure the master detail relationship between the master and the detail blocks on the form are as follows:
* CLEAR_ALL_MASTER_DETAILS
* QUERY_MASTER_DETAILS

The use and execution of each of the triggers and procedures is explained as below.

Retrieving records in the Master and Detail Blocks:

When an Execute_Query is fired for the master block, corresponding detail records for the retrieved master record are also retrieved.

Before executing the query, Oracle Forms runtime gets the name of the detail block and then checks if there are any changes done to data visible in the detail block. If data changes are made in any detail block Oracle Form runtime asks for confirmation to save changes. An Execute_Query for the master blocks triggers a block level trigger named ON-POPULATE-DETAILS defined in the master block. This trigger checks if the join column value in the master block is Null or not. If the join column value is not Null, a procedure named QUERY_MASTER_DETAILS is executed.

The QUERY_MASTER_DETAILS moves the cursor to the detail block and retrieves the records using the Execute_Query function.

The *Execute_Query* function called in the QUERY_MASTER_DETAILS procedure uses the value retrieved for the 'Join' column in the master block as its 'Where' clause. Hence records from the detail table that match the record from the master table are retrieved.

Example:
If the master and the detail blocks with the join conditions are defined as follows:

      Master Block   : *Challan_Header* connected to base table *Challan_Header*
      Detail Block   : *Challan_Details* connected to base table *Challan_Details*
      Join Condition : *Challan_Header.Challan_No = Challan_Details.Challan_No*

and the first master record retrieved *Challan_No* 'CH0001' then, execute_query called in QUERY_MASTER_DETAILS generates a 'Where' clause using the 'Join' column in the detail, '=' operator and the value retrieved in the master record i.e. 'CH0001'. The generated where clause will be as follows:

      where challan_no = 'CH0001'

Adding Records in the Master and Detail Block:

When a new record is inserted into the master block, new records are also added to the detail block i.e. both the master as well as the detail blocks are in add mode.

When a new record is inserted into the master block, a form level trigger named ON-CLEAR_DETAILS is triggered. ON-CLEAR-DETAILS calls a procedure named CLEAR_ALL_MASTER_DETAILS, which is created when a master detail relation is set. The CLEAR_ALL_MASTER_DETAILS procedure moves the cursor to the detail block and clears the blocks using *Clear_Block*.

Adding Records in the Detail Block and Setting the value for the Join Column in the Detail Block:

Whenever a new record is added to the detail block, the value of the join column in the detail block is set automatically. This functionality is achieved by setting the properties of the join column in the detail block as follows:

Copy Value from Item : challan_header.challan_no

When a new record is added to the detail block Oracle Forms Runtime checks the *Copy Value from Item* property. If the value is set, Oracle Forms Runtime retrieves the value from the specified item and sets the value for the join column in the detail block.

Deleting Records in the Master block along with corresponding records in the Detail Block:

The delete operation for the master detail block is controlled by a property named **Delete Record Behavior** of the 'Relation' object. The *Delete Record Behavior* property specifies how the deletion of a record in the master block effects records in the detail block. This property can take following values:

Non-Isolated:

The *Delete Record Behavior* property is set to *Non-Isolated* by default. If the *Delete Record Behavior* Property is set to **Non-Isolated**, Oracle Forms Runtime displays an error message and prevents the deletion of a master record when associated detail records exist.

If the *Delete Record Behavior* property is set to *Non-Isolated*, Oracle Forms Builder creates a trigger named ON-CHECK-DELETE-MASTER. This trigger is executed when a master record is deleted.

ON-CHECK-DELETE-MASTER trigger checks if the detail records for the current master exists. If the detail records are present, an error message is displayed as follows:

Cannot delete master record when matching detail records exists.

Cascading:

If the *Delete Record Behavior* property is set to **Cascading**, Oracle Forms Runtime automatically deletes any associated detail records along with the master record.

When the *Delete Record Behavior* property is set to **Cascading**, Oracle Forms Builder replaces the ON-CHECK-DELETE-MASTER with a PRE-DELETE trigger. When an attempt is made to delete the master record, ON-CLEAR-DETAILS trigger is executed. This trigger calls a procedure named CLEAR_ALL_MASTER_DETAILS to clear the records in the detail block.

Since the master record is deleted by using *delete_record*, Oracle form runtime will display next record after the deleted record if the master block contains more than one record. Corresponding detail records are retrieved for the new master will also be displayed. If the number of records before deletion in the master block is one, both the master and the detail blocks are cleared and show blank records in both the blocks.

When data is committed, Oracle Forms Runtime executes PRE-DELETE trigger for every master record deleted using *Delete_Record*. The values of the deleted record can be accessed in the PRE-DELETE trigger using *:blockname.columnname*. The *challan_no* of the master record i.e. :challan_header.challan_no is then used in the delete statement to delete the corresponding detail records from the table.

Example:
> Delete from challan_details
> > where challan_no = :challan_header.challan_no;

Isolated:

If the *Delete Record Behavior* property is set to **Isolated**, Oracle Forms Runtime calls ON-CLEAR-DETAILS trigger that invokes CLEAR_ALL_MASTER_DETAILS procedure. This procedure clears all the records from the detail block. The master record is then deleted.

Caution

When data is committed, Oracle Forms runtime generates *Delete* statements for the deleted master records and attempts to delete the master records from the table.

If a foreign key constraint is defined at table level, and an attempt to delete a master record when child records exist is done this gives rise to a violation of the foreign key constraint defined at the table level. Thus Oracle Forms runtime displays an error message as follows:

FRM-40510 - ORACLE error : unable to delete record.

Click on **Help..Display Error** in the default textual menu to view the database error. The database error displayed is as follows:

ORA-02292: integrity constraint (username.FK_CHALLAN_NO) violated - child record found

The above error message points to violation of a foreign key constraint defined at the table level.

To prevent a Foreign Key constraint from being violated when a master record is being deleted, the associated value in the foreign key column of the detail table must be programmatically set to NULL.

This is done by writing a PRE-DELETE trigger at the block level that updates corresponding detail records (*for a master record being deleted*) and sets the foreign key column value to **NULL**.

```
BEGIN
        update challan_details
                set challan_no = null
                where challan_no = :challan_header.challan_no ;
END;
```

Setting the properties of the relation object:

1. Double click on the Master block in the Object Navigator. The Master block node expands and displays three nodes. These are:
   - Triggers
   - Items
   - Relation

Double click on the relation node in the master block. The relation object is displayed in the Object Navigator as shown in diagram 6.14.

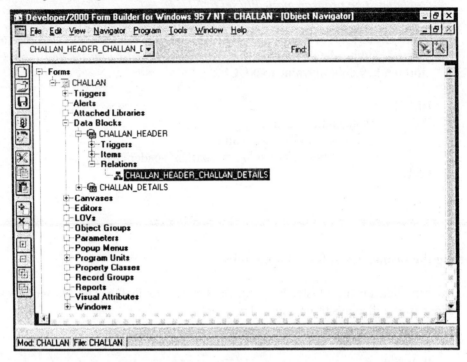

Diagram 6.14 : Relation Object Displayed in the Object Navigator

2. Right click on the relation object and select **Properties Palette** from the popup menu. The properties of the relation object are displayed. Set the **Delete Record Behavior** property to **Cascading** as shown in diagram 6.15.

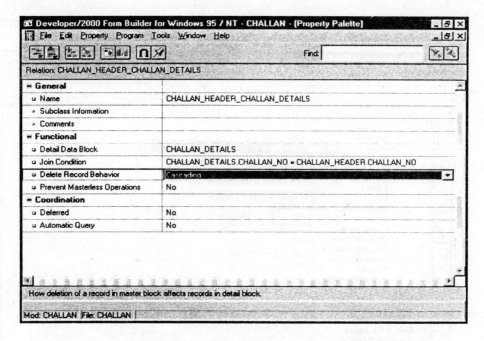

Diagram 6.15 : Setting the 'Delete Record Behavior' property.

CREATING A BUTTON PALETTE BLOCK

To make data manipulation and navigation user-defined; a control block needs to be added to the form. This control block will *control* the functionality of the form's data aware blocks.

The control block will largely consist of push buttons, which will have suitable PL/SQL code that will control the data aware blocks behavior when the push button is *pressed*.

The push buttons can be divided into three categories based on their functionality.
- Data Navigation : First, Next, Prior and Last used for data navigation in the master block.
- Data Manipulation : Add Master, Add Detail, Update, Delete Master, Delete Detail, View, Save
- Close Form : Exit

Since this control block consists of push buttons, each push button having a specific functionality, the block is traditionally called *Button_Palette*.

1. Thus to further customize the form, a *Button_Palette* block must be created. To create a new block, select the *Data Blocks* Node in the *Object Navigator* and click on **N**avigator**..Create** menu option.

Confirmation to use a wizard for the block creation is asked. Select the second option i.e. *'Build a new Block Manually'* as shown in diagram 6.16 and click on OK.

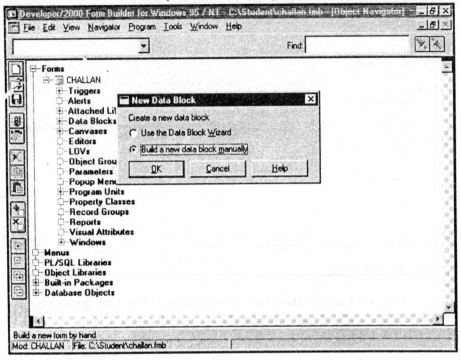

Diagram 6.16 : Selecting the *'Build a new Block Manually'* option

2. A new block with default name is created and displayed in the *Object Navigator*.

3. Right click on the block name and select *Property Palette* from the popup menu. Change the name of the block to **Button_Palette**.

4. Right click on *Button_Palette* block in the *Object Navigator* and Select Layout Editor from the popup menu. From the item palette on the left of the layout editor select the push button item and place it on the layout. Change the Name and the Label property of the push button to *pb_view* and *View* respectively.

Similarly place required number of push buttons as shown in the table below and set the *Name* and the *label* property of each pushbutton.

Push Button Name	Label
pb_add	Add
pb_view	View
pb_modify	Modify
pb_delete	Delete
pb_save	Save
pb_exit	Exit

Push Button Name	Label
pb_first	First
pb_prior	Prior
pb_next	Next
pb_last	Last
pb_adddet	Add Detail
pb_deldet	Delete Detail

5. The push buttons included in any form must have the same width, height and background color. Each push button must also be iconic. The properties of the form objects can be standardized using a user-defined property class. A property class named *PClass_Button* is already created. The properties in the property class are as follows:

Name	: PClass_Button
Width	: 23
Height	: 23
Iconic	: Yes
Background Color	: Gray

Connect this property class to the push buttons and instant standardization is available. The push buttons must thus be connected to this property class. Property class *PClass_Button* is included in *Comobj.olb* object library. Open *Comobj.olb* object library by clicking on **File..Open**. Forms Builder displays *File Open* dialog box. Select the object library file and click on *Open*.

6. Object library is displayed in the Object library. Click on the '+' next to the *Library Tabs* node. The library tabs as shown in diagram 6.17 is displayed.

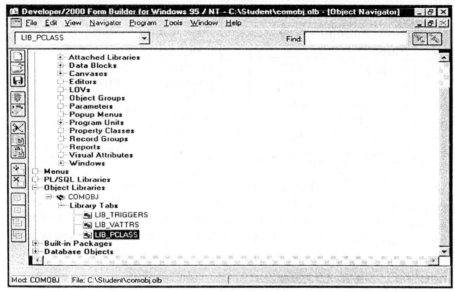

Diagram 6.17 : Library Tabs defined in the Object Library

7. Click on **Tools..Object Library** menu items. The *Library Tabs* node is opened and the objects in the first library tab are displayed. Since the property classes were stored in the Pclass tab at the time of creation, the *Pclass* tab must be selected. The objects in the Pclass tab are displayed as shown in diagram 6.18.

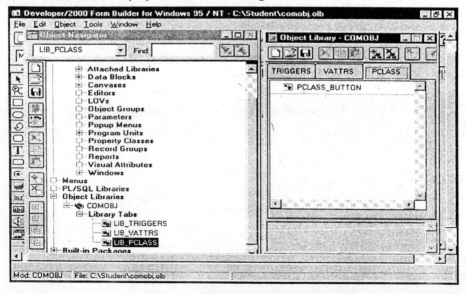

Diagram 6.18 : Objects in the *Pclass* Tab

8. Drag and drop property class *PClass_Button*. The mouse cursor changes as shown in diagram 6.19.

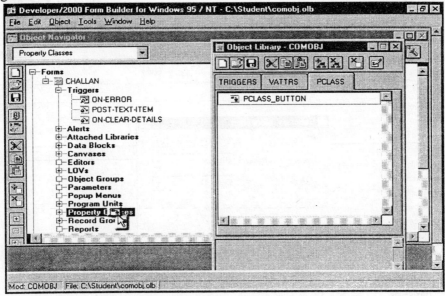

Diagram 6.19 : Dragging Pclass_Button to the Challan Form

9. Confirm to Subclass or copy the dragged object. Click on *Subclass*. A reference to the property class object in the object library is created and displays the property class in the property class node of the challan form.

10. To attach *PClass_Button* object to the buttons, select the pushbuttons one at a time in the *button_palette* block button and open the property sheet.

11. Select the *SubClass Information* property. It displays **More...** as the property value.

12. Click on **More...** *SubClass Information* dialog box is displayed. Select **Property Class** radio button. *SubClass Information* dialog box now displays two properties i.e. *Property Class Name* and *Module Name* as shown in diagram 6.20.

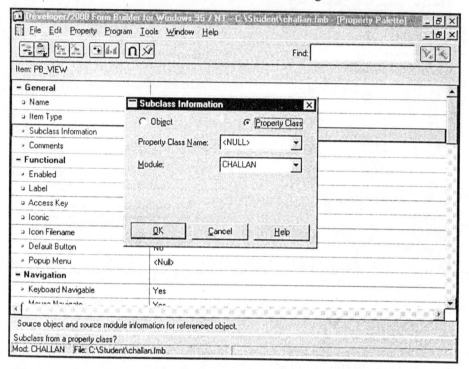

Diagram 6.20 : Accessing the Property Class Interface

13. Set the property class name to *PClass_Button* using the list available. Note that the properties of the push buttons that are inherited form the property class will display an arrow.

14. Close the property sheet. The Object Navigator displays the push button with a referenced icon.

15. Setting the *Iconic* property to 'Yes', enables display of pictures on the face of the button. Select each push buttons individually and set the *Icon Name* property as follows.

Button Name	Icon Name
pb_search	c:\orawin95\tools\devdem20\bin\icon\rt_quer1
pb_view	c:\orawin95\tools\devdem20\bin\icon\rt_quer2
pb_first	c:\orawin95\tools\devdem20\bin\icon\rt_rec1
pb_prior	c:\orawin95\tools\devdem20\bin\icon\rt_rec2
pb_next	c:\orawin95\tools\devdem20\bin\icon\rt_rec3
pb_last	c:\orawin95\tools\devdem20\bin\icon\rt_rec4
pb_add	c:\orawin95\tools\devdem20\bin\icon\rt_radd
pb_delete	c:\orawin95\tools\devdem20\bin\icon\rt_rdel

pb_modify	c:\orawin95\tools\devdem20\bin\icon\clear
pb_save	c:\orawin95\tools\devdem20\bin\icon\rt_save
pb_adddet	c:\orawin95\tools\devdem20\bin\icon\adddet
pb_deldet	c:\orawin95\tools\devdem20\bin\icon\delrow
pb_exit	c:\orawin95\tools\devdem20\bin\icon\exit

16. Open the Layout Editor. Align the push buttons as shown in them as shown in the diagram 6.21.

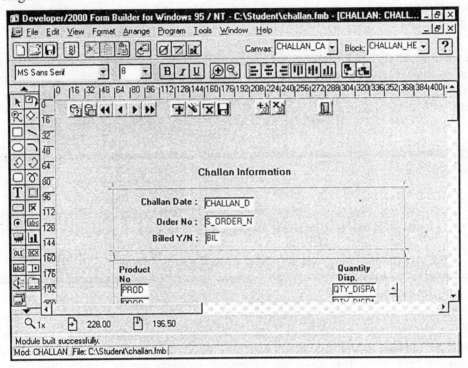

Diagram 6.21 : Push Buttons displayed in the Layout Editor

CHANGES REQUIRED IN THE COMMON LIBRARY PROCEDURES

The text items in the master as well as detail block must be enabled or disabled based on the data entry form's mode of operation. For example if the mode of operation is 'View' all the text items in the master and detail block must be disabled. Similarly, if the mode of operation is 'Add' all the text items in the detail block must be enabled.

A simple way of achieving the above functionality is to write a procedure that loops through the text items in the master and detail block and based on the form's mode of operation enables or disables the text item.

Note that the detail block includes text items that are related to the master block. These text items are set by the system and not displayed on the form at runtime. Such text items are not displayed on the form by the system setting the 'Canvas' property of each text item to 'Null'.

The *Updateable* property cannot be set for the objects if the 'Canvas' property is set **Null**. At runtime, when the *Set_Item_Property* function is called in the user-defined procedure, to set the enabled property of such text items, it causes a runtime error and thus an error message is displayed as follows:

FRM-41014: Cannot set attribute of null canvas item

The updateable property of the items that are not displayed cannot be set. Thus the PL/SQL code for the user-defined procedure named *item_enable_disable* defined in *SalesLib.pll* must be changed so that the procedure does not attempt to set the updateable property of text items that have the 'Canvas' property set to 'Null'. Similarly the updateable property of the *display items* can be set since updateable property does not exist for display items.

Open the *SalesLib.pll* library. Open the user-defined procedure named *'Item_enable_disable'* in the PL/SQL Editor and change the PL/SQL code as follows:

```
PROCEDURE ITEM_ENABLE_DISABLE( blk_name IN char, item_on_off IN
NUMBER)IS
        nxt_itemname varchar2(70);
        itemtype varchar2(25); /* Variable used to store the item type */
        itemcanvas varchar2(25); /* Variable used to store the name of the canvas on
                             which item is placed */
BEGIN
    nxt_itemname := blk_name||'.'|| get_block_property(blk_name, first_item);
    loop
                /* Get the item type and the name of the canvas on which item is placed */
                itemtype := get_item_property(nxt_itemname, item_type);
                itemcanvas := get_item_property(nxt_itemname, item_canvas);

                /* If the item type is not display item and the canvas is not blank then */
                if itemtype <> 'DISPLAY ITEM' and itemcanvas is not null then
                        set_item_property(nxt_itemname, updateable, item_on_off);
                end if;
                nxt_itemname := blk_name||'.'|| get_item_property(nxt_itemname,
                             next_navigation_item);
                if (nxt_itemname = blk_name||'.ROWID') THEN
                        exit;
                end if;
    end loop;
END;
```

ATTACHING THE COMMON PL/SQL LIBRARY

Since the triggers for the items in the *Button_Palette* reference two common procedures i.e. *scroll_control* and *item_enable_disable* which are included in the PL/SQL library named *SalesLib.pll*, the *SalesLib.pll* library must be attached to the form.

Attach the library by clicking on the *Attached Library* node in the Object Navigator. Forms Builder displays the *Attach Library* dialog box. Enter the library name as *C:\Student\SalesLib.pll* as shown in diagram 6.22.

Tip

SalesLib.pll library has been saved in a directory named *'Student'* in Drive 'C'. Please specify a sub-directory and / or path in which the library was saved as a file appropriate to the computer being worked on.

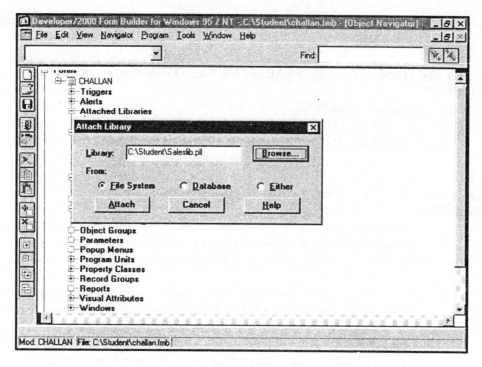

Diagram 6.22 : Attaching SalesLib.pll Library

14. Click on *Attach*. When a library file is attached to a form, the library name is stored in the form module. Library file path can be stored in the form module or an instruction to look into the default path can be given. If the path is not specified in the form module, the named library file is searched in the default path specified in the Windows Registry using the FORM50_PATH parameter.

When a library file is attached Oracle asks for confirmation to remove the library file path in the form module as shown in diagram 6.23. Click on 'Yes'. *SalesLib.pll* will be attached to the challan form without the library path and displayed under the *Attached Library* node.

Note

If an application is deployed at the client site, the file tree structure must be the same as specified in the development environment if the Library path is included in the form module. Thus from deployment point of view, this will cause administrative and deployment problems.

Instead if the library path is picked up from the FORMS45_PATH parameter, the library files can be stored in any sub directory and the FORMS45_PATH must be changed accordingly.

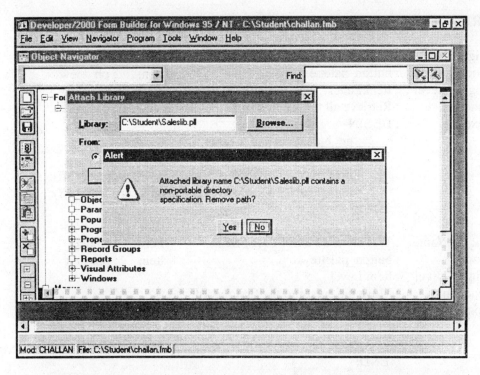

Diagram 6.23 : Removing Library path from the Form Module

15. Attached library will be displayed in the Object Navigator as shown in diagram 6.24.

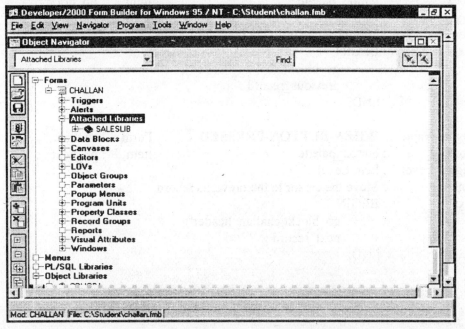

Diagram 6.24 : Attached Library displayed in Object Navigator

TRIGGERS

Trigger Name	: **WHEN-BUTTON-PRESSED**	Form	: challan
Block	: button_palette	Item	: pb_view
Trigger Level	: Item Level		
Function	: Retrieve all the records from the master and detail tables.		
Text	: BEGIN		

```
        go_block('challan_header');
        execute_query ;
        item_enable_disable('challan_header', property_off);
        item_enable_disable('challan_details', property_off);
    END;
```

Trigger Name	: **WHEN-BUTTON-PRESSED**	Form	: challan
Block	: button_palette	Item	: pb_first
Trigger Level	: Item Level		
Function	: Move the cursor to the first record.		
Text	: BEGIN		

```
        go_block('challan_header');
        first_record;
    END;
```

Trigger Name	: **WHEN-BUTTON-PRESSED**	Form	: challan
Block	: button_palette	Item	: pb_prior
Trigger Level	: Item Level		
Function	: Move the cursor to the previous record.		
Text	: BEGIN		

```
        go_block('challan_header');
        previous_record ;
    END;
```

Trigger Name	: **WHEN-BUTTON-PRESSED**	Form	: challan
Block	: button_palette	Item	: pb_next
Trigger Level	: Item Level		
Function	: Move the cursor to the previous record.		
Text	: BEGIN		

```
        go_block('challan_header');
        next_record ;
    END;
```

Trigger Name	: **WHEN-BUTTON-PRESSED**	Form	: challan
Block	: button_palette	Item	: pb_last
Trigger Level	: Item Level		
Function	: Move the cursor to the previous record.		
Text	: BEGIN		

```
        go_block('challan_header');
        last_record ;
    END;
```

Note

The Buttons first, prior, next and last allow scrolling in the master block. The detail records will change when the master record changes because of the *Relation* object on the form.

Trigger Name	: **WHEN BUTTON-PRESSED**	Form	: challan
Block	: button_palette	Item	: pb_add
Trigger Level	: Item Level		
Function	: Add new records in the challan form.		
Text	: BEGIN		

```
        go_block('challan_header');
        create_record ;

        /* Item_enable_disable is a user-defined is called twice i.e. for the
        master and detail block to enable the items of both the blocks. */
        item_enable_disable('challan_header', property_on);
        item_enable_disable('challan_details', property_on);
    END;
```

Trigger Name	: **WHEN-BUTTON-PRESSED**	Form	: challan
Block	: button_palette	Item	: pb_modify
Trigger Level	: Item Level		
Function	: Set the primary key i.e. *challan_no* not enterable and set all other fields enterable so that the record in the *Challan_Header* table can be modified.		
Text	: BEGIN		

```
        go_block('challan_header');
        item_enable_disable('challan_header', property_on);
        item_enable_disable('challan_details', property_on);
        set_item_property('challan_header.challan_no',
                    updateable, property_off);
    END;
```

Trigger Name	: **WHEN-BUTTON-PRESSED**	Form	: challan
Block	: button_palette	Item	: pb_delete
Trigger Level	: Item Level		
Function	: Delete the current challan record along with its corresponding detail records.		
Text	: BEGIN		

```
       BEGIN
            go_block('challan_header');
            delete_record ;
       END;
```

Note

The **Delete Record Behavior** property of the Relation Object is set to **Cascading**. Hence when a 'master' record is deleted, all associated detail records are deleted as well.

Trigger Name	: **WHEN-BUTTON-PRESSED**	Form	: challan
Block	: button_palette	Item	: pb_save
Trigger Level	: Item Level		
Function	: Save the changes to the challan tables.		
Text	: BEGIN		

```
       BEGIN
            if :system.form_status = 'CHANGED' then
                    /* If the form status is changed then commit changes */
                    commit_form ;
                    if :system.form_status = 'QUERY' then
                        item_enable_disable('challan_header', property_off);
                        item_enable_disable('challan_details', property_off);
                    end if ;
            end if;
       END;
```

Note

Trigger *When-Button-Pressed* on item pb_modify, pb_add and pb_save calls a user-defined procedure named *Item_Enable_Disable*. This procedure is included in the library *Saleslib.pll*.

Trigger Name	: **WHEN-BUTTON-PRESSED**	Form	: challan
Block	: button_palette	Item	: pb_adddet
Trigger Level	: Item Level		
Function	: Insert an item in the challan.		
Text	: BEGIN		

```
        go_block('challan_details');
        create_record ;
        item_enable_disable('challan_details', property_on);
    END ;
```

Trigger Name	: **WHEN-BUTTON-PRESSED**	Form	: challan
Block	: button_palette	Item	: pb_deldet
Trigger Level	: Item Level		
Function	: Delete the current item in the challan.		
Text	: BEGIN		

```
        go_block('challan_details');
        delete_record ;
    END;
```

Trigger Name	: **WHEN·BUTTON-PRESSED**	Form	: challan
Block	: button_palette	Item	: pb_exit
Trigger Level	: Item Level		
Function	: Quit challan form.		
Text	: DECLARE		

```
        answer number;
    BEGIN
        /* If there are any changes in the form the system must asks for
           confirmation to save changes */
        If :System.form_status = 'CHANGED' then
            set_alert_property('confirm_alert',title, 'Save Changes');
            set_alert_property('confirm_alert', alert_message_text,
                'Would you like to make Changes Permanent?');
            answer := Show_Alert('confirm_alert');
            If answer = Alert_Button1 then
                commit_form;
            End If;
        End If;
        /* Close the form. */
        exit_form(No_Commit);
    END ;
```

Trigger Name	: **WHEN-BUTTON-PRESSED**	Form	: challan
Block	: button_palette	Item	: pb_search
Trigger Level	: Item Level		
Function	: Search for a specific record in the master table.		
Text	: BEGIN		

```
              go_block('challan_header');
              enter_query ;
              item_enable_disable('challan_header', property_off);
              item_enable_disable('challan_details', property_off);
        END;
```

DISABLING DEFAULT FORMS TOOLBAR

The default toolbar provided by Oracle Forms Runtime must not be visible since a set of user-defined pushbuttons has been placed on the form.

An appropriate form property must be set to make the default toolbar invisible. Select *Product* form in the Object Navigator. Right click and open the property palette of the form. The form property palette includes a property named **Menu Module**. Menu Module has a default value of **DEFAULT&SMARTBAR** where DEFAULT displays the default textual menu and SMARTBAR displays the default toolbar.

To make the default toolbar invisible, set the *Menu Module* property to '**DEFAULT**' (i.e. disabling SMARTBAR) as shown in diagram 6.25.

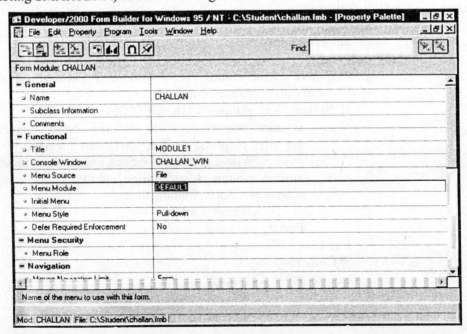

Diagram 6.25 : Setting the Menu Module Property to Default

ENABLING AND DISABLING NAVIGATIONAL BUTTONS

The navigational buttons i.e. pb_first, pb_prior, pb_next and pb_last must be enabled or disabled based on the total number of records and the current record position of the form cursor. The procedure named *scroll_control* used for enabling and disabling the navigational buttons is included in the *saleslib.pll* PL/SQL library.

Thus a call must be made to the *scroll_control* procedure when the current record focus changes. The trigger that is fired when the record focus changes is called WHEN-NEW-RECORD-INSTANCE.

Trigger Name	: **WHEN-NEW-RECORD-INSTANCE**	Form	: challan
Block	: challan_header	Item	:
Trigger Level	: Block Level		
Function	: calls procedure scroll_control that enables or disables the navigational Push buttons i.e. pb_first, pb_prior, pb_next and pb_last based on the total number of records on the form and the current record.		
Text	: BEGIN		

```
          BEGIN
              scroll_control ;
          END;
```

VALIDATIONS

Table data integrity must be ensured. Table data integrity can be achieved by
- Defining Constraints on the table
- By writing database triggers and database packages that either validate data or generate a correct value automatically.
- Setting the *properties* of the form objects.
- Writing validation code and attaching this code to form objects.

Using Database Triggers and Database Package to ensure Table Data Integrity:

Generating Primary key value for the master table:
In the *Challan_Header* table, *Challan_No* is a primary key. In a multi-user environment, data entry operators are not allowed to enter a primary key value. The primary key value is generally generated by the system.

A simple but effective approach that can be used to generate a primary key value is by using a Sequence. Once the sequence is created using SQL*Plus, a database trigger can be written such that it retrieves the next value from a sequence and uses the same as a part *or whole* of the primary key value.

The value created by the sequence must be used as the primary key value of the master table as well as the foreign key value of the detail table.

Thus the primary key value generated for the master table must be retained and then used as a foreign key value for the detail table where applicable.

If a sequence is used in a database trigger to generate the primary key, such a value is not retained by the database trigger i.e. all the variables defined in the database trigger get initialized as soon as trigger execution is completed. Hence, an object that retains values must be created and used.

One such object that Oracle provides is called a **Database Package**. Database Packages allow declaration of variables that retain values for future use. A Database Package is divided into two components:

- *Package Specification* used to declare variables, functions and procedures.
- *Package Body* specifies the PL/SQL code for the functions and procedures declared in the Package Specification.

In the current example the value for *Challan_No* as the primary key of the *Challan_Header* table needs to be generated using a sequence. The same must also be retained so that it can be used as the foreign key value for the *Challan_Detail* table.

The primary key value can be generated in the *Before Insert* database trigger by using a sequence. The database trigger must also set a variable declared in a package specification object to the newly generated *Challan_No* for later use.

Setting Foreign Key value for the Detail table:
A *Before Insert* database trigger that gets executed when new records are inserted in the *Challan_Details* table, can be used to set a foreign key. Thus insertions in the *Challan_Details* table can be done for an existing *Challan_Header* record.

The foreign key of the detail records for a challan must be set to the newly generated primary key value only if a completely new challan is generated.

If detail records are added to an existing challan, the existing *challan number* value must be used to set the value of the foreign key.

Since the master detail relation exists on the form, if detail records are added to the existing challan, the foreign key value will be set automatically by the triggers generated by Forms Builder to maintain master detail relationship.

Since the value for the challan_no is generated using a sequence in a database trigger, if a completely new challan is generated, the *Challan_No* in the master block will be Null and thus the value set for the foreign key in the detail block will also be set to Null. Thus the foreign key must be set to the value held in the package variable only if the foreign key value is Null.

The steps to generate a primary key for the master table and use the same as the foreign key for the detail table are summarized as under:

Syntax for Sequence Creation:
The syntax for creating a sequence for product_no is as follows:

> **CREATE SEQUENCE** *challan_seq*
> **INCREMENT BY** *1*
> **START WITH** *1;*

Creating a Package Specification Object:
In the current example the newly generated *Challan_No* is stored in a variable declared in a package specification. Thus a database package specification must be created.

A database package specification can be created in SQL*Plus. The Forms Builder Tool also provides an interface for creating, compiling and storing database triggers. The steps in creating a database package specification using the *Database Object Interface* of Forms Builder are:

1. Select *Database Objects* Node in the *Object Navigator*. Oracle Forms Builder will display a list of users as shown in diagram 6.26.

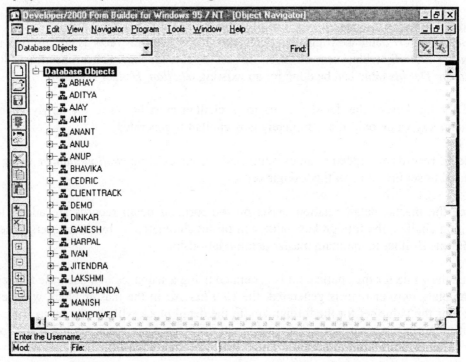

Diagram 6.26 : List of Users displayed in Database Object Node

2. Select the user for which the database trigger must be created. Oracle Forms Builder displays a list of objects that can be created and stored in the database. These include
    *   Stored Program Units i.e. procedures and functions
    *   PL/SQL Libraries
    *   Tables
    *   Views

3. Since Database Package Specification form a part of the Stored Program Unit; double click on the *Stored Program Units* Node in the Object Navigator. Oracle Forms Builder displays *New Program Unit* dialog box as shown in diagram 6.27.

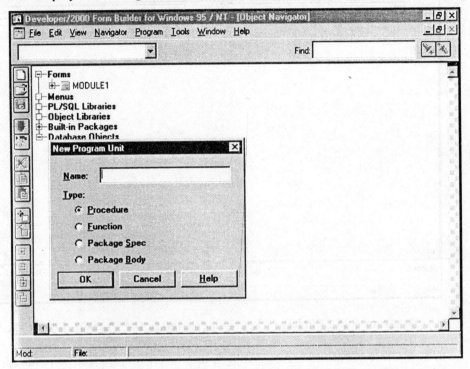

Diagram 6.27 : New Program Unit dialog box

4. Select *Package Spec* and enter the name of the package *'pkey_gen'*. Click on OK.

5. Oracle Form Builder displays the PL/SQL Editor. Declare a variable in the package as follows:

```
PACKAGE pkey_gen IS
        master_key varchar2(6);
END;
```

The completed screen will be as shown in diagram 6.28.

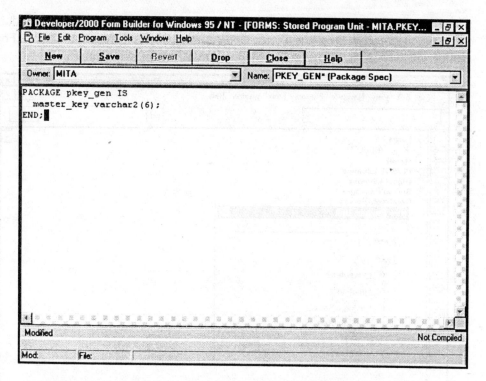

Diagram 6.28 : Package pkey_gen created in the PL/SQL Editor

6. Click on Close. Confirmation to 'Apply', or 'Revert' or 'Cancel' is required. Click on Apply. Close the Stored Program Unit Node.

Creating a Database Trigger for the master and detail tables:
Once the package is created a database trigger must be created to generate the primary key for the master table and another database trigger must be created to set the foreign key. The steps in creating the database trigger are:

1. Since a database trigger is connected to a table click on the *Tables* Node. A list of tables belonging to a specific user is displayed.

2. Each *Table* Node is further subdivided into *Triggers* and *Columns*. The *Triggers* Node will display a list of triggers if any currently created exists for the selected table. To create a new trigger, select the table on which the database trigger must be created and click on **N**avigator**..Cr**eate menu option.

An interface that allows database trigger creation appears.

3. Click on New. A new trigger with a default name is created. Change the name of the trigger to *Challan_No_Gen* and set the database trigger parameters as follows:

Triggering Time   : Before
Statement   : Insert

Also check the *For Each Row* check box.

Note

The primary key must be generated using a database trigger. Thus a Before Insert trigger Statement Level or Row Level trigger must be created.

The generated primary key value must then be set for the challan_no column in the newly inserted record. **Table column only be accessed in a Row Level trigger.**

Checking the **For Each Row** check box creates a Row Level trigger. If the **For Each Row** is not checked, a Statement Level trigger is created.

Enter the PL/SQL statements that must be included in the trigger. Enter the text as required. The equivalent Oracle PL/SQL syntax will be:

```
CREATE OR REPLACE TRIGGER challan_no_gen
     BEFORE INSERT
     ON s_challan_header
     FOR EACH ROW
DECLARE
      primary_key_value varchar2(4);
BEGIN
     SELECT lpad(to_char(challan_seq.nextval) , 4 , '0')
            INTO primary_key_value FROM dual;
     /* Set the value of the variable in the package to the newly generated
        primary key value. */
     pkey_gen.master_key := 'CH' || primary_key_value;
     /* Assign the newly generated primary key value to the challan_no column */
     :new.challan_no := pkey_gen.master_key;
END;
```

4. Click on 'Save'. Forms Builder Interface will convert the text into an appropriate PL/SQL trigger block and pass the same to the Oracle engine. The Oracle engine will execute the PL/SQL block and create a database trigger. *The Object Navigator displays the newly created trigger.*

Since the primary key is generated by the system, the primary key must not be visible on the screen. Thus we need to set the *Canvas* property of *Challan_No* item in the master block to Null.

Open the property sheet of the *Challan_No* item. Set the *Canvas* property to Null.

Note

Challan_No item is also being referenced in the *When-Button-Pressed* trigger of *pb_modify*. Updateable property of an item cannot be set if the item is not visible i.e. if the canvas property of the item is set to Null. The line of code to set the updateable property of the *Challan_No* item must be deleted from the *When-Button-Pressed* trigger of *pb_modify*.

After creating Database trigger to generate the primary key for the *Challan_Header* table, a Database trigger to set the foreign key for the *Challan_Detail* table must be created. The same steps need to be performed for creating the Before Insert Database trigger for the *Challan_Details*. The Oracle PL/SQL syntax to set a foreign key for the *Challan_Details* table will be:

```
CREATE OR REPLACE TRIGGER challan_no_gen
        BEFORE INSERT
        ON challan_details
        FOR EACH ROW
BEGIN
        /* The foreign key value must be set only for a newly
           generated challan. */

        if :new.challan_no is null then
                :new.challan_no := pkey_gen.master_key;
        end if;
END;
```

Implementing Business Rules using When-Validate-Item Trigger:

The business rules can be defined using the *When-Validate-Item* trigger. If an invalid value is entered, an appropriate error message can be displayed and the text color can be changed to RED to indicate an error condition.

The visual properties of any item can be set by attaching appropriate a Visual Attribute object. There are two visual attributes created and stored in the Object Library. These are:
- VA_ERRORS
- VA_NOERRORS

This technique of visually representing an error based on the data entered is used extensively where the data entry operator may not be completely comfortable using 'English'.

Thus if invalid value is entered, the *current_record_attribute* property is used to set the visual attribute to VA_ERRORS. If a valid value is entered, the *current_record_attribute* property is used to set the visual attribute to VA_NOERRORS.

VA_ERRORS and VA_NO_ERRORS visual attributes are defined and stored in the object library. Thus these objects must be referenced in the form. The steps are as follows:

1. Click on **File..Open** to open the Object Library. Oracle Forms Builder will display the *Open File* dialog box. Select *comobj.olb* file from the appropriate directory. *Comobj.olb* object library will be displayed in the Object Navigator under the Object Libraries Node.

2. Click on **Tool..Object Library** menu items to open the library tabs. The *Comobj.olb* currently includes three library tabs. These library tabs are named *Triggers*, *VATTRS* and *Pclass* that store the common triggers, visual attributes and property classes respectively.

3. Select *VATTRS* library tab. Oracle Forms Builder displays the VA_ERRORS, VA_NOERRORS visual attribute objects as shown in diagram 6.29.

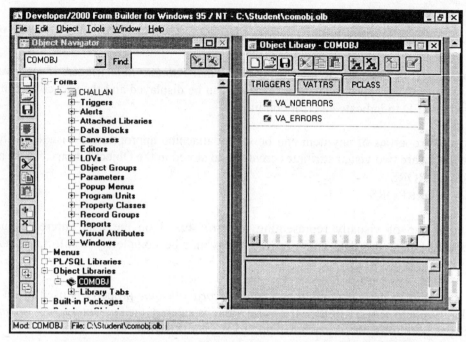

Diagram 6.29 : Object Library tabs opened in Forms Builder

4. Drag and drop the both the visual attributes from the library tab to the *Visual Attributes* node. Confirmation to subclass or copy the Visual Attribute objects are asked for. Select *SubClass*. The visual attribute reference will be included in the form as shown in diagram 6.30.

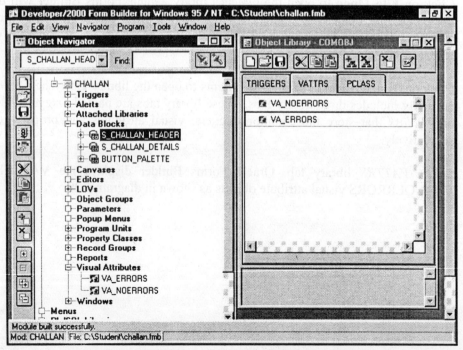

Diagram 6.30 : Sub-Classing a Visual Attribute

Tip

The visual attributes stored in the object library but referenced in the form will be shown using this icon.

5. Write When-Validate-Item triggers to validate the contents of specific text items.

_Challan_Date_ must be less than or equal to system date.

Trigger Name	: **WHEN-VALIDATE-ITEM**	Form	: challan
Block	: challan_header	Item	: challan_date
Trigger Level	: Item Level		
Function	: Check that _challan_date_ is less than or equal to the system date.		
Text	: BEGIN		

```
BEGIN
    if :challan_header.challan_date is not null then
        if :challan_header.challan_date > sysdate then
            message('Challan Date cannot be greater than ' ||
                        to_char(sysdate));
            set_item_property('challan_date', current_record_attribute,
                        'VA_ERRORS');
            raise form_trigger_failure;
        end if;
    end if;
END;
```

Quantity dispatched cannot be 0.

Trigger Name	: **WHEN-VALIDATE-ITEM**	Form	: challan
Block	: challan_details	Item	: qty_dispatched
Trigger Level	: Item Level		
Function	: Check that qty_dispatched is not 0.		
Text	: BEGIN		

```
BEGIN
    if :challan_details.qty_dispatched = 0 then
        message('Quantity Dispatched cannot be 0.');
        set_item_property('qty_dispatched',
                current_record_attribute, 'VA_ERRORS');
        raise form_trigger_failure;
    end if;
END;
```

Not Null Check using ON-ERROR Form Trigger:

If the column is defined as a NOT NULL column at the table level, Oracle Forms Builder sets the 'Required' attribute to 'Yes'. If the 'Required' attribute is set to 'Yes', Oracle Forms Runtime will display an error message if the item is exited without any value being entered.

Note

If the item is left blank, Oracle Forms Runtime displays an FRM Error as follows:

FRM-40202 : Field must be entered

To handle this error appropriate code can be written in the ON-ERROR trigger defined at the form level.

In case of an error Oracle Forms Runtime checks if an ON-ERROR trigger is written at form level. If the ON-ERROR trigger is written, Oracle Forms Runtime executes the statements specified in the ON-ERROR trigger.

Generalized PL/SQL code for the ON-ERROR trigger is written and stored in the Object Library. The ON-ERROR trigger can be subclassed or inherited from the object library leading to standardization of error handling. The steps in subclassing the ON-ERROR trigger, are:

1. Click on **File..Open** to open the Object Library. Oracle Forms Builder will display the *Open File* dialog box. Select *comobj.olb* file from the appropriate directory. *Comobj.olb* object library will be displayed in the Object Navigator under the Object Libraries Node.

2. Click on **Tool..Object Library** menu items to open the liorary tabs. The *Comobj.olb* currently includes three library tabs. These library tabs are named *Triggers*, *VATTRS* and *Pclass* that store the common triggers, visual attributes and property classes respectively.

3. Select *Triggers* library tab. Oracle Forms Builder displays the ON-ERROR trigger object included in the *Triggers* library tab as shown in diagram 6.31.

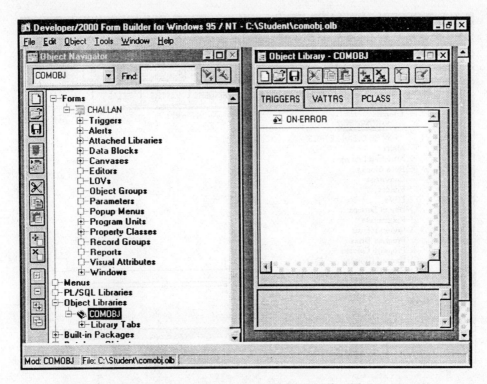

Diagram 6.31 : Object Library tabs opened in Forms Builder

4. Drag and drop the ON-ERROR trigger from the library tab to the *Triggers* node under the form name such that the ON-ERROR trigger will be a form level trigger. Oracle Forms Builder will then ask for confirmation to subclass or copy ON-ERROR trigger. Select *SubClass*. ON-ERROR trigger reference will be included in the form as shown in diagram 6.32.

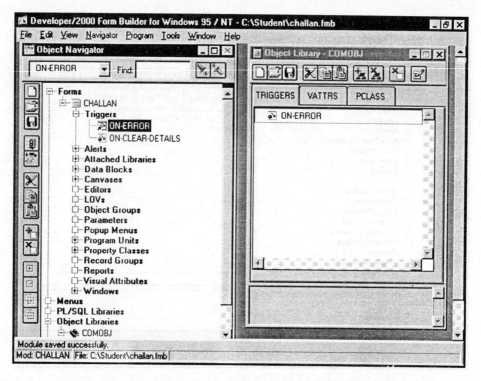

Diagram 6.32 : Object Library Tabs opened in Forms Builder

Tip

Triggers defined and stored in the form will be shown using the icon. The triggers stored in the object library but referenced in the form will be shown using this icon.

5. Set the required property to True for all the items that require a NOT NULL check.

Trigger Name	: **ON-ERROR**	Form	: challan
Block	:	Item	:
Trigger Level	: Form Level		

Function : Check for Not Null. In case of any other error display default error message and set the visual attribute to VA_ERRORS.

Text :
```
DECLARE
        error_item varchar2(50);
        current_item_label varchar2(100);
BEGIN
        error_item := :system.trigger_item;
        If error_type = 'FRM' and error_code = 40202 THEN
                current_item_label := get_item_property(error_item,
                        prompt_text);
                current_item_label := replace(current_item_label, ':', '');
                current_item_label := replace(current_item_label, ' ', '');
                Message(current_item_label || ' cannot be left blank.');
        Else
                Message(error_text);
                set_item_property(error_item,
                        current_record_attribute, 'VA_ERRORS');
        End if;
END;
```

<u>Resetting the visual attribute to VA_NO_ERRORS after the error is corrected:</u>
After entering a value in any item when the focus moves to another item Oracle Forms Runtime performs default checks on the data that it entered. For example in case of an item connected to a column defined with the Date data type, the Oracle Forms Runtime will check if date is entered in the correct format i.e. DD-MON-YYYY.

If the data does not pass default validation checks, Oracle Forms Runtime executes the ON-ERROR trigger else Oracle Forms Runtime executes the WHEN-VALIDATE-ITEM trigger.

In the current example the challan form has an ON-ERROR trigger defined at the form level and the WHEN-VALIDATE-ITEM trigger defined at the item level. PL/SQL code is written in both these triggers to display an error message and set the visual attribute to VA_ERRORS.

In case of ON-ERROR, Oracle Form Runtime will not allow movement from the current item to any other item on the form. In case of WHEN-VALIDATE-ITEM trigger, PL/SQL code i.e. *'raise form_trigger_failure'*, stops navigation to any other item unless the error is corrected.

Thus form cursor navigation is possible only if the errors are corrected. If the errors are corrected, the item text color must be set to Black i.e. the visual attribute must be set to VA_NO_ERRORS.

The trigger that gets executed when the form cursor moves from one item to the other is called POST-TEXT-ITEM. The POST-TEXT-ITEM trigger can be written for each item to ensure that the visual attribute of the text item is set to VA_NOERRORS.

Tip

If the code for any trigger defined at the item level is same for items in the same block the same trigger can be written at the block level. If an item level trigger is defined at the block level the trigger gets executed for every item in that block.

Similarly, if the PL/SQL code in the trigger for items in different blocks is same then the trigger can be defined at the form level. If an item level trigger is defined at the form level the trigger gets executed for every item in all the blocks of the form.

In the current example, the PL/SQL code for the POST-TEXT-ITEM trigger to set the visual attribute to VA_NO_ERRORS is same for all the text items in both the master and the detail block. If the POST-TEXT-ITEM trigger is written at the form level i.e. it will be executed when the cursor moves out of any text item in the *Challan_Header* or *Challan_Details* block.

The code written in the POST-TEXT-ITEM trigger is a call to the built-in *set_item_property()* to set the visual attribute of the current item to VA_NO_ERRORS. Thus there is a need to know the name of the current item. The name of the current item is stored in a system variable that can be accessed using '**:system.cursor_item**'. Thus the PL/SQL code written at block level will be as follows:

Trigger Name	: **POST-TEXT-ITEM**	Form	: challan
Block	:	Item	:
Trigger Level	: Form Level		
Function	: Set the visual attribute of the current item to VA_NO_ERRORS.		
Text	: DECLARE		

```
DECLARE
    str_current_item varchar2(50);
BEGIN
    str_current_item := :system.cursor_item;
    set_item_property(str_current_item, current_record_attribute,
        'VA_NOERRORS');
END;
```

Creating Display Items:

A Sales Challan document generated using a manual system generally displays the Challan Number, Challan Date, the Sales Order Number against which the challan is generated, the name of the client, and the details of the material delivered. Thus the data entry challan form must also display the same details.

<u>Using a Display Item in the Master Block:</u>
Order Number, Order Date and Client Number are displayed as text items belonging to the *Sales_Order* block on the Order form. These text items are connected to the columns of the *Sales_Order* table.

The Order form must also display the name of the client to whom material is being delivered. Details of each client are stored in the *Client_Master* table. Each client is identified by a unique *Client_No*.

The *Client_No* is used to identify the client when an order is placed. The *Client_No* is recorded when the client places an order. Client name can be retrieved based on the *Client_No* entered.

The relationship between S_Order_*No*, *Client_No* and *Name* can be depicted as follows:

In the master section, as soon as a valid order number is loaded into the text item S_Order_No item, the system must display the corresponding client name from the *Client_Master* table. Create a display item to display the *Client_Name* (i.e. an item to which cursor navigation is not allowed).

1. Open the layout editor of the *challan* form. Create a new display field by selecting the *display item* tool from the toolbar and dropping it on the form.

2. Set the following properties of the display field.

Name	: client_name
Item Type	: **Display Item**
Data Type	: Char
Maximum Length	: 20
Database Item	: **No**
Prompt	: Name :

Caution

STOP *Client_Name* is not included in the *Challan_Header* table i.e. *Client_Name* is not a part of the base table. If the column is not included in the base table, its **Database Item** property must be set to '**No**'.

Using a Display Item in the Detail Block:
Challan Number, Product Number and Qty Delivered are displayed as text items belonging to the *Challan_Detail* block on the Challan form. These text items are connected to the columns of the *Challan_Detail* table.

The challan form must also display the description and unit measure of the material delivered. Product description and unit measure are stored in the *Product_Master* table. Each product is identified by a unique *Product_No*.

The *Product_No* is recorded when an order accepted for delivery. Description and unit measure can be retrieved based on the *Product_No* entered. The relationship between *Product_No* and *Description* can be depicted as follows:

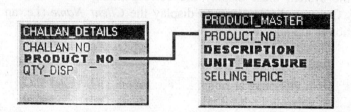

In the detail section, as soon as a valid product number is loaded into the text item *Product_No* item, the system must display the corresponding description and unit measure from the *Product_Master* table. Create a display item to display the *Description* and *Unit Measure* (i.e. an item to which cursor navigation is not allowed).

1. Select detail block in the layout editor and place a *display item* it. Set the following properties of the display field.

Name	: description
Item Type	**: Display Item**
Data Type	: Char
Maximum Length	: 20
Database Item	**: No**
Prompt	: Description
Prompt Adjustment Edge	: Top

2. Place another *display item* on the form. Set the properties of display field as follows:

Name	: unit_measure
Item Type	**: Display Item**
Data Type	: Char
Maximum Length	: 20
Database Item	**: No**
Prompt	: Unit Measure
Prompt Adjustment Edge	: Top

Note

The label or the prompt for an item must be displayed on top of the items since the detail block displays multiple records. The property that determines the position of the item prompt is **Prompt Adjustment Edge**. Set the value of this property to **Top**. The other values that this property can take are **Start**, **End**, **Top** and **Bottom**.

3. Since all prompts are displayed with the bold font style, select the prompts of the display items and click on **B** to set the font style to bold.

WORKING WITH L.O.V. OBJECTS

As seen earlier, a sales transaction starts with when a client places an order. Each Order is uniquely identified by its *S_Order_No*. Sales Order details like *S_Order_No*, *S_Order_Date*, client details and *Order_Status* are recorded in the *Sales_Order* table. *Order_Status* is a flag set to indicate whether the material ordered is not yet delivered (NP), partially delivered (IP) or fully delivered (FP).

The details of material ordered like *Product_No* and *Qty_Ordered* are stored in the *Sales_Order_Details* table.

Material ordered is then delivered and a delivery challan is prepared for the same. Material delivered to the client must be based on the order placed by the client. Thus *Challan_No*, *Challan_Date* and *S_Order_No* are stored in *Challan_Header* table.

Since a delivery challan and the sales order are related, the *S_Order_No* must exist in the *Sales_Order* table and the delivery challan must be prepared for the order that is not fully processed.

Such a business rule can be implemented by providing a selection list from which appropriate value can be selected. The method of providing a selection list is called LIST OF VALUES or simply L.O.V.

Example:
A selection list consisting of *S_Order_No* from the *Sales_Order* table can be used to select *S_Order_No* for the Challan data entry form.

List Of Values (L.O.V) is an object that opens up a separate window displaying the values from one or more tables as shown in diagram 6.33 when an appropriate key sequence is pressed.

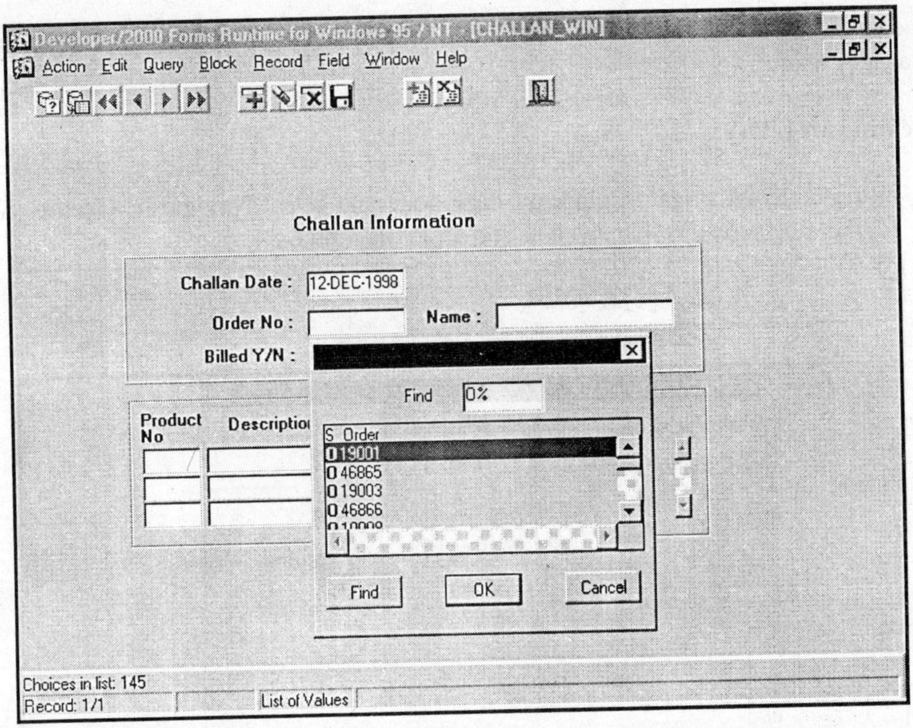

Diagram 6.33 : L.O.V window showing a list of S_Order_No

The values displayed in an L.O.V window are based on an SQL select statement defined for the LOV object. The L.O.V window must be displayed when an appropriate key sequence is pressed _and_ the form cursor is on the required item.

When a value is selected from the list and the OK push button is pressed, the selected value must be displayed in appropriate text item.

Thus to create and use a L.O.V the following distinct operations must be carried out:

- Define the data that will be displayed in the L.O.V.
- Specify the name of the text item where the selected value is displayed.
- Connect the L.O.V to a specific text item in a block.

An LOV that displays _S_Order_No_ from the _Sales_Order_ table must be created. This list of values will be connected to _S_Order_No_ text item in the _Challan_Header_ block. Since data is selected from a pre-determined number of values i.e. selected dynamically from the table column, no validation code needs to be written.

A Sales Challan document generally displays the _Challan Number_, _Challan Date_, the _S_Order_No_ against which the challan is generated, and the _Name_ of the client. Thus an L.O.V must also display the _Client Name_ along with the _S_Order_No_.

When a S_Order_No is selected, the Client Name must also be displayed on the challan data entry form.

Creating an L.O.V:

1. In the Object Navigator, click on *LOV* node and select **Navigator..Create**. A *NEW LOV* dialog screen is displayed as shown in diagram 6.34.

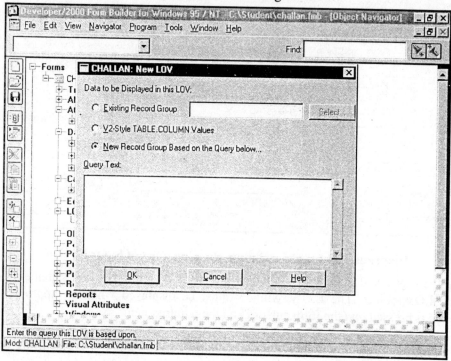

Diagram 6.34 : New LOV Dialog Window

2. A L.O.V. retrieves data based on the select statement specified for the L.O.V. Thus a select statement must be entered in the *Query Text* property of the L.O.V.

```
SELECT s_order_no, name
    INTO :s_order_no, :client_name
    FROM client_master, sales_order
    WHERE client_master.client_no = sales_order.client_no and
            sales_order.order_status <> 'FP';
```

The above query retrieves data from two tables i.e. *Sales_Order* and *Client_Master*. These tables are linked using the *Client_No* column. The relation between these tables can be shown as follows:

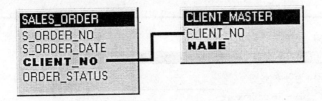

Thus the SQL statement depicting the relation will be:

SELECT s_order_no, name
    FROM client_master, sales_order
    WHERE client_master.client_no = sales_order.client_no

The L.O.V. must include *S_Order_No* which are not fully processed i.e. the material ordered is not fully delivered. Each record in the Sales_Order table holds the Order Status as (NP - Not processed, IP - In Process or FP- fully Processed) in the column named Order_Status. Thus an additional where clause is required as follows:

    sales_order.order_status <> 'FP';

As soon as a value is selected from the LOV it must be displayed in the *S_Order_No* text item. Thus the select statement includes an INTO clause that passes the selected values to the *S_Order_No* and *Client_Name* text item.

    INTO :s_order_no, :client_name

The completed *NEW LOV* screen is as shown in diagram 6.35.

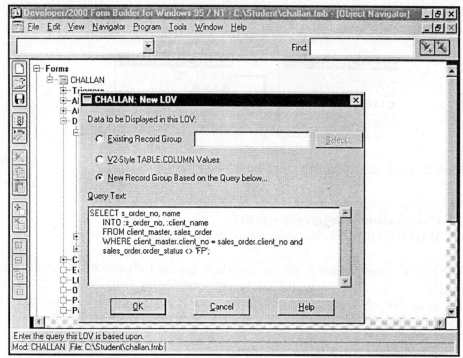

Diagram 6.35 : New LOV dialog along with Completed Select Statement

3. Click on OK. A List of values with a default name is displayed in the Object Navigator. When an LOV is created in this manner, two objects are created. These are

* A '**Record Group**' object i.e. a collection of records fetched, based on the select statement specified.

* An '**LOV**' object that display the records from the *Record Group* and when a record is selected, sets the values of the items specified in the INTO clause.

 Note

 The Record Group object is displayed in the *Record Group* Node and the LOV is displayed in the *LOV* node of the object Navigator as shown in diagram 6.35.

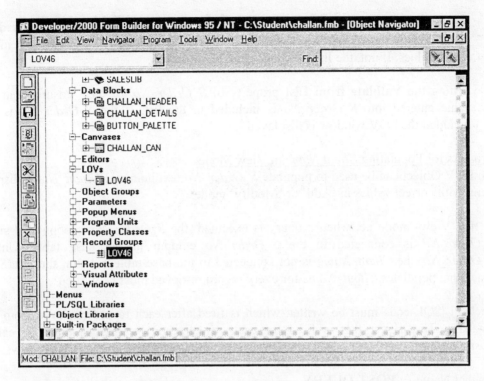

Diagram 6.35 : LOV and Record Group displayed in the Object Navigator

4. Change the name of the L.O.V to *Order_Lov* and the record group to *Order_Recgrp*.

5. L.O.V, *Order_lov* must be connected to the *S_Order_No* text item by selecting the *Order_Lov* in L.O.V property of the text item *S_Order_No*. The following properties are set for the text item.

List of Values	: *Order_Lov*
List X Position	: 158
List Y Position	: 147

The '*List of Values*' property connects the text item to the L.O.V. The '*List of values*' property thus allows selection of *S_Order_No* by pressing appropriate key sequence at runtime. The LOV X Position and LOV Y Position properties specifies the X and Y co-ordinates where the list of values must be displayed.

 Tip

The default key sequence used to display the L.O.V. window is **F9**.

A value can also be entered without using the list of values. If data entry is done without using the L.O.V, the system must check if the entered value is present in the list of values. If not, the list of values must be displayed.

Setting the **Validate from List** property of *S_Order_No* to '**Yes**' ensures that the value entered into *S_Order_No* is included in the list. If the *S_Order_No* is not included the LOV window is displayed.

Triggers for Populating *Client Name* in View Mode:
An LOV Object can be used to populate *S_Order_No* text item and *Client_Name* display item, with correct values in 'Add' or 'Modify' mode.

In the 'View' mode i.e. when a query is executed, the *S_Order_No* is populated since *S_Order_No* is connected to the *S_Order_No* column in the base table. Unlike *S_Order_No*, the *Client_Name* is not connected to the base table column, thus PL/SQL block that populates *Client_Name* for every record retrieved must be written.

Such PL/SQL code must be written which is fired after each record retrieved from the database. The trigger that is fired for each row fetched by *execute_query* is called *Post-Query* trigger. The PL/SQL block written in the *Post-Query* trigger is as follows:

Trigger Name   : **POST-QUERY**   Form   : challan
Block   : challan_header   Item   :
Trigger Level : Block Level
Function   : Populates the display item *Client_Name* for every row retrieved from
                 the *challan_header* table.
Text   : BEGIN
                         select name into :challan_header.client_name
                         from client_master, sales_order
                         where client_master.client_no = sales_order.client_no and
                                 sales_order.s_order_no = :challan_header.s_order_no;
                 END;

L.O.V IN THE DETAIL SECTION

As seen earlier, a sales transaction starts with when a client places an order. The details of material ordered like *Product_No* and *Qty_Ordered* are stored in the *Sales_Order_Details* table.

A delivery challan is prepared when the material delivered as per the Sales Order specification. Thus *S_Order_No* is recorded *Challan_Header* and the *Product_No* is selected from the *Sales_Order_Details* table for the selected *S_Order_No* in the *Challan_Header* and recorded into the *Challan_Details* table.

In the detail section the entered *Product_No* must be present in the *Sales_Order_Details* table for a selected *S_Order_No*. Thus the *Product_No* values must be selected using an L.O.V as shown in diagram 6.37.

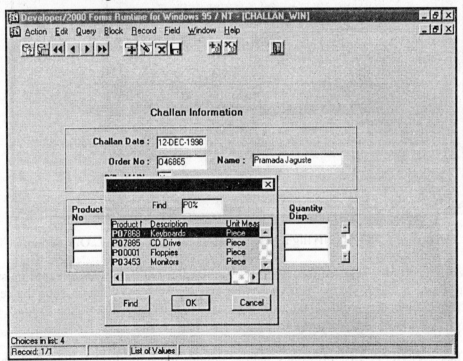

Diagram 6.37 : L.O.V of Products Ordered

The steps in creating the L.O.V for the *Product_No* text item will be as follows:

1. In the Object Navigator, click on *L.O.V.* node and select **Navigator..Create**. A *NEW L.O.V* dialog screen is displayed.

2. A L.O.V. retrieves data based on the select statement specified for the L.O.V. Thus a select statement must be entered in the *Query Text* property of the L.O.V as shown in diagram 6.38.

SELECT sales_order_details.product_no, description, unit_measure
    INTO :product_no, :description, unit_measure
    FROM product_master, sales_order_details
    WHERE product_master.product_no = sales_order_details.product_no and
        s_order_no = :challan_header.s_order_no

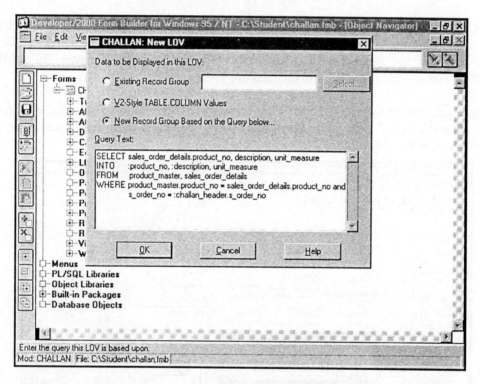

Diagram 6.38 : Specifying a Select Statement in the New L.O.V screen

When a record is selected from the L.O.V, the values of the selected record must be displayed in the *Product_No*, *Description* and *Unit_Measure* items. Thus the select statement includes an INTO clause that passes the selected values to the *Product_No*, *Description* and *Unit_Measure* items.

3. Click on OK. A List of values with a default name is displayed in the Object Navigator. When an L.O.V is created, two objects i.e. record group and L.O.V. object gets created.

4. Change the name of the L.O.V to *Product_Lov* and the record group to *Product_Recgrp*.

5. L.O.V *Product_Lov* must be connected to the *Product_No* item by selecting the *Product_Lov* in L.O.V property of the *Product_No*. The properties set for *Product_No* are as follows:

List of Values	: Product_Lov
List X Position	: 158
List Y Position	: 147
Validate from List	: Yes

CHANGING THE LIST VALUES DYNAMICALLY AT RUNTIME

Ensuring that the combination of *Challan_No* and *Product_No* must be unique:

In the detail section, the combination of *Product_No* and *Challan_No* is the primary key. Thus the *Product_No* for a specific challan should not be repeated. Since an L.O.V is used for selecting and validating the *Product_No*, the L.O.V must be changed dynamically to guarantee that same the *Product_No* is not repeated for a challan.

An L.O.V is used to select a *Product_No* by setting '*List of values*' and the '*Validate from list*' properties. If the '*Validate from list*' property is set to 'Yes' and an invalid value is entered, the L.O.V window is displayed.

As soon as the *Product_No is* selected for a challan the *Product_No* must be removed from the L.O.V. If the selected *Product_No* is removed, such value will not be available for selection when another detail record is inserted for the same challan.

If the *Product_No* is keyed-in instead of being selected from the list, the default validation of '*Validate from list*' will be executed to check if the value is present in the list or not. Since the value is removed, the validation test will fail and thus the L.O.V. window will be displayed to select a new value.

This method will thus guarantee that the *Product_No* is not only present in the *Sales_Order_Details* table for the selected *S_Order_No* but also not repeated in the challan.

There is a need to understand how a list of values is displayed in the L.O.V. window, if the L.O.V. values have to change dynamically.

How is L.O.V. Window populated with list of values:

Two objects are created when an L.O.V. is created. These are:
- L.O.V. Object
- Record Group

Record group is an object that stores multiple records. The fields in the record group are defined based on the SQL select statement specified at the time of creating the L.O.V. This record group is used to populate the L.O.V. window. Oracle Runtime environment refreshes

- The Record Group and
- The corresponding L.O.V. window from time to time

Thus the values displayed in the L.O.V. window reflect the changes made to the source table i.e. the table used to populate the values using a SQL select statement.

Tip

Form Runtime executes the query to populate an L.O.V.'s underlying record group whenever the L.O.V. is invoked or whenever a text item that has the '*Validate from list*' property set to 'Yes'.

Unique values in the *Product_No* item can be guaranteed by removing the records in the record group.

Since the L.O.V. window is refreshed by Oracle Runtime environment from time to time if the records in the record group are changed, the same will be reflected in the L.O.V. window.

Caution

Oracle Forms runtime not only refreshes the L.O.V. window but also refreshes the record group. Thus any programmatic change to the record group will be reset automatically by Oracle Forms Runtime.

To avoid this, appropriate properties must be set to disable the automatic refresh of the record group and ensuring that the L.O.V. is refreshed automatically.

Setting Properties to 'Disable' refreshing of the record group:

L.O.V. object includes a number of properties that determine the behavior of L.O.V. object and the corresponding record group. The property that controls the refresh behavior of the record group is called **Automatic Refresh**.

When the '*Automatic Refresh*' property is set to 'Yes' (default value), Oracle Form runtime refreshes the record group when the L.O.V. is invoked or when a text item is validated against L.O.V. values.

If the '*Automatic Refresh*' property is set to 'No', Oracle Form runtime executes the query for the first time only. Once the record group is populated with the query, the record group is not repopulated automatically. Records from the initial query remain stored in the record group until they are removed or replaced. Thus records can be manipulated programmatically when the '*Automatic Refresh*' property is set to 'No'.

To set the '*Automatic Refresh*' property to 'No', click on L.O.V. node in the object navigator and select *product_lov*. Click on **Tools..Property Palette** to invoke the property sheet of *product_lov*. Set the set the '*Automatic Refresh*' property to 'No'.
To change L.O.V. dynamically, PL/SQL code blocks must be written in the appropriate triggers. Thus there is a need to identify the instances when the L.O.V. must be changed and appropriate triggers must be chosen where PL/SQL code can be written. The instances where the L.O.V. must be changed are defined as under:

There is a movement from one challan to the other:
L.O.V. must show all the *Product_No* that are not included in the current challan. Thus when navigating between different challans, the L.O.V. must first be populated with all the product numbers from the *Sales_Order_Details* table for the selected *S_Order_No* and then each *Product_No* that is present in the current challan must be removed.

When a new challan is generated:
When a new challan is generated, the detail section includes only blank records. Thus all the product numbers from the *Sales_Order_Details* table for the selected *S_Order_No* must be available for selection. *Create_Record* function inserts a new challan and positions the cursor on the new record.

When a challan is deleted:
When a challan is deleted, the cursor moves to the challan after the deleted challan. Thus deletion of a challan also results into cursor navigation. The L.O.V. must first be populated with all the product numbers from the *Sales_Order_Details* table for the selected *S_Order_No* and then each *Product_No* that is present in the current challan must be removed.

The *When-New-Record-Instance* trigger gets executed when there is navigation from one challan to the other or when a new challan is generated. Thus PL/SQL code must be written in the *When-New-Record-Instance* trigger.

Trigger Name	: **WHEN-NEW-RECORD-INSTANCE**	Form	: challan
Block	: challan_header	Item	:
Trigger Level	: Block Level		
Function	: Dynamically changing the L.O.V.		
Text	: DECLARE		

```
           form_name varchar2(50);
           current_rec_no number(3); /* Stores current record number */
           cur_val varchar2(60); /* Stores current product_no */
           row_count number(3); /* counter used in the for loop */
           last_rec_no number(3); /* total number of rows */
           product_group recordgroup;
           group_rec_id number; /* record number in the record group */
           status number;
       BEGIN
           /* Call the scroll control procedure to enable / disable the
           navigation buttons based on the current record and the total
           number of records */
           scroll_control;

           /*Find the record group associated with the L.O.V. for
           product_no so that the records can be manipulated */
           product_group := find_group('product_recgrp');

           /* Whenever the focus of the master record changes, the record
           group must be populated with all the records from the
           product_master table irrespective of the record status i.e. NEW,
           INSERT, CHANGED or QUERY. The SQL select statement used
           to populate the record group is specified in the Record Group
           Query property */

           /* If record group is populated successfully, it returns 0. If the
           record group is not populated it returns a negative number. */
           status := populate_group(product_group);

           /* The record is not blank i.e. the record status is not NEW then
           appropriate records must be removed from the record group */

           If :system.record_status <> 'NEW' then
               /* Record removal results into record navigation in the detail
               block and thus the validations checks will be executed. The
               validation for the current form must be set to false so that
               oracle forms runtime does not execute validation checks. */

           form_name := get_application_property(current_form_name);
           set_form_property(form_name, validation, property_false);
```

/ * Set the focus on the detail block and get the current record number. The current record number is required to reposition the cursor on the current record after the records are deleted from the record group */

```
go_block('challan_details');
current_rec_no := to_number(:system.cursor_record);
```

/* Position the cursor on the last record and get total number of records. Reposition the cursor on the first record. */

```
last_record;
last_rec_no := to_number(:system.cursor_record);
first_record;
```

```
For row_count in 1..last_rec_no Loop
```

/* get the current product_no and store it in a variable */
```
    cur_val := :product_no;
```

/* Find the record number that matches the current product_no. The column in the record group for which the value is searched and the value itself must be specified. The columns in the record group can be referenced as record_group_name.column_name. */

```
    group_rec_id := get_group_record_number(
            'product_recgrp.product_no', cur_val);
```

/* Get_group_record_number returns 0 if no records are found. If the record position is not 0 the record at that position must be deleted from the record group. The delete_group_row function accepts record group and the record position as parameters */

```
    if group_rec_id > 0 then
        delete_group_row(product_group, group_rec_id);
    end if;
```

/* Move to the next record in the detail block */
```
    next_record;
End Loop;
```

/* After deleting appropriate records in the record group the focus must return to the record on which the focus was before executing this trigger */
go_record(current_rec_no);

/* Enable the validations of the form and reposition the cursor on the master block */

set_form_property(form_name, validation, property_true);
go_block('challan_header');
End If;
END;

Note

The columns in the record group can be referenced as record_group_name.column_name. For example if the record group is named *Product_Recgrp* and the column is *product_no*, the record group column can be accessed as *Product_Recgrp.Product_No.*

When-Validate-Item Trigger:
When-Validate-Item trigger is executed when the value in the *Product_No* item is modified. The value in the *Product_No* item will be changed when
• A new record is inserted in the detail section and the *Product_No* is entered.
• An existing record's *Product_No* is modified.

When a new record is inserted and a Product_No is entered or selected from the L.O.V.:
When a new record is inserted in the detail section and the *Product_No* is entered or selected the selected *Product_No* must be removed from the L.O.V.

When the product_no of an existing record is modified:
When an existing record is modified, the record in the record group for the newly selected *Product_No* must be removed from the record group. The record group for the old value of *Product_No* must be inserted in the record group. Thus a hidden item named *B_Product_No* must be maintained to store the old value of the *Product_No* item. This item will be populated whenever the focus is set on the *Product_No* item.

The steps for creating this hidden item is as follows:

1. Show the layout editor by clicking on **Tools..Layout Editor**. Place a display item on the canvas and set the following properties:

Name	: B_Product_No
Item Type	: Display Item
Data Type	: Char
Maximum Length	: 6
Database Item	: No
Canvas	: <Null>
Prompt	:

2. Write necessary PL/SQL code to populate the display item and make changes to the records in the record group.

Trigger Name	: **WHEN-NEW-ITEM-INSTANCE**	Form	: challan
Block	: challan_details	Item	: product_no
Trigger Level	: Item Level		
Function	: Populate the hidden with the *Product_No* value in the detail block.		
Text	: BEGIN		

```
        :b_product_no := :product_no;
    END;
```

Trigger Name	: **WHEN-VALIDATE-ITEM**	Form	: challan
Block	: challan_details	Item	: product_no
Trigger Level	: Item Level		
Function	: Changes in the record group after selecting a *Product_No*.		
Text	: DECLARE		

```
        cur_val varchar2(6); /* Stores current product_no */
        product_group recordgroup;
        group_rec_id number; /* record number in the record group */
        current_row number;
    BEGIN
        product_group := find_group('product_recgrp');
        cur_val := :product_no;
        /* If a blank record is inserted and the product_no is selected, the
        record status is INSERT and the old value of product_no is null. The
        selected product_no must be removed from the record group */

        If :system.record_status = 'INSERT' Then
            If :b_product_no is null Then
                group_rec_id := get_group_record_number(
                        'product_recgrp.product_no', cur_val);
                delete_group_row(product_group, group_rec_id);
```

```
        else
                /* if the record status is INSERT and the b_product_no
                i.e. is not null, it indicates that the record that is yet not
                saved to the table is being modified. Thus the record with
                the value as specified in the product_no item is deleted
                and the record with the value as specified in
                b_product_no is added. */

                group_rec_id := get_group_record_number(
                        'product_recgrp.product_no', cur_val);
                delete_group_row(product_group, group_rec_id);

                /* add_group_row function inserts a blank record in the
                record group. This function accepts record group and the
                position where the record is inserted. Blank record is
                inserted at the end if END_OF_GROUP is specified. */

                add_group_row(product_group, END_OF_GROUP);

                /* Row count can be used to get the last record in the
                record group i.e. the newly inserted row */

                current_row := get_group_row_count(product_group);

                /* Set the product_no value of the newly inserted record
                to the old value held in b_product_no. Char data type
                values can be set using set_group_char_cell */

                set_group_char_cell('product_recgrp.product_no',
                        current_row, :b_product_no);

        End If;
    Elsif :system.record_status = 'CHANGED' Then
                group_rec_id := get_group_record_number(
                        'product_recgrp.product_no',cur_val);
                delete_group_row(product_group, group_rec_id);
                add_group_row(product_group, END_OF_GROUP);
                current_row := get_group_row_count(product_group);
                set_group_char_cell('product_recgrp.product_no',
                        current_row, :b_product_no);
        End If;
    END;
```

<u>When the detail record is deleted:</u>
When a detail record is deleted, a new record must be added to the record group and the value must be set to the *Product_No* of the record that has to be the deleted. Since the value is not available once the record is deleted, new record must be added to the record group before deletion. Thus the PL/SQL code for adding the record will be written in the *When-Button-Pressed* event of 'Pb_Delete'. The code for the delete button will be changed as follows:

Trigger Name	: **WHEN-BUTTON-PRESSED**	Form	: challan
Block	: button_palette	Item	: pb_delete
Trigger Level	: Item Level		
Function	: Adding a record in the record group when a detail record is deleted.		

Text   : DECLARE

```
        cur_val varchar2(20);
        product_group recordgroup;
        group_rec_id number;
        current_row number;
BEGIN
        product_group := find_group('product_recgrp');
        cur_val := :product_no;

        /* If the record is not a blank record */
        If :b_product_no is not null and curval is not null Then
            /* Add a blank record at the end of the record group */
            add_group_row(product_group, END_OF_GROUP);

            /* Get the record number of the newly inserted record */
            current_row := get_group_row_count(product_group);

            /* Set the value of the newly inserted row to the value held in
            the product_no item */
            set_group_char_cell('product_recgrp.product_no',
                current_row, :product_no);
        End If;
            /* Set the focus on the detail block and delete the current
            detail block */

            go_block('challan_details');
            delete_record ;
END;
```

<u>Triggers for Populating Description In 'View' Mode:</u>

In the view mode the *Product_No*, *Unit_measure* and *qty_dispatched* will be populated automatically when an *execute_query* is fired. *Description* is not connected to the base table and thus it has to be populated using PL/SQL code. A trigger named *Post-Query* is executed for every row fetched by *execute_query*. The PL/SQL block in the *Post-Query* will be changed as follows:

Trigger Name	: **POST-QUERY**	Form	: challan
Block	: s_challan_detail	Item	:
Trigger Level	: Block Level		
Function	: Populates *Description* and *Unit_Measure* from *Product_Master* table for every detail row retrieved.		
Text	: BEGIN		

```
          select description, unit_measure
                into :description, unit_measure
                from product_master
                where product_no = :product_no;
      EXCEPTION
          When No_Data_Found Then
                   null;
      END;
```

Similarly in insert or modify mode A trigger named *When-Validate-Item* fires when the *Product_No* is entered and the cursor is moved to another item. PL/SQL code must be written in this trigger to populate *Description* and *Unit_Measure* from the *Product_Master* table. The changes in the *When-Validate-Item* trigger is as follows:

Trigger Name	: **WHEN-VALIDATE-ITEM**	Form	: challan
Block	: challan_detail	Item	: product_no
Trigger Level	: Item Level		
Function	: Changes the record in the record group dynamically and populates *Description* and *Unit_Measure* from *Product_Master* table.		
Text	: DECLARE		

```
          cur_val varchar2(20);
          product_group recordgroup;
          group_rec_id number;
          current_row number;
      BEGIN
          product_group := find_group('product_recgrp');
          cur_val := :product_no;
          If :system.record_status = 'INSERT' Then
             If :b_product_no is null Then
                 group_rec_id := get_group_record_number(
                     'product_recgrp.product_no', cur_val);
                 delete_group_row(product_group, group_rec_id);
```

```
                    Else
                        group_rec_id := get_group_record_number(
                                'product_recgrp.product_no', cur_val);
                        delete_group_row(product_group, group_rec_id);
                        add_group_row(product_group, END_OF_GROUP);
                        current_row := get_group_row_count(product_group);
                        set_group_char_cell('product_recgrp.product_no',
                                current_row, :b_product_no);
                    End If;
                Elsif :system.record_status = 'CHANGED' Then
                    group_rec_id := get_group_record_number(
                        'product_recgrp.product_no', cur_val);
                    delete_group_row(product_group, group_rec_id);
                    add_group_row(product_group, END_OF_GROUP);
                    current_row := get_group_row_count(product_group);
                    set_group_char_cell('product_recgrp.product_no',
                            current_row, :b_product_no);
                End If;
                select description, unit_measure
                        into :description, unit_measure
                        from product_master
                        where product_no = :product_no;
        EXCEPTION
                When No_Data_Found Then
                        null;
        END;
```

SETTING DEFAULT VALUES FOR THE ITEMS

The default value for *Challan_Date* must be set to system date:
Every item includes a property named *Initial Value* that allows default value setting. Set the *initial value* of *Challan_Date* item to $$date$$ as follows:

Initial Value   : $$date$$

Note

$$date$$ is a system variable that records the current date. It can be used to designate a default value for an item only via the default value item characteristics. The item must be of *Char* or *Date* data type.

CROSS TABLE UPDATION

A very commonly used technique in commercial applications is that when data is being manipulated using a data entry form, data in several other tables will get affected immediately depending upon the processing taking place on the data entry form.

A very simple example of this is as described below:

product_no	quantity

Product_no	qty_on_hand

Challan_details table
(When goods are dispatched
  records in inserted in the
  challan_details table)

Product_master table
(The qty_on_hand in the
  product_master table will reduce when
  goods are dispatched)

Cross Table Updation required for the Challan form:

Whenever a record is inserted, updated, deleted in the *Challan_Detail* table the *Quantity_On_Hand* in the *Product_Master* table must reflect a change in the stock level. The quantity delivered against a challan would change the *Qty_On_Hand* of *Product_Master* as follows:

- Whenever an *insert* is performed decrease the *Qty_on_Hand*.
- Whenever a *delete* is performed increase the *Qty_on_Hand*.
- Whenever an *update* is done the *Qty_on_Hand* is adjusted appropriately.

Order status flags i.e. not processed (NP), in process (IP) or fully processed (FP) is maintained in the *Sales_Order* table. The order status will be updated from the challan data entry form. If the *Qty_Ordered* and *Qty_Disp* of all the products is the same the status is set to 'FP' i.e. fully processed and if the *Qty_Disp* is greater than 0 for any item in the order then the status is set to 'IP' i.e. In Process. If *Qty_Disp* is 0 for all the items included in the order, the status is set to 'NP'.

The tables related to the *challan_header* and *challan_details* must be updated using appropriate PL/SQL code blocks when the data manipulation operations are made permanent by clicking on *Save* push button. Data manipulation operations can be made permanent by executing *Commit_form* packages procedure.

Thus triggers that get executed when a *commit_form* is executed must be recognized and appropriate PL/SQL code must be written.

Working of *Commit_Form* and Sequence of Triggers that get executed:

When the *commit_form* packaged procured is executed, the contents of *form_status* system variable (:system.form_status) is read to determine whether the form requires a commit operation. *:system.form_status* can hold following values:

Value	Description
NEW	Form contains blank records that need not be saved to the base table
QUERY	Form contains records retrieved from the base table but none of these records have been modified
CHANGED	Records in the blocks defined in the form have been modified i.e. • new records have been inserted • existing records have been modified • records have been deleted

If *:system.form_status* is CHANGED, the contents of *block_status* system variable (:system.block_status) is read for each data block in the form to determine the block in which records have changed. :system.block_status can hold following values:

Value	Description
NEW	Data Block contains blank records that need not be saved to the base table
QUERY	Data block contains records retrieved from the base table but none of these records have been modified
CHANGED	Records in the data block have been modified i.e. • new records have been inserted • existing records have been modified • records have been deleted

If *:system.block_status* is CHANGED, the contents of *record_status* system variable (:system.record_status) is read for each record in the data block to determine the SQL statement that must be generated for the records that have been changed, inserted or deleted. :system.record_status can hold following values:

Value	Description
NEW	It is a blank record
QUERY	The record has been queried but not modified.
INSERT	A blank record was inserted and data entry for the same is done and thus an insert statement must be executed.
CHANGED	Existing record is modified and thus an update statement must be executed.

If the records are inserted or modified, appropriate insert or update statements are generated. Similarly delete statements are generated for the records deleted using the *delete_record* syntax.

Based on operation performed for a specific record, a set of triggers also get executed for each record as follows:

Operation	Triggers Executed	
INSERT	PRE-INSERT	Is executed before the insert statement is generated and sent to the Oracle engine
	ON-INSERT	The insert statement is not generated instead the PL/SQL code in the ON-INSERT trigger is executed.
	POST-INSERT	Is executed after the insert statement is generated and sent to the Oracle engine
CHANGED	PRE-UPDATE	Is executed before the update statement is generated and sent to the Oracle engine
	ON-UPDATE	The update statement is not generated instead the PL/SQL code in the ON-UPDATE trigger is executed.
	POST-UPDATE	Is executed after the update statement is generated and sent to the Oracle engine
DELETE	PRE-DELETE	Is executed before the delete statement is generated and sent to the Oracle engine
	ON-DELETE	The delete statement is not generated instead the PL/SQL code in the ON-DELETE trigger is executed.
	POST-DELETE	Is executed after the delete statement is generated and sent to the Oracle engine

The PL/SQL code for cross table updation in case of an insert and update operation must be executed after the insert / update statement associated with the detail block is sent to the Oracle engine. The PL/SQL code must be written at block level i.e. on challan_details block defined in the POST-INSERT and POST-UPDATE triggers.

Trigger Name	: **POST-INSERT**	Form	: Challan
Block	: challan_details	Item	:
Function	: Cross table updation when a record is inserted in the challan detail table.		
Trigger Level	: Block Level		
Trigger Text	: DECLARE		

```
            current_quantity number(8);
        BEGIN
            current_quantity := :Challan_details.quantity;
            update product_master
              set qty_on_hand =
              qty_on_hand - current_quantity
              where rtrim(product_no) = :challan_details.product_no;

            /* Procedure called to set order_status of the sales_order table */
            update_order_status;
        EXCEPTION
            When No_data_found Then
                    message('Error while updating details of new records');
                    raise form_trigger_failure;
        END;
```

Trigger Name	: **POST-UPDATE**	Form	: Challan
Block	: challan_details	Item	:
Function	: Cross table updation when a record is updated in the challan detail table.		
Trigger Level	: Block Level		
Trigger Text	: DECLARE		

```
            old_qty Number(8);
            current_qty number(8);
        BEGIN
            current_qty := :challan_details.quantity;

            select quantity into old_qty
                from challan_details
                where rtrim(challan_no) =:challan_details.challan_no
                and rtrim(product_no) = :challan_details.product_no;

            update product_master
                set qty_on_hand = qty_on_hand + old_qty - current_qty
                where rtrim(product_no) = :challan_details.product_no;

            /* Procedure called to set the status field of the sales_order table */
            update_order_status;
        END;
```

For table updation for delete operation the **when-button-pressed** trigger on the pb_delete and pb_deldet must be changed. The triggers will be as follows:

Trigger Name : **WHEN-BUTTON-PRESSED**   Form : Challan
Block   : challan_details   Item : pb_delete
Function   : Delete the corresponding detail records and the master record.
       Cross table updation when a record is deleted in the challan detail table.
Trigger Level : Item Level
Trigger Text : DECLARE

```
                old_qty Number(8);
                total_records number(8);
                row_cntr number(8);
        BEGIN
                select count(challan_no) into total_records
                        from    challan_details
                        where challan_no = :challan_header.challan_no;
                go_block('challan_details');
                first_record;
                for row_cntr in 1..total_records
                loop
                        select quantity into old_qty
                        from challan_details where rtrim(challan_no) =
                                :challan_details.challan_no and
                        rtrim(product_no) = :challan_details.product_no;

                        update product_master
                        set qty_on_hand = qty_on_hand + old_qty
                        where rtrim(product_no) = :challan_details.product_no;

                        /* Procedure called to set order_status of the sales_order */
                        update_order_status;
                        delete_record;
                end loop;
                go_block('challan_header');
                delete_record ;
        EXCEPTION
                when no_data_found then
                        message('Error while updating details of delete records');
        END;
```

Trigger Name	: **WHEN-BUTTON-PRESSED**	Form	: Challan
Block	: challan_details	Item	: pb_deldet
Function	: Delete the current detail record.		

Cross table updation when a record is deleted in the challan detail table.

Trigger Level : Item Level

Trigger Text : DECLARE

```
            old_qty Number(8);
    BEGIN
            go_block('challan_details');
            select quantity into old_qty
                    from challan_details
                    where rtrim(challan_no) =
                            :challan_details.challan_no and
                    rtrim(product_no) = :challan_details.product_no;

            update product_master
                    set qty_on_hand = qty_on_hand + old_qty
                    where rtrim(product_no) =
                    :challan_details.product_no;

            /* Procedure called to set Order status field of sales_order
            table */
            update_order_status;

            delete_record;
    EXCEPTION
            when no_data_found then
                    message('Error while updating details of delete records');
    END;
```

The **post-insert**, **post-update** on challan_details and the **when-button-pressed** trigger on pb_delete and pb_deldet call a procedure named **update_order_status**.

The **update_order_status** is used to update the order status field in the sales_order table based on the quantity ordered and the quantity dispatched.

UPDATE_ORDER_STATUS (Procedure Body)

```
PROCEDURE update_order_status IS
    total_qty_ordered number(8);
    total_qty_disp number(8);
BEGIN
    select sum(qty_ordered), sum(challan_details.qty_disp)
            into total_qty_ordered, total_qty_disp
            from sales_order_details, challan_details, challan_header
            where challan_header.s_order_no = sales_order_details.s_order_no and
            challan_header.challan_no = challan_details.challan_no and
            challan_header.s_order_no = :challan_header.s_order_no
    if total_qty_ordered = total_qty_disp  Then
            update sales_order
            set order_status = 'FP'
            where rtrim(s_order_no) = :challan_header.s_order_no;
    elsif total_qty_disp = 0 then
            update sales_order
            set order_status = 'NP'
            where s_order_no = :challan_header.s_order_no;
    else
            update sales_order
            set order_status = 'IP'
            where s_order_no = :challan_header.s_order_no;
    end if;
END;
```

SELF REVIEW QUESTIONS

TRUE OR FALSE

1. The master detail relationship can be set only if foreign key / primary key is defined at the table level.

   A) True   B) False

2. An LOV can be connected to Display Item.

   A) True   B) False

3. An LOV is created by specifying static values for an LOV.

   A) True   B) False

4. If ON DELETE CASCADE is specified at the time of defining a foreign key, the Delete Record behavior property must not be set to Cascading.

   A) True   B) False

5. The updateable property cannot be set for the objects if the 'Canvas' property is set to Null.

   A) True   B) False

6. Database Item property must be set to 'No' if the item is not connected to a base table column.

   A) True   B) False

7. Prompt Adjustment Edge property is used to determine the position of the label relative to the associated item.

   A) True   B) False

8. To change the list of values dynamically at runtime, the Automatic Refresh property must be set to True.

   A) True   B) False

FILL IN THE BLANKS

1. A Master detail relation defined in the form creates _____ object.

2. An LOV can be used as a validation tool by setting _____ property.

3. A Pre-Delete trigger is created if the Master Deletes property is set to _____.

4. Oracle Forms determines the SQL statement to be generated when a commit is fired based on the _____ variable.

5. On-check-delete-master trigger is created if the Master Deletes property is set to _____.

6. LOV creation creates two objects. These are _____ and _____.

7. The triggers that will fire when all the records are newly inserted and a commit is fired are

   - _____

   - _____

   - _____.

8. The form behavior when deleting a master record can be determined by _____ property. This property can take three values. These are :

   - _____

   - _____

   - _____.

9. The properties that determine data coordination in view mode between the master and the detail block are:

   - _____

   - _____

10. In the Object Navigator, the Relation object appears in the **Relations** Node under the block defined as a _____ block.

11. The properties of the relation object **Master Block** and **Join Condition** are taken from the foreign key constraint at the table level if the _____ check box is on.

12. Whenever a new record is added to the detail block, the value of the join column in the detail block is set to the value of the join column in the master block by using _____ property.

13. _____ property is used to determine the type of item.

PICK THE RIGHT OPTION

1. SYSTEM.FORM_STATUS can take the following values:

    A) CHANGED, NEW, QUERY
    B) NEW, INSERT, CHANGED, QUERY

2. SYSTEM.RECORD_STATUS can take the following values:

    A) CHANGED, NEW, QUERY
    B) NEW, INSERT, CHANGED, QUERY

CHAPTER SEVEN

Using Multiple Canvases

IN THIS CHAPTER

> Need for Multiple Canvases

> Types of Canvases

> Displaying / Hiding the Canvas at runtime

> Working with Radio Groups and Radio Buttons

7. USING MULTIPLE CANVASES

The Forms example so far deals with a single form with
- One command window
- One canvas object
- Multiple blocks

Sometimes the number of columns in a table cannot be contained on a standard canvas or the system requires that information on the form be displayed either on a click of a button or on some condition being set for the system.

Example:

In a sales order system the client contact information can be displayed when the button labeled **Contact Info...** is clicked.

Multiple canvases can be placed on the same form. Additional items can be included in the second canvas and code can be written to make the canvas visible / invisible when a button is pressed.

Stacked Canvas:

In earlier examples all items in all blocks were placed on the *same* Canvas. Thus the form includes:
1. One Window
2. One Canvas connected to the window
3. Items in the blocks that are placed on the Canvas.

Since the canvas is placed on the window the size of the canvas is restricted to the size of the window. Similarly if the window is resized, the canvas must also be resized. The type of the canvas determines the canvas-resizing behavior. The default value for the *Canvas Type* is 'Content'. This property value ensures that the canvas is automatically resized horizontally and vertically based on the size of the window.

There may be a need to place some items on the content canvas and other items on a new canvas such that the content canvas and the new canvas are stacked one on top of the other.

A canvas that that can be stacked on the content canvas is called a *Stacked Canvas*. The stacked canvas is displayed in the same window along with the window's content canvas. There can be any number of stacked canvases placed on the content canvas.

If the form includes multiple canvases, a common practice is to make the stacked canvases visible or invisible programmatically.

FOCUS

Create a client master data-entry screen to manipulate the data being loaded into the *Client_Master* and the *Client_Contact* table. The Client Contact Information is placed on a different canvas and is presented in a tabular format. Contact information must be displayed only when the push button for Contact Information is clicked.

Provide a set of data manipulation operations (Add, View, Modify and Delete). In the view mode, allow browsing through the data table, one record at a time i.e. First, Last, Previous, Next operations have to be provided for.

Add mode   : All the fields in the master and detail block must be updateable.
Modify mode   : All the fields other than primary key can be modified.
View mode   : No fields must be updateable.
Delete Mode   : Delete cascading must be on.

Include a search operation that searches a table to find a match for a client number entered.

The Table structures are as under:

Table Name   : Client_master (Master)
Description   : Use to store information about clients.

Column Name	Data Type	Size	Column Description
client_no	varchar2	6	Access key via which we shall seek data. (Primary Key)
name	varchar2	20	Client's name.
address1	varchar2	30	First line in the client's address.
address2	varchar2	30	Second line in the client's address.
City	varchar2	15	City in which the client is located.
State	varchar2	15	State in which the client is located.
Pincode	number	6	Pin code
bal_due	number	10,2	Balance amount payable by the client.

Integrity Constraints:
- PK_Client_No Primary Key on Client_no.

Validations in the *Client Master* data entry screen are as follows:
- The *Client_No* column is a Primary Key. Duplicate values are not allowed in *Client_No*. It cannot be left blank.
- The first letter of *Client_No* must start with 'C'.
- The *name* column cannot be left blank
- The *Bal_Due* column should have a default value of 0. The *Bal_Due* field is not enterable.

Table Name : Client_Contact (Detail)

Description : Use to store information about clients contact information.

Column name	Data Type	Size	Column Description
client_no	varchar2	6	Access key via which we shall seek data (Foreign Key that references client_no of the client_master table).
contact_no	varchar2	25	Correspondence Number for the client.
Device	Char	1	Type of contact number. The values that this field can take are Tel, Fax, Email address, Pager No etc.

Validations in the client contact information, data entry screen, are as follows:

- *Client_No* must be present in the *Client_Master* table.
- *Contact_No* or *Device* cannot be left null.
- *Device* field can take only following values - 'T' for telephone number, 'F' for fax number, 'E' for email, 'P' for pager number, 'M' for mobile number. Implement the device field using radio group.

THE SOLUTION

Creating Master Block:

1. Click on **Start..Programs..Developer 2000 R2.0..Forms Builder** to invoke *Forms Builder*.

2. The *'Welcome to the Form Builder'* opening screen is shown. From the **'Designing'** option select *'Use the Data Block Wizard'* to create a new block.

3. The Data Block wizard is invoked and a *'Welcome to Data Block Wizard'* screen is displayed. Click on Next.

4. Enter details for the data source. The available options are:
   - Tables or View
   - Stored Procedure

   Select *Table* data source.

5. In the next step enter the name of the table as *Client_Master* and the columns that must be included in the form.

6. A list of columns is displayed. Select all columns from the column list.

7. Confirmation to invoke the Layout is asked for. Click on Finish.

8. Since the option selected is *'Create Data Block, and then call Layout Wizard'*, the welcome screen of the layout editor is displayed.

9. Click on Next. The layout wizard asks for the canvas *name* and the *type* of canvas. If the canvas name is set to (New Canvas) the Layout wizard creates a new canvas.

10. The next screen displays items to be included in the block. Click on to select all the columns from the block.

11. The Label / Prompt is displayed for each item along with the height and width. If required change the prompt, width or height and click on Next.

12. The next step is to choose the Layout style. The layout style for the Master Block must be set to *'Form'*. Click on Next.

13. The selected items are grouped within a frame. In the next screen enter the frame title, the number of records to be displayed and the distance between the records. It also asks for the confirmation to display a scrollbar.

14. Finally a congratulation screen is displayed. Click on Finish.

15. The required objects will be created and the Object Navigator will be displayed.

Creating Detail Block:

1. Create a new block for the detail section. Click on **Tools..New Block**. *New Data Block* dialog box asking for confirmation to start the data block wizard or create a data block manually is invoked.

2. Ensure that *'Use Data Block Wizard'* is selected and click on OK. A *'Welcome to Data Block Wizard'* screen is displayed. Click on Next.

3. Next select the data source as *Table* and click on Next.

4. In the next step the name of the table and the columns that must be included in the form is to be specified. Enter the table name as *Client_Contact*.

5. After selecting the table from the list, a list of columns is displayed to select from. Select all columns from the column list.

6. Since the master block is already created, a dialog box that allows creation of a relation object that connects the detail block to the master block is displayed.

If Foreign Key constraint is defined in the detail table, the **Auto Join Data Blocks** checkbox can be checked and when the *Create Relation* push button is clicked, Forms Builder automatically creates a relation between the primary key and the foreign key of the master and details tables.

If the foreign key constraint is not defined, the **Auto Join Data Blocks** checkbox must be unchecked. When the *Create Relation* push button is clicked, Forms Builder automatically displays a list of blocks in the current form.

Caution

 If the foreign key constraint is not defined, the **Auto Join Data Blocks** checkbox must be unchecked else it displays the following error message:

FRM-10757: No Master blocks are available.

8. Select *Client_master* and click on OK. Selected block is displayed in the *Master Data Block* list box and *Master Item* is set to *(No Join)*.

9. Select *Client_No* from the list of columns from the master block. The completed join condition will be displayed.

10. Confirmation to invoke the Layout is asked for. Click on Finish.

11. The *Welcome* dialog box of the Layout Wizard appears. Enter the canvas name in the next screen. The master canvas is selected by default. Change it to '*New Canvas*'. Change the type of canvas to **Stacked** as shown in diagram 7.1. Click on Next.

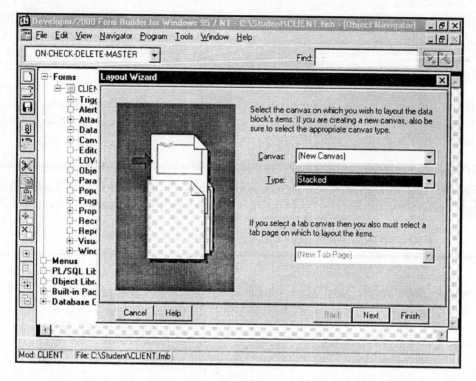

Diagram 7.1 : Setting Canvas properties for the detail block

12. A list of columns belonging to the detail block is displayed. The detail block must display all columns except the foreign key column. By default all the columns are selected. Deselect *Client_No* column by using <CTRL> + <Left Click>. Move the selected columns to *Displayed Items* list box.

13. The list of selected items with the *Prompt, Width* and *Height* properties is displayed. Accept default values by clicking on Next. Choose the *Presentation Type* as *Tabular*.

14. Enter the *Frame Title, Records Displayed, Distance between Records*. Set *Records Displayed* to 3.

15. Click on Finish. A detail block with the master detail relation will be created and displayed in the layout editor.

16. The master-detail form is ready. Save the form by selecting **File..Save** menu items.

17. Open the property sheet of the detail block and set the scrollbars properties.

Show Scrollbar	: Yes
Scrollbar Canvas	: Client_Contact_Can
Scrollbar Orientation	: Vertical
Scrollbar X Position	: 357
Scrollbar Y Position	: 181

18. Open the Property sheet of the Detail Canvas and set the properties as shown in diagram 7.2.

Name : Client_Contact_Can
Canvas View Type : Stacked
Viewport Width : 256
Viewport Height : 70
Viewport X Position : 250
Viewport Y Position : 126

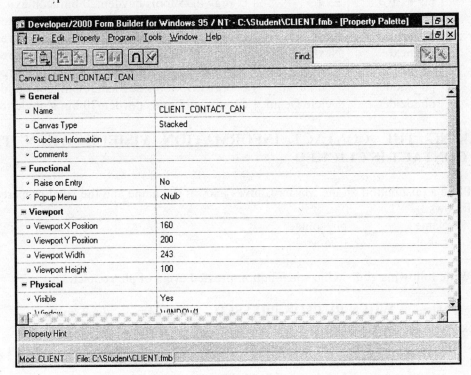

Diagram 7.2 : Setting Canvas Properties

Creating Button Palette Block with push buttons and writing PL/SQL code:

To customize data manipulation, form creator must disable the toolbar provided by Forms Runtime and place push buttons as required. The push buttons for data manipulation are placed in a separate block named as *Button_Palette*. The properties of the buttons on the form are as follows:

Push Button Name	Label	Icon File Name
pb_add	Add	c:\orawin95\tools\devdem20\bin\icon\rt_radd
pb_view	View	c:\orawin95\tools\devdem20\bin\icon\rt_quer2
Pb_search	Search	c:\orawin95\tools\devdem20\bin\icon\rt_quer1
pb_modify	Modify	c:\orawin95\tools\devdem20\bin\icon\clear
pb_delete	Delete	c:\orawin95\tools\devdem20\bin\icon\rt_rdel
pb_save	Save	c:\orawin95\tools\devdem20\bin\icon\rt_save
pb_exit	Exit	c:\orawin95\tools\devdem20\bin\icon\exit
pb_first	First	c:\orawin95\tools\devdem20\bin\icon\rt_rec1
pb_prior	Prior	c:\orawin95\tools\devdem20\bin\icon\rt_rec2
pb_next	Next	c:\orawin95\tools\devdem20\bin\icon\rt_rec3
pb_last	Last	c:\orawin95\tools\devdem20\bin\icon\rt_rec4
pb_adddet	Add Detail	c:\orawin95\tools\devdem20\bin\icon\adddet
pb_deldet	Delete Detail	c:\orawin95\tools\devdem20\bin\icon\delrow

MAKING THE CONTACT INFORMATION VISIBLE WHEN THE PB_CONTACT IS CLICKED

1. Place a pushbutton on the Master Canvas and set the name and the label property as follows :

   Name   : pb_contact
   Label   : Contact Info...

2. Write following code in the when-button-pressed event of pb_contact.

Trigger Name	: **WHEN-BUTTON-PRESSED**	Form	: client_master
Block	: button_palette	Item	: pb_contact
Function	: Making the Client_Contact_Can visible.		
Text	: DECLARE		

/* Variable that will hold the value returned by the get_item_property built-in function. */

label_value varchar2(30);
BEGIN

/* *Show Contact Info...* label is shown on the face of the push button pb_contact when the form opens. But once the push button is pressed and the contact detail canvas is displayed, the label must change to **Hide Contact Info...** Thus the code in the When-Button-Pressed will include code to: */

- If the label is set to 'Show Contact Info...' the 'Visible' property of the canvas must be set to False. If the label is set to 'Hide Contact Info...' the 'Visible' property of the canvas must be set to False..

- *Change the label of the button based on whether the canvas is visible or not.*

*In order to get the label property of the button, a built procedure named **get_item_property** is used that returns the value in the **Label** property is used. */*

```
        label_value:= get_item_property('pb_contact', label);
```

/ A Canvas can be made visible using the 'Show_View' procedure. * /*

```
        if label_value = 'show contact info...' then
          go_block ('client_master');
          show_view ('client_contact_can');
          set_item_property ('pb_contact', label, 'Hide Contact Info...');
        elsif label_value = 'Hide Contact Info...' then
          hide_view ('client_contact_can');
          set_item_property ('pb_contact', label, 'Show Contact Info...');
        end if;
    END;
```

3. Ideally until the push button labeled 'Show Contact Info...' is clicked, the *Client_Contact_Can* canvas must not be displayed. Hence when the form comes up the canvas can be hidden.

Trigger Name	: **WHEN-NEW-FORM-INSTANCE**	Form	: client_master
Block	:	Item	:
Function	: Hiding the Client_Contact_can canvas when the form comes up.		
Text	: BEGIN		

```
            /* The hide_view procedure hides the specified canvas in the
               window. show_view procedure can be used to show canvas */

        hide_view('client_contact_can');
    END;
```

4. The completed client screen when run will be as shown in diagram 7.3

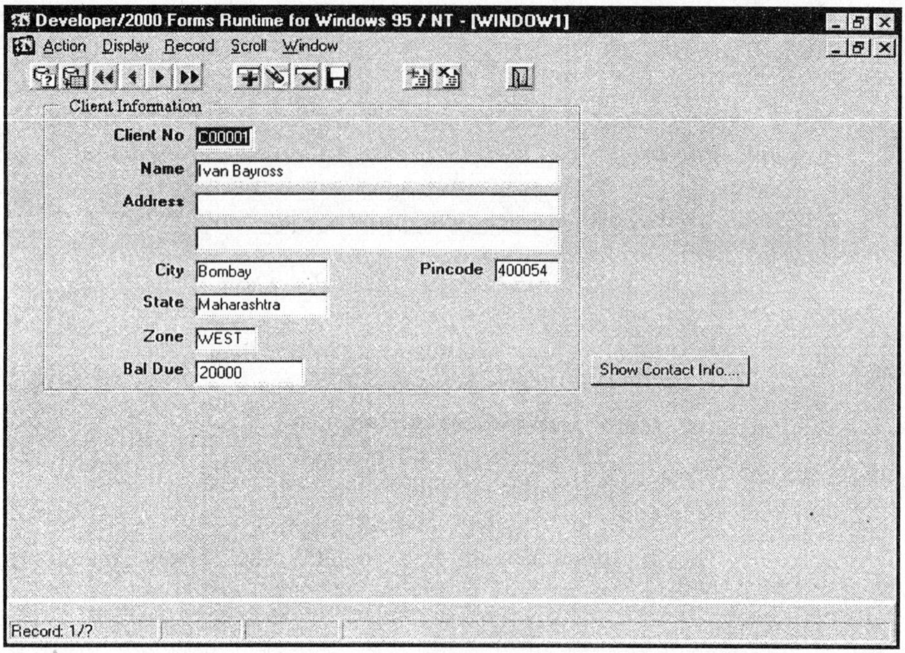

Diagram 7.3 : Runtime screen

5. After the push button 'Show Contact Info...' is pressed the screen with the contact information will be as shown in diagram 7.4.

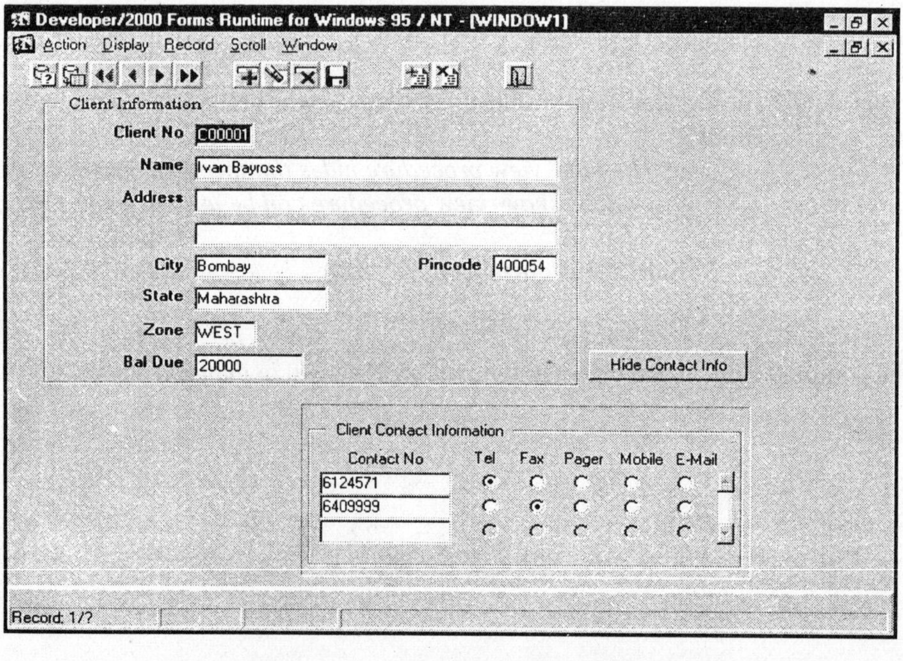

Diagram 7.4 : Screen showing Contact Details

6. When the button 'Hide Contact Info...' is pressed the *contact_info_can* canvas is closed and also the label on the button is set to 'Show Contact Info....'

ATTACHING COMMON PL/SQL LIBRARY

Since the triggers for the items in the *Button_Palette* reference two common procedures i.e. *scroll_control* and *item_enable_disable* which are included in the PL/SQL library named *SalesLib.pll*, the *SalesLib.pll* library must be attached to the form.

Attach the library by clicking on the *Attached Library* node in the Object Navigator. Forms Builder displays the *Attach Library* dialog box. Enter the library name as *C:\Student\SalesLib.pll*.

Click on *Attach*. Confirm to remove the path. Click on '**No**'. *SalesLib.pll* will be attached to the challan form and displayed under the *Attached Library* node.

TRIGGERS

Trigger Name	: **WHEN-BUTTON-PRESSED**	Form	: client
Block	: button_palette	Item	: pb_view
Trigger Level	: Item Level		
Function	: Retrieve all the records from the master and detail tables.		
Text	: BEGIN		

```
        go_block('client_master');
        execute_query ;
        item_enable_disable('client_master', property_off);
        item_enable_disable('client_contact', property_off);
    END;
```

Trigger Name	: **WHEN-BUTTON-PRESSED**	Form	: client
Block	: button_palette	Item	: pb_first
Trigger Level	: Item Level		
Function	: Move the cursor to the first record.		
Text	: BEGIN		

```
        go_block('client_master');
        first_record;
    END;
```

Trigger Name	: **WHEN-BUTTON-PRESSED**	Form	: client
Block	: button_palette	Item	: pb_prior
Trigger Level	: Item Level		
Function	: Move the cursor to the previous record.		
Text	: BEGIN		

```
        go_block('client_master');
        previous_record ;
    END;
```

Trigger Name	: **WHEN-BUTTON-PRESSED**	Form	: client
Block	: button_palette	Item	: pb_next
Trigger Level	: Item Level		
Function	: Move the cursor to the previous record.		
Text	: BEGIN		

```
        go_block('client_master');
        next_record ;
    END;
```

Trigger Name	: **WHEN-BUTTON-PRESSED**	Form	: client
Block	: button_palette	Item	: pb_last
Trigger Level	: Item Level		
Function	: Move the cursor to the previous record.		
Text	: BEGIN		

```
        go_block('client_master');
        last_record ;
    END:
```

Note

The Buttons first, prior, next and last allow the scrolling in the master block. The detail records will change when the master record will change because of the Master Detail Relation.

Trigger Name	: **WHEN-BUTTON-PRESSED**	Form	: challan
Block	: button_palette	Item	: pb_add
Trigger Level	: Item Level		
Function	: Add new records in the client form.		
Text	: BEGIN		

```
        go_block('client_master');
        create_record ;
        item_enable_disable('client_master', property_on);
        item_enable_disable('client_contact', property_on);
    END:
```

Trigger Name	: **WHEN-BUTTON-PRESSED**	Form	: client
Block	: button_palette	Item	: pb_delete
Trigger Level	: Item Level		
Function	: Delete the current client record along with the corresponding detail records.		
Text	: BEGIN		

```
BEGIN
        go_block('client_master);
        delete_record ;
    END;
```

Trigger Name	: **WHEN-BUTTON-PRESSED**	Form	: client
Block	: button_palette	Item	: pb_save
Trigger Level	: Item Level		
Function	: Save the changes to client tables.		
Text	: BEGIN		

```
BEGIN
        if :system.form_status = 'CHANGED' then
                /* If the form status is changed then commit changes */
                commit_form ;
                if :system.form_status = 'QUERY' then
                    item_enable_disable('client_master', property_off);
                    item_enable_disable('client_contact',property_off);
                end if ;
        end if;
    END;
```

Trigger Name	: **WHEN-BUTTON-PRESSED**	Form	: client
Block	: button_palette	Item	: pb_search
Trigger Level	: Item Level		
Function	: Search for a specific record in the master table.		
Text	: BEGIN		

```
BEGIN
        go_block('client_master');
        enter_query ;
        item_enable_disable('client_master', property_off);
        item_enable_disable('client_contact', property_off);
    END;
```

Note

Trigger *When-Button-Pressed* on item pb_view, pb_search, pb_modify, pb_add, pb_save calls a procedure named *Item_Enable_Disable*. This procedure is included in the library *Saleslib.pll*.

Trigger Name	: **WHEN-BUTTON-PRESSED**	Form	: client
Block	: button_palette	Item	: pb_adddet
Trigger Level	: Item Level		
Function	: Insert an item in the client contact.		
Text	: BEGIN		

```
            go_block('client_contact');
            create_record ;
            item_enable_disable('client_contact' , property_on);
        END;
```

Trigger Name	: **WHEN-BUTTON-PRESSED**	Form	: client
Block	: button_palette	Item	: pb_deldet
Trigger Level	: Item Level		
Function	: Delete the current item in the client contact.		
Text	: BEGIN		

```
            go_block('client_contact');
            delete_record ;
        END;
```

Trigger Name	: **WHEN-BUTTON-PRESSED**	Form	: client
Block	: button_palette	Item	: pb_exit
Trigger Level	: Item Level		
Function	: Quit the client form.		
Text	: DECLARE		

```
            answer number;
        BEGIN
        /* If there are any changes in the form the system must asks for
            confirmation to save changes */
        If :System.form_status = 'CHANGED' then
                set_alert_property('confirm_alert', title, 'Save Changes');
                set_alert_property('confirm_alert', alert_message_text,
                    'Would you like to make Changes Permanent?');
                answer := Show_Alert('confirm_alert');
                If answer = Alert_Button1 then
                        commit_form;
                End If;
        End If;
        /* Close the form. */
        exit_form(No_Commit);
    END;
```

DISABLING DEFAULT FORMS TOOLBAR

The default toolbar provided by Oracle Forms Runtime must not be visible since a set of user-defined pushbuttons has been placed on the form.

Appropriate form property must be set to make the default toolbar invisible. Select *Product* form in the Object Navigator. Right click and open the property palette of the form. The form property palette includes a property named **Menu Module**. To make the default toolbar invisible, set the *Menu Module* property to **Default**.

ENABLING AND DISABLING NAVIGATIONAL BUTTONS

The navigational buttons i.e. pb_first, pb_prior, pb_next and pb_last must be enabled or disabled based on the total number of records and the current record position. The procedure named *scroll_control* for enabling and disabling the navigational buttons is included in the *saleslib.pll* PL/SQL library.

Thus a call to the scroll_control procedure must be made when the current record focus changes. The trigger that that is fired when the record focus changes is called WHEN-NEW-RECORD-INSTANCE.

Trigger Name	: **WHEN-NEW-RECORD-INSTANCE**	Form	: client
Block	: client_master	Item	:
Trigger Level	: Block Level		
Function	: calls procedure scroll_control that enables or disables the navigational Push buttons i.e. pb_first, pb_prior, pb_next and pb_last based on the total number of records on the form and the current record.		
Text	: BEGIN		

```
          scroll_control ;
      END;
```

VALIDATIONS

To modify the form to include the following validations:
- *Client_No* is a Primary Key. Duplicate values are not allowed in *Client_No*. It cannot be left blank.
- The first letter of *Client_No* must start with 'C'.
- Client *Name* cannot be left blank.
- The *Bal_Due* should have a default value of 0. Item *Bal_Due* is not enterable.

Validation Rule Implementation:

- *Client_No* is a Primary Key. Duplicate values are not allowed in *Client_No*. It cannot be left blank.
- The first letter of *Client_No* must start with 'C'.

Using Database Triggers and database package to ensure Table Data Integrity:

In the *Client_master* table, *client_no* is a primary key. In a multi-user environment, if the data entry operator is not allowed to enter the primary key value and the primary key value is generated by the system, it is possible to conserve on time and other resources.

In the current example the value for the *client_no* as the primary key of the *Client_Master* table needs to be generated using a sequence. Also the same must also be retained so that it can be used as a foreign key value in the *Client_Contact* table.

The primary key value can be generated in the *Before Insert* database trigger by using a sequence. The database trigger must also set the variable declared in the package specification to the newly generated *Client_No*.

A *Before Insert* database trigger that gets executed when new records are inserted in the *Client_Contact* table, can be written to set the foreign key. Insertions in the *Client_Contact* table can be done for an existing *Client_Master* record or when a completely new client including the master and the detail section is created.

The foreign key of the detail records for a client must be set to the newly generated number only if a completely new client is inserted. If detail records are added to an existing client, the existing *client number* value must be used to set the value of the foreign key.

The steps to generate the primary key for the master table and use the same as the foreign key in the detail table are summarized as under:

Syntax for Sequence Creation:

The syntax for creating a sequence for client_no is as follows:

> **CREATE SEQUENCE** *client_seq*
> **INCREMENT BY** *1*
> **START WITH** *1;*

Package Specification Creation:

In the current example the newly generated *Client_No* is stored in the variable declared in the package specification. Thus a database package specification must be created.

A database package specification can be created in SQL*Plus. The Forms Builder Tool also provides an interface for creating, compiling and storing database triggers. The steps in creating a database package specification using *Database Object Interface* of Forms Builder are:

1. Select *Database Objects* Node in the *Object Navigator*. Oracle Forms Builder will display a list of users.

2. Select the user for which the database trigger must be created. Oracle Forms Builder displays a list of objects that can be created and stored in the database. These include
   - Stored Program Units i.e. procedures and functions
   - PL/SQL Libraries
   - Tables
   - Views

3. Since Database Package Specification form a part of the Stored Program Unit; double click on the *Stored Program Units* Node in the Object Navigator. Oracle Forms Builder displays *New Program Unit* dialog box.

4. Select *Package Spec* and enter the name of the package *'pkey_gen'*. Click on OK.

5. Oracle Form Builder displays the PL/SQL Editor. Declare a variable in the package as follows:

   ```
   PACKAGE pkey_gen IS
           master_key varchar2(6);
   END;
   ```

6. Click on Close. Confirmation to 'Apply' or 'Revert' the changes or 'Cancel' the close operation is asked for. Click on Apply. Close the Stored Program Unit Node.

Creating Database Trigger for the master and detail tables:
Once the package is created a database trigger must be created to generate the primary key for the master table and another database trigger must be created to set the foreign key. The steps in creating the database trigger

1. Since a database trigger is connected to a table click on the *Tables* Node. A list of tables belonging to a specific user is displayed.

2. Each *Table* Node is further subdivided into *Triggers* and *Columns*. The *Triggers* Node will display a list of triggers if any currently created on the selected table. To create a new trigger, select the table on which the database trigger must be created and click on **Navigator..Create** menu option.

   An interface that allows database trigger creation.

3. Click on New. A new trigger with a default name is created. Change the name of the trigger to *Client_No_Gen* and set the database trigger parameters as follows:

Triggering Time	: Before
Statement	: Insert

   Also check the *For Each Row* check box. Oracle Forms Builder also provides space to enter the PL/SQL statements that must be included in the trigger. Enter the text as required. The equivalent Oracle PL/SQL syntax will be:

```
CREATE OR REPLACE TRIGGER client_no_gen
        BEFORE INSERT
        ON client_master
        FOR EACH ROW
DECLARE
        primary_key_value varchar2(4);
BEGIN
        SELECT lpad(to_char(client_seq.nextval) , 4 , '0')
                INTO primary_key_value FROM dual;
        /* Set the value of the variable in the package to the newly generated
            primary key value. */
        pkey_gen.master_key := 'C' || primary_key_value;
        /* Assign the newly generated primary key value to the challan_no column */
        :new.client_no := pkey_gen.master_key;
END;
```

4. Click on 'Save'. Forms Builder Interface will convert the text into appropriate PL/SQL trigger block and pass the same to the Oracle Engine. The Oracle engine will execute the PL/SQL block and thus a database trigger will be created. Once created the name of the trigger cannot be modified. The *Object Navigator* displays the newly created trigger.

5. The same steps need to be performed for the Before Insert trigger for the *Client_Contact* table. The equivalent Oracle PL/SQL syntax will be:

> **CREATE OR REPLACE TRIGGER** *client_no_gen*
> > **BEFORE INSERT**
> > **ON** *client_contact*
> > **FOR EACH ROW**
>
> **BEGIN**
> > if :new.Client_no is null then
> > > :new.client_no := pkey_gen.master_key;
> >
> > end if;
>
> **END;**

Since the primary key is generated by the system, the primary key must not be visible on the screen. Thus we need to set the canvas of *client_no* column to Null.

Open the property sheet of the *client_no* item. Set the *Canvas* property to Null. *Client_No* item is also being referenced in the *When-Button-Pressed* trigger of *pb_modify*. Updateable property of an item cannot be set if the item is not visible i.e. if the canvas property of the item is set to Null. Thus code to set the updateable property of the *Client_No* item must be removed.

Not Null Check using ON-ERROR Form Trigger:

If the column is defined as a NOT NULL column at the table level, Oracle Forms Builder sets the '*Required*' attribute to '*Yes*'. If the '*Required*' attribute is set to '*Yes*', Oracle Forms Runtime will display an error message if the item is exited without entering value in the item.

Note

If the item is left blank, Oracle Forms Runtime displays an FRM Error as follows:

FRM-40202 : Field must be entered

Generalized PL/SQL code for the ON-ERROR trigger is written and stored in the Object Library. The ON-ERROR trigger can be subclassed or inherited from the object library leading to standardization of error handling. The steps in subclassing the ON-ERROR trigger are:

1. Click on **File..Open** to open the Object Library. Oracle Forms Builder will display the *Open File* dialog box. Select *comobj.olb* file from the appropriate directory. *Comobj.olb* object library will be displayed in the Object Navigator under the Object Libraries Node.

2. Click on **Tool..Object Library** menu items to open the library tabs. The *Comobj.olb* currently includes three library tabs. These library tabs are named *Triggers, VATTRS* and *Pclass* that store the common triggers, visual attributes and property classes respectively.

3. Select *Triggers* library tab. Oracle Forms Builder displays·the ON-ERROR trigger object included in the *Triggers* library tab.

4. Drag and drop the ON-ERROR trigger from the library tab to the *Triggers* node under the form name such that the ON-ERROR trigger will be a form level trigger. Oracle Forms Builder will then ask for confirmation to subclass or copy ON-ERROR trigger. Select *SubClass*. ON-ERROR trigger reference will be included in the form.

5. Set the required property to True for all the items that require a NOT NULL check.

```
Trigger Name   : ON-ERROR              Form   : client
Block          :                       Item   :
Trigger Level  : Form Level
Function       : Check for Not Null. In case of any other error display default error
                 message and set the visual attribute to VA_ERRORS.
Text           : DECLARE
                     error_item varchar2(50);
                     current_item_label varchar2(100);
                 BEGIN
                     error_item := :system.trigger_item;
                     If error_type = 'FRM' and error_code = 40202 THEN
                         current_item_label := get_item_property(error_item,
                             prompt_text);
                         current_item_label := replace(current_item_label, ':', '');
                         current_item_label := replace(current_item_label, ' ', '');
                         Message(current_item_label || ' cannot be left blank.');
                 Else
                         Message(error_text);
                         set_item_property(error_item,
                             current_record_attribute, 'VA_ERRORS');
                     End if;
                 END;
```

MAKING THE BALANCE DUE ITEM NOT ENTERABLE

Bal_Due item in the *Client_Master* table shows the balance amount due from the client. This column will be updated when an invoice for the client is generated or when the client makes payment against an invoice.

Thus this item will not be enterable from the *Client_Master* data entry form. The *Item Type* property of *Bal_Due* can be set to Display Item. Select *Bal_Due Item* in the Object Navigator. Select **Tools..Property Palette** from the main menu. It displays the properties of the *bal_due* Item. Set the *Item Type* property to *Display Item* and the *Initial Value* property to *0* as sown in diagram 7.5.

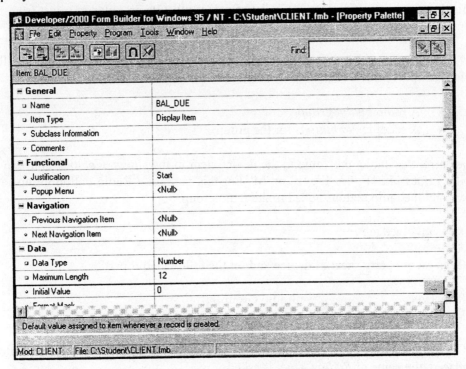

Diagram 7.5 : Changing the Item Type and Initial Value property of bal_due

VALIDATION FOR THE CLIENT_CONTACT BLOCK

- Device field must not be left blank

The *'Required'* property of the item *device* to 'True'. The ON-ERROR trigger for checking not null written at the form level takes care of this.

Using RADIO GROUPS for Validations

Device field can take only following values - 'T', 'F', 'E', 'P' or 'M':

If a field can take only fixed values, a list of values must be provided to select from. This will make the form user-friendly. It will also eliminate the data entry errors.

A set of object via which data entry can be done from a selected set of values is called a **Radio Group**. A selected set of values consist of two distinct objects:

- A *radio button group*.
- A set of *radio buttons* for the group.

In the current example, the value in the device item in the *Client_Contact* table can take specific values like 'T', 'F', 'E', 'P' or 'M'. For this purpose a Radio button group can be created and the radio buttons added to the radio group.

The steps involved are:

1. Open the property sheet of device and set the following properties :

   Item Type   : Radio Group
   Mapping of other values   : Null

2. Open the Layout editor and place the radio buttons. Each time a radio button is placed, the name of *Radio Group* is asked.

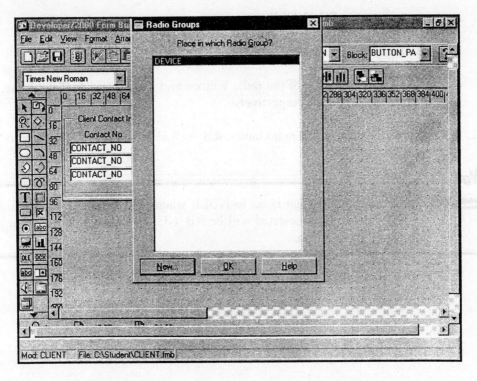

Diagram 7.6 : Choosing the right radio group

3. Click on OK. Set the properties of each of the radio buttons as follows :

    Name   : RB_TEL
    Label   :
    Radio Button Value : T

    Name   : RB_FAX
    Label   :
    Radio Button Value : F

    Name   : RB_EMAIL
    Label   :
    Radio Button Value : E

    Name   : RB_ PAGER
    Label   :
    Radio Button Value : P

    Name   : RB_ MOBILE
    Label   :
    Radio Button Value : M

Name   : RB_ NULL
Label   :
Radio Button Value : NULL

4. Place Text Labels for each of the radio buttons and set the text as **Telephone**, **Fax**, **E-Mail** and **Pager, Mobile** respectively.

12. In the property palette of the radio button RB_NULL set the *Visible* property to No.

Note

        Since the default value is set to NULL when there is no value specified the default radio button selected will be RB_NULL. But this radio button is not displayed on the form.

Need for Multiple Canvases

Types of Canvases
- Content Canvas
- Stacked Canvas
- Tab Canvas

Displaying / Hiding the Canvas at runtime

Working with Radio Groups and Radio Buttons
- Creating Radio Groups
- Including Radio Buttons in the Radio Group
- Setting the Properties of Radio Buttons

Using Tab Canvas

IN THIS CHAPTER

8. USING TAB CANVAS

Information pertaining to related business processes are recorded in different documents and stapled together. Generally such documents are divided into a number of pages and each page holds information pertaining to a business process

Thus when a business process is computerized the data entry form must also be designed to map to the information gathering and storing method used in the manual system.

For Example,
When a sales order is created for a client the following is recorded,
- The details of the sales order like sales order number, sales order date, client name, along with the product information like product specification, quantity ordered, the rate applicable at the time of ordering.
- The Delivery Schedule for the sales order
- Most sales orders also document terms and conditions of the sale to avoid future conflicts.

The business process of accepting the sales order is divided into distinct sub-processes as:
- Sales Order Information
- Delivery Schedule
- Terms and Conditions

Since these segments are associated with a single business process, a single form could be used to capture this data.

Just like the paper form is made of multiple pages, the data entry form could also be created with multiple pages.

Items on any form are placed on a canvas, the type of the canvas must be changed so that it can include multiple pages. The type of canvas that can include multiple tab pages is called '**Tab Canvas**'. Thus, the sales order form should be created using a 'Tab Canvas'.

Focus: Sales Order Data Entry Form

When a client places an order with the supplier a sales order details must be recorded. The Sales Order form is divided into three pages
- The first page includes information like Order Number, Order Date and Client Name along with the items ordered by the client.
- The second page includes delivery schedule for the sales order recorded on the first page.
- The third page includes terms and conditions for the sale.

Design a data-entry screen that allows data manipulation in the following tables:
- *Sales_Order and Sales_Order_Details*
- *Delivery_Schedule*
- *Order_TermsConditions*

The master-detail relationship between these tables is as under.

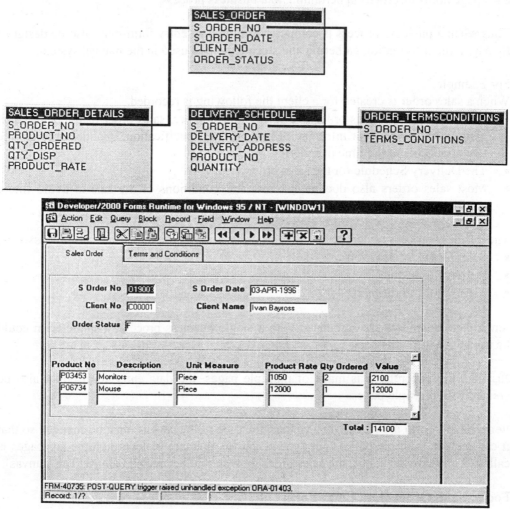

Diagram 8.1 : Sales Order Data-Entry Screen

Provide a set of complete data manipulation operations (Add, View, Modify and Delete). In the view mode, allow browsing through table data, one record at a time i.e. First, Last, Previous, Next operations have to be provided for.

Add mode   : All items in the master and detail block must be updateable.
Modify mode   : All items other than the Primary Key can be updateable.
View mode   : items are not updateable in view mode.
Delete mode   : Delete *Cascading* must be 'Activated'.

Include a search operation that searches and retrieves data from the *Sales_Order* table to match a *S_Order_No* entered. In the detail section, automatically display the *Description* and *Unit_Measure* from the *Product_Master* table when an appropriate *Product_No* is entered.

Table Name : Sales_Order (Master)
Description : Use to store order header information.

Column Name	Data Type	Size	Attributes
S_order_no	Varchar2	6	Unique primary key allotted to each order.
Order_date	Date		Date on which order is generated.
Client_no	Varchar2	6	Client for whom the sales order is created.
Order_Status	Varchar2	1	The delivery status of the Order.

Integrity Constraints:

Constraint Name	Description
PK_order_no	A primary key based on the column *S_Order_No* of the *Sales_Order* table.
FK_client	Foreign Key based on the column *Client_No* that References *Client_No* from the *Client_Master* table.

Table Name : Sales_Order_Details
Description : Use to store information about order details.

Column Name	Data Type	Size	Attributes
S_order_no	Varchar2	6	Order number against which Order details are stored.
Product_no	Varchar2	6	Product identity of the material being Ordered.
Product_rate	Number	8,2	Rate at which the Material is sold.
Qty_ordered	Number	8	Quantity of material Ordered.

Integrity Constraints:

Constraint Name	Description
PK_order_details	Composite Primary Key that is based on the *S_Order_No* and *Product_No* column of the *Order_Details* table.
FK_product_details	Foreign Key based on the column *Product_No* that References *Product_No* from the *Product_Master* table.
FK_order	Foreign Key based on the column *S_Order_No* that References *S_Order_No* from the *Sales_Order* table.

Table Name : Delivery_Schedule
Description : Use to store information about order delivery schedule.

Column Name	Data Type	Size	Attributes
S_Order_no	Varchar2	6	Order number against which Order details are stored.
Delivery_date	Date		Date when material must be delivered
Delivery_address	Varchar2	100	Delivery address
Product_no	Varchar2	6	Product identity of the material being Ordered.
Quantity	Number	8	Quantity of material to be delivered.

Integrity Constraints:

Constraint Name	Description
PK_delivery	Composite Primary Key that is based on the S_Order_No and Delivery_Date column of the Delivery_Header table.
FK_order	Foreign Key based on the column S_Order_No that References S_Order_No from the Sales_Order table.

Table Name : Order_TermsConditions
Description : Use to store information about order details.

Column Name	Data Type	Size	Attributes
S_Order_no	Varchar2	6	Order number against which Order details are stored.
Terms_Conditions	Varchar2	1000	Terms and Conditions specified for the order

Integrity Constraints:

Constraint Name	Description
FK_order	Foreign Key based on the column S_Order_No that References S_Order_No from the Sales_Order table.

I/O and Business Rules to be enforced in the Order Form:

- *S_Order_No* is a Primary Key column i.e. *S_Order_No* cannot be left blank and duplicate values are not allowed in *Challan_No*.
  Implement this by generating Primary key value using a database trigger.

- *Order_Date* cannot be greater than system date.
  Implement this by writing appropriate validation code.

- *Client_No* must be present in the *Client_Master* table.
  Implement this by using an LOV.

- *Product_No* in the Sales_Order details table must be present in the *Product_Master* table.
  Implement this by using an LOV.

- *Quantity_Ordered* must not be left empty and cannot be 0.
  Implement this by writing appropriate validation code.

- *Product_Rate* must not be left empty and cannot be 0.
  Implement this by writing appropriate validation code.

- *Delivery_Date* cannot be less than system date. *Delivery_Date* cannot be less than *Order_Date*.
  Implement this by writing appropriate validation code.

- *Quantity_Dispatched* must not be left empty and cannot be 0. *Quantity_Dispatched* cannot be greater than *Qty_Ordered*
  Implement this by writing appropriate validation code.

Setting Default Values:

- Set the default value of *Order_Date* to system date.

Displaying Additional Information on the Form in View, Add and Modify Mode:

- *Client Name* must be displayed using a display item when a valid value for *Client_Name* is entered or when a global query is fired.
- The data entry form must display the *Description, Unit_Measure* in the detail block using display items when the *Product_No* item is exited or when the records are retrieved.

The Lookup Master Tables used with Order Data Entry are:

Table Name : Client_Master
Description : Stores information about clients.

Column Name	Data Type	Size	Column Description
Client_No	Varchar2	6	Unique primary key for each client
Name	Varchar2	20	Client's name
Address1	Varchar2	30	First, line in the client's address.
Address2	Varchar2	30	Second, line in the client's address.
City	Varchar2	15	City in which client's is located.
State	Varchar2	15	State in which client's is located.
Pincode	Number	6	Pin code
Bal_Due	Number	10,2	Balance amount receivable from the Client.

Table Name : Product_Master
Description : Stores information about products supplied by the company.

Column Name	Data Type	Size	Column Description
Product_No	Varchar2	6	Unique primary key for each product.
Description	Varchar2	25	Description of the product.
Unit_Measure	Varchar2	10	Unit by which the product is measured.
Qty_On_Hand	Number	8	Quantity which is available in the stock.
Reorder_Lvl	Number	8	Quantity level when the stock should be re-ordered.
Cost_Price	Number	8,2	Cost price of the product
Selling_Price	Number	8,2	Selling price of the product

Creating the Master Block:

1. Invoke the *Forms Builder Tool*.

2. The *'Welcome to the Form Builder'* opening screen is shown. From the **'Designing'** option select *'Use the Data Block Wizard'* to create a new block.

3. The Data Block wizard is invoked and a *'Welcome to Data Block Wizard'* screen is displayed. Click on Next.

4. Enter details for the data source. Select *Table* data source.

5. In the next step enter the name of the table and the columns that must be included in the form. Click on the **Browse** push button to select the table from the list. If not connected to the database a *Connect* dialog box is displayed. Enter the *Username*, *Password* and *Connect String*.

6. Data block can be created using tables, views and synonyms. 'Table' object is selected by default. Click on OK.

7. The list of tables is displayed. Select *Sales_Order* table.

8. After selecting the table from the list, a list of columns is displayed. Select all columns from the column list.

9. Confirmation to invoke the Layout Wizard is displayed. Click on Finish.

10. Since the option '*Create Data Block, and then call Layout Wizard*' is selected, the welcome screen of the layout editor is displayed.

11. Click on Next. The layout wizard asks for the canvas name and the type of canvas. If the canvas name is set to (New Canvas) the Layout wizard creates a new canvas. The canvas type must be set to 'Tab' as shown in diagram 8.2.

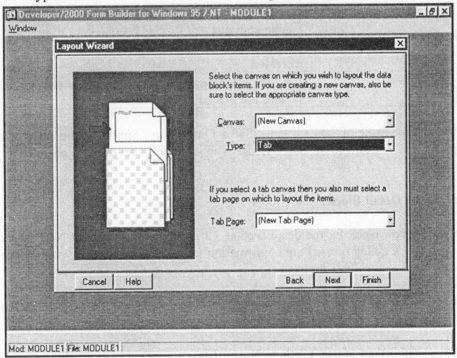

Diagram 8.2 : Specifying Canvas Type as 'Tab' Properties

12. The Tab Page property must be set to '(New Tab Page)' thus a tabbed canvas with a new tab page will be created.

13. The next screen displays the items to be included in the block. Select items that must be displayed on the canvas from the list provided. Click on ⟩⟩ to select all the columns from the block.

14. The Label / Prompt is displayed for each item along with the height and width. If required change the prompt, width or height and click on Next.

15. The next step is to choose the Layout style. Set the layout style for the Master Block to 'Form'. Click on Next.

16. The selected items are grouped within a frame. In the next screen, enter the frame title, the number of records to be displayed and the distance between the records.

17. Finally, a congratulation screen is displayed. Click on Finish.

18. The objects created by using a wizard and displayed in the Object Navigator are as follows:

Object Type	Object Details
Block	Sales_Order
Text Items	Text Item will be created for the selected table columns.
Canvas	A new canvas of 'Tab' type will be created.
Tab Page	A single tab page on which all the text items are placed.

19. Change the name of the canvas to 'Sales_Order_Can'. Similarly, the name of the tab page must be changed to 'Sales_Order_Tab' and the Label must be changed to 'Sales Order'.

Creating the Detail Block:

1. Create a new block for the detail section. Click on **Tools** and select **New Block**. *New Data Block* dialog box asking confirmation to start the data block wizard or create a data block manually is invoked.

2. Ensure that *'Use Data Block Wizard'* is selected and click on OK. A *'Welcome to Data Block Wizard'* screen is displayed. Click on Next.

3. Select *Table* data source. Click on Next.

4. Specify the name of the table as *Sales_Order_Details*.

5. A list of columns is displayed to select from. Select all columns from the column list.

6. Since the master block is already created, a dialog box that allows creation of a relation object that connects the detail block to the master block is displayed.

If Foreign Key constraint is defined in the detail table, the **Auto Join Data Blocks** checkbox can be checked and when the *Create Relation* push button is clicked, Forms Builder automatically creates a relation between the primary key and the foreign key of the master and details tables.

8. Select *Sales_Order* and click on OK. The selected block is displayed in the *Master Data Block* list box and *Master Item* is set to *(No Join)*.

7. Select *S_Order_No* from the list of columns from the master block. The completed join condition will be displayed.

8. Confirmation to invoke the Layout Wizard is asked for. Click on Finish.

9. The *Welcome* dialog box of the Layout Wizard appears. Click on Next. The next screen shows canvas properties for the new block. The '*Sales_Order_Can*' canvas is selected by default. Since the Sales_Order_Details information must be displayed on the same tab page, the tab page must be '*Sales_Order_Tab*'. The completed screen is as shown in diagram 8.3. Click on Next.

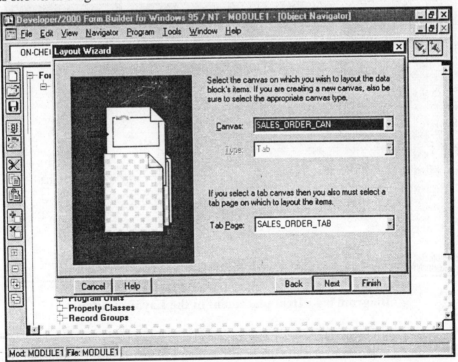

Diagram 8.3 : Specifying Canvas Properties for the detail block

10. A list of columns belonging to the detail block is displayed. The detail block must display all columns except the foreign key column. Select all the columns except *S_Order_No*. Click on > to move the selected columns to *Displayed Items* list box.

11. The list of selected items with the *Prompt, Width* and *Height* properties is displayed. Accept default values by clicking on Next. Choose the *Presentation Type* as *Tabular*.

12. Enter the *Frame Title, Records Displayed, Distance Between Records*. Set *Records Displayed* to 3.

13. Click on Finish. A detail block with the master detail relation will be created and displayed in the Object Navigator.

14. The master-detail form is ready. Save the form by selecting **File..Save** menu items.

15. Arrange the items as shown in diagram 8.4.

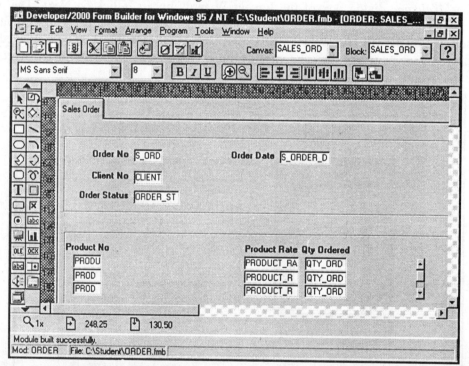

Diagram 8.4 : Item placement in the Layout Editor

Note

Space is left between the items in the detail block to insert additional objects to display 'Description' and 'Unit_Measure' and 'Sales Value'.

RUNNING A MASTER DETAIL FORM

Run the Form by selecting the **Program..Run Form** menu option. The completed master detail data entry screen is displayed as shown in diagram 8.5.

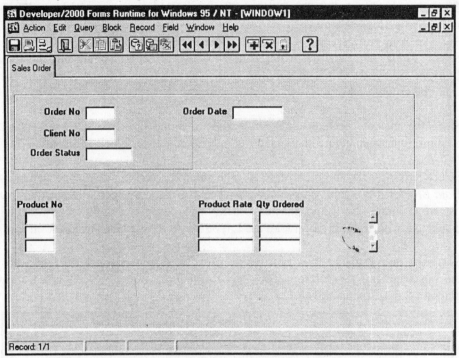

Diagram 8.5 : Runtime Order Form

Setting the Properties of the Relation Object:

1. Click on the relation object in the master block. It displays the relation object in the object navigator.

2. Right click on the relation object and select **Properties Palette** from the popup menu. The properties of the relation object are displayed. Set the **Delete Record Behavior** property to **Cascading**.

CREATING A BLOCK AND PLACING BLOCK ITEMS ON A NEW TAB PAGE

New Tab page for Delivery Schedule Block:

1. Create a new block for the *Delivery_Schedule* table section. Click on **Tools** and select **Data Block Wizard**.

2. Select *Table* data source. Click on Next. Specify the name of the table as *Delivery_Schedule.* A list of columns is displayed to select from. Select all columns from the column list.

3. Since the master block is already created, a dialog box that allows creation of a relation object that connects the detail block to the master block is displayed.

4. Select *Sales_Order* and click on OK. The selected block is displayed in the *Master Data Block* list box and *Master Item* is set to *(No Join)*. Select *S_Order_No* from the list of columns from the master block. The completed join condition will be displayed. Confirmation to invoke the Layout Wizard is asked for. Click on Finish.

5. Since the delivery schedule information must be displayed on a different tab page, the tab page must be '(New Tab Page)'. The completed screen is as shown in diagram 8.6. Click on Next.

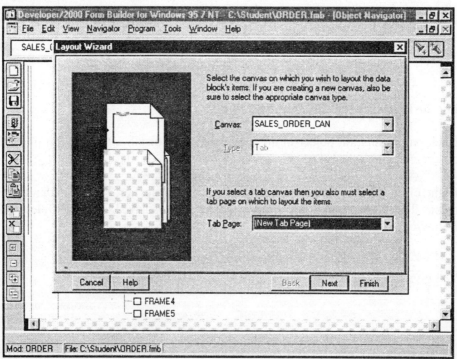

Diagram 8.6 : Creating a New Tab Page to display items from Delivery_Schedule

6. A list of columns belonging to the terms and conditions block is displayed. This block must display all columns except the foreign key column. Select Terms and Conditions column and click on 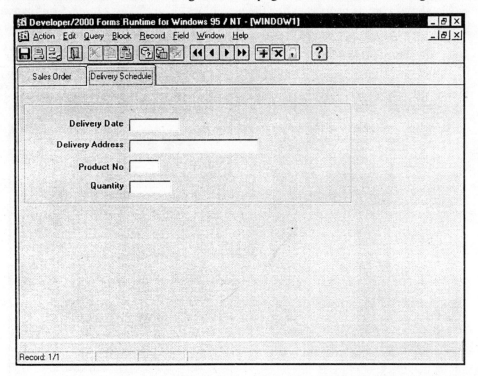 to move the selected columns to *Displayed Items* list box.

7. The list of selected items with the *Prompt, Width* and *Height* properties is displayed. Accept default values by clicking on Next. Choose the *Presentation Type* as *Tabular*.

8. Enter the *Frame Title, Records Displayed, Distance Between Records*. Set Records Displayed to 4. Click on Finish. A detail block with the master detail relation will be created and displayed in the Object Navigator.

15. The name of the tab page must be changed to 'DeliverySchedule_Tab' and the Label must be changed to 'Delivery Schedule'.

16. The runtime screen after creating a new tab page will be as shown in diagram 8.7.

Diagram 8.7 : Forms Runtime for the Delivery Schedule Tab Page

New Tab page for Terms and Conditions Block:

1. Create a new block for the terms and conditions table section. Click on **Tools** and select **Data Block Wizard**.

2. Select *Table* data source. Click on Next. Specify the name of the table as *Order_TermsConditions*. A list of columns is displayed to select from. Select all columns from the column list.

3. Since the master block is already created, a dialog box that allows creation of a relation object that connects the detail block to the master block is displayed.

4. Select *Sales_Order* and click on OK. The selected block is displayed in the *Master Data Block* list box and *Master Item* is set to *(No Join)*. Select *S_Order_No* from the list of columns from the master block. The completed join condition will be displayed. Confirmation to invoke the Layout Wizard is asked for. Click on Finish.

5. The *Welcome* dialog box of the Layout Wizard appears. Click on Next. The next screen shows canvas properties for the new block. The '*Sales_Order_Can*' canvas is selected by default.

6. Since the Terms and Conditions information must be displayed on a different tab page, the tab page must be '(New Tab Page)'. The completed screen is as shown in diagram 8.6. Click on Next.

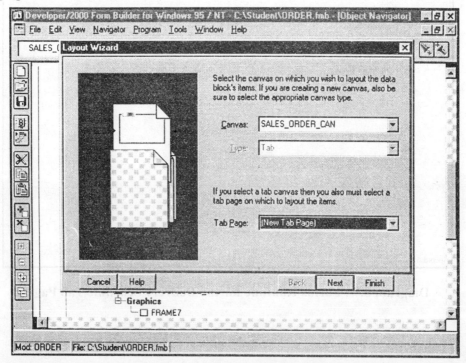

Diagram 8.8 : Specifying Canvas Properties for the Terms and Conditions block

7. A list of columns belonging to the terms and conditions block is displayed. This block must display all columns except the foreign key column. Select Terms and Conditions column and click on ⟩ to move the selected columns to *Displayed Items* list box.

8. The list of selected items with the *Prompt, Width* and *Height* properties is displayed. Accept default values by clicking on Next. Choose the *Presentation Type* as *Tabular*.

9. Enter the *Frame Title, Records Displayed, Distance Between Records.* Set *Records Displayed* to 4.

10. Click on Finish. A detail block with the master detail relation will be created and displayed in the Object Navigator.

11. The name of the tab page must be changed to 'TermsConditions_Tab' and the Label must be changed to 'Terms and Conditions'.

12. The runtime screen after creating a new tab page will be as shown in diagram 8.9.

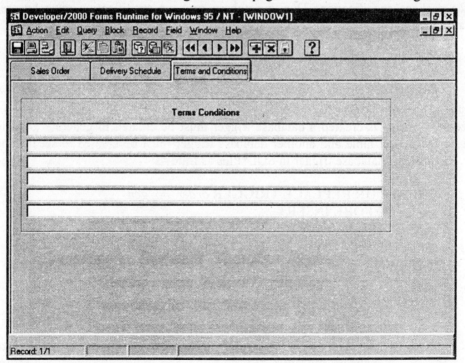

Diagram 8.9 : Forms Runtime for the Terms and Conditions Tab Page

VALIDATIONS

Modify the form to include the following validations:

- *S_Order_No* is a Primary Key. Duplicate values are not allowed in S_Order_*No*. It cannot be left blank.
- The first letter of *S_Order_No* must start with 'O'.

Database triggers and a Database Package is used to generate a primary key value and set the foreign key to the newly generated value. The steps to generate the primary key for the master table and use the same as the foreign key in the detail table are summarized as under:

Syntax for Sequence Creation:

The syntax for creating a sequence for s_order_no is as follows:

> **CREATE SEQUENCE** *order_seq*
> **INCREMENT BY** *1*
> **START WITH** *1;*

Package Specification Creation:

In the current example the newly generated *S_Order_No* is stored in the variable declared in the package specification. Thus a database package specification must be created. Create a PACKAGE USING SQL*Plus as follows:

> **CREATE PACKAGE** *orderpkey_gen* **IS**
> **master_key varchar2(6);**
> **END;**

Creating Database Trigger for the master and detail tables:

Once the package is created a database trigger must be created to generate the primary key for the master table and another database trigger must be created to set the foreign key. Creating the database trigger in SQL*Plus as follows:

> **CREATE OR REPLACE TRIGGER** *order_no_gen*
> **BEFORE INSERT**
> **ON** *sales_order*
> **FOR EACH ROW**
> **DECLARE**
> primary_key_value varchar2(4);
> **BEGIN**
> SELECT lpad(to_char(order_seq.nextval) , 4 , '0')
> INTO primary_key_value FROM dual;
> /* Set the value of the variable in the package to the newly generated
> primary key value. */
> orderpkey_gen.master_key := 'O' || primary_key_value;
> /* Assign the newly generated primary key value to the challan_no column */
> :new.s_order_no := orderpkey_gen.master_key;
> **END;**

The same steps need to be performed for the Before Insert trigger for the *sales_order_details* table. The equivalent Oracle PL/SQL syntax will be:

```
CREATE OR REPLACE TRIGGER fk_order_no_gen
        BEFORE INSERT
        ON sales_order_details
        FOR EACH ROW
BEGIN
        if :new.s_order_no is null then
                :new.s_order_no := orderpkey_gen.master_key;
        end if;
END;
```

Since the primary key is generated by the system, the primary key must not be visible on the screen. Thus we need to set the canvas of *s_order_no* column to Null. Open the property sheet of the *s_order_no* item. Set the *Canvas* property to Null.

Implementing Business Rules using When-Validate-Item Trigger:

To modify the form to include the following validations:
- *Order_Date* **cannot be greater than system date.**
- *Quantity_Ordered* must not be left empty and **cannot be 0 or less than 0.**
- *Product_Rate* must not be left empty and **cannot be 0 or less than 0.**
- *Delivery_Date* **cannot be less than system date.**
- *Delivery_Date* **cannot be less than** *Order_Date*.
- *Quantity_Dispatched* must not be left empty and cannot be 0 or less than 0.
- *Quantity_Dispatched* cannot be greater than *Qty_Ordered*

Business rules can be defined using the *When-Validate-Item* trigger. If an invalid value is entered, an appropriate error message can be displayed and the text color can be changed to RED to indicate an error condition.

The visual properties of any item can be set by attaching appropriate a Visual Attribute object. There are two visual attributes created and stored in the Object Library. These are:
- VA_ERRORS
- VA_NOERRORS

VA_ERRORS and VA_NO_ERRORS visual attributes are defined and stored in the object library. Thus these objects must be referenced in the form. The steps are as follows:

1. Click on **File..Open** to open the Object Library. Oracle Forms Builder will display the *Open File* dialog box. Select *comobj.olb* file from the appropriate directory. *Comobj.olb* object library will be displayed in the Object Navigator under the Object Libraries Node.

2. Click on **Tool..Object Library** menu items to open the library tabs. The *Comobj.olb* currently includes three library tabs. These library tabs are named *Triggers*, *VATTRS* and *Pclass* that store the common triggers, visual attributes and property classes respectively.

3. Select *VATTRS* library tab. Oracle Forms Builder displays the VA_ERRORS, VA_NOERRORS visual attribute objects. Drag and drop the both the visual attributes from the library tab to the *Visual Attributes* node. Confirmation to subclass or copy the Visual Attribute objects are asked for. Select *SubClass*. The visual attribute reference will be included in the form.

4. Write When-Validate-Item triggers to validate the contents of specific text items.

<u>*Order Date* must be less than or equal to system date.</u>

Trigger Name	: **WHEN-VALIDATE-ITEM**	Form	: order
Block	: sales_order	Item	: s_order_date
Trigger Level	: Item Level		
Function	: Check that *s_order_date* is less than or equal to the system date.		
Text	: BEGIN		

```
           if :sales_order.s_order_date > sysdate then
                   message('Order Date cannot be greater than ' ||
                                    to_char(sysdate));
                   set_item_property('s_order_date', current_record_attribute,
                                    'VA_ERRORS');
                   raise form_trigger_failure;
               end if;
           elsif :s_order_date > :delivery_date Then
                   message('Order Date cannot be greater than Delivery Date.');
                   set_item_property('s_order_date',
                           current_record_attribute, 'VA_ERRORS');
                   raise form_trigger_failure;
               end if;
       END;
```

<u>Quantity ordered cannot be 0.</u>

Trigger Name	: **WHEN-VALIDATE-ITEM**	Form	: order
Block	: sales_order_details	Item	: qty_ordered
Trigger Level	: Item Level		
Function	: Check that qty_ordered is not 0.		
Text	: BEGIN		

```
           if :sales_order_details.qty_ordered = 0 then
                   message('Quantity Ordered cannot be 0.');
                   set_item_property('qty_ordered', current_record_attribute,
                                    'VA_ERRORS');
                   raise form_trigger_failure;
               end if;
       END;
```

Product Rate cannot be 0.

Trigger Name	: **WHEN-VALIDATE-ITEM**	Form	: order
Block	: sales_order_details	Item	: product_rate
Trigger Level	: Item Level		
Function	: Check that product_rate is not 0.		
Text	: BEGIN		

```
        if :sales_order_details.product_rate = 0 then
                message('Product Rate cannot be 0.');
                set_item_property('product_rate', current_record_attribute,
                        'VA_ERRORS');
                raise form_trigger_failure;
        end if;
    END;
```

Delivery Date must be greater than or equal to system date.

Trigger Name	: **WHEN-VALIDATE-ITEM**	Form	: order
Block	: delivery_schedule	Item	: delivery_date
Trigger Level	: Item Level		
Function	: Check that *delivery_date* is less than or equal to the system date.		
Text	: If :delivery_date < sysdate Then		

```
        message('Delivery Date cannot be less than ' || to_char(sysdate) || ' .');
        set_item_property('delivery_date', current_record_attribute,
                'VA_ERRORS');
        raise form_trigger_failure;
    ElsIf :s_order_date > :delivery_date Then
        message('Delivery Date cannot be greater than Order Date.');
        set_item_property('delivery_date', current_record_attribute,
                'VA_ERRORS');
        raise form_trigger_failure;
    End If;
```

Quantity dispatched in the delivery schedule cannot be 0.

Trigger Name	: **WHEN-VALIDATE-ITEM**	Form	: order
Block	: delivery_schedule	Item	: quantity
Trigger Level	: Item Level		
Function	: Check that quantity in the delivery schedule is not 0.		
Text	: BEGIN		

```
        if :delivery_schedule.quantity = 0 then
                message('Quantity Delivered cannot be 0.');
                set_item_property('quantity', current_record_attribute,
                        'VA_ERRORS');
                raise form_trigger_failure;
        end if;
    END;
```

Not Null Check using ON-ERROR Form Trigger:

If the column is defined as a NOT NULL column at the table level, Oracle Forms Builder sets the '*Required*' attribute to '*Yes*'. If the '*Required*' attribute is set to '*Yes*', Oracle Forms Runtime will display an error message if the item is exited without any value being entered.

To handle this error appropriate code can be written in the ON-ERROR trigger defined at the form level.

Generalized PL/SQL code for the ON-ERROR trigger is written and stored in the Object Library. The ON-ERROR trigger can be subclassed or inherited from the object library leading to standardization of error handling. The steps in subclassing the ON-ERROR trigger, are:

1. Click on **File..Open** to open the Object Library. Oracle Forms Builder will display the *Open File* dialog box. Select *comobj.olb* file from the appropriate directory. *Comobj.olb* object library will be displayed in the Object Navigator under the Object Libraries Node.

2. Click on **Tool..Object Library** menu items to open the library tabs. The *Comobj.olb* currently includes three library tabs. These library tabs are named *Triggers*, *VATTRS* and *Pclass* that store the common triggers, visual attributes and property classes respectively.

3. Select *Triggers* library tab. Oracle Forms Builder displays the ON-ERROR trigger object included in the *Triggers* library tab.

4. Drag and drop the ON-ERROR trigger from the library tab to the *Triggers* node under the form name such that the ON-ERROR trigger will be a form level trigger. Oracle Forms Builder will then ask for confirmation to subclass or copy ON-ERROR trigger. Select *SubClass*. ON-ERROR trigger reference will be included in the form.

5. Set the required property to True for all the items that require a NOT NULL check.

Trigger Name	: **ON-ERROR**	Form	: order
Block	:	Item	:
Trigger Level	: Form Level		
Function	: Check for Not Null. In case of any other error display default error message and set the visual attribute to VA_ERRORS.		
Text	: DECLARE		

```
        DECLARE
                error_item varchar2(50);
                current_item_label varchar2(100);
        BEGIN
                error_item := :system.trigger_item;
                If error_type = 'FRM' and error_code = 40202 THEN
                        current_item_label := get_item_property(error_item,
                                prompt_text);
                        current_item_label := replace(current_item_label, ':', '');
                        current_item_label := replace(current_item_label, ' ', '');
                        Message(current_item_label || ' cannot be left blank.');
                Else
                        Message(error_text);
                        set_item_property(error_item,
                                current_record_attribute, 'VA_ERRORS');
                End if;
        END;
```

Resetting the visual attribute to VA_NO_ERRORS after the error is corrected:
In the current example the order form has an ON-ERROR trigger defined at the form level and the WHEN-VALIDATE-ITEM trigger defined at the item level. PL/SQL code is written in both these triggers to display an error message and set the visual attribute to VA_ERRORS.

If the errors are corrected, the item text color must be set to Black i.e. the visual attribute must be set to VA_NO_ERRORS.

The trigger that gets executed when the form cursor moves from one item to the other is called POST-TEXT-ITEM.

In the current example, the PL/SQL code for the POST-TEXT-ITEM trigger to set the visual attribute to VA_NO_ERRORS is same for all the text items in both the master and the detail block. If the POST-TEXT-ITEM trigger is written at the form level i.e. it will be executed when the cursor moves out of any text item in any block on the form.

The code written in the POST-TEXT-ITEM trigger is a call to the built-in *set_item_property()* to set the visual attribute of the current item to VA_NO_ERRORS. Thus there is a need to know the name of the current item. The name of the current item is stored in a system variable that can be accessed using '**:system.cursor_item**'. Thus the PL/SQL code written at block level will be as follows:

Trigger Name	: **POST-TEXT-ITEM**	Form	: order
Block	:	Item	:
Trigger Level	: Form Level		
Function	: Set the visual attribute of the current item to VA_NO_ERRORS.		

```
Text           : DECLARE
                     str_current_item varchar2(50);
                 BEGIN
                     str_current_item := :system.cursor_item;
                     set_item_property(str_current_item, current_record_attribute,
                         'VA_NOERRORS');
                 END;
```

Creating Display Items:

A Sales Order document generated using a manual system generally displays the Order Number, Order Date, Client Number, Client Name and the details of the material ordered. Thus the data entry sales order form must also display the same details.

Using a Display Item in the Master Block:

Order Number, Order Date and Client Number are displayed as text items belonging to the *Sales_Order* block on the Order form. These text items are connected to the columns of the *Sales_Order* table.

The Order form must also display the name of the client to whom material is being delivered. Details of each client are stored in the *Client_Master* table. Each client is identified by a unique *Client_No*.

The *Client_No* is used to identify the client when an order is placed. The *Client_No* is recorded when the client places an order. Client name can be retrieved based on the *Client_No* entered.

The relationship between *S_Order_No*, *Client_No* and *Name* can be depicted as follows:

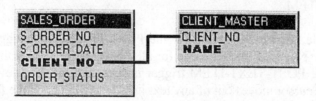

In the master section, as soon as a valid client number is loaded into the text item *Client_No* item, the system must display the corresponding client name from the *Client_Master* table. Create a display item to display the *Client_Name* (i.e. an item to which cursor navigation is not allowed).

1. Open the layout editor of the *Order* form. Create a new display field by selecting the *display item* tool from the toolbar and dropping it on the form.

2. Set the following properties of the display field.

Name	: client_name
Item Type	**: Display Item**
Data Type	: Char
Maximum Length	: 20
Database Item	**: No**
Prompt	: Name :

Caution

> *Client_Name* is not included in the *Sales_Order* table i.e. *Client_Name* is not a part of the base table. If the column is not included in the base table, its **Database Item** property must be set to 'No'.

Using a Display Item in the Detail Block:

Order Number, Product Number and Qty Ordered are displayed as text items belonging to the *Sales_Order_Details* block on the order form. These text items are connected to the columns of the *Sales_Order_Details* table.

The order form must also display the description and unit measure of the material delivered. Product description and unit measure are stored in the *Product_Master* table. Each product is identified by a unique *Product_No*.

Description and unit measure can be retrieved based on the *Product_No* entered. The relationship between *Product_No* and *Description* can be depicted as follows:

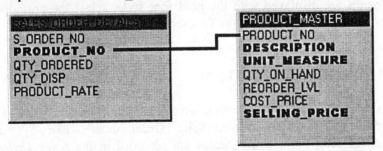

In the detail section, as soon as a valid product number is loaded into the text item *Product_No* item, the system must display the corresponding Description and Unit Measure from the *Product_Master* table. Create a display item to display the *Description* and *Unit Measure* (i.e. an item to which cursor navigation is not allowed).

1. Select detail block in the layout editor and place a *display item* it. Set the following properties of the display field.

Name	: description
Item Type	: Display Item
Data Type	: Char
Maximum Length	: 20
Database Item	: No
Prompt	: Description
Prompt Adjustment Edge	: Top

2. Place another *display item* on the form. Set the properties of display field as follows:

Name	: unit_measure
Item Type	: Display Item
Data Type	: Char
Maximum Length	: 20
Database Item	: No
Prompt	: Unit Measure
Prompt Adjustment Edge	: Top

Note

The label or the prompt for an item must be displayed on top of the items since the detail block displays multiple records. The property that determines the position of the item prompt is **Prompt Adjustment Edge**. Set the value of this property to **Top**. The other values that this property can take are **Start**, **End**, **Top** and **Bottom**.

5. Since all prompts are displayed with the bold font style, select the prompts of the display items and click on $\boxed{\text{B}}$ to set the font style to bold.

CREATING AND USING A LIST ITEM

As seen earlier, a sales transaction starts with when a client places an order. Each Order is uniquely identified by its *S_Order_No*. Sales Order details like *S_Order_No*, *S_Order_Date*, client details and *Order_Status* are recorded in the *Sales_Order* table. *Order_Status* is a flag set to indicate whether the material ordered is not yet delivered (NP), partially delivered (IP) or fully delivered (FP).

Client_No must exist in the *Client_Master* table. Such a business rule can be implemented by providing an item that displays a selection list from which appropriate value can be selected and placed in the item. The Item that displays a selection list is called **List Item**.

List Item is a list of text elements that can be displayed as a poplist, text list, or combo box. List Item displays a fixed number of elements from which an operator can select a single text element. Each element in a list is a text string up to 30 characters long.

Poplist:
The poplist style list item appears initially as a single ▭ item. When the list item is clicked, a list of available choices appears as shown below.

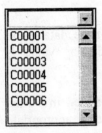

TLIST
The text list style list item appears as a rectangular box, which displays a fixed number of values. When the text list contains values that cannot be displayed in the display area (due to the displayable area of the item), a vertical scroll bar appears.

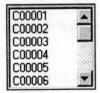

ComboList
The combo box style list item combines the features found in list and text items. Unlike the poplist or the text list style list items, the combo box style list item will display fixed values and accept operator-entered value as well. The combo box list item appears as an empty box with an icon to the right. Text can be entered directly into the combo list item or click the list icon to display a list of available values.

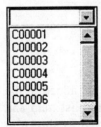

List Element Elements:
When a list item is created, **list item elements** must also be created. Each list element comprises of:
- Display Value
- Data Value

Display Values:
A set of values displayed when the list item is clicked is called Display Value.

Data Values:
Each display value is associated with a data value. Thus when a display value is selected, the list item internal holds the corresponding data value that can be accessed by using **:listitemname**.

Similarly, when a value is fetched from the database, the element whose data value matches the fetched value is searched for and the corresponding display value is displayed in the list item.

List item can include a list of **static list elements** i.e. list elements added in Forms Builder or the list elements can be added programmatically by writing appropriate PL/SQL code.

Creating A List Item:
A list item can be created in two ways as explained below.

Method 1 - Creating a New List Item:
1. Click and drag the list item tool until the item's bounding box is the desired size. The default list item is displayed as a **Poplist**.

2. If required, open the Property Palette window for the list item and change the **List Style** to **Combo** or **Tlist**.

Method 2 - Converting a Text Item to a List Item:
1. Select the text item and open the Properties Palette window. Change the **Item Type** property to **list item**.

2. If required, open the Property Palette window for the list item and change the **List Style** to **Combo** or **Tlist**.

Adding Static List Elements:

The steps in adding Static list element are as follows:
1. Static List elements i.e. display value and associated data value can be added in the List Item Property Palette. Open the Property Palette window for the list item and select **Elements in List** property. A **More...** push button is displayed as shown in diagram 8.10.

2. Click on More. *List Item Elements* dialog box is displayed. Enter the display value and the data value for the selected item as shown in diagram 8.11.

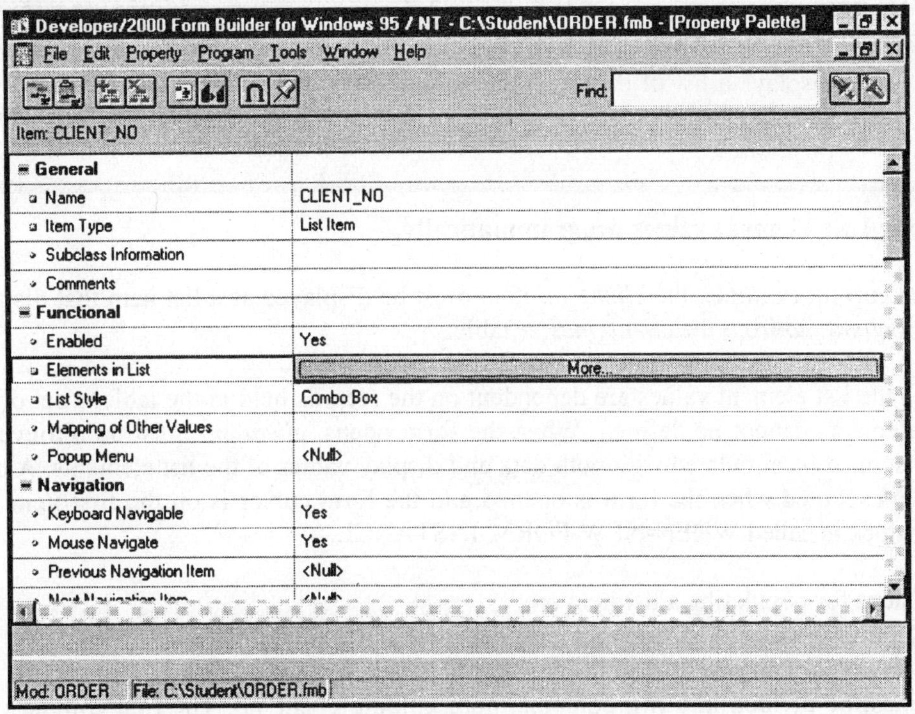

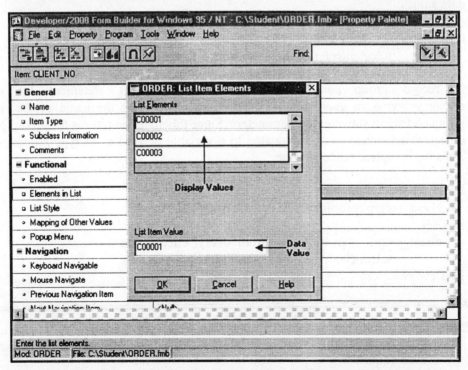

Diagram 8.10 : Elements in List Property displayed in the Property Palette

Diagram 8.11 : Setting Display and Data values for the List Item

Note

As seen in diagram 8.11, the first half of *List Item Elements* dialog box displays a list of display values. The lower half of *List Item Elements* dialog box displays the data value for the display value on which the form cursor is positioned.

Setting List Element values programmatically:

In the current example, the *client_no* item must be displayed as a list item that displays a list of *client_no* from the *client_master* table.

Since the list element values are dependent on the records held in the table, a set of static list elements cannot be defined. When the form opens, *client_no* must be retrieved and the list must be populated with both data and display values of the list elements. A trigger that is executed when the form is opened and the form cursor is on the first item in the first block is called WHEN-NEW-FORM-INSTANCE.

The steps for populating a list item are:
- Define an object that can hold multiple rows and column:
  An object that can hold multiple records is called a record group. This record group must be divided into two columns, both holding client_no. The first column can be used for populating display value and the second column can be used for populating data values.

```
create_group_from_query('clientrecgrp',
        'select client_no, client_no from client_master');
```

A record group can be defined from a select statement by using *create_group_from_query* function. This function accepts the name of the record group and select statement as parameters. Since this function returns the record group object, this function must be equated to a variable defined as of type *recordgroup*. Thus the complete syntax will be:

```
DECLARE
    client_recgrp recordgroup;
BEGIN
    client_recgrp := create_group_from_query('clientrecgrp',
            'select client_no, client_no from client_master');
END;
```

Note

The Select statement used to populate a list item must include two columns. The first column is used as display value and the second column is used as data value.

- Populate the record group using the select statement:
  The select statement specified at the time of creating a record group must be executed to populate the record group. *Populate_group* function is used to populate a record group. This function accepts a variable defined of type recordgroup as a parameter. This function returns an integer value 0 if the select statement is successfully executed. In case of an error query this function returns a negative number indicating the type of error.

```
DECLARE
    status number;
BEGIN
    status := populate_group(clientrecgrp);
END;
```

- Populate list item from the record group:
  Once the record group is populated, the *populate_list()* can be used to populate the list item from the record group. This function accepts a list item name and a record group variable as parameters.

```
populate_list('client_no', client_recgrp);
```

Thus the PL/SQL code written in the WHEN-NEW-FORM-INSTANCE is as follows:

Trigger Name	: **WHEN-NEW-FORM-INSTANCE**	Form	: order
Block	:	Item	:
Trigger Level	: Form Level		
Function	: Populates List Item with List Item Elements.		
Text	: DECLARE		

```
        DECLARE
                client_recgrp recordgroup;
                status number;
        BEGIN
                client_recgrp := create_group_from_query('client_recgrp',
                        'select client_no, client_no from client_master');

                /* Record group must be populated only if the record group is
                successfully created. If an object is created, a unique object id is
                assigned. Thus id_null() can be used to check if an object id
                exists. */
                if not id_null(client_recgrp) then
                        status := populate_group(client_recgrp);
                        populate_list('client_no', client_recgrp);
                end if;
        END;
```

Changing product_no text item into list item and populating it:

Product_no item in the detail section must display product_no form the product_master table. Thus the **Item Type** property of product_no must be set to **List Item**.

Additional PL/SQL code must be written to populate *product_no* list item at runtime as follows:

Trigger Name	: **WHEN-NEW-FORM-INSTANCE**	Form	: order
Block	:	Item	:
Trigger Level	: Form Level		
Function	: Populates List Item with List Item Elements.		
Text	: DECLARE		

```
          client_recgrp recordgroup;
          product_recgrp recordgroup;
          status number;
       BEGIN
          client_recgrp := create_group_from_query('client_recgrp',
                    'select client_no, client_no from client_master');
          if not id_null(client_recgrp) then
                 status := populate_group(client_recgrp);
                 populate_list('client_no', client_recgrp);
          end if;

          product_recgrp := create_group_from_query('product_recgrp',
                 'select product_no, product_no from product_master');
          if not id_null(product_recgrp) then
                 status := populate_group( product_recgrp);
                 populate_list('sales_order_details.product_no',
                          product_recgrp);
          end if;
       END;
```

Populating Client Name based on the selected client_no:

When a *client_no* list element is selected from the list item, the corresponding *client_name* must be displayed from the *client_master* table. Trigger that is fired when a list element in a list item is selected is called WHEN-LIST-CHANGED. The PL/SQL code written to populate *client_name* is as follows:

Trigger Name	: **WHEN-LIST-CHANGED**	Form	: order
Block	: sales_order	Item	: client_no
Trigger Level	: Item Level		
Function	: Populates *client_name* based on the selected *client_no*.		
Text	: DECLARE		

```
          select name into :client_name from client_master
                    where client_no = :client_no;
       EXCEPTION
          when no_data_found then
                    message('Invalid Client Number');
                    raise form_trigger_failure;
       END;
```

Populating Description, Unit_Measure and Product_Rate based on selected Product_No:

When a *product_no* list element is selected from the list item, the corresponding *description*, *unit_measure* and *product_rate* must be displayed from the *product_master* table. Trigger that is fired when a list element in a list item is selected is called WHEN-LIST-CHANGED. The PL/SQL code written to populate *description*, *unit_measure* and *product_rate* is as follows:

Trigger Name	: **WHEN-LIST-CHANGED**	Form	: order
Block	: sales_order_details	Item	: product_no
Trigger Level	: Item Level		
Function	: Populates *description*, *unit_measure* and *product_rate* based on the selected *product_no*.		
Text	: BEGIN		

```
        select description, unit_measure, selling_price
            into :description, :unit_measure, :product_rate
            from product_master
            where product_no = :sales_order_details.product_no;
    EXCEPTION
        when no_data_found then
            message ('Invalid Product Number');
            raise form_trigger_failure;
END;
```

WORKING WITH FORMULA AND SUMMARY ITEMS
Formula Items:

Since the rate and quantity for the selected products are entered, the sales value for the same can be calculated as *Product_Rate * Qty_Ordered*. Oracle forms tool provides a set of properties associated with text items and display items that can be set to calculate values based on a pre-defined formula.

The steps in creating a formula item are as follows:
1. Create a display item in the sales_order_details block and set following properties:

Name	: Amount
Item Type	: Display Item
Data Type	: Number
Maximum length	: 12
Database Item	: No
Prompt	: Amount
Prompt Attachment Edge	: Top

2. The property sheet of a display item also includes a section named **Calculation**. The first property is called **Calculation Mode**, which is set to **None** by default (No calculations required). Set the **Calculation Mode** property to **Formula**. Define the formula in the **Formula** property as **:sales_order_details.product_rate * :sales_order_details.qty_ordered**. The completed property sheet is as shown in diagram 8.12.

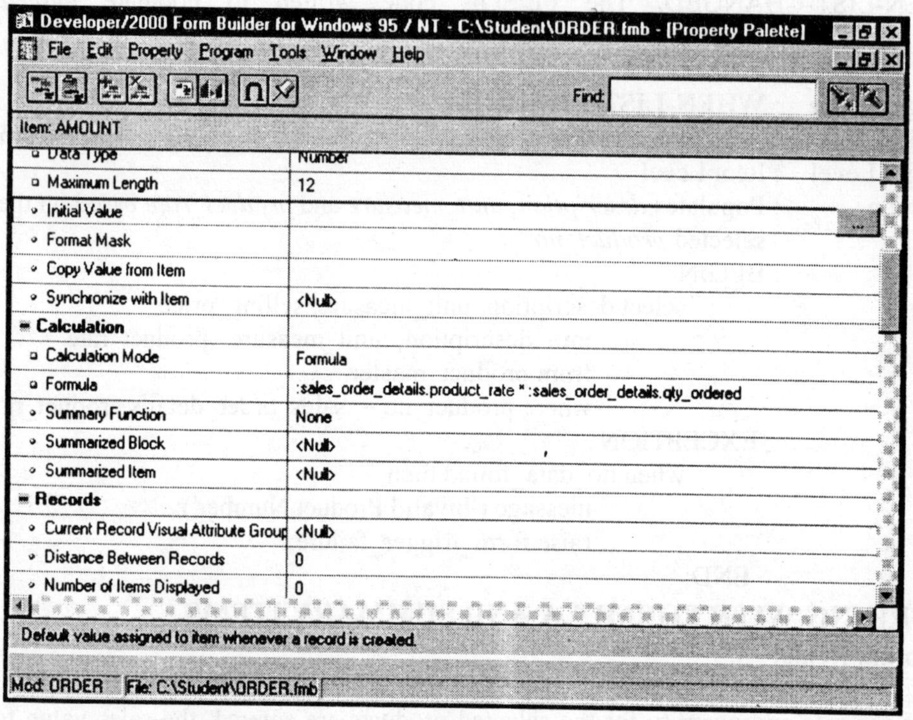

```
Developer/2000 Form Builder for Windows 95 / NT - C:\Student\ORDER.fmb - [Property Palette]
File   Edit   Property   Program   Tools   Window   Help

                                                              Find:
Item: AMOUNT
   □ Data Type                          Number
   □ Maximum Length                     12
   ◦ Initial Value
   ◦ Format Mask
   ◦ Copy Value from Item
   ◦ Synchronize with Item              <Null>
 ▬ Calculation
   □ Calculation Mode                   Formula
   □ Formula                            :sales_order_details.product_rate * :sales_order_details.qty_ordered
   ◦ Summary Function                   None
   ◦ Summarized Block                   <Null>
   ◦ Summarized Item                    <Null>
 ▬ Records
   ◦ Current Record Visual Attribute Group  <Null>
   ◦ Distance Between Records           0
   ◦ Number of Items Displayed          0

Default value assigned to item whenever a record is created.

Mod: ORDER   File: C:\Student\ORDER.fmb
```

Diagram 8.12 : Setting Calculation Properties

Summary Items:

After calculating the amount for the selected products the total order amount must be calculated as the sum of the amount for individual products. Oracle forms tool provides a set of properties associated with text items and display items that can be set to calculate values based on a pre-defined summary function.

The steps in creating a summary item are as follows:

1. Create a display item in the sales_order_details block and set following properties:

Name	: Total
Item Type	: Display Item
Data Type	: Number
Maximum length	: 14
Database Item	: No
Prompt	: Total :
Prompt Attachment Edge	: Start

2. The property sheet of a display item also includes a section named **Calculation**. The first property is called **Calculation Mode**, which is set to **None** by default (No calculations required). Set the **Calculation Mode** property to **Summary**. Set additional properties for creating a summary column as follows:

Summary Function	: Sum
Summarized Block	: Sales_Order_Details
Summarized Item	: Amount

3. Currently the sales_order_details block displays three records and thus any item placed in the sales_order_details block will be displayed thrice once for each record. Summary column must be displayed only once irrespective of the number of records displayed in the detail block. To do so set the **Number of Items Displayed** property to 1. Completed property sheet for the summary column is as shown in diagram 8.13.

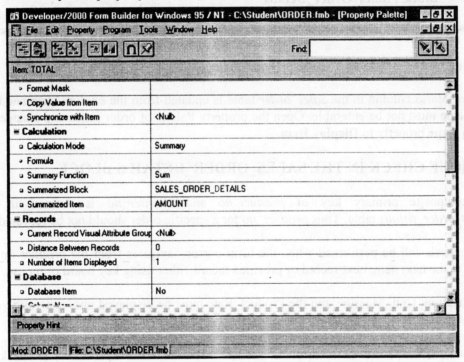

Diagram 8.13 : Properties of a Summary Item

4. **Query All Records** property determines how data is retrieved from the database. By default this property is set to **No** i.e. retrieve as needed.

Note

When an execute_query is fired, the Oracle runtime tool reads the **Number of Displayed Records** to determine the number of records that must be fetched from the server. Additional records if any are retrieved when based on form navigation.

To calculate summary values all the records must be retrieved. Thus **Query All Records** property of *sales_order_details* block must be set to **Yes**.

Caution

If Thus **Query All Records** property is set to **No** and a summary column is used, Oracle Forms Builder displays a compilation error as follows:

FRM-30426: Summarized control item must reside in a control block or in a block with Query All Records set to Yes.
Item : Total
Block : Sales_Order_Details

Setting Order_Status as a Display Item:

Order_Status column in the *sales_order* table is updated from the *challan* form and thus the same must not be enterable. Open the property Palette of order status and change the **Item Type** property to **Display Item**.

UNIQUE CHECK IN THE SALES_ORDER_DETAILS BLOCK

A composite primary key of *product_no* and *s_order_no* is defined in the *sales_order_details* table. Thus *product_no* for a specific order should not be repeated.

This check will be performed when the form cursor navigates from the *product_no* list item to the next item, next record or previous record either using key board or mouse.

Description, Unit_Measure and the Product_Rate must be displayed only if a valid value is entered.

To achieve this, a user-defined function is written in the *Saleslib.pll* library to check for duplicate values in the detail section. This function is called from different key and mouse triggers. It returns 1 if a duplicate is found else it returns 0.

Open the *Saleslib.pll* library and include function *f_dup_detail*.

FUNCTION **F_DUP_DETAIL** (item_name varchar) RETURN NUMBER IS
       is_duplicate char(5);
       current_rec_no number(3);
       last_rec_no number(3);
       cur_val varchar2(20);
       row_count number(3);
       form_name varchar(40);
BEGIN
       is_duplicate := 'FALSE';

       /* Store the current record position */
       current_rec_no := to_number(name_in('system.cursor_record'));

       /* Store the current record's product number */
       cur_val := name_in(item_name);

       /* *When form cursor navigates from one record to the other, in the detail
          block of the Master / Detail form all the default Oracle triggers fire. Any user
          defined validation code attached to any of these triggers will thus get
          executed.*

       *The F_Dup_Detail function will deliberately cause the form cursor to navigate
       through all the records in the detail section while checking for the uniqueness
       of the data held in Product_No column.*

       *Thus all the other triggers attached to each field in the record will
       automatically fire and the PL/SQL code block will get executed. This is
       completely unnecessary.*

       *To temporarily disable all these triggers the **Validation** property must be set to
       property_false at the form level. Thus we need to use the function
       set_form_property that accepts the name of the form, the form property name
       and the property value.*

       *To generalize the procedure we need to get the current form name. The form
       name can be accessed by using the **current_form_name** property of the
       application. */
       form_name := get_application_property(current_form_name);
       set_form_property(form_name,validation,property_false);

       last_record; /* position cursor on the last record */
       /* check if current record is the only record in the detail block */
       if name_in('system.cursor_record') <> '1' then

          /* *The system variable defined in Forms do not give information on the
            total number of records. Thus to get the total number of records we need
            to position the cursor on the last record and get the current record
            number */*

```
        last_rec_no := to_number(name_in('system.cursor_record'));
        first_record;

        /* set up a loop from one to maximum number of records to compare
           each record's product_no with the variable cur_val */
        for row_count in 1..last_rec_no loop

                /* Ensure comparison is not made with the entered product_no,
                   stored in variable cur_val */
                if current_rec_no <> row_count then
                        if cur_val = name_in(item_name) then
                                is_duplicate := 'TRUE';
                                exit;
                        end if;
                end if;

                /* Ensure that the cursor doesn't go to a record that does not exist */
                if last_rec_no < > row_count then
                        next_record;
                end if;
        end loop;
end if;

/* Reposition the cursor to the record number when function was called */
go_record(current_rec_no);
set_form_property(form_name,validation,property_true);
/* check if a duplicate is found; if yes, return 1 else return 0 */
if is_duplicate = 'TRUE' then
        return(1);
else
        return(0);
end if;
END;
```

Trigger Name	: **KEY-NEXT-ITEM**	Form	: sales_order
Block	: sales_order_details	Item	: product_no
Trigger Level	: Field Level		
Function	: Check that product number is not duplicated for a specified order.		
Text	: BEGIN		

```
                if f_dup_detail('sales_order_details.product_no') = 0  then
                        next_Item;
                else
                        message('product "' || :sales_order_details.product_no
                                || '" cannot be included twice in the order "' ||
                                :sales_order_details.s_order_no || '".');
                        raise form_trigger_failure;
                End if;
        END;
```

Trigger Name	: **KEY-UP**	Form	: sales_order
Block	: sales_order_details	Item	:
Trigger Level	: Block Level		
Function	: Check that product number is not duplicated for a specified order.		
Text	: BEGIN		

```
        BEGIN
            if :system.cursor_block = 'sales_order_details' and
                    :system.cursor_record <> 1 then
                if f_dup_detail('sales_order_details.product_no') = 0 then
                    previous_record;
                else
                    message('Product ''' || :sales_order_details.product_no
                        || ''' cannot be included twice in the order ''' ||
                        :sales_order_details.s_order_no || '''.');

                    raise form_trigger_failure;
                end if;
            end if;
        END;
```

Trigger Name	: **KEY-DOWN**	Form	: sales_order
Block	: sales_order_details	Item	:
Trigger Level	: Block Level		
Function	: Check that product number is not duplicated for a specified order.		
Text	: BEGIN		

```
        BEGIN
            if :system.cursor_block = 'sales_order_details' and
                    :system.last_record <> 'TRUE' then
                if f_dup_detail('sales_order_details.product_no') = 0 then
                    next_record;
                else
                    message('Product ''' || :sales_order_details.product_no
                        || ''' cannot be included twice in the order ''' ||
                        :sales_order_details.s_order_no || '''.');

                    raise form_trigger_failure;
                end if;
            end if;
        END;
```

CREATING AND USING AN EDITOR

The current application accepts data for terms and conditions where the user would enter data in paragraph format i.e. multi-line information. If the data is entered in a paragraph format an editor can be displayed and used to accept input.

Oracle Forms tool can call text editors like Notepad. This can be achieved by setting the Oracle Form Builders system editor to Notepad. All that is required is to specify the type of the editor that must be opened for items that accept multi-line text. Customized editors can also be created to accept input. The name of the custom editor created can then be specified to display data.

Focus:

Create a User-defined editor for terms and conditions. The editor must be displayed when the user presses CTRL E in the **Terms_Conditions** item as shown in diagram 8.14.

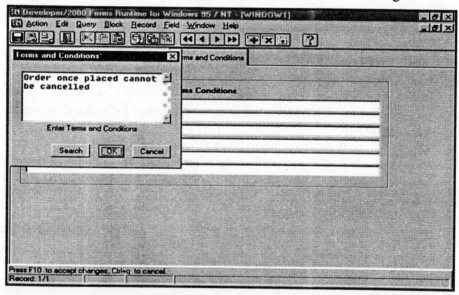

Diagram 8.14 : Customized Editor displayed in Sales Order Form

Solution:
1. To create a new editor, select the **Editors** node in the Object Navigator and click on **Navigator..Create**. A new editor named *Editor30* as shown in diagram 8.15 is created.

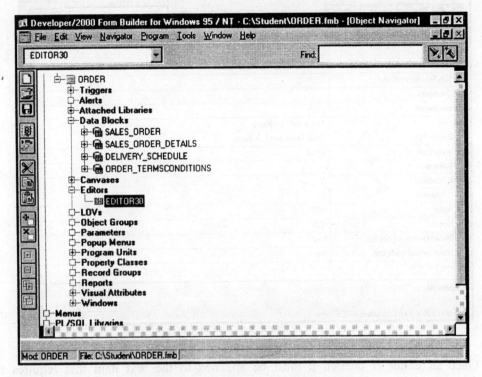

Diagram 8.15 : Creating a New Editor

2. Open Property Palette of the editor and set the *Name*, *Title*, *Bottom Title* property of the editor to customize the editor to suit the users needs. The properties are:

Name	: Terms_Conditions_Editor
Title	: Terms and Conditions
Bottom Title	: Enter Terms and Conditions
Show Horizontal Scrollbar	: Yes
Show Vertical	: Yes

The completed property sheet is as displayed in diagram 8.16.

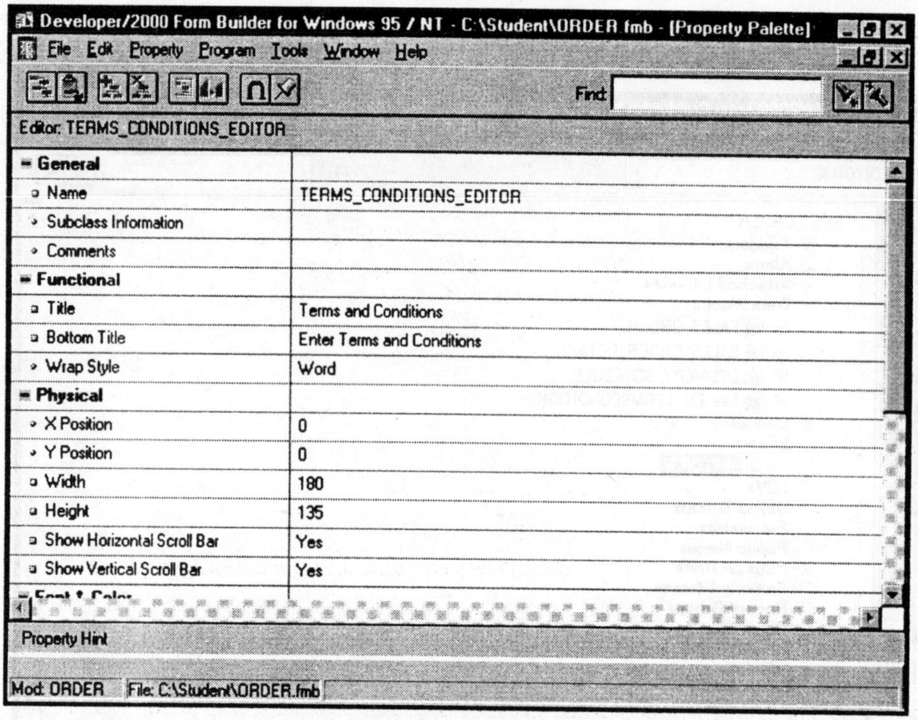

8.16 : Properties of Editor

3. Once an editor is created it must be attached to the text item that requires the customized editor. Open the property sheet of the Terms_Conditions Text Item and set the **Editor** property to Terms_Conditions_Editor as shown in diagram 8.17.

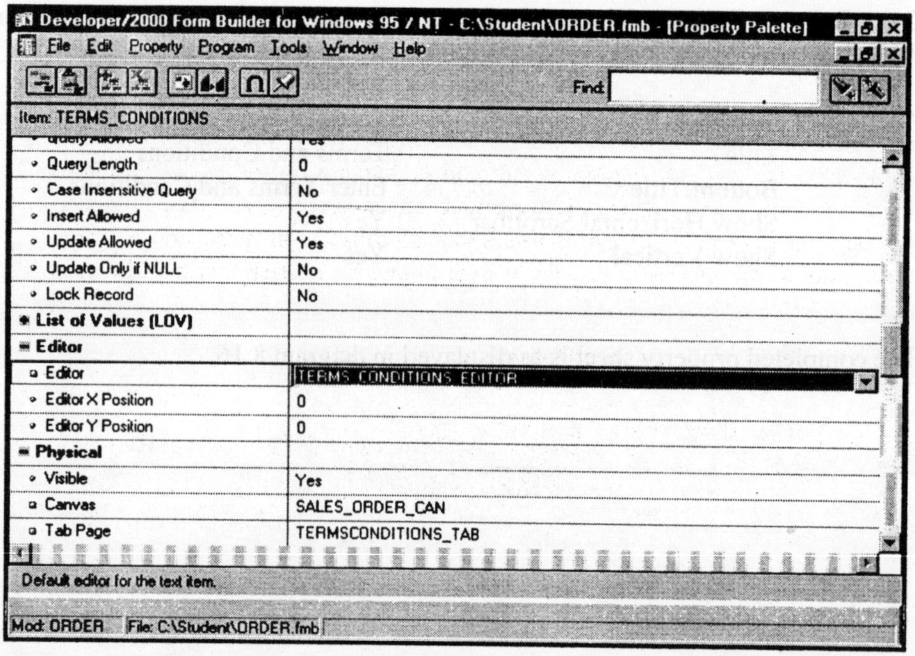

Diagram 8.17 : Connecting an Editor to a Text Item

Note

The Editor property displays a list of custom editors along with a list element as SYSTEM_EDITOR. If SYSTEM_EDITOR is selected, Notepad Editor is displayed by default. If FORM50_EDITOR parameter from the windows registry to determine the system editor that must be opened. By default the SYSTEM_EDITOR is set to Notepad.

4. Run the form. Press <CTRL E> when the cursor is in TERM_CONDITIONS item. Enter Terms and Conditions as required. The completed Terms and Conditions will be displayed as shown in diagram 8.18.

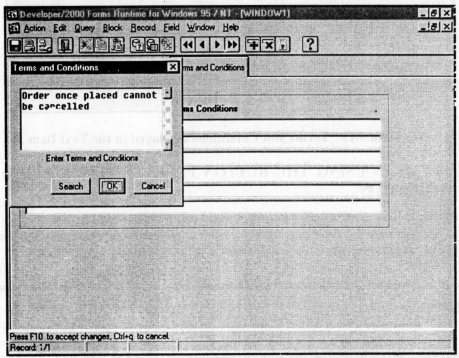

Diagram 8.18 : Custom Editor Displayed at runtime

5. Click on OK. The Terms and Conditions will be displayed in a single line in the Terms_Conditions item as shown in diagram 8.19.

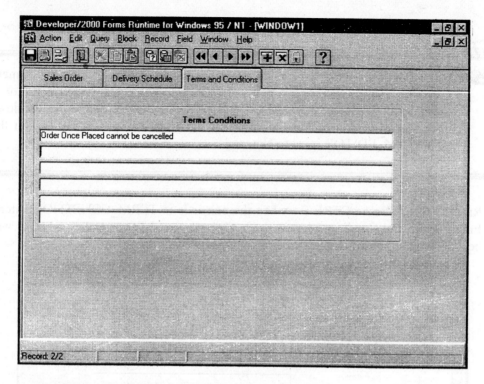

Diagram 8.19 : Terms and Conditions displayed in the Text Item

PROBLEMS IN USING THE BUTTON PALETTE BLOCK FOR DATA MANIPULATION

As seen earlier, once the data blocks are created and validation code written, the next step is to create the *button_palette* block that includes a number of push buttons that are used for data navigation and manipulation.

 Note

 Any item placed on a tab page will be displayed only for that tab page. Thus in case of a form which displays two tab pages, two sets of push buttons must be created **one set for each tab page**.

A more workable approach is a new canvas that looks like a vertical or horizontal toolbar. Data manipulation and navigation push buttons can be created and placed on this canvas. The type of canvas that resembles a horizontal toolbar is called '**Horizontal Toolbar Canvas**' and the type of canvas that resembles a vertical toolbar is called '**Vertical Toolbar Canvas**'.

The push buttons placed on the toolbar canvas in turn can be associated with a data block via program code. This technique gives a set of push buttons being used to control data navigation and / or manipulation on a form that has multiple tab pages.

Creating a horizontal toolbar canvas and placing push buttons on it:

1. Select the **Canvases** node in the Object Navigator and click on **Navigator..Create**. A new canvas with the default name will be created.

2. Open the Property Palette of the new canvas and set the following properties:

Name	: Buttons_Can
Canvas Type	: Horizontal Toolbar
Height	: 23

    Close the Property Palette. The newly created canvas will be displayed as shown in diagram 8.20.

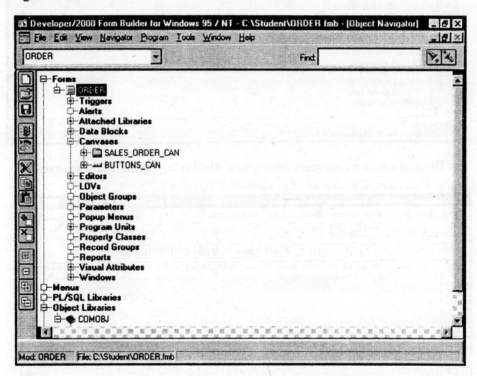

Diagram 8.20 : New Horizontal Toolbar canvas displayed in Object Navigator

3. Select **Data Blocks** node in the Object Navigator and click on **Navigator..Create** to create a new block. *New Data Block* dialog box asking for confirmation to use the Data block wizard is displayed. *Since the new block is not a data block, the block must be created manually.* To do so, select *Build a New Block Manually* option and click on OK. A new block with the default name is displayed. Change the name of the block to *Button_Palette*.

4. Click on **Tools..Layout Editor** to open the Layout editor. Since the current form includes two canvases, the *Canvases* dialog box is displayed with a list of available canvases as shown in diagram 8.21. Select *button_can* and click on OK.

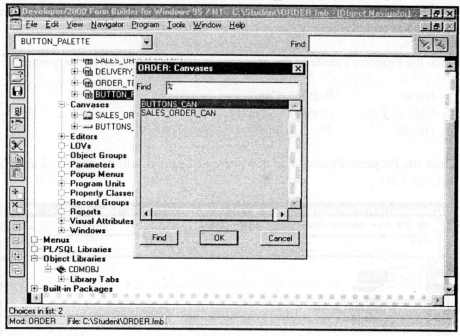

Diagram 8.21 : Canvases dialog box displaying Available Canvases

5. Button_Can canvas is displayed as shown in diagram 8.22.

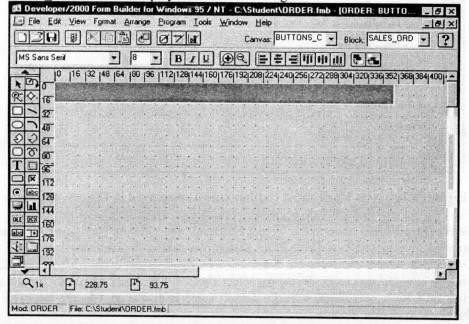

Diagram 8.22 : Button_Can displayed in Layout Editor

6. From the item palette on the left of the layout editor select a *push button* item and place it on the canvas displayed in the Layout Editor. Change the Name and the Label property of the push button to *pb_view* and *View* respectively.

   Similarly place required number of push buttons as shown in the table below and set the *Name* and the *label* property of each pushbutton.

Push Button Name	Label	Push Button Name	Label
pb_add	Add	pb_exit	Exit
pb_view	View	pb_first	First
pb_modify	Modify	pb_prior	Prior
pb_delete	Delete	pb_next	Next
pb_save	Save	pb_last	Last

7. The push buttons included in any form must have the same width, height and background color. Each push button must also be iconic. The properties of the form objects can be standardized using a user-defined property class. A property class named *PClass_Button* is already created. The properties in the property class are as follows:

Name	: PClass_Button
Width	: 23
Height	: 23
Iconic	: Yes
Background Color	: Gray

   Connect this property class to the push buttons and instant standardization of the push buttons is available.

Note

Property class *PClass_Button* is included in *Comobj.olb* object library.

Open *Comobj.olb* object library by clicking on **File..Open**. Forms Builder displays *File Open* dialog box. Select the object library file and click on *Open*.

Object library is displayed in the Object library. Click on the '+' next to the *Library Tabs* node. The library tabs are displayed. Click on **Tools..Object Library** menu items. The *Library Tabs* node is opened and the objects in the first library tab are displayed. Since the property classes were stored in the Pclass tab at the time of creation, the *Pclass* tab must be selected. The objects in the Pclass tab are displayed. Drag and drop property class *PClass_Button* on the Property Classes node of the current form displayed in the Object Navigator.

8. Confirmation to Subclass or copy the dragged object is asked for. Click on *Subclass*. A reference to the property class object in the object library is created and displays the property class in the property class node of the challan form.

9. To attach *PClass_Button* object to the buttons, select the pushbuttons one at a time in the *button_palette* block button and open the property sheet. Select the *SubClass Information* property. It displays **More...** as the property value. Click on **More...** *SubClass Information* dialog box is displayed. Select **Property Class** radio button. *SubClass Information* dialog box now displays two properties i.e. *Property Class Name* and *Module Name*. Set the property class name to *PClass_Button* using the list available.

10. Setting the *Iconic* property to 'Yes', enables display of pictures on the face of the button. Select each push buttons individually and set the *Icon Name* property as follows.

Button Name	Icon Name
pb_search	c:\orawin95\tools\devdem20\bin\icon\rt_quer1
pb_view	c:\orawin95\tools\devdem20\bin\icon\rt_quer2
pb_first	c:\orawin95\tools\devdem20\bin\icon\rt_rec1
pb_prior	c:\orawin95\tools\devdem20\bin\icon\rt_rec2
pb_next	c:\orawin95\tools\devdem20\bin\icon\rt_rec3
pb_last	c:\orawin95\tools\devdem20\bin\icon\rt_rec4
pb_add	c:\orawin95\tools\devdem20\bin\icon\rt_radd
pb_delete	c:\orawin95\tools\devdem20\bin\icon\rt_rdel
pb_modify	c:\orawin95\tools\devdem20\bin\icon\clear
pb_save	c:\orawin95\tools\devdem20\bin\icon\rt_save
pb_exit	c:\orawin95\tools\devdem20\bin\icon\exit

11. Open the Layout Editor. Align the push buttons as shown in them as shown in the diagram 8.23.

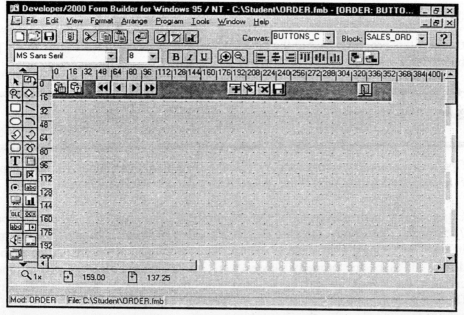

Diagram 8.23 : Iconic Push Buttons displayed in the Layout Editor

12. Since the triggers for the items in the *Button_Palette* reference two common procedures i.e. *scroll_control* and *item_enable_disable* which are included in the PL/SQL library named *SalesLib.pll*, the *SalesLib.pll* library must be attached to the form.

Attach the library by clicking on the *Attached Library* node in the Object Navigator. Forms Builder displays the *Attach Library* dialog box. Enter the library name as *C:\Student\SalesLib.pll*. Click on *Attach*.

13. Write PL/SQL code blocks in the WHEN-BUTTON-PRESSED trigger of each of the push buttons.

Note

The PL/SQL code must be written for Data Navigation and manipulation operations performed on the current data block.

When any push button is clicked, the sequence of operations is as follows:

- The form cursor moves out of the data block and is positioned on the clicked push button. The current item is the clicked push button and the current block is *button_palette*.
- PL/SQL code in the When-Button-Pressed trigger is executed.

When the form cursor navigates from the data block to the *button_palette* block the current data block name is lost and *thus data navigation and / or manipulation operations cannot be performed*.

To avoid this the cursor must not move from the current block to the *button_palette* block when any of the push buttons in the button palette blocks is clicked. To achieve this, the **Mouse Navigate** property must be set to **No** (i.e. Do not Navigate to the object that is clicked) for each push button on the toolbar canvas.

Tip

When **Mouse Navigate** property is set to '**No**' default navigation to the push button is stopped. Thus the form cursor will still be in the data block. in the When-Button-Pressed trigger will be executed. But while the form cursor stays on the data block, the when-button-pressed trigger will fire.

This is because form cursor navigation and firing of when-button-pressed trigger on the push button are two isolated form processes.

This eliminates the code for moving to an appropriate data block written in the when-button-pressed trigger of the push buttons.

Open the property Palette of each push button and set the Mouse Navigate Property to 'No' as shown in diagram 8.24.

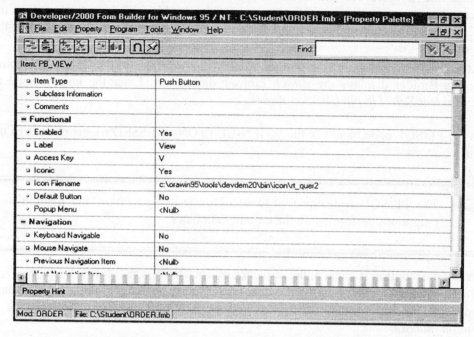

Diagram 8.24 : Setting Mouse Navigate property to No

TRIGGERS

Trigger Name	: **WHEN-BUTTON-PRESSED**	Form	: order
Block	: button_palette	Item	: pb_view
Trigger Level	: Item Level		
Function	: Retrieve all the records from the master and detail tables.		
Text	: BEGIN		

```
        /* Execute query retrieves records for the current block. */
        execute_query ;

        /* If the current block is master block then updateable property
        of the master and all the detail blocks must be set to property
        off */
    if :system.cursor_block = 'SALES_ORDER' then
        item_enable_disable('sales_order',property_off);
        item_enable_disable('sales_order_details', property_off);
        item_enable_disable('delivery_schedule', property_off);
        item_enable_disable('order_termsconditions', property_off);
    else
        /* The current block's property must be set to property false */
        item_enable_disable(:system.cursor_block, property_off);
    end if;
END ;
```

Trigger Name	: **WHEN-BUTTON-PRESSED**	Form	: order
Block	: button_palette	Item	: pb_search
Trigger Level	: Item Level		
Function	: Retrieve all the records from the master and detail tables.		
Text	: BEGIN		

/* *Enter query sets the form in query mode waiting for user input for search value.*

*Press F8 after entering required values in the text items, the user must. Oracle Forms generates a query with a **WHERE** clause as text item 'name' = value entered. The Forms tool then executes the query and retrieves appropriate records.*

PL/SQL code written after a call to enter_query will be executed only after exiting the query mode. */

```
enter_query ;

/* After executing the query, the mode of operation is View and
   thus all the items must be non-updateable */
if :system.cursor_block = 'SALES_ORDER' then
        item_enable_disable('sales_order', property_off);
        item_enable_disable('sales_order_details', property_off);
        item_enable_disable('delivery_schedule', property_off);
        item_enable_disable('order_termsconditions', property_off);
else
        item_enable_disable(:system.cursor_block, property_off);
end if;
END ;
```

Trigger Name	: **WHEN-BUTTON-PRESSED**	Form	: order
Block	: button_palette	Item	: pb_first
Trigger Level	: Item Level		
Function	: Move to the first record in the current block.		
Text	: BEGIN		

```
        first_record;
END ;
```

Trigger Name	: **WHEN-BUTTON-PRESSED**	Form	: order
Block	: button_palette	Item	: pb_prior
Trigger Level	: Item Level		
Function	: Move to the previous record in the current block.		
Text	: BEGIN		

```
        previous_record;
END ;
```

Trigger Name	: **WHEN-BUTTON-PRESSED**	Form	: order
Block	: button_palette	Item	: pb_next
Trigger Level	: Item Level		
Function	: Move to the next record in the current block.		
Text	: BEGIN		

```
            next_record;
        END ;
```

Trigger Name	: **WHEN-BUTTON-PRESSED**	Form	: order
Block	: button_palette	Item	: pb_last
Trigger Level	: Item Level		
Function	: Move to the last record in the current block.		
Text	: BEGIN		

```
            last_record;
        END ;
```

Trigger Name	: **WHEN-BUTTON-PRESSED**	Form	: order
Block	: button_palette	Item	: pb_add
Trigger Level	: Item Level		
Function	: Add a blank record in the current block and enable all the fields.		
Text	: BEGIN		

```
        /* Insert a new record in the current block and position the
           cursor on the newly inserted record */
        create_record ;

        if :system.cursor_block = 'SALES_ORDER' then
                item_enable_disable('sales_order',property_on);
                item_enable_disable('sales_order_details', property_on);
                item_enable_disable('delivery_schedule', property_on);
                item_enable_disable('order_termsconditions', property_on);
        else
                item_enable_disable(:system.cursor_block, property_on);
        end if;
        END ;
```

Trigger Name	: **WHEN-BUTTON-PRESSED**	Form	: order
Block	: button_palette	Item	: pb_delete
Trigger Level	: Item Level		
Function	: delete current record in the current block.		
Text	: BEGIN		

```
            delete_record ;
        END ;
```

Trigger Name	: **WHEN-BUTTON-PRESSED**
Block	: button_palette
Trigger Level	: Item Level
Function	: Enable the fields so that it can be modified.
Text	: DECLARE

Form : order
Item : pb_modify

```
DECLARE
        blk_name varchar2(60);
        str_itemname varchar2(60);
        itemtype varchar2(60);
        itemcanvas varchar2(60);
BEGIN
        blk_name := :system.cursor_block;
        if blk_name = 'SALES_ORDER' then
                item_enable_disable('sales_order', property_on);
                item_enable_disable('sales_order_details', property_on);
                item_enable_disable('delivery_schedule', property_on);
                item_enable_disable('order_termsconditions', property_on);
                set_item_property('sales_order.s_order_no',
                                        updateable, property_on);
                set_item_property('sales_order_details.product_no',
                        updateable, property_off);
        else
            item_enable_disable(:system.cursor_block, property_on);
            str_itemname := blk_name || '.' ||
                        get_block_property(blk_name, first_item);
            loop
                itemtype := get_item_property(str_itemname, item_type);
                itemcanvas := get_item_property(str_itemname, item_canvas);
                if itemtype <> 'DISPLAY ITEM' and
                        itemcanvas is not null then
                    if get_item_property(str_itemname, primary_key) = 'TRUE' then
                        set_item_property(str_itemname, updateable,
                                        property_off);
                    end if;
                end if;
                str_itemname := blk_name || '.' ||
                    get_item_property(str_itemname, next_navigation_item);
                if (str_itemname = blk_name||'.ROWID') then
                    exit;
                end if;
            end loop;
        end if;
END ;
```

Trigger Name	: **WHEN-BUTTON-PRESSED**	Form	: order
Block	: button_palette	Item	: pb_save
Trigger Level	: Item Level		
Function	: Delete current record in the current block.		
Text	: BEGIN		

```
            if :system.form_status = 'CHANGED' THEN
                /* If the form status is changed then commit changes */
                commit_form ;
                if :system.form_status = 'QUERY' then
                    item_enable_disable('sales_order', property_off);
                    item_enable_disable('sales_order_details', property_off);
                    item_enable_disable('delivery_schedule', property_off);
                    item_enable_disable('order_termsconditions', property_off);
                end if ;
            end if;
        END ;
```

Trigger Name	: **WHEN-BUTTON-PRESSED**	Form	: order
Block	: button_palette	Item	: pb_exit
Trigger Level	: Item Level		
Function	: Close Application		
Text	: DECLARE		

```
            answer number;
        BEGIN
            if :system.form_status = 'CHANGED' then
                set_alert_property('confirm_alert',title,'Save Changes');
                set_alert_property('confirm_alert',alert_message_text,
                    'Would you like to make Changes Permanent ?');
                answer := show_alert('confirm_alert');
                if answer = ALERT_BUTTON1 then
                        commit_form;
                else
                        exit_form(No_Validate);
                end if;
            else
                exit_form;
            end if;
        END ;
```

SELF REVIEW QUESTIONS

TRUE OR FALSE

1. Summary items can either be defined in the control block or in a block with '*Query All Records*' property set to Yes.

   A) True   B) False

2. Items placed on a specific tab page are visible only on the tab page on which the items are placed.

   A) True   B) False

FILL IN THE BLANKS

1. The type of canvas that can include multiple pages is called _____.

2. A New Tab Page is created in the Layout wizard if the Tab Page property is set to _____.

3. An item that can display a set of values to select from is called _____ item.

4. Each List Element comprises of
   - _____

   - _____

5. The List styles available for a List Item are
   - _____

   - _____

   - _____

6. List Elements can be added using the _____ property in the property sheet.

7. A list item can be populated at runtime using _____ object.

8. _____ function is used to create a record from an SQL Select statement.

9. _____ function is used to populate the record group.

10. _____ function is used to populate a list item from a record group.

11. When an object is created a unique _____ is assigned.

12. _____ function is used to check whether the object was created or not.

13. _____ trigger is associated with list item.

14. The calculation mode property can taken following values:
   - _____
   - _____
   - _____

15. _____ property is used to specify the expression for the formula column.

16. The properties that must be set for the summary column are:
   - _____
   - _____
   - _____

17. In a Multi-Record block, the summary item defined in the same block must be displayed only once. To do so _____ property must be set.

18. If summary columns are used, all records must be retrieved to calculate the summary value. To do so the _____ property must be set to Yes.

19. The name of the current form name can be known by using _____ function.

20. _____ property is used to enable or disable form validations at runtime.

21. User defined editors are created in the _____ node of the forms module.

22. _____ Oracle parameter is used to define the system editor.

23. To ensure that the cursor does not move from the data block to the push button when the push button is clicked the _____ property must be set to No.

A QUICK REVIEW

Need for a Tab Canvas

Creating a Tab Canvas

Adding Tab Pages to the Tab Canvas

Creating and Using a List Item
- Changing the Item Type to List Item
- Populating a List Item with Static values entered at design time.
- Populating a List Item by specifying a Select Statement in PL/SQL code
- The When-List-Changed Trigger

Working with Formula and Summary Columns

Creating and Using an Editor
- Working with the System Editor
- Creating an Editor and Attaching the editor to an Item

Creating Horizontal Toolbar Canvas
- The need to Place Push Buttons on another Canvas
- Creating a New canvas of the type Horizontal Toolbar
- Placing Buttons on the Horizontal Toolbar canvas
- Setting the Mouse Navigation Property of Push Buttons items

Duplicate check in the Form Buffer

CHAPTER NINE

Interlinking Related Forms and Passing Parameters Between Forms

IN THIS CHAPTER

> Need for Interlinking Forms

> The 'Calling' and 'Called' Forms

> Opening the 'Called' Form and Passing Parameters from the calling Form to the called Form

> Types of Parameters

> Conditionally Retrieving records by Setting the Default_Where Block Property at Runtime

9. INTERLINKING RELATED FORMS AND PASSING PARAMETERS BETWEEN FORMS

A sales transaction starts when a client places an order. When an order is received, the client's details are recorded in the *client_master* table. Information regarding the orders received from the client is recorded in the *sales_order* and *sales_order_details* tables.

The information in the *sales_order* and the *client_master* table is linked using a common column like *client_no*.

As per the delivery schedule specified in the sales order, material will be delivered to the client on a specific date and at a specified destination. Each time material is delivered to the client a delivery challan will be generated and delivery challan information will be recorded in the *challan_header* and *challan_details* table. A delivery challan is based on the sales order. Thus each sales order is linked to the one or more delivery challans by using a common column called *s_order_no*. The relation between the *client_master* table, the *sales_order* and the *challan_header* tables can be shown as follows:

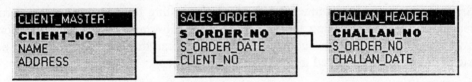

When designing forms based commercial applications for such an entity relationship the *client* form should allow the processing of information for the *sales_order* and the *sales_order_details* tables as well.

This can be achieved in a number of ways. The techniques that can be applied are:
- Extra data aware blocks linked to the *sales_order* and *sales_order_details* tables respectively can be created in the *client* form itself. Thus all the three tables will be manipulated via a single form.
- A commonly used, commercial application development technique is to create separate forms. Data in the *client_master* table can be manipulated using the <u>*client data entry form*</u> and Data in the *sales_order* and *sales_order_details* tables can be manipulated using the <u>*order data entry form*</u>.

When required the *order data entry form* can be called from the *client data entry form*. Here the *client data entry form* can be viewed as the '**calling form**' and the *order data entry form* can be viewed as the '**called form**'. This can be programmed to occur when a push button labeled and placed appropriately on the calling form is pressed.

When the *order data entry form* is called the *'client_no'* from the current record in the *client data entry form* must be passed to the *order data entry form* so that from that moment onwards a sales order will be linked to a specific client.

This chapter will focus on simple but essential techniques available in Oracle Forms Builder used for:

- Calling one form from another.
- Passing vital information from the 'calling form' to the 'called form'. In this case vital information will be passed from the *client data entry form* to the *order data entry form*.

OPENING ANOTHER FORM FROM THE CURRENT FORM

The OPEN_FORM or the CALL_FORM procedure is used to open a form from the current form. Forms can be opened in one of two modes:

- Document
- Dialog

Document Form:

If the form is opened in document mode, both the calling form and the called form are independent. A list displaying the name of the window associated with each form is shown under the WINDOWS sub menu. These forms can be accessed by clicking on the name of the window displayed in the WINDOW sub menu.

The OPEN_FORM function opens the form in document mode.

Dialog Form:

If the form is opened in dialog mode, the calling form can be accessed only after the called form is closed. The calling form is also known as **Parent Form** and the called form is known as **Child Form**.

The CALL_FORM function opens the form in dialog mode.

PASSING PARAMETERS TO THE CALLED FORM

As seen earlier, interlinking between forms can be achieved by opening required forms from the current form and passing required information to the called form.

When opening related forms, in a commercial application it is appropriate that the mode of operation in the called form and the calling form are the same.

Example:
If the mode of operation in the *client* form is QUERY, the mode of operation in the *order* form must also be QUERY and information regarding the sales orders placed by the current client must be retrieved from the table.

Similarly, if the mode of operation in the *client* form is INSERT, the mode of operation in the *order* form must also be INSERT and information pertaining to the current client must be set by the system in INSERT mode.

Thus the *mode of operation* must be passed to the *order* form. The *client_no* associated with the current client must also be passed to the *order* form. The *client_no* passed from the *client* form can then be used to retrieve corresponding order information if the mode of operation is QUERY. If the mode of operation is INSERT, *client_no* can be used to set the value of the text item associated with the *client_no* column in the *sales_order* table.

Parameter values from a calling form can be passed to a called form, when any form is invoked by using the OPEN_FORM or CALL_FORM procedures.

The basic steps in parameter passing are:
- Creating a list of parameters in the calling form and passing the list of parameters to the called form using the OPEN_FORM or CALL_FORM procedure.
- Defining parameters in the called form and using them to accept values from the list of parameters passed by the calling form.
- Referencing the values held in the parameters defined in the called form.

Specifying the Parameter List in the Calling Form:

Parameters can be passed from a calling form to the called form by using an object called parameter **list**. A Parameter list is a three-column data structure that contains the name, the type (*Text_Parameter* or *Data_Parameter*) and the value of each parameter added to the parameter list.

Example:
The parameter list used to pass the mode of operation and the client_no to the order form will be created as follows:

Parameter Name	Parameter Type	Parameter Value
P_mode	Text_Parameter	INSERT
P_client_no	Text_Parameter	C00001

◄——— Parameter List

The steps in passing these parameters from a calling form to the called form are:
- Create a Parameter list object
- Add parameters to the parameter list
- Pass the parameter list to the called form via the *open_form ( )* or the *call_form ( )* oracle procedure.

Creating a Parameter List:

A Built-in package procedure named CREATE_PARAMETER_LIST creates a parameter list and returns the memory address (i.e. specific location) of the parameter list. A variable of type PARAMLIST must be declared to hold the memory address (i.e. a pointer) returned by the function. The variable declaration is as follows:

        DECLARE
                client_param_list paramlist;

Each parameter list created using CREATE_PARAMETER_LIST( ) must be assigned a unique name. The parameter list name must be passed as an argument to the CREATE_PARAMETER_LIST( ) procedure as explained below. A parameter list can then be referenced by its 'Name' or the 'Variable' that holds the pointer to the parameter list.

Example:
Create a parameter list named *client_list* and assign the pointer value to the variable named *client_param_list*.

        client_param_list := create_parameter_list('client_list');

Tip

If the creation of parameter list is successful, a unique object id is assigned to the parameter list. This object id will then be assigned to the variable client_param_list.

If parameter list creation fails the object id will be NULL and as such NULL will be assigned to the variable client_param_list. Hence the ID_NULL( ) function can be used to check if the parameter list is created successfully or not. If ID_NULL(client_param_list) returns FALSE the parameter list is created successfully else its creation has failed.

Adding Parameters to a Parameter List:

A Built-in package procedure ADD_PARAMETER adds parameters to the parameter list. This procedure accepts the following parameters:
- Name of the parameter list (The Parameter List variable can also be specified)
- The Name of the parameter
- The Type of parameter
- The Value of the parameter

Types of Parameters:
Parameters added to the parameter list can be used to pass a single value to the called form. Alternatively parameters can be used to pass a record group or a set of records to the called form. The parameter type determines whether the parameter can hold a single value or can hold a record group. The Parameters type can be any one of the following:
- TEXT_PARAMETER.
- DATA_PARAMETER

Text Parameter:
When a **single value** is passed as a parameter to the called form, the parameter type must be set to 'TEXT_PARAMETER'.

Note

 'TEXT_PARAMETER' can store values with a maximum length of 255 characters. The Data Type for a 'TEXT_PARAMETER is always CHAR.

Example:
When *client_no* 'C00001' is passed as a parameter from the *client* form to the *order* form the Parameter Type, set for a parameter will be 'TEXT_PARAMETER'.

Data Parameter:
When a record group is being passed as a parameter, the parameter type must be set to 'DATA_PARAMETER'.

Note

 The **value** for a DATA_PARAMETER will be a string specifying the name of a record group defined in the calling form.

Example:

Create a parameter list named *client_list* and assign the memory address of the parameter list to a memory variable called *client_param_list*. Add a parameter named *p_client_no* and specify its value as 'C00001'. Since a single value is being passed as a parameter, the type of parameter will be 'TEXT_PARAMETER'.

```
DECLARE
    client_param_list paramlist;
BEGIN
    client_param_list := create_parameter_list ('client_list');
    add_parameter(client_param_list, 'p_client_no',
            text_parameter, 'C00001');
END;
```

Tip

Multiple parameters can be added to a parameter list by calling the *add_parameter( )* procedure for each parameter that must be added to the parameter list.

Passing the Parameter List to the Called Form:

After creating a parameter list and populating its parameters with appropriate values, the form to which the parameters are to be passed must be opened. A form can be opened using OPEN_FORM( ) **or** CALL_FORM( ) procedures. The name of the form must be passed as an argument to any of these procedures as in

OPEN_FORM('order.fmx');

The parameter list is to be passed as the *last argument* to the OPEN_FORM( ) or the CALL_FORM( ) procedure. *The name of the form is the only mandatory argument to any of these procedures*. To ensure that the last position is maintained, all other parameters, normally optional to the OPEN_FORM( ) or the CALL_FORM ( ) procedure become mandatory. The values for these arguments are pre-defined by Oracle Forms and thus null values are not allowed. The complete syntax for opening the form and passing parameter list is:

CALL_FORM('form name', display, switch menu, query mode, ***parameter list***) ;

The arguments specified in the CALL_FORM( ) procedure are as follows:

Display:
This argument can be set to HIDE or NO_HIDE. If this argument is set to HIDE, the calling form will be made invisible before calling the called form. If this argument is set to NO_HIDE, the called form will be opened without hiding the calling form.

Switch Menu:
This argument can be set to NO_REPLACE or DO_REPLACE. If this argument is set to NO_REPLACE, the menu of the called form will not be replaced with the menu of the calling form. If this argument is set to DO_REPLACE, the menu of the called form will be replaced with the menu of the calling form.

Query Mode:
This argument can be set to NO_QUERY_ONLY or QUERY_ONLY. If this argument is set to QUERY_ONLY, the called form is opened for query purpose only. If this argument is set to NO_QUERY_ONLY, the called form can be used for data insertion, updation, deletion and viewing.

Parameter List:
This argument must be set to the name of the parameter list created using CREATE_PARAMETER( ) function.

Along with the above-mentioned arguments, if the called form and the calling form use PL/SQL libraries, an additional parameter called *Data Mode* can be specified.

Data Mode:
If the called form and the calling form share the same set of libraries by default, the form runtime tool loads multiple copies of the library file i.e. one copy for every form. Thus, the memory resources of the system are inefficiently used. If same set of libraries are attached to the called form and the calling form, the *Data Mode* argument can be set to SHARE_LIBRARY_DATA. This ensures that only one copy of the PL/SQL library is loaded and used by both the forms. The system resources are thus efficiently used.

If different set of libraries are attached the forms then the *Data Mode* argument can be set to NO_SHARE_LIBRARY_DATA.

Tip

 Data Mode argument is set to NO_SHARE_LIBRARY_DATA by default.

Defining Parameters in the Called Form:

Values passed by the calling form to the Called Form must be stored in special variables that can be accessed by any PL/SQL code used in the Called Form. Variables that hold these values passed from the Calling Form are called **Parameters**.

Each parameter has the following properties:
- Parameter Name
- Data Type
- Maximum Length
- Default Value.

These parameters can be created in the **Parameters Node** of the Called Form. The parameter node is found in the Object Navigator in Forms Builder.

The steps in defining parameters in the Called Form are as follows:

1. Ensure that the Called Form is open in the Forms Builder tool. Select the **Parameters Node** in the Called Form via the Object Navigator and click on **Navigator..Create** menu option. A new parameter is created as shown in diagram 9.1.

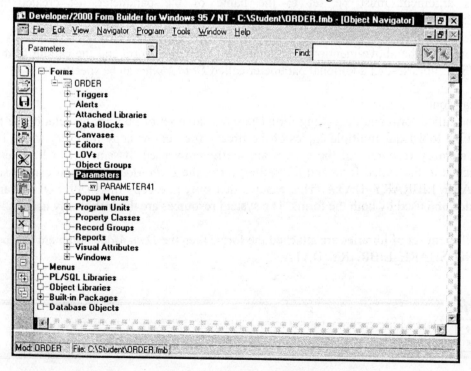

Diagram 9.1 : New Parameter created in the Parameters Node

2. Open the property sheet of the parameter and specify the Name, Data Type and Maximum Length of the parameter as shown in diagram 9.2.

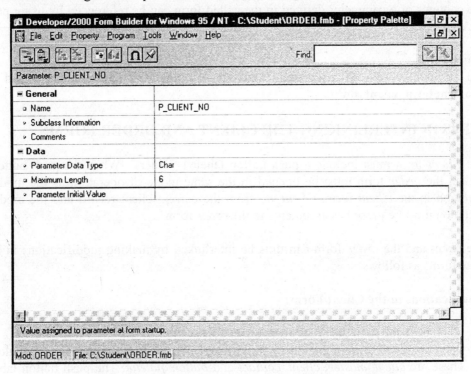

Diagram 9.2 : Setting the Properties of the Parameter

Tip

Following Rules must be followed when defining parameters in the called form:

- The names of the parameters defined in the called form must be identical to the names of the parameters added to the parameter list using *add_parameter( )* procedure in the calling form.
- The number of parameters in the called form must be the same as the number of parameters added to the parameter list defined in the calling form.

Note

If the calling form is passing a single parameter named *p_client_no*, the number of parameters defined in the called form must be <u>one</u> and the name of that parameter must be *p_client_no*.

Using the Parameters in the Called Form:

The contents of a parameter defined in the called form can be referenced by using prefix '**:PARAMETER**' before the parameter name.

Example:
The contents of a parameter named *p_client_no* can be accessed as '**:parameter.p_client_no**'.

STEPS IN INTERLINKING THE CLIENT AND ORDER FORMS

The *Client* form must include a push button labeled 'Orders'. When the push button is clicked the *order* form must be opened in the same mode of operation as the mode of operation in the *Client* form. *Client_no* from the current client record and the mode of operation must be passed as arguments to the *order* form.

The *client* and the *order* form can thus be interlinked by making modifications in both these forms as follows:

Modifications in the Client Form:

The changes required in the *client* form are as follows:
1. Open the *client* form in the Forms Builder tool. The *client* form includes three blocks. These are *client_master*, *client_contact* and *button_palette*. The push button labeled 'Orders' must be added to the button_palette block.

2. Click on **Tools..Layout Editor** to open the layout editor. Select *button_palette* block, as the push button labeled 'Orders' must be added to this block.

3. Place a push button on the form layout and set the following properties.

    Name : Pb_Orders
    Label : Orders

The completed screen will be as shown in diagram 9.3.

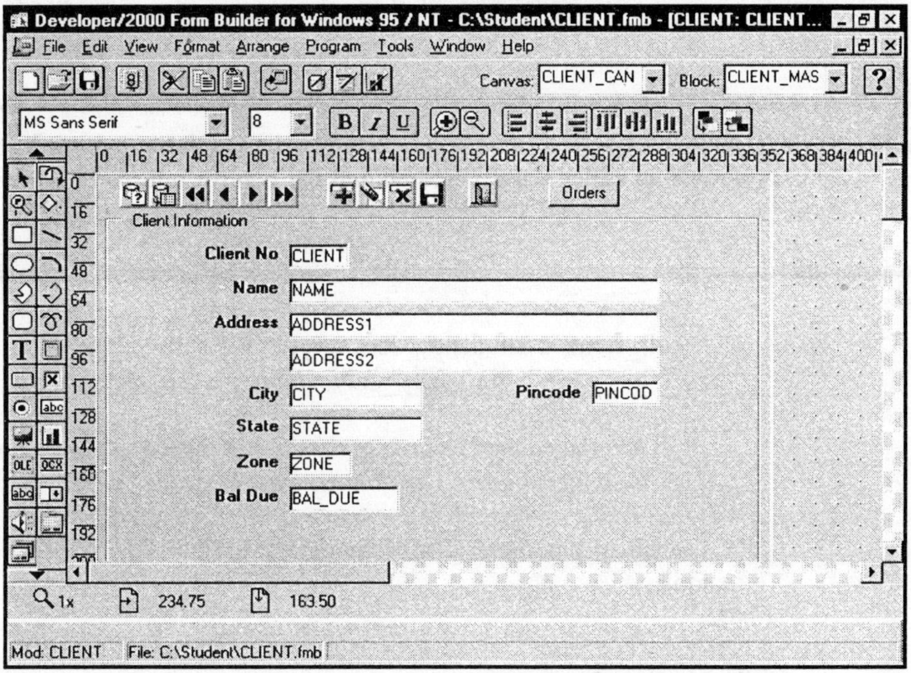

Diagram 9.3 : Push Button placed on the Form Layout

4.   Write required PL/SQL code in the *When-Button-Pressed* trigger of pb_orders.

Trigger Name	: **WHEN-BUTTON-PRESSED**	Form	: client
Block	: button_palette	Item	: pb_orders
Trigger Level	: Item Level		
Function	: To open the order form and pass client_no and mode of operation as parameter to the order form.		
Text	: DECLARE		

```
          order_param_list paramlist;
      BEGIN
              order_param_list := create_parameter_list('order_list');
              if not id_null(order_param_list) then
                      add_parameter(order_param_list, 'p_client_no',
                              text_parameter, :client_no);
                      add_parameter(order_param_list, 'p_mode',
                              text_parameter, :system.record_status);
```

/ Call_form is used to open order form. It takes the
form name(along with the path) as the parameter. */*

Note

PL/SQL code lines defined after a call to the CALL_FORM ( ) procedure will
be executed when called form is exited and the control returns to the calling
form.

call_form(' c:\student\order.fmx', no_hide, no_replace,
no_query_only, ***client_param_list***);

/ When the control returns to the calling form, the parameter list
is no longer required and thus it must be destroyed. */*

destroy_parameter_list(order_param_list);
      end if;
END;

5. Save and compile the client form.

6. Open the order form.

7. Two parameters must be created in the order form and the properties of the sales
order block must be set as per the mode of operation for the client form.

Select Parameter Node and click on **Navigator..Create** to create a new parameter. A
New parameter with a default name will be created. Set the following properties of
the parameter created.

Name   : p_client_no
Data Type   : Char
Maximum Length   : 6

8. Similarly create another parameter and set the following properties:

Name   : p_mode
Data Type   : Char
Maximum Length   : 10

The Object Navigator with the completed **Parameters** Node is displayed in diagram 9.4.

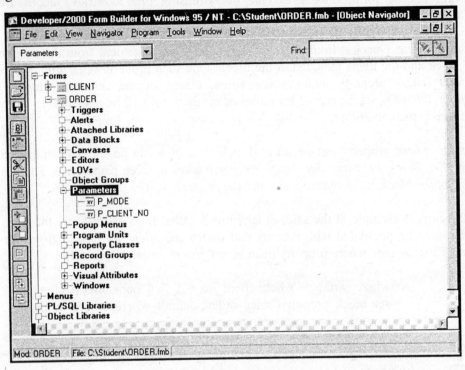

Diagram 9.4 : Object Navigator displaying Parameters in the Parameter Node

9. Write required PL/SQL code in the order form to handle a 'View' operation.

Trigger Name   : **WHEN-NEW-FORM-INSTANCE**   Form   : order

Block   :   Item   :

Trigger Level   : Form Level

Function   : If p_mode is set to 'QUERY', the default_where property of the sales_order block must be set to *client_no = 'client_no passed as parameter'*. An execute_query must then be fired for the sales_order block.
parameter to the order form.

Text   : DECLARE

       where_string varchar2(40);

   BEGIN

      if :parameter.p_mode = 'QUERY' then

         where_string := 'where client_no = ' || "" ||

               :parameter.p_client_no || "" ;

        set_block_property('sales_order', default_where, where_string) ;

        execute_query;

      end if ;

   END ;

If the mode of operation in the client form is QUERY, the mode of operation must be QUERY in order form. Thus, an *execute_query* must be fired to retrieve records from the *sales_order* table.

When *Execute_Query* is fired, Oracle creates the select statement from the properties of the block and the items included in the block. One such property is *Default_Where*. The *Default_Where* property includes the where clause of the select statement. If the *Default_Where* is set the record set retrieved on the form will be restricted to the records that satisfy the condition the *Default_Where* clause.

Default_Where property can be set at design time or it can be set programmatically by using *Set_Block_Property*. *Set_Block_Property* takes in three parameters. These are the *name of the block*, the *property name* and the *property value*.

In the current example, if the sales order form is called from client form, the sales order block must be populated with records that match the *client_no* passed from the client form. Thus, *default_where* property must be set programmatically as follows:

where_string := 'where client_no = ' || "" || :parameter.p_client_no || "" ;
set_block_property('sales_order', default_where, where_string);

Tip

order.fmb form has been being saved in a directory named '*Student*' in Drive 'C'. When compiled it creates a file named *order.fmx* in the same directory. When calling the form, please specify a sub-directory and / or path in which the form was saved as a file appropriate to the computer being worked on.

Note

Value for a varchar2 column when included in the where clause must be enclosed in single quotes. Thus single quotes becomes a part of the string as.

where client_no = 'C00001'

As seen in the above example, the value in the where clause is enclosed in the single quotes.

Note

> By default a single quote is used to enclose character values as part of syntax. Thus single quotes do not become a part of the string itself. To include single quotes as a part of the string *each quote included in the string* must be represented as *two single quotes* as part of proper syntax.

Use of single quotes can be explained by using a set of variables and the syntax for assignment as follows:

Syntax Used for assignment	Contents of the variables
Var1 := 'where client_no = ' ;	where client_no =
Var2 := '''' /* two single quotes enclosed inside single quotes. */	' /* Output is a single quote */
Var3 := 'C00001'	C00001
Var4 := '''' /* two single quotes enclosed inside single quotes. */	' /* Output is a single quote */
Concatenation of all above variables	Where client_no = 'C00001'

Note

> It is assumed that variables used in the above example are defined of type varchar2. *Any assignments to a varchar2 variable must be done using single quotes.*

10. Write required PL/SQL code in the order form to handle the add operation.

Trigger Name	: **WHEN-CREATE-RECORD**	Form	: order
Block	: sales_order	Item	:
Trigger Level	: Block Level		
Function	: If the order form is called from the client form, and a blank record is inserted, the *client_no* item must be set to the *p_client_no*.		
Text	: BEGIN		

```
        if :parameter.p_mode = 'INSERT' then
                :client_no := :parameter.p_client_no ;
        end if;
END ;
```

WHEN-CREATE_RECORD trigger fires when a blank record is inserted in the block. A blank record is inserted in the block under following circumstances.

- If no PL/SQL code is written, the form is opened in INSERT mode and thus a blank record is inserted.
- If *execute_query* does not retrieve any records from the table, a blank record is inserted.
- A blank record is inserted by clicking on the add push button.

Note

If the *order* form is executed as a standalone form, parameter *p_mode* will be set to NULL. Thus the code required for the integration of the *client* and *order* form will not be executed.

SELF REVIEW QUESTIONS

TRUE OR FALSE

1. Text_Parameter is used to pass a Record Group as a parameter.

    A) True   B) False

2. A Variable of Type ParameterList is required to create a parameter list.

    A) True   B) False

3. The name of the parameters in the called form and the calling form must be the same.

    A) True   B) False

FILL IN THE BLANKS

1. Forms can be opened in two modes. These are:
    *   _____
    *   _____

2. Calling Form is also called _____ Form.

3. Called Form is also called _____ Form.

4. Parameters are passed to the called form by using _____.

5. The _____ Function is used to check if a parameter List is created or not.

6. Text_Parameters are defined with the data type as _____ and a maximum length of _____.

7. If display argument in the call_form( ) procedure is set to _____, the calling form will be made invisible before calling the called form.

8. To open the form such that insert, update and delete are not allowed, the Query Mode property must be set to _____.

9. If the PL/SQL libraries between forms can be shared, the _____ argument in the call_form ( ) procedure must be set to _____.

10. Parameter List is divided into three sections. These are:

- _____

- _____

- _____

11. Data from a table can be retrieved conditionally by setting the _____ property for a data block.

12. A single quote can be included as a part of a string held in a varchar2 variable, by specifying _____ single quotes.

13. _____ trigger is fired when a blank record is inserted in a block.

PICK THE RIGHT OPTION

1. The number of parameters in the calling form and the called form must
    A) be same.
    B) can be different.

2. Parameter values can be referenced in the called form using
    A) :parameter.parametername
    B) :parametername
    C) :param.parametername

Need for Interlinking Related Forms

Concept of a 'Calling' and 'Called' Form

Opening a Form
- *Modes in which a form can be Opened*
- *Using Open_Form ( ) and Call_Form ( ) Procedures*
- *Sharing PL/SQL Libraries between Called Form and Calling Form*

Passing Parameters to the 'Called' Form
- *Creating a Parameter List in the Calling Form*
- *Checking whether the Parameter List is created or not*
- *Adding Parameters to the Parameter List*
- *Types of Parameters*
- *Passing Parameter List from the 'Calling' Form to the 'Called' Form*
- *Defining Parameters in the 'Called' Form to hold the values sent by the 'Calling' Form*
- *Referencing Parameter values in PL/SQL code blocks defined in the 'Called' Form*

CHAPTER TEN

User Defined Search Form

IN THIS CHAPTER

➢ Creating a User Defined Search Form that can be called from any data entry form

➢ Passing an SQL Statement as a parameter to the search form

➢ Setting Canvas and Window Properties

➢ Working with Global Variables

➢ Use of List Item Functions

10. USER DEFINED SEARCH FORM

INTRODUCTION

The data entry forms based on commercial applications are used for
- Data Manipulation - Insert, Update, Delete Operations
- Data Retrieval

The commonly used techniques for data retrieval are:
1. Use *execute_query* to retrieve data from the table without a where clause. This causes the Oracle engine to attempt to return all the rows of the base table to the form. Push buttons *first*, *prior*, *next* and *last* can be used to view data of choice. *This approach leads to a waste of computer and network resources*.

2. Use *enter_query* to reduce resource waste and retrieve data conditionally from a table. *Enter_query* clears the block and places the form in 'Query' mode. Search criteria can then be entered in any item or combination of items in a block. The F8 key or the 'execute' menu item can be used to generate an SQL statement with a where clause based on search criteria and retrieve data from the base table. An inherent drawback of this technique is that specific search criteria to be entered into a form needs to be *memorized*.

3. A method that displays values to choose from, based on values currently in the base table, will eliminate the drawback of the second technique.

   A specific value from those displayed can be selected conveniently. Based on the selected value, a matching data set can be retrieved from a base table. This technique thus results into less resource waste leading to efficient and low cost (of query) data retrieval from the base table.

   A search push button can be place on the data entry forms, both Master and Master / Detail which when clicked, displays a form with a set of appropriate values from a base table to choose from. Such a form could easily be understood as a 'Search' form that helps retrieve (search) the appropriate data set from a base table with the least load on resources.

The focus of the chapter is to achieve this functionality.

FOCUS - GENERIC SEARCH FORM

When the search button in any form is clicked, a pop up search form is displayed. The search form must display a list of values, which can be used to search for and retrieve a specific data set from a base table. When a value is selected and the OK button on the search window is clicked the search window closes. The selected value must be used to retrieve information from a table and display this information in the form used to 'call' the 'search' form.

The layout of the search form as displayed at runtime is as follows:

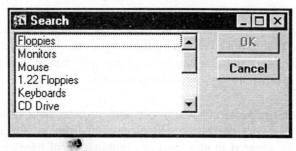

Diagram 10.1 : Layout of the Search Form displayed at Runtime

The objects included in the search form are:
- List Item named search_list
- A push button named pb_ok.
- A push button named pb_cancel

Each of these objects are used in the form as follows:
<u>List Item:</u>
The search form must display a list of values to select from. An item that allows selection from a list of values is called **List Item**.

When designing the search form, search values can be conveniently displayed in the search form are based on a table column on which a search done. For example, it is a common practice to search for a product based on the product description from the product / stock register.

A search on such descriptive column will be very easy for the end-user but time consuming for the Oracle engine. Data retrieval speed is faster if data set is retrieved based on a column which is a primary key or unique index.

The search form must be designed such that the advantage of both the speedy retrieval of data using unique column values and user friendliness is achieved. To facilitate such data retrieval, the list item provides two types of values. These are:
- Display Value
- Data Value

Display Value is a value that will be displayed on the form. Each Display value is associated with a Data Value which is a part of the list item but not displayed to the end-user. The end-user can then select a Display value from the list and PL/SQL code can be written to retrieve data based on the associated data value. Each combination of data value and display value is called a **List Element**.

Thus a list item must be populated with a set of values made of two parts i.e. a display value and a data value for each element in the list item.

The data value and the display value must be set based on the form from which the search form is called. The technique used for achieve this is:

- Design a search form for each data entry screen where the list item is populated using a specific pre-determined set of values from the base table.
- Create a generic form that can be called from any data entry screen. The list item's display and data values are determined by a 'Select Statement' passed as a parameter from the data entry screen. For example if the search form is called from the *product* form, the list item must be populated with *description* as **display** value and *product_no* as **data** value.

The search window called from the product form is as displayed in diagram 10.2.

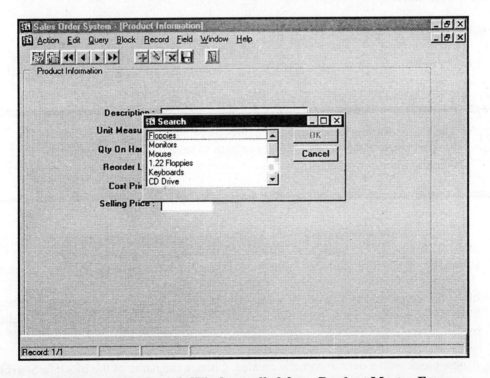

Diagram 10.2 : Search Window called from Product Master Form

Similarly, if the search window is called from the client form, the list item can be populated with *client name* as **display** value and *client_no* as the **data** value.

Note

A list item can be populated using a select statement that retrieves two columns. The first item is used as display value and the second column is used as data value. *Since the select statement will change based on the form that calls the search form, the select statement must be passed as a parameter to the search form.*

1. A ***push button*** labeled *OK.* The OK push button must be enabled only if the search value is selected. When the OK push button is clicked, the selected value must be sent to the calling form and the search window must be closed. This search value will then be used to retrieve data appropriately in the calling form.

2. A ***push button*** labeled *Cancel.* When the cancel push button is clicked, the search window must be closed and control must return to the calling form.

THE SOLUTION

Creating a User-Defined Search Form:

1. Open a new form and save the form as *search.fmb*.

Tip

The search form is being saved in a directory named '*Student*' in Drive 'C'. Please choose a sub-directory and / or path to save the file appropriate to the computer being worked on.

2. Click on the **Data Blocks** node in the Object Navigator and select **Navigator..Create** to create a new block. The *New Data Block* dialog box is displayed. As seen in the layout the search form includes items that are not connected to a table. Thus the items in the search form are control items that must be placed inside a control block i.e. a block not connected to a table. A control block can be created by selecting the *Build Data Block manually* radio button in the *New Data Block* dialog box. Select and click on OK.

A new block with a default name is created. Change the name of the block to **Search**.

3. When a data block is created manually, a new canvas is not created. Thus before opening the layout editor, a new canvas must be created and named appropriately.

   Click on Canvas node in the Object Navigator and select **Navigator..Create**. A new canvas with a default name is created. Change the name of the canvas to **Search_can**.

4. Open the layout editor by clicking on **Tools..Layout Editor**. Reduce the size the canvas as shown in diagram 10.3.

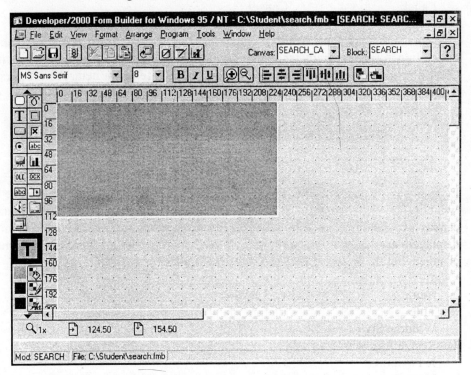

Diagram 10.3 : Resized Search Canvas

5. Place a list item and set the following properties of the list item:

Name	: search_list
List Style	: Tlist
Database Item	: No
Width	: 143
Height	: 70

6. Place a push button and set the following properties:

Name	: pb_ok
Label	: OK
Enabled	: No

7. Place another push button and set the following properties:

| Name | : pb_cancel |
| Label | : Cancel |

8. Since an SQL statement used to populate the list item is passed as a parameter from the calling form, a parameter that must hold the SQL statement must be created. Click on parameter node and select **Navigator..Create** menu item. A new parameter with a default name is created. Set the properties of the parameter as follows:

Name	: p_search_sql
Data Type	: Char
Maximum Length	: 255

7. Every form created in forms Builder includes a window with a default name set to 'window1'. When the form is executed the canvas along with the items placed on canvas are displayed in this window. For the search form, this window must be displayed as a pop up window and thus the properties of the window must be changed. Set the following properties of the window:

Name	: search_win
Title	: Search
Window Style	: Dialog
Resize Allowed	: No
X Position	: 130
Y Position	: 100
Width	: 214
Height	: 76

As shown in diagram 10.2, the search window must be displayed as a popup window in the center of the screen. The *X Position* and *Y Position* attribute sets the position of the window on the VDU. The *Height* and *Width* attribute sets the size of the window.

The *Resize Allowed* attribute is set to *No* to ensure that the search window cannot be resized at runtime.

8. Write the PL/SQL code in the search form described.

Trigger Name	: **PRE-FORM**	Form	: search
Block	:	Item	:
Trigger Level	: Form Level		
Function	: To populate the list item with appropriate SQL statement passed as a parameter from the calling form.		
Text	: DECLARE		

```
        DECLARE
                search_recgrp recordgroup;
                status number;
        BEGIN
                /* Create a record group object using the SQL statement
                assigned to :p_search_sql parameter. */
                search_recgrp := create_group_from_query('search_list',
                                        :parameter.p_search_sql);

                /* Populate the group with the records fetched by the
                select statement associated with the group. */
                status := populate_group(search_recgrp);

                /* Populate the list with the records in the group */
                populate_list('search_list', search_recgrp);
        END;
```

Trigger Name	: **WHEN-LIST-CHANGED**	Form	: search
Block	: search	Item	: search_list
Function	: To set the enable property of the OK button to true		
Text	: BEGIN		

```
        BEGIN
                set_item_property('search.pb_ok', enabled, property_on);
        END;
```

Trigger Name	: **WHEN-BUTTON-PRESSED**	Form	: search
Block	: search	Item	: pb_ok
Function	: To assign the selected list value to global variable and quit the search form. The value in this global variable will be used in the default_where property of the main block.		
Text	: BEGIN		

```
        BEGIN
                /* Assigning the selected value to a global variable.
                The value in the global variable can then be
                 used in any form.
                Any variable prefixed with :global is considered to a
                global variable. Global variables are not explicitly
                declared. They are of data type char size 255 */

                :global.search_value := :search_list;
                exit_form;
        END;
```

Trigger Name	: **WHEN-BUTTON-PRESSED**	Form	: search
Block	: search	Item	: pb_cancel
Function	: To assign spaces to global variable and quit the search form.		
Text	: BEGIN		

```
          /* Set the value of the global variable to single space and
          quit form */
          :global.search_value := ' ';
          exit_form ;
    END;
```

Tip

Rules applicable for global variables are:
- Global variables cannot be declared in the declare section of a PL/SQL block
- Global variables are created as Char(255) variables.
- Global variables come into existence only when a value is assigned to it.
- Global variables ceases to exists if a NULL value is assigned.

If the push button *pb_cancel* is clicked, the search form must be closed without passing any search value. Thus the global variable does not exist when the cancel button is clicked. When the search form is closed by clicking on cancel and the control returns to the calling form and the next line after the *call_form ( )* procedure is executed.

Thus when the global variable is accessed in the WHEN-BUTTON-PRESSED trigger defined on *pb_search* push button in the called form (as explained on page 366), an error indicating that the global variable is not available is displayed. To avoid this, although no value is required for if the cancel button is clicked, a value must be assigned to global variable.

Since a null or empty string cannot be assigned to global variable, a single space is assigned to the global variable.

MODIFICATIONS IN THE CALLING FORM

1. Open the *product* form and check to see that the form has a Search button with the following properties.

Name	: pb_search
Iconic	: Yes
Icon Name	: c:\orawin95\tools\devdem20\bin\icon\rt_quer1
Height	: 16
Width	: 16
Background Color	: Gray
Hint	: Search for a Specific Product
Tooltip	: Search

When calling the search form it is assumed that the form is saved in a directory named '*Student*' in Drive 'C'. Please specify a sub-directory and / or path to call the search form from a location appropriate to the computer being worked on.

2. Write PL/SQL code in the search button in *product* form as shown below:

Trigger Name	: **WHEN-BUTTON-PRESSED**	Form	: product
Block	: button_palette	Item	: pb_search
Function	: To open the search form. Pass the valid value accepted in the search form to the default_where property of the product_master block and execute the query.		
Trigger Level	: Item Level		
Text	: DECLARE		

```
            search_list paramlist; /* Parameter list declaration */
            where_string varchar2(100);
        BEGIN
            search_list := create_parameter_list('search_paramlist');
            if not id_null(search_list) then
                add_parameter(search_list, 'p_search_sql', text_parameter,
                        'select description, product_no
                            from product_master order by description');
            call_form('c:\student\search.fmx', no_hide, no_replace,
                no_query_only, search_list);

            /* The parameter list is no longer required and thus it must
            be destroyed */
            destroy_parameter_list(search_list);
```

/* If the product_no is not set to a single space then set the default_where property of the product_master block. Set the form cursor on the product_master block and execute the query. The default_where of the product_master block must then be set to an empty string. */

```
if not (:global.search_value = ' ') then
        where_string := 'where product_no = ' || "" ||
                                :global.search_value || "";
        set_block_property('product_master', default_where,
                                where_string);
        go_block('product_master') ;
        execute_query;
        set_block_property('product_master', default_where, " );
    end if;
end if;
END;
```

When *Execute_Query* is fired, Oracle creates a select statement from the properties of the block and the items included in the block. One such property is *Default_Where*. The *Default_Where* property could hold the where clause of a select statement or NULL. If the *Default_Where* is set the record set retrieved by the form will be restricted to the records that satisfy the condition the *Default_Where* clause. If the *default_where* holds NULL, all the records from the base table will be retrieved.

Default_Where property can be set at design time or it can be set programmatically by using *Set_Block_Property*( ) procedure. *Set_Block_Property* ( ) procedure takes in three parameters. These are the *name of the block*, the *property name* and the *property value*.

In the current example, *execute_query* must populate the block with a global select statement when the view push button is clicked. If the search push button is clicked, a search form must be displayed for selection. A selected value can then be used to help specify a where clause. The where clause can be set programmatically as follows:

```
where string := 'where product_no = ' || "" || :global.search_value || "" ;
set_block_property('product_master', default_where, where_string) ;
```

search_value is a global variable that holds the value selected in the search form if the OK push button is clicked. The contents of this variable can be accessed as **:global.search_value**.

INTRODUCING PATTERN MATCHING IN THE SEARCH FORM

If the list of search values is very large, the time taken to select the value to search on is equally large. Search for an element can be simplified and the selection time can be reduced as explained below:

- The search form can have its list item selectively populated. To achieve this the query that populates the list item must itself have an appropriate where clause based on the search pattern entered.

  An inherent drawback of this technique is if the search criterion is changed frequently, network traffic and database activity increases sharply.

- Another commonly used technique is to position the cursor on the first element in the list item that matches criteria entered by a user. The network traffic and database activity will be less.

To achieve this the following changes could be incorporated into the 'search' form.
1. A text item for entering a required pattern must be added above the list item.

2. Appropriate PL/SQL code must be written to move to an element in the list item who's value is mapped to a pattern entered.

The steps in introducing pattern matching are:
1. Ensure that the search form is opened in Forms Builder tool.

2. The height *search* canvas must be increased to accommodate the text item required for entering a pattern. Select *search_can* canvas in the Object Navigator and set the height property to **103**.

3. Since the height of the window is set based on the height of the canvas, the height of the window must also be increased accordingly. Select *search_win* window in the Object Navigator and set the height **103**.

4. Open the layout editor by selecting **Tools..Layout Editor**. Rearrange the objects in the layout as shown in diagram 10.4.

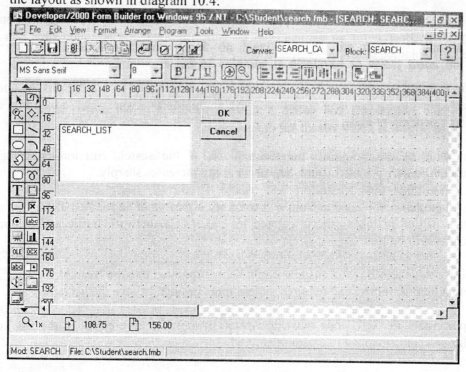

Diagram 10.4 : Rearranged Search Layout

5. Place a Text Item above the list item and set the following properties of the text item.

Name	: pattern
Data Type	: Char
Maximum Length	: 100
Database Item	: No

The complete search layout is displayed in diagram 10.5.

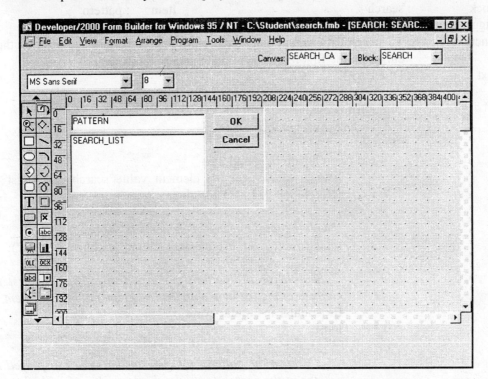

Diagram 10.5 : Search Layout with Pattern Text Item

6. At runtime, a pattern can be entered in the *pattern* text item. When the <Tab> or <Enter> key can be pressed, the list item elements must be searched to find an item that matches the entered pattern. If a match is found, the list item value can be set to the first list element value that matches the pattern specified in the *pattern* text item.

    The trigger that fires when a <Tab> or <Enter> key is pressed and the value in the text item has changed is called WHEN-VALIDATE-ITEM trigger. Thus PL/SQL code to achieve the above functionality must be written

Trigger Name	: **WHEN-VALIDATE-ITEM**	Form	: search
Block	: search	Item	: pattern
Trigger Level	: Item Level		
Function	: To search list element that matches the entered pattern and position the cursor on the first list element that matches the pattern.		
Text	: DECLARE		

```
           DECLARE
               listdisplayvalue   varchar(100);
               listdatavalue varchar(100);
               total_rows number;
           BEGIN
               if :search.pattern is null then
                   listdatavalue := get_list_element_value('search.search_list', 1);
                   :search_list := ListDataValue;
               else
                   /* Get the total number of elements in the list */
                   total_rows := get_list_element_count('search.search_list');

                   /* Search for the pattern match starting from the first list
                   element of the list item upto the last element of the list item */
                   for counter in 1..total_rows
                   loop

                       /* Since the pattern is based on the values displayed to
                       the in the search form, the display value of each element
                       must be stored in a variable for further comparison. */

                       listdisplayvalue := get_list_element_label(
                                       'search.search_list', counter);

                       /* Since a case insensitive search is be implemented, the
                       element value and the search pattern must be converted
                       to the same case. In the current example, the list element
                       stored in the variable value and is converted to upper
                       case. */

                       listdisplayvalue := upper(listdisplayvalue);
```

/ Check for pattern matching and return the first value that matches the pattern. Pattern matching is implemented using the **Like** operator. */*
if listdisplayvalue like upper(:search.pattern) || '%' then

   /* If a match is found then the data value associated with the current list element must be retrieved. */

   listdatavalue := get_list_element_value(
            'search.search_list', counter);

   /* The current element can be selected by setting the value of the list item to the data value of the current item */
   :search_list := listdatavalue;

   /* Since a value is selected, push button OK must be enabled */
   set_item_property('search.pb_ok', enabled,
                                    property_on);

   /* Exit from the loop as no further check is required. */
   exit;
      end if;
   end loop;
   end if;
END;

SELF REVIEW QUESTIONS

TRUE AND FALSE

1. Parameters can be referenced outside the form in which they are declared.

    A) True   B) False

2. A parameter list consists of three parts.

    A) True   B) False

3. If NULL value is assigned to a Global Variable, it ceases to exist.

    A) True   B) False

FILL IN THE BLANKS

1. Global Variables are defined with _____ data type and _____ size.

2. _____ function is used to get the display value from the list item.

3. _____ function is used to get the data value from a list item.

4. _____ is used to get the total number of elements in the list item

PICK THE RIGHT OPTION

1. When a new form is created, the Forms Builder creates _____ by default.

    A) a window named window0.
    B) a canvas named canvas0.
    C) a block named block0.

2. Popup forms can be displayed by using

    A) Open_form ( ) procedure with parameter value set to NO_HIDE.
    B) Call_form ( ) procedure with parameter value set to NO_HIDE.
    C) Call_form ( ) procedure with parameter value set to HIDE.

Create a User Defined Search form that can be called from any data entry form
- Creating a List Item
- Populating a List item using an SQL Statement passed from the calling form to the search form
- Calling a pop up Search Form

Setting Object Properties
- Setting Canvas Properties
- Setting Window Properties

Working with Global Variables
- Assigning value to a Global Variable
- Global variables Rules

List Item Functions
- Accessing Display value of a List Element
- Accessing Data value of a List Element
- Counting the number of List Elements
- Selecting a List Element programmatically

CHAPTER ELEVEN

Working With Menus

IN THIS CHAPTER

> Components of a Custom Menu

> Creating a Custom Menu

> Attaching a PL/SQL Library to a Menu Module

> Attaching PL/SQL code to Menu Items

> Attaching a Menu Module to a Form

> Checked and Enabled Property of Menu Items

> Creating an Iconic Toolbar

11. WORKING WITH MENUS

Every form runs with one of the following:

- The Default textual menu and a Default Toolbar menu built into the form
- A custom textual menu that the user defines as a separate module and then attaches to the form for runtime execution. A custom toolbar created by the user.

At runtime, a form can have only one menu module active at a time, either the Default menu or a custom menu.

The Default menu is part of the form module. Custom menu modules, however, are separate from form modules. So, when an application, based on a single form that uses a custom menu is delivered, following files must be provided:

- An .FMX form module.
- An .MMX menu module.

In a multi-form application, several form modules and several menu modules may be delivered to a client. Multiple forms can share the same menu, or each form can invoke a different menu.

USING A CUSTOM MENU

A Custom menu is built by creating a Menu Module in Forms Builder and then defining objects for the menu.

A Menu Module includes different types of objects as shown in diagram 11.1.

1. The Main Menu encompasses all Sub menu and menu items in a menu module. The Main Menu is the first item in the *Menus* node in the Object Navigator. The Main Menu includes menu items displayed on the Menu Bar.
2. Sub Menus that encompass menu items.
3. Menu items attached to a Sub Menu with their associated commands and procedures.

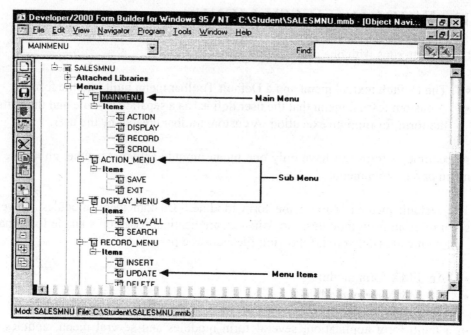

Diagram 11.1 : Menu Module Along with Objects in it

FOCUS

Create a textual menu named *salesmnu.mmb* for the product form allowing Data manipulation and Navigation.

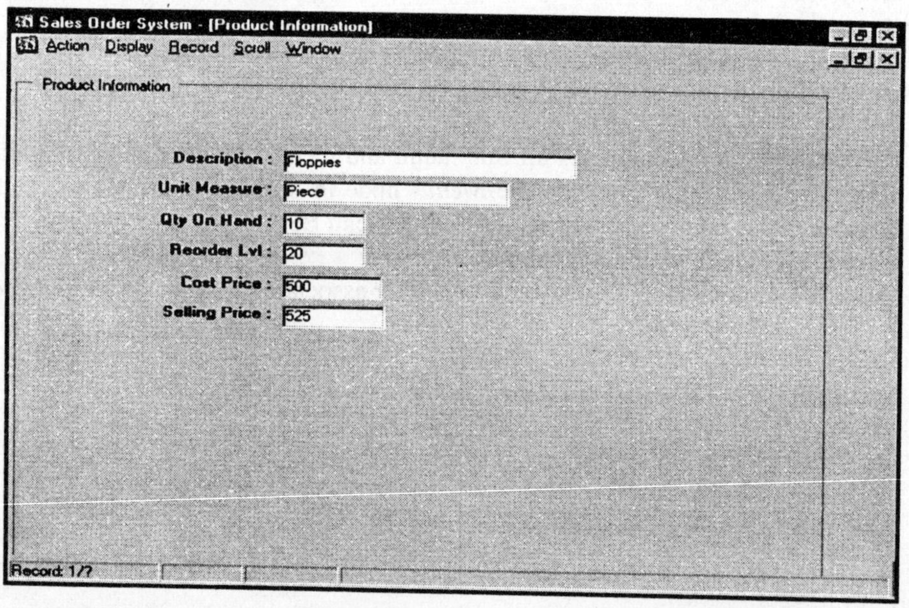

Diagram 11.2 : Product Data Entry Screen with Custom Menu

THE SOLUTION

Creating A Menu Module:

1. Create a new menu module by selecting **File..New..Menu**. Or, in the Navigator, select the Menus node and click on the Create icon in the toolbar. A new menu module is created and displayed in the Navigator with a default name such as MODULE2 as shown in diagram 11.3.

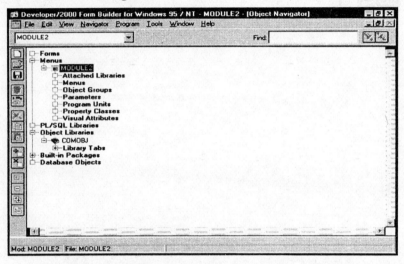

Diagram 11.3 : New menu module Screen

2. Replace the default name with a more meaningful name by setting the *Name* property of the menu module as shown in diagram 11.4.

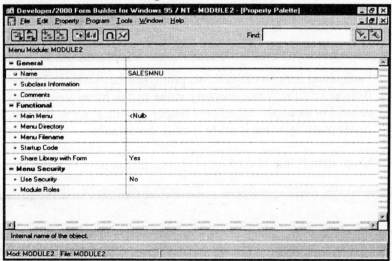

Diagram 11.4 : Setting the Menu Module Name

3. After creating a new menu module appropriate Sub Menus and Menu Items must be created in the Menu Editor. Select **Tools..Menu Editor** to open the Menu Editor. By Default a new menu item, labeled **<New Item>** is shown as in diagram 11.5.

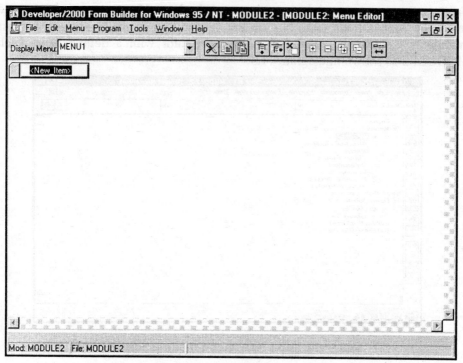

Diagram 11.5 : New Menu Item displayed in the Menu Editor

4. Replace the default label of the first menu item to 'Action'.

Note

Each menu item has atleast two properties i.e. *Name* and *Label*. Oracle Forms Builder sets the *Name* property value of the menu item to its *Label* property value. For example if the *Label* property value is set to 'Scroll', the menu item *Name* property value is set to 'Scroll' by default.

Menu item Name is used for programmatic control of menu items.

5. Before creating other menu items, organization and display of menu items in a runtime window must be understood. As shown in diagram 11.6, the space between the window title bar and the canvas is called a **Menu Bar** and the menu items included in the Menu Bar are called **Menu Bar Items**.

Each Menu Bar item, based on the functionality, can be further categorized into
- Menu Bar items that call a form or a block of PL/SQL code
- Menu Bar items that drop-down a sub menu as shown in diagram 11.6.

Each sub menu includes a number of menu items and these menu items are called **Sub Menu Items**.

While creating a Menu module, a common practice is to create the menu bar items first and then create sub menu items that make up a sub menu.

As seen in diagram 11.6, menu bar items are items placed one besides the other and thus a menu bar item can be created by creating a menu item to the right of the menu item provided by default.

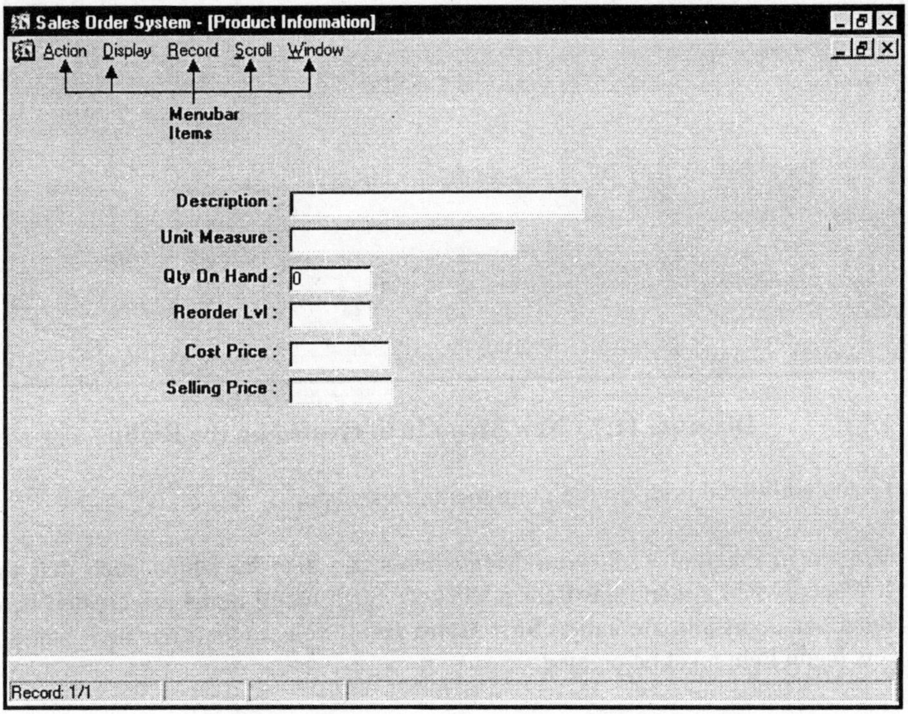

Diagram 11.6 : Menubar Items

Select **Menu..Create Right** to add a new menu item to the main bar. Or, click the Create Right icon. A menu item labeled **<New Item>** is created in the Menu Editor as shown in diagram 11.7. Change the menu item label to 'Display'.

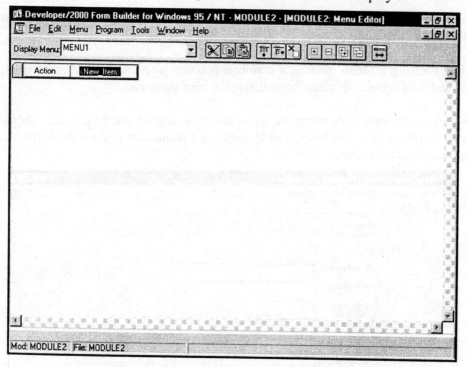

Diagram 11.7 : New Menu Item created on the Right

5. To add additional items to the main menu, repeat step 5.

6. As seen in diagram 11.8, New Menu items can also be added such that they are displayed when a menu bar item is clicked. Such menu items are created below the menu bar items and are called **Sub Menu Item**. Select menu bar item below which new menu item must be created.

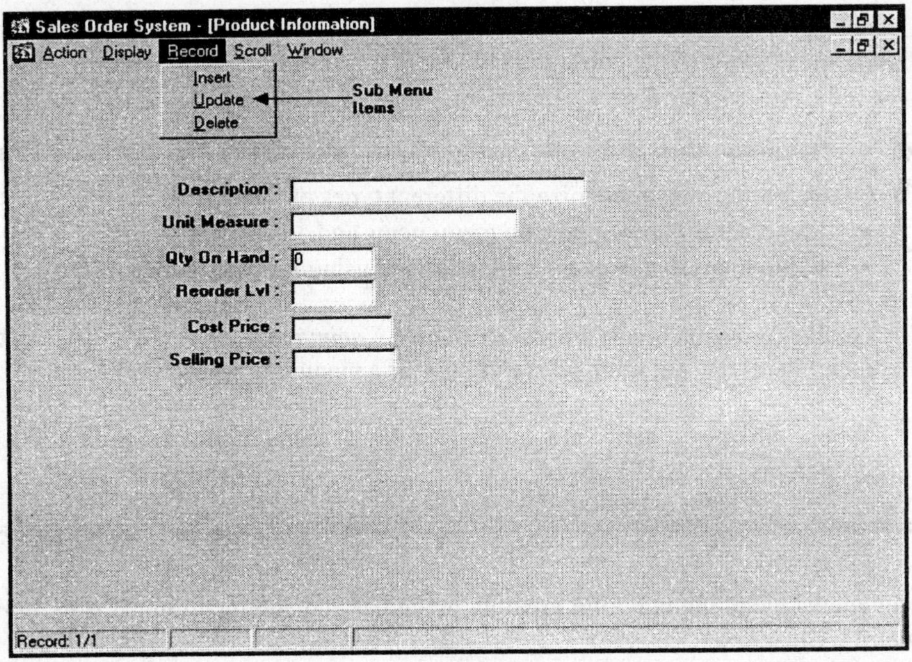

Diagram 11.8 : Sub Menu Items

Select **Menu..Create Down** to create a sub menu item below the current menu item or click on the Create Down icon. Oracle Forms creates a new menu item with the label **<New Item>** as shown in diagram 11.9.

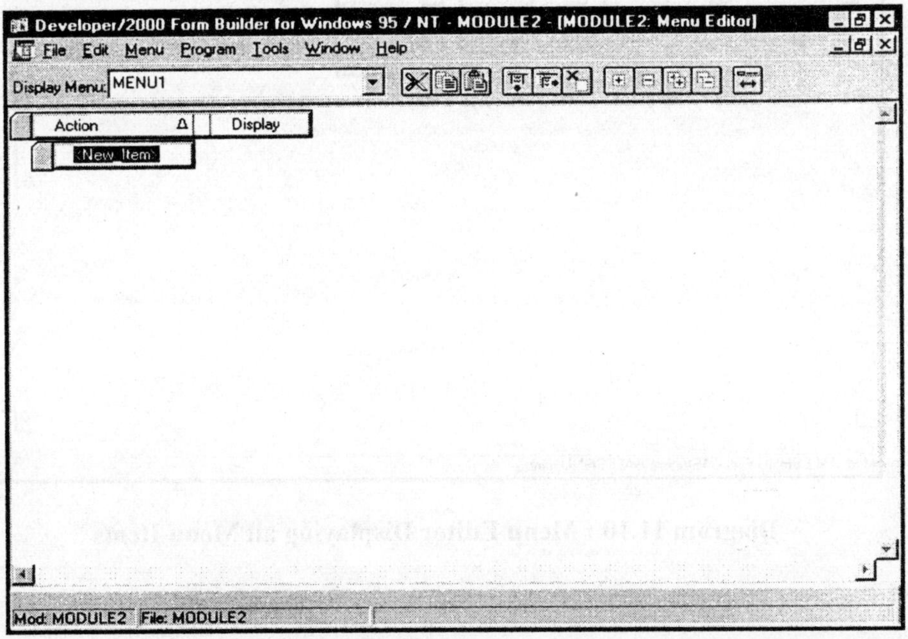

Diagram 11.9 : New Menu Item Created under the Action Menu Item

6. Change the label of the new menu item as required. Repeat steps 2 and 3 to add further menu items to the current menu.

Tip

Oracle Forms must recognize the different types of menu items i.e.
*   Menu items that display sub menu items and
*   Menu items that execute action defined using PL/SQL code.

Oracle Forms maintains a property named *Command Type* to distinguish between menu items. By default *Command Type* of a menu item is set to *PL/SQL*.

When sub menu items are created under a menu item, the *Command Type* property is changed to *Menu*.

The completed menu module after creating menu bar and sub menu items is as shown in diagram 11.10.

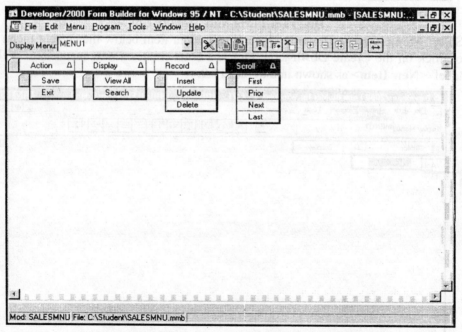

Diagram 11.10 : Menu Editor Displaying all Menu Items

PROCEDURES

The current menu module is used for data manipulation and navigation in the product form. The text items in the master form must be enabled or disabled based on the data entry form's mode of operation. For example if the mode of operation is 'View' all the text items in the master form must be disabled. Similarly, if the mode of operation is 'Add' all the text items must be enabled.

PL/SQL code block to achieve this functionality is defined in a PL/SQL library named *Saleslib.pll* as a procedure named *item_enable_disable*. This procedure can then called in the triggers defined for the menu items. Thus *Saleslib.pll* library must be attached to the menu module as follows:

1. Select the 'Attached Libraries' node in the menu module. Double click on the Attached Libraries node. It displays the *Attached Library* dialog box. Specify the name of the library as *Saleslib.pll* as shown in diagram 11.11.

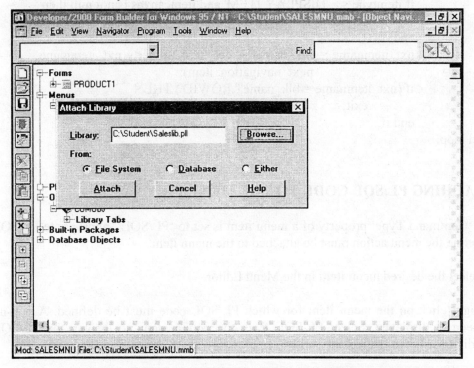

Diagram 11.11 : Attaching a Library to a Menu Module

The Procedures used in the library are defined below:

Procedure Name   : **ITEM_ENABLE_DISABLE**

Function   : To enable the fields so that the contents of the field can be modified or new values can be entered. To disable fields so that the contents of the field cannot be modified.

```
PROCEDURE ITEM_ENABLE_DISABLE (blk_name IN char, item_on_off IN NUMBER) IS
        nxt_itemname varchar2(70);
        itemtype varchar2(25);
        itemcanvas varchar2(25);
BEGIN
    nxt_itemname := blk_name||'.'|| get_block_property(blk_name, first_item);
    loop

            itemtype := get_item_property(nxt_itemname, item_type);
            itemcanvas := get_item_property(nxt_itemname, item_canvas);

            if itemtype <> 'DISPLAY ITEM' and itemcanvas is not null then
                    set_item_property(nxt_itemname, updateable, item_on_off);
            end if;
            nxt_itemname := blk_name||'.'|| get_item_property(nxt_itemname,
                    next_navigation_item);
            if (nxt_itemname = blk_name||'.ROWID') THEN
                    exit;
            end if;
    end loop;
END;
```

ATTACHING PL/SQL CODE TO THE MENU ITEMS

If the 'Command Type' property of a menu item is set to 'PL/SQL', appropriate PL/SQL that define the menu action must be attached to the menu item.

1. Select the desired menu item in the Menu Editor.

2. Right click on the menu item for which PL/SQL code must be defined. A pop-up menu is displayed. Select PL/SQL from the popup menu to display the PL/SQL Editor as shown in diagram 11.12.

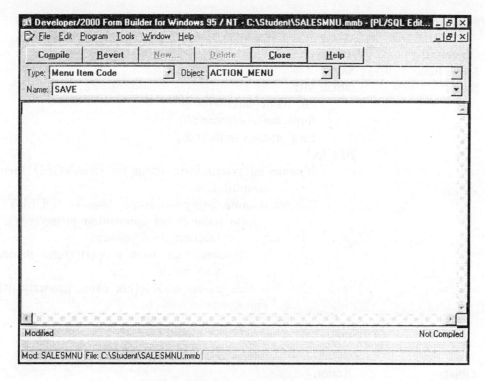

Diagram 11.12 : PL/SQL Editor

4. In the PL/SQL Editor, enter appropriate PL/SQL code.

Note

The PL/SQL Editor sets the *Type of PL/SQL* to *Menu Item Code*. The object is set to the submenu or main menu name. The Name of the PL/SQL block is the same as the name of the menu item.

5. Click Compile to compile the PL/SQL code. Click Close to close the PL/SQL editor.

Tip

A Trigger Name need not be selected since there is only one event connected to a menu item i.e. click of the menu item.

PL/SQL Code Written for the menu Items:

1. Object   : Action
   Menu Item   : Save
   Script   : DECLARE

```
        blk_name varchar(60);
        form_name varchar(60);
        item_name varchar(60);
    BEGIN
        if name_in('system.form_status') = 'CHANGED' then
            commit_form ;
            if name_in('system.form_status') = 'QUERY' then
                form_name := get_application_property
                    (current_form_name);
                blk_name := get_form_property(form_name,
                    first_block);
                item_enable_disable(blk_name, property_off);
            end if;
        end if;
    END;
```

2. Object   : Action
   Menu Item   : Exit
   Script   : exit_form;

3. Object   : Display
   Menu Item   : View
   Script   : DECLARE

```
        blk_name varchar(60);
        form_name varchar(60);
        item_name varchar(60);
    BEGIN
        execute_query ;
        form_name :=
            get_application_property(current_form_name);
        blk_name := get_form_property(form_name, first_block);
        item_enable_disable(blk_name, property_off);
    END;
```

4. Object   : Display
   Menu Item   : Search
   Script   : DECLARE

```
        blk_name varchar(60);
        form_name varchar(60);
        item_name varchar(60);
```

```
BEGIN
        enter_query;
        form_name :=
                get_application_property(current_form_name);
        blk_name := get_form_property(form_name, first_block);
        item_enable_disable(blk_name, property_off);
END;
```

5. Object   : Record
    Menu Item : Insert
    Script   : DECLARE

```
        blk_name varchar(60);
        form_name varchar(60);
        item_name varchar(60);
BEGIN
        create_record ;
        form_name :=
                get_application_property(current_form_name);
        blk_name := get_form_property(form_name, first_block);
        item_enable_disable(blk_name, property_on);
END;
```

6. Object   : Record
    Menu Item : Modify
    Script   : DECLARE

```
        blk_name varchar(60);
        form_name varchar(60);
BEGIN
        form_name :=
                get_application_property(current_form_name);
        blk_name := get_form_property(current_form_name,
                first_block);
        item_enable_disable(blk_name, property_on);
END;
```

Note

Menu Items *View, Search, Insert, Modify* and *Save* call a procedure named ITEM_ENABLE_DISABLE. This procedure is explained in the section PROCEDURES in chapter WORKING WITH MENUS on page 377.

It is assumed that the data block is the first block. Alternately the user can check for every block whether the base table is null or not to determine if the block is a data block.

7. Object   : Record
    Menu Item   : Delete
    Script   : delete_record ;

8. Object   : Scroll
    Menu Item   : First
    Script   : first_record ;

9. Object   : Scroll
    Menu Item   : Prior
    Script   : previous_record ;

10. Object   : Scroll
    Menu Item   : Next
    Script   : next_record ;

11. Object   : Scroll
    Menu Item   : Last
    Script   : last_record;

Delete Items from a Menu Bar or Submenu:

To delete items from a menu Bar or submenu:

1. Select the item that must be deleted. Select **Menu..Delete** or click on the Delete icon. Oracle Forms displays an alert for confirmation to delete the menu item. Click Yes.

Caution

When deleting menu items care must be taken to check that appropriate value is specified for the *Command Type* property.

If *all* the menu items in the sub menu are deleted, the *Command Type* property of item that called the sub menu items is set to *Null*. If no further sub menu items are required, the *Command Type* must be set to *PL/SQL*. If new sub menu items are created the *Command Type* must be set to *Menu*.

SAVING COMPILING AND ATTACHING A MENU MODULE

Saving and Compiling Menu Module:

After creating menu items as required and writing appropriate PL/SQL code, the menu module must be saved by selecting **File..Save** or **File..Save As**. A menu module i.e. menu source file is saved with an extension of .MMB as shown in diagram 11.13.

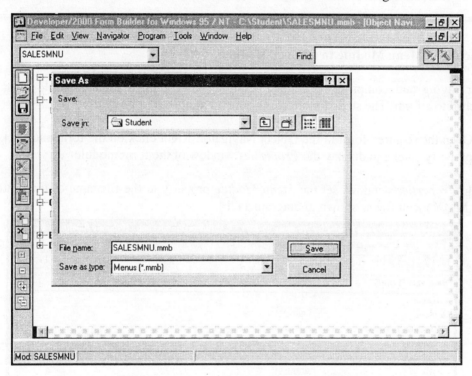

Diagram 11.13 : Saving a Menu Module

Menu module cannot be executed by itself. Menu module must be compiled and then attached to the form module.

Click on **File..Administration..Compile File** menu options to compile the menu module. When a menu module is compiled Oracle Forms creates an executable file with the same name as the MMB file but with an extension of MMX.

Caution

Before compiling check that appropriate PL/SQL code is written for menu items with *Command Type* set as *PL/SQL*.

If PL/SQL code is not written, Oracle Compiler will display error messages and create an error file.

Attaching a Menu Module to a Form Module:

After saving and compiling the menu module, the compiled menu module must be attached to a form. The steps for attaching a menu module to a form are:

1. Open the required form in the Object Navigator. Right click on the form and click on property palette to display the *Properties* window of the form module.

2. In *Properties* window, set the *Menu Module* property to the filename of the runtime .MMX menu file as shown in diagram 11.14.

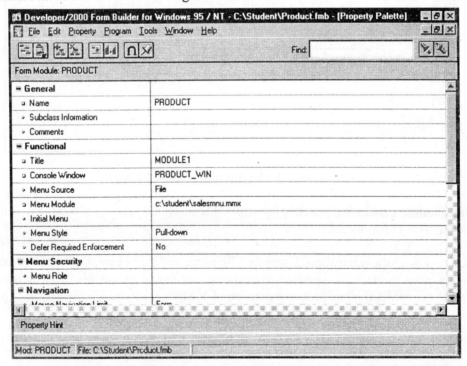

Diagram 11.14 : Attaching a Menu Module to a Form Module

Once a menu is attached to a form, Oracle forms automatically loads the .MMX menu file when the form is run.

3. Select **File..Save** or **File..Save As** to save the form module.

4. Select **File..Administration..Generate** to generate the form module.

CHECKED, ENABLED AND DISPLAYED PROPERTY OF MENU ITEMS

The displayed, enabled and checked property specifies the state of the menu item. The three properties are explained below.

Checked Property:

Specifies the state of a check-box or radio-style menu item, either CHECKED or UNCHECKED. This property is set programmatically only for the menu items with the **Menu Item Type** property set to **Check** or **Radio**.

Enabled Property:

Specifies whether the menu item should be displayed as an enabled (normal) item or disabled (grayed) item. This property is set programmatically.

Note

Programmatically enabling or disabling a menu item that is hidden as a result of the following conditions is **not allowed**:

- The menu module **Use Security** property is TRUE.
- The menu item **Display w/o Privilege** property is set to FALSE.
- The current operator is not a member of a role that has access to the menu item.

Displayed Property:

Determines whether the menu item is visible or hidden at runtime. This property is set programmatically.

Getting the Value of the Menu Property:

The state of the menu item for the above three properties can be obtained using the following functions:

get_menu_item_property(menuitem_id, property)
get_menu_item_property(menu_name.menuitem_name, property)

The above function returns the state of the menu item given the specific property. The return value is either TRUE or FALSE depending on the state of property(i.e. if above function is used to check the enabled property of menu item, then it returns TRUE if the menu item is enabled and FALSE if it is disabled.)

Focus:

Create a menu where the scroll menu items like first, next, last and prior will be enabled or disabled according to current record position (i.e. if the current record is the first record then first and prior menu items will be disabled. If the current record is the last record then the last and prior menu items will be disabled. If the current record is the only record then all the scroll menu items will be disabled. The menu item first will be checked if the current record is the first record and the menu item last will be checked if the current record is the last record.

The *Scroll_control* procedure is called in the When-New-Record-Instance of the product form. When-New-Record-Instance will fire whenever there is a change in the row focus.

Similarly create a procedure named *menu_scroll* as follows and call the same in the When-New-Record-Instance trigger:

Solution:

1. Make the **Menu Item Type** property for first and last menu items equal to **check.**

2. Create a procedure named menu_scroll in the common library as shown below.

The Procedures is defined below:

Procedure Name   : **MENU_SCROLL**

```
PROCEDURE menu_scroll IS
BEGIN
        if name_in('system.last_record')= 'TRUE' and   name_in('system.cursor_record') = '1' then
        /* Setting the enabled property for all the menu items if there is only one record. */
                set_menu_item_property('scroll_menu.next',enabled,property_false);
                set_menu_item_property('scroll_menu.last',enabled, property_false);
                set_menu_item_property('scroll_menu.first',enabled, property_false);
                set_menu_item_property('scroll_menu.prior',enabled, property_false);
        elsif name_in('system.last_record') = 'TRUE' then
            /* Setting the enabled property for the menu items last and next to off if focus
              is on the  last record. */
                set_menu_item_property('scroll_menu.next',enabled, property_false);
                set_menu_item_property('scroll_menu.first',enabled, property_true);
                set_menu_item_property('scroll_menu.prior',enabled, property_true);
                set_menu_item_property('scroll_menu.last',enabled, property_false);
                /* Setting the checked property for the menu item  last  on and first to off
                  if focus is on the  last record.  */
                set_menu_item_property('scroll_menu.last',checked,property_true);
                set_menu_item_property('scroll_menu.first',checked,property_false);

        elsif  name_in('system.cursor_record') = '1' then
            /* Setting the enabled property for the menu items first and prior to off if
              focus is on the first record. */
                set_menu_item_property('scroll_menu.prior',enabled, property_false);
                set_menu_item_property('scroll_menu.next',enabled, property_true);
                set_menu_item_property('scroll_menu.last',enabled, property_true);
                set_menu_item_property('scroll_menu.first',enabled, property_false);

                /* Setting the checked property for the menu item first on and last to off
                  if focus is on the  last record */
                set_menu_item_property('scroll_menu.last',checked,property_false);
                set_menu_item_property('scroll_menu.first',checked,property_true);

        ELSE
                set_menu_item_property('scroll_menu.first',enabled, property_true);
                set_menu_item_property('scroll_menu.prior',enabled, property_true);
                set_menu_item_property('scroll_menu.next',enabled, property_true);
                set_menu_item_property('scroll_menu.last',enabled, property_true);
        END IF ;
END;
```

The *scroll_control* and *menu_scroll* procedure is called in the form as shown below:

Trigger Name : **WHEN-NEW-RECORD-INSTANCE** Form Name : product
Block Name : product_master_blk   Item Name :
Trigger level : Block level
Text : scroll_control;
        menu_scroll ;

Note

A call to a user-defined procedure named *menu_scroll* must be made in the When-new-record-instance trigger in all the forms where the menu is attached.

CREATING AN ICONIC TOOLBAR

Menu items created in a menu module can also be displayed as iconic buttons on a vertical or horizontal toolbar by setting additional properties for the menu items.

Focus:

Create an iconic horizontal toolbar by altering the properties of the menu items defined in menu module *salesmmu.mmb* as shown in diagram 11.15.

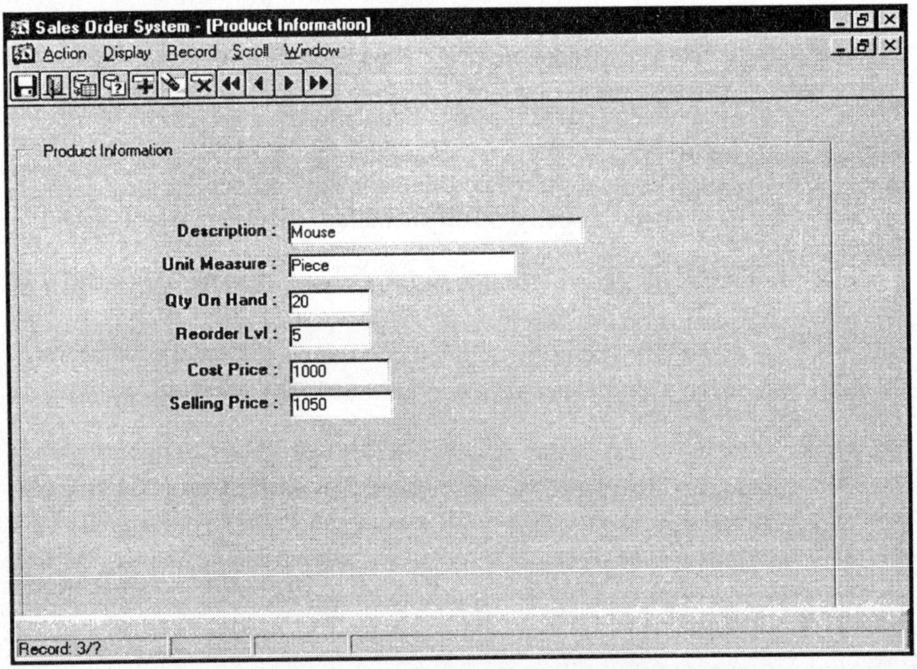

Diagram 11.15 : Toolbar Menu displayed at runtime

The steps in creating an iconic toolbar are:

1. Click on File..Open to Open menu module named *salesmmu.mmb* in c:\student directory.

2. Right click on the menu module and select Menu Editor from the pop up menu. Menu editor displays the menu items defined in the menu module as shown in diagram 11.16.

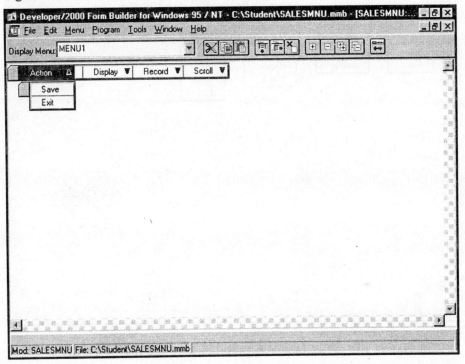

Diagram 11.16 : Menu Editor displaying Menu Items defined in Menu Module

3. The menu module displays *Action* menubar item with the sub menu items *Save* and *Exit*.

   Click on 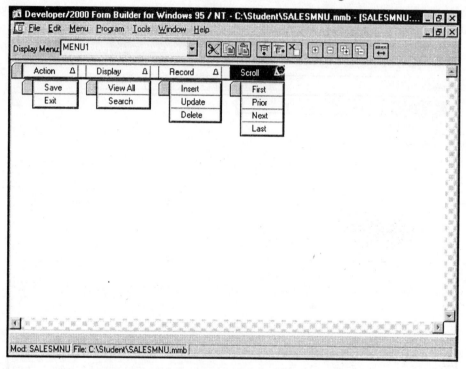 icon in each menubar item to expand other menubar items. The expanded menubar items will be displayed as shown in diagram 11.17.

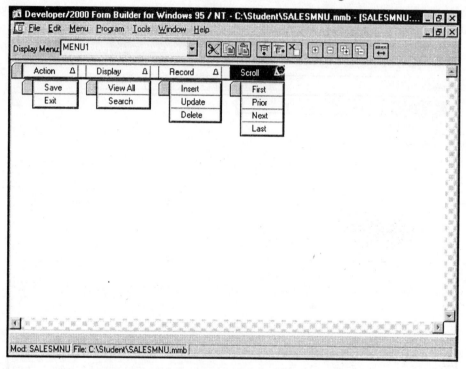

Diagram 11.17 : Expanded Menubar Items

4. Right click on submenu item *Save* and select Property Palette from the pop up menu. Set the properties of the *Save* submenu item as shown in diagram 11.18.

   Icon Filename   : c:\orawin95\tools\devdem20\bin\icon\rt_save
   Visible in Horizontal Toolbar   : Yes

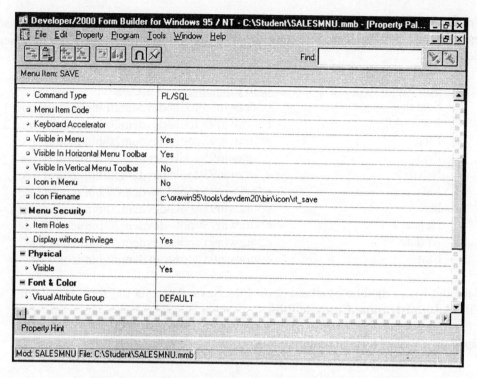

Diagram 11.18 : Properties of the Save Submenu Item

Note

Icon Filename property is used to specify the name of the icon filename that must be used to create an iconic button. The icon can be made visible in horizontal or vertical toolbar by setting **Visible in Horizontal Toolbar** or **Visible in Vertical Toolbar** property respectively to **Yes**.

Ensure that the **Visible in Menu** property is set to **Yes**. If the **Visible in Menu** property is set to **No**, the menu item is not displayed in the textual menu.

5. Set the **Visible in Menu** and **Visible in Horizontal Toolbar** to **Yes** for all the sub menu items. Set the Icon Filename property as follows for each of the submenu items.

Sub Menu Item	Icon Filename
Search	c:\orawin95\tools\devdem20\bin\icon\rt_quer1
View_All	c:\orawin95\tools\devdem20\bin\icon\rt_quer2
First	c:\orawin95\tools\devdem20\bin\icon\rt_rec1
Prior	c:\orawin95\tools\devdem20\bin\icon\rt_rec2
Next	c:\orawin95\tools\devdem20\bin\icon\rt_rec3
Last	c:\orawin95\tools\devdem20\bin\icon\rt_rec4
Insert	c:\orawin95\tools\devdem20\bin\icon\rt_radd
Delete	c:\orawin95\tools\devdem20\bin\icon\rt_rdel
Update	c:\orawin95\tools\devdem20\bin\icon\clear
Exit	c:\orawin95\tools\devdem20\bin\icon\exit

6. Save the Menu module by clicking on **File..Save**. Compile the form by clicking on **File..Administration..Compile File**.

7. Open the *Product* form and run the form.

Caution

The product form currently includes a set of iconized push buttons defined within the button palette block. Thus two sets of icons will be displayed on the form. Close the Object Navigator and delete the button_palette block from the *Product* Form.

The navigation buttons pb_first, pb_prior, pb_next and pb_last defined in the button_palette block are referenced in the scroll_control procedure called in the WHEN-NEW-RECORD-INSTANCE trigger. Thus the call to the scroll_control procedure must also be removed.

8. Run the form after making the changes. The product form will be displayed as shown in diagram 11.19.

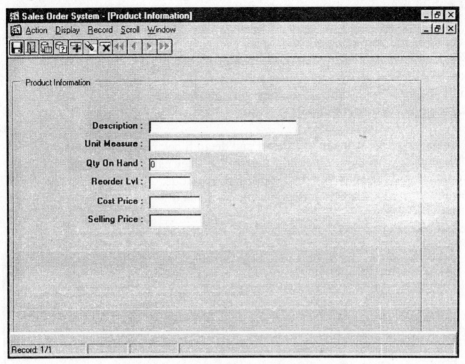

Diagram 11.19 : Iconic Buttons displayed at runtime

The WHEN-NEW-RECORD-INSTANCE trigger calls a user-defined procedure named *menu_scroll* that enables / disables the menu items. Since the number of records in the Oracle form is 1 i.e. a new record inserted when the form starts up, the menu items first, prior, next and last are disabled. If the menu items in the textual menu are disabled, the corresponding icons in the horizontal toolbar are also disabled as shown in diagram 11.19.

MASTER DETAIL MENU

FOCUS

Create a generalized menu for the Master / Detail forms as shown in diagram 11.20. Provide complete data manipulation operations i.e. Add, View, Modify and Delete for the master block. Also allow Add Detail and Delete Detail operations for any master detail form. In the view mode, allow browsing through table data, one record at a time i.e. First, Last, Previous, Next operations.

Add mode   : All items in the master and detail block must be updateable.
Modify mode   : All items other than the Primary Key can be updateable.
View mode   : Items are not updateable in view mode.
Delete mode   : Delete *Cascading* must be 'Activated'.

Include a search operation that searches and retrieves data from the master table.

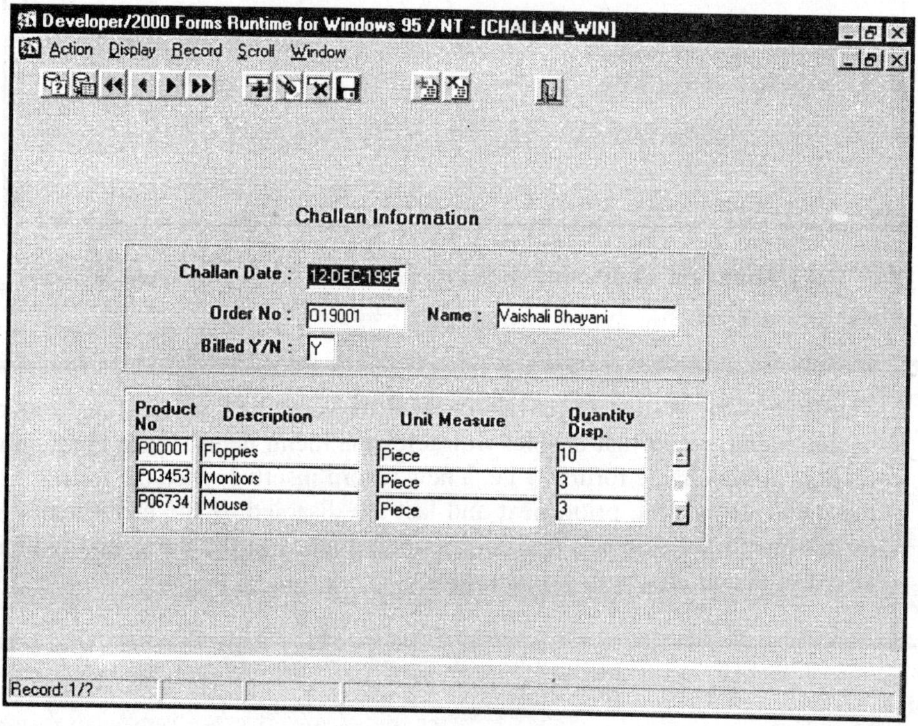

Diagram 11.20 : Generalized menu for a Master / Detail Form

THE SOLUTION

A generalized menu for Master / Detail forms can be created in the same way as the generalized menu for the master form. Menu for the Master Details form will include additional menu items to manipulate data in the detail block as well.

The PL/SQL code for data manipulation must be written to suit the requirements of manipulation for a Master / Detail form. Thus menu items required in a Master / Detail form are as shown in diagram 11.21.

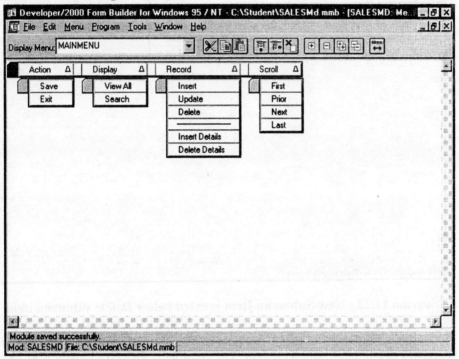

Diagram 11.21 : Menu Items defined for a Menu connected to a Master / Detail Form

As seen in diagram 11.21, the *Record* menubar item includes <u>five</u> submenu items Insert, Update and Delete that are used to perform data manipulation for the Master block and the Insert Detail and Delete Detail that perform data manipulation for the Detail block.

The sub menu items for the Master block and the Detail block is separated by a submenu item of a special type called **Separator**. A separator menu item can be created as follows:

1. Select the *Delete* Submenu Item and click on **Menu..Create Down**. A submenu item is created below the *Delete* submenu item as shown in diagram 11.22.

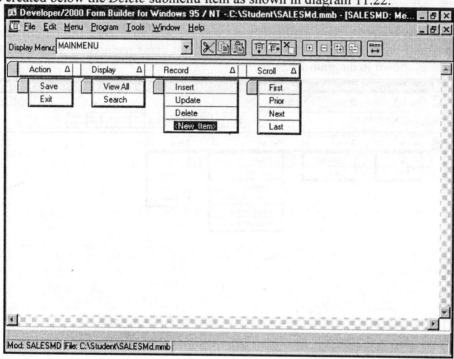

Diagram 11.22 : New Submenu Item created below *Delete* submenu item

2. Right click on the menu submenu item and select Property Palette. Set the following properties of the menu submenu item. The completed Property Palette is as shown in diagram 11.23.

        Name   : MENU_SEPARATOR1

        Menu Item Type   : Separator

        Label   : -

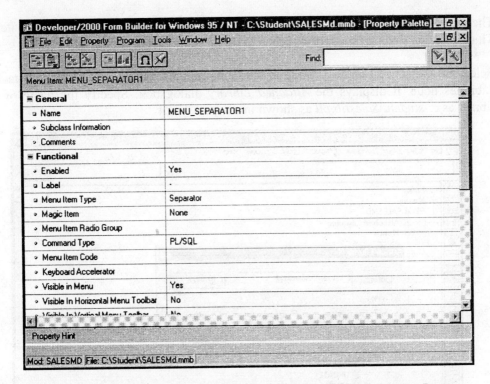

Diagram 11.23 : Completed Property Palette for New Submenu Item

After creating the separator items, the Insert Details and Delete Detail submenu items can be created by clicking on **Menu..Create Down** and setting the name and the Label property.

After creating the required menu items, PL/SQL code for each of the menu items must be written. The PL/SQL code for the menu item references a procedure named *item_enable_disabled* defined in the PL/SQL library named *saleslib.pll*.

The PL/SQL library must be attached before writing PL/SQL code for the menu items. Thus *Saleslib.pll* library must be attached to the menu module as follows:

Select the 'Attached Libraries' node in the menu module. Double click on the Attached Libraries node. It displays the *Attached Library* dialog box. Specify the name of the library as *c:\student\Saleslib.pll* as shown in diagram 11.24.

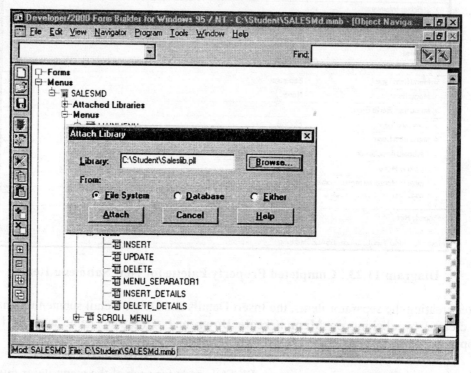

Diagram 11.24 : Attaching a Library to a Menu Module

The PL/SQL library *saleslib.pll* was saved in a directory named '*Student*' in Drive 'C'. Please choose a sub-directory and / or path to save the file appropriate to the computer being worked on.

PL/SQL Code Written for the Menu Items:

1. Object   : Action
   Menu Item   : Exit
   Script   : DECLARE

```
            answer number;
       BEGIN
            /* If there are any changes in the form the system must
            asks for confirmation to save changes */
              if :system.form_status = 'CHANGED' then
                  set_alert_property('confirm_alert',title, 'Save Changes');
                  set_alert_property('confirm_alert', alert_message_text,
                  'Would you like to make Changes Permanent ?');
                  answer := show_alert('confirm_alert');
                  if answer = ALERT_BUTTON1 then
                      commit_form;
                      /* If the commit form is not successful, the
                      form_status will not change to QUERY. In
                      such a case, confirmation to quit without
                      saving must be asked for. */
                      if :system.form_status <> 'QUERY' then
                          set_alert_property('confirm_alert', title,
                                  'Quit Without Saving');
                          set_alert_property('confirm_alert',
                            alert_message_text, 'Errors Encountered
                            while saving. Quit without Saving?');
                          answer := show_alert('confirm_alert');
                          if answer = ALERT_BUTTON1 then

                          /* If the answer is 'Yes', the form must be
                          closed    without    validating.    The
                          No_Validate   parameter   passed   to
                          exit_form   closes   the   form   without
                          validating or committing. */
                              exit_form(No_Validate);
                          end if;
                      end if;
                  end if;
              end if;
              /* Close the form. */
              exit_form(No_Commit);
       END;
```

2. Object   : Action
    Menu Item   : Save
    Script   : DECLARE

```
            blk_name varchar(60);
            form_name varchar(60);
            str_base_table varchar2(60);
    BEGIN
            if :system.form_status = 'CHANGED' then
                commit_form ;
                if :system.form_status = 'QUERY' then
                    form_name := get_application_property
                                        (current_form_name);
                    blk_name := get_form_property(form_name,
                                        first_block);
                loop
                            /* Get the name of the base table
                            associated with the block */
                            str_base_table := get_block_property(
                                blk_name, DML_Data_Target_Name);
                            /*  DML_Data_Target_Name  property
                            returns null in case of a control block */
                            if str_base_table is not null then
                                item_enable_disable(blk_name, property_off);
                            end if;
                            blk_name := get_block_property(
                                            blk_name,nextblock);
                            if blk_name is null then
                                    exit;
                            end if;
                    end loop;
                end if;
            end if;
    END;
```

3. Object : Display
   Menu Item : View_All
   Script : DECLARE

```
        blk_name varchar(60);
        form_name varchar(60);
        str_base_table varchar2(60);
BEGIN
        execute_query;
        form_name := get_application_property(
                        current_form_name);
        blk_name := get_form_property(form_name, first_block);
        loop
            str_base_table := get_block_property(blk_name,
                    DML_Data_Target_Name);
            if str_base_table is not null then
                item_enable_disable(blk_name, property_off);
            end if;
            blk_name := get_block_property(blk_name, nextblock);
            if blk_name is null then
                exit;
            end if;
        end loop;
END;
```

3. Object : Display
   Menu Item : Search
   Script : DECLARE

```
    blk_name varchar(60);
    form_name varchar(60);
    str_base_table varchar2(60);
BEGIN
    enter_query;
    form_name := get_application_property(current_form_name);
    blk_name := get_form_property(form_name, first_block);
    loop
        str_base_table := get_block_property(blk_name,
                DML_Data_Target_Name);
        if str_base_table is not null then
          item_enable_disable(blk_name, property_off);
        end if;
        blk_name := get_block_property(blk_name, nextblock);
        if blk_name is null then
          exit;
        end if;
    end loop;
END;
```

4.   Object   : Record
    Menu Item   : Insert
    Script   : DECLARE

```
            blk_name varchar(60);
            form_name varchar(60);
            str_base_table varchar2(60);
        BEGIN
        create_record ;
        form_name := get_application_property(current_form_name);
        blk_name := get_form_property(form_name, first_block);
        loop
            str_base_table := get_block_property(blk_name,
                            DML_Data_Target_Name);
            if str_base_table is not null then
                    item_enable_disable(blk_name, property_on);
            end if;
            blk_name := get_block_property(blk_name, nextblock);
            if blk_name is null then
                exit;
            end if;
        end loop;
        END;
```

5.   Object   : Record
    Menu Item   : Delete
    Script   : BEGIN

```
          delete_record ;
        END;
```

6. Object   : Record
   Menu Item   : Update
   Script   : DECLARE

```
            blk_name varchar(60);
            form_name varchar(60);
            str_base_table varchar2(60);
            str_itemname varchar2(60);
            itemtype varchar2(60);
            itemcanvas varchar2(60);
        BEGIN
            form_name := get_application_property(current_form_name);
            blk_name := get_form_property(form_name, first_block);
            loop
                str_base_table := get_block_property(blk_name,
                                DML_Data_Target_Name);
                if str_base_table is not null then
                    item_enable_disable(blk_name, property_on);
                    str_itemname := blk_name || '.' ||
                        get_block_property(blk_name, first_item);
                    loop
                        itemtype := get_item_property(str_itemname,
                                        item_type);
                        itemcanvas := get_item_property(
                                    str_itemname, item_canvas);
                        if itemtype <> 'DISPLAY ITEM' and
                                    itemcanvas is not null then
                            if get_item_property(str_itemname,
                                    Primary_Key) = 'TRUE' then
                                set_item_property(str_itemname,
                                    updateable, property_off);
                            end if;
                        end if;
                        str_itemname := blk_name || '.' ||
                            get_item_property(str_itemname,
                                    next_navigation_item);
                            if (str_itemname = blk_name||'.ROWID') then
                                exit;
                            end if;
                    end loop;
                end if;
                blk_name := get_block_property(blk_name,nextblock);
                if blk_name is null then
                    exit;
                end if;
            end loop;
        END;
```

7. Object   : Record
   Menu Item   : Insert Details
   Script   : DECLARE

```
        blk_name varchar(60);
        item_name varchar(60);
        detail_block varchar2(60);
   BEGIN
        create_record ;
        blk_name := name_in('system.cursor_block');
        item_enable_disable(blk_name, property_on);
   END;
```

8. Object   : Record
   Menu Item   : Details
   Sub-Menu Item : Delete
   Script   : BEGIN

```
        delete_record;
   END;
```

9. Object   : Scroll
   Menu Item   : First
   Script   : BEGIN

```
        first_record;
   END;
```

10. Object   : Scroll
    Menu Item   : Prior
    Script   : BEGIN

```
        previous_record;
   END;
```

11. Object   : Scroll
    Menu Item   : Next
    Script   : BEGIN

```
        next_record;
   END;
```

12. Object   : Scroll
    Menu Item   : Last
    Script   : BEGIN

```
        last_record;
   END;
```

Enabling and Disabling Menu Items:

1. Make the **Menu Item Type** property for first and last menu items equal to **check.**

2. Menu_Scroll a user-defined procedure is created in the library *saleslib.pll*. This library is attached to all the master detail forms. Thus a call must be made to menu_scroll procedure to enable / disable the navigation menu item i.e. first, prior, next and last as follows:

Trigger Name	: **WHEN-NEW-RECORD-INSTANCE**	Form Name	: challan
Block Name	: challan_header	Item Name	:
Trigger level	: Block Level		
Text	: BEGIN		
	menu_scroll;		
	END;		

SELF REVIEW QUESTIONS

TRUE AND FALSE

1. If the menu item type is PL/SQL, the menu object can be successfully compiled even if no PL/SQL code is written.

    A) True   B) False

2. Checked Property is available for menu items of type CHECK or RADIO

    A) True   B) False

FILL IN THE BLANKS

1. A menu can be attached to a form by using the _____ property.

2. Menu Item property can be set at runtime by using _____ function.

3. Menu Module is saved with an extension of _____ and when compiled the executable is created using _____ extension.

4. The menu items included in the Menu Bar are called _____.

5. Each sub menu includes a number of menu items and these menu items are called _____.

6. Oracle Forms maintains a property named _____ to distinguish between menu items.

7. _____ and _____ property is used to create an iconic toolbar item.

A QUICK REVIEW

Components of a Custom Menu
- Menu Bar
- Menu Bar Items
- Sub Menu Items

Creating a Custom Menu
- Creating a new Menu Module
- Adding Menu Items
- Deleting Menu Items

Attaching a PL/SQL Library to a Menu Module

Attaching PL/SQL code to Menu Items

Attaching a Menu Module to a Form

Checked and Enabled Property of Menu Items

Creating an Iconic Toolbar

CHAPTER TWELVE

Working with Reports

IN THIS CHAPTER

- ➤ Features of Reports Tool

- ➤ Report Data Model

- ➤ Report Layout

- ➤ Parameter Form

- ➤ Oracle Report Interface

- ➤ Creating a Default Tabular Report

- ➤ Creating Computed Columns

- ➤ Customizing Report Layout

12. WORKING WITH REPORTS

After validated data is stored in Oracle tables, it is necessary to extract this data and display it on VDU or printer. Business managers then can make business decisions based on how they interpret the displayed data.

The process of data extraction and its display is called Report creation. For this purpose, Oracle provides a GUI based report writer tool called Oracle Reports Builder. Oracle Reports is a tool for developing, displaying, and printing production-quality reports.

FEATURES

Oracle Reports enables creation of a variety of reports, such as a tabular report, form report, master/detail reports, nested matrix reports and mailing labels. Its major features include:

- Data model and layout editors in which the structure and format of the report can be created.
- Object Navigator that permits navigation among the data and layout objects in the report.
- Packaged functions for computations
- Support for fonts, colors, and graphics
- Conditional printing capabilities
- Fully-integrated Previewer for viewing report output.
- A unique **Non-procedural Approach** of Oracle Reports helps concentrate design improvements instead of programming. It is easy-to-use, fill in the form interface and powerful defaults make developing and maintaining even the most complex reports fast and simple.
- Oracle Reports adheres to the native look-and-feel of the host environment. Thus, it brings about **Portability with GUI Conformance**. Oracle Reports can be created on bit-mapped platforms and run on character-mode, bit-mapped, and block-mode platforms with the guarantee of identical functionality and complete compatibility across all systems.
- Oracle Reports can be **fully integrated with Other Oracle Products** such as Oracle Forms, Oracle Graphics and Oracle Mail. For example, graphics and charts can be included in a report, and send output to other users via Oracle Mail.
- Report's **Open Architecture** enables incorporating user-defined routines written in COBOL, C and most other programming languages, as well as the powerful PL/SQL language. Information can be presented exactly as per the report specification provided.

BASIC CONCEPTS

In the following few pages, the tool in general and its basic components are explained. There are three steps to building a report with Oracle reports
- Create a new report definition.
- Define the data model. Data along with their relationships and calculations can be specified to produce report output.
- Specify layout (i.e. design). Default or customized report layouts can be used.

CREATING A REPORT USING ORACLE REPORTS BUILDER

A New report can be created
- By using a Report Wizard
- Create a report Manually

Before a new report is created, the components of an Oracle Report must be understood.

DEFINING A DATA MODEL FOR A REPORT

To specify data for a report, a data model should be defined. A Data model is composed of some or all of the following data definition objects
- Queries
- Groups
- Columns
- Parameters
- Links

A sample data model in the data model editor is as shown in diagram 12.1.

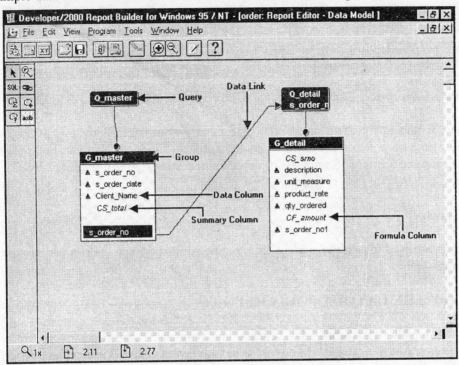

Diagram 12.1 : Sample Data Model

Queries:

As in diagram 12.1 Queries are SQL SELECT statements that fetch data from the Oracle database. These statements are fired each time the report is run.

Groups:

Groups determine the hierarchy of data appearing in the report, and are primarily used to group columns selected in the query as shown in diagram 12.1. Oracle report automatically creates a group for each query.

Data Columns:

Data Columns contain the data values for a report. Default data columns, corresponding to the table columns included in each query's SELECT list are automatically created by Oracle Reports. Each column is placed in the group associated with the query that selected the column.

Formula Columns:

Formulas can be entered in Formula columns to create computed columns. Formulas can be written using PL/SQL syntax. Formula columns names are generally preceded by **CF_** to distinguish them from data columns.

Summary Columns:

Summary Columns are used for calculating summary information like sum, average etc. This column uses a set of predefined Oracle aggregate functions that can be applied to data or formula columns. Summary columns named are generally preceded by **CS_** to distinguish them from data columns.

Data Links:

Data links are used to establish parent-child relationships between queries and groups via column matching.

SPECIFY THE LAYOUT FOR A REPORT

After defining the data model, the report's layout must be specified. There are eight default layout styles provided. One of these default layouts can be selected and modified as required. These are:
- Tabular,
- Form
- Master / Detail,
- Form Letter,
- Mailing Label,
- Matrix,
- Group Above
- Group Left

A report layout can contain following layout objects:
- Repeating frames
- Frames
- Fields
- Boilerplate

In the diagram 12.2, a sample layout, in the Layout Editor is shown.

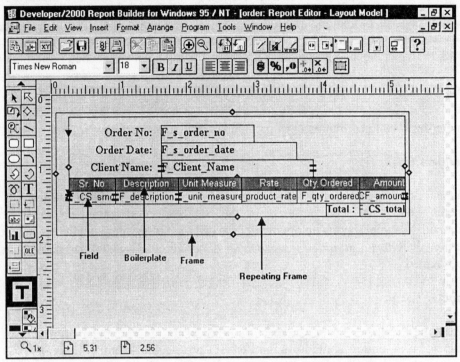

Diagram 12.2 : Sample LayoutShown in the Layout Editor

Frames:

Frames as shown in diagram 12.2 surrounds other layout objects, enabling control of multiple objects simultaneously; e.g., ensuring that they maintain their positions relative to each other in the output.

Repeating Frames:

Repeating frames as shown in diagram 12.2 act as placeholders for groups (i.e. repeating values) and present rows of data retrieved from the database. Repeating frames repeat as often as the number of rows retrieved.

Fields:

Fields act as placeholders for columns values. They define the formatting attributes for all columns displayed in the report. A field can be placed inside a frame as shown in diagram 12.2 or a repeating frame.

Boilerplate:

Boilerplate consists of text and graphics that appear in a report each time it is run; e.g., a label as shown in diagram 12.2 appearing above a column of data is boilerplate text. Graphics drawn in the layout as well as text added to the layout are called boilerplates.

SPECIFY A RUNTIME PARAMETER FORM FOR A REPORT

Parameter form includes a number of parameters used to accept input from the user.

Parameters:

Parameters are variables for a report that accept input from the user at runtime. The parameter values can then be used in the SQL select statement to retrieve data conditionally. Oracle Reports automatically creates a set of system parameters at runtime. These include *report destination type*, *number of copies* etc. User-defined parameters can also be created.

Parameter Form:

The Runtime Parameter Form can be customized using the Parameter Form editor. The Parameter Form editor contains a subset of the Layout editor's functionality, and determines the positions of objects, as they should appear in the Runtime Parameter Form.

A Runtime Parameter Form can contain following objects:
*   Fields
*   Boilerplates

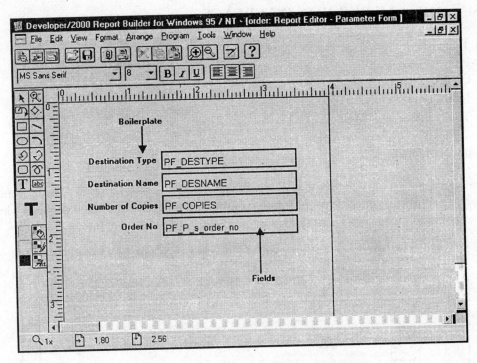

Diagram 12.3 : Parameters Form Editor

In diagram 12.3, a sample layout in the parameter form editor is shown.

Fields:

Fields in the parameter form editor act as placeholders for parameters. They define the formatting attributes for all parameters displayed in the Runtime Parameter Form.

Boilerplates:

Boilerplate in the Parameter Form editor refers to text and graphics that appear in the Runtime Parameter Form each time it is run; e.g., a label denoting a particular parameter is boilerplate text. Lines or boxes drawn in the layout are also considered boilerplate, as well as any added text.

USING ORACLE REPORTS INTERFACE

The following interface components are to define report objects:
- Property Sheets
- Object Navigator
- Editors
- Tool palettes and Toolbars

Property Sheets:

A property sheet is a window that displays the settings for defining an Oracle Reports object. Each object (query, group, frame, column, parameter, etc.) has a property sheet. An example of the property sheet of a computed field is as shown in the diagram 12.4.

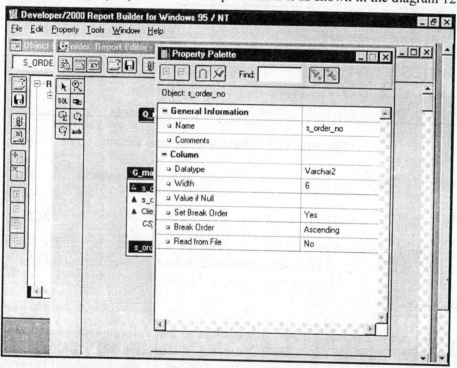

Diagram 12.4 : Property Sheet of a Database Column

Object Navigator:

The Object Navigator shows a hierarchical view of objects in the report. Object Navigator can be used to gain an overview of a report's organization. Each item listed is called a node, and represents an object or type of object the report can contain or reference.

Editors:

An editor is a work area that contains graphical representations of related objects. The Data Model editor is used to manipulate (create, delete, move, resize, copy, paste, etc.), data model objects, the Layout editor is used to manipulate layout objects, and the Parameter Form editor is used to manipulate parameter form objects.

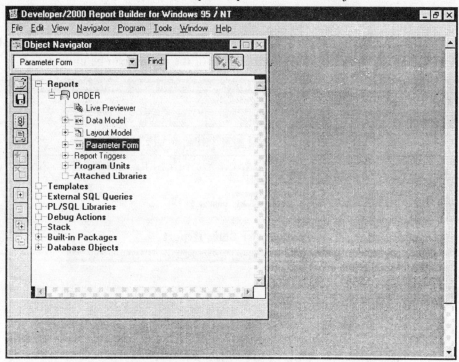

Diagram 12.5 : Editor Displayed in the Object Navigator

- The *Data Model editor*, in which the data for the report (i.e. defining Query, groups, computation fields etc. for the report) is defined.
- The *Layout editor*, in which the report layout (i.e. designing the looks of the reports) is created.
- The *Parameter Form Editor* is used to customize the appearance of the Runtime Parameter Form that optionally appears at runtime and enables data entry for the parameter values that affect report execution).

Palettes and Toolbars:

The Tool palettes and toolbars contain tools used to manually create or manipulate objects in editors. Each editor has a tool palette and a toolbar; each tool appears as an icon on the palette or toolbar. Some tools, such as the Select tool, are common to all the palettes. Other tools are specific to the editors in which they appear. Toolbar items also have textual menu equivalents.

CREATING A DEFAULT TABULAR REPORT

Creating a tabular '*Productwise Sales Report*' from *sales_order*, *sales_order_details* and *Product_master* tables. In this exercise, we will go step-by-step to create a report, as shown in diagram 12.6.

For ease of understanding, the tables described below are populated with around 50 records so that pages handling either on the VDU or the printer can be understood.

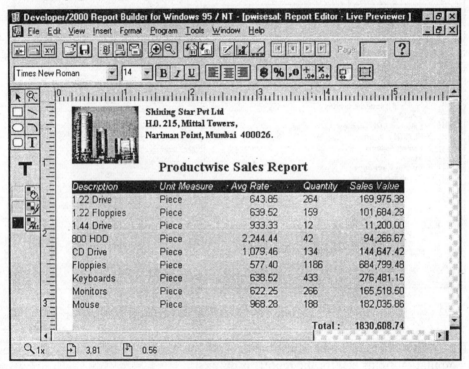

Diagram 12.6 : Productwise Sales Report

The definitions of the tables used are as mentioned below:

Table Name : product_master
Description : stores information about products supplied by the company.

Column Name	Data Type	Size	Column Description
product_no	varchar2	6	Unique primary key allotted to each product.
description	varchar2	25	Description of the product
unit_measure	varchar2	10	Unit by which the product is measured.
qty_on_hand	number	8	Quantity which is available in the stock.
reorder_lvl	number	8	Quantity level when the stock should be re-ordered.
cost_price	number	8,2	Cost price of the product.
selling_price	number	8,2	Selling price of the product.

Table Name   : sales_order (Master)
Description   : Use to store information about orders placed by the clients.

Column Name	Data Type	Size	Attributes
s_order_no	varchar2	6	Unique primary key allotted to each order.
s_order_date	date		Date on which the order is placed.
client_no	varchar2	6	Client No., who places the order.
status	varchar2	2	Order Status (In Process IP, FullFilled FP, Not Processed NP)

Table Name : sales_order_details
Description : Use to store information about order details.

Column Name	Data Type	Size	Attributes
s_order_no	varchar2	6	Order No. for which details have to be stored.
product_no	varchar2	6	Product No. for which details have to be stored.
product_rate	number	8,2	The rate agreed upon.
qty_ordered	number	8	Quantity of goods ordered.

The following steps are used to crate the report shown in the diagram 2.1:

- Create a new report definition.
- Connect to the database and select the data columns.
- Specify a default report layout.
- Save and run the report.
- View the report output.
- Create formulae columns, specify a default report layout.
- Create summary columns, specify a default report layout.
- Create user parameters.
- Arrange the layout and run the report.

Creating a new Report Definition:

The screen that will be displayed, as soon as the Oracle Report is invoked is as shown in diagram 12.7. The Object Navigator will display a new report definition.

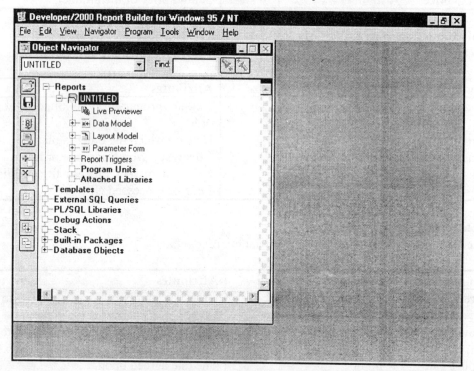

Diagram 12.7 : New Report Definition

Connecting to the Database:

1. Select **File**, **Connect** menu options. The *Connect* dialog box will appear, prompting you for your username and password.

2. Click in the *User Name* field and type your username.

3. Click in the *Password* field and type password and connect string.

Specifying the Data and Layout for the Report:

1. After invoking the Report Builder and connecting to the database, the next step is to specify the data for the report. Click on **Tools..Report Wizard...** to start the report wizard for a new report. Report Wizard shows a number of Tab pages to enter information required for report creation. The different tab pages are:
   - Style
   - Data
   - Fields
   - Totals
   - Labels
   - Template

Select **Tabular** as the report style as shown in diagram 12.8 and click on Next.

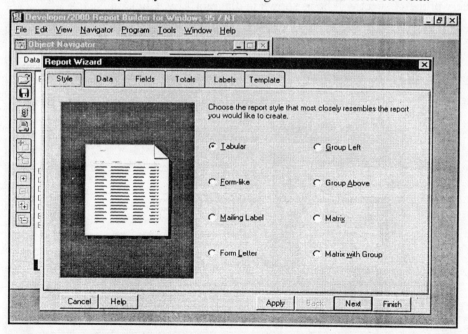

Diagram 12.8 : Specifying Tabular Presentation Style

2. Any report created using Report Builder requires a query via which data will be retrieved for the report. The **Data** Tab allows creation of an SQL statement using Query Builder. The SQL statement can also be entered in the multi line edit box provided in the data tab.

Create a query with a select statement as follows:

```
select   product_master.description,
         product_master.unit_measure,
         avg( sales_order_details.product_rate ) "avg_product_rate",
         sum( sales_order_details.qty_ordered) "sum_quantity"
from     sales_order, product_master,
         sales_order_details
where (product_master.product_no = sales_order_details.product_no ) and
      ( sales_order_details.s_order_no = sales_order.s_order_no )
group by product_master.description ,
         product_master. unit_measure
order by product_master.description  asc
```

This select will actually get the data of the report from a base table. The completed query property sheet will be as shown in diagram 12.9. Click on Next.

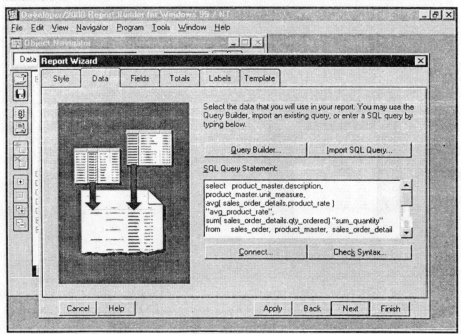

Diagram 12.9 : Completed Query Property Sheet

3. Fields Tab is used to specify the fields that must be displayed in tabular format. Select all fields by clicking on [>] icon. Completed screen will be as displayed in diagram 12.10.

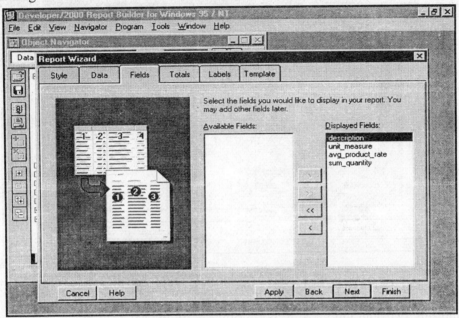

Diagram 12.10 : Selecting the Fields that must be displayed in Tabular format

4. Click on Next. The **Totals** tab is displayed that allows creation of summary columns using aggregate functions. This report does not include totals for the selected fields and thus click on Next.

5. The Labels for the columns can be changed using the **Labels** tab. Change the Label of *Sum_Quantity* column to *Quantity* and *Avg_Product_Rate* to *Avg. Rate*. The completed screen will be displayed as shown in diagram 12.11.

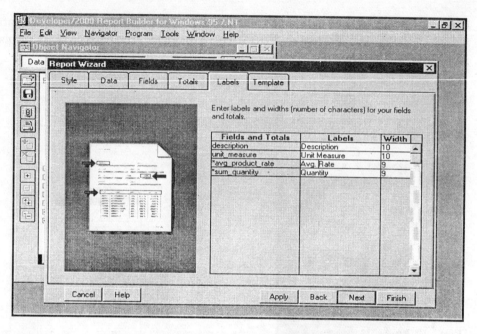

Diagram 12.11 : Changing Column Labels

6. Report can be created from templates. There are a number of pre-determined templates available in Oracle Reports Builder. By default reports are created using pre-determined template named *Corporate 1* as shown in diagram 12.12. Click on Finish.

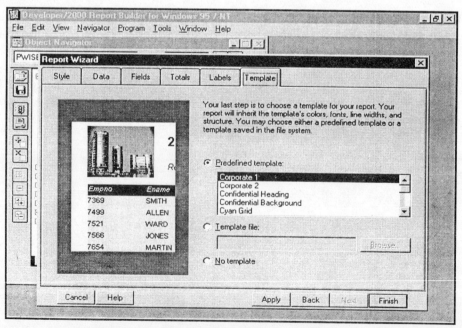

Diagram 12.12 : Selecting a Pre-Defined Report Template

7. Reports Builder includes a Live Previewer that is used to display... Finish button is clicked, the Report Runtime is invoked as shown in d...

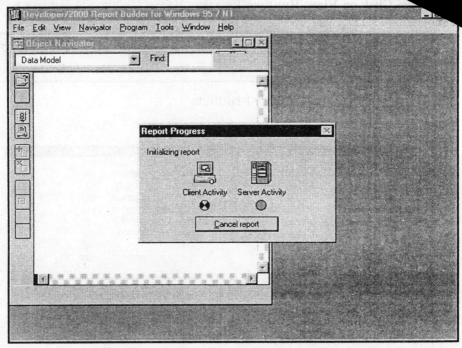

Diagram 12.13 : Invoking Reports Runtime

The Report format with live data is then displayed as shown in diagram 12.14.

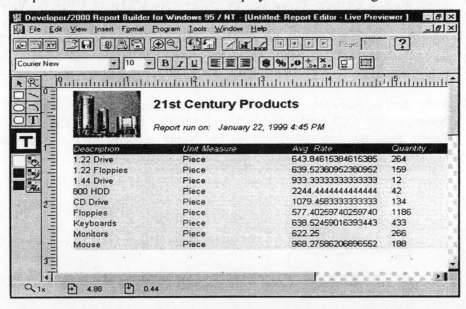

Diagram 12.14 : Report Displayed with Live Data

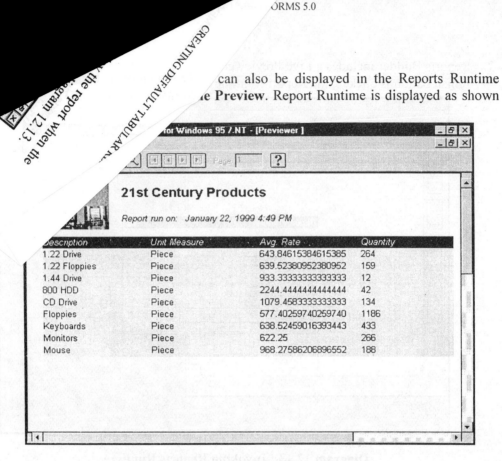

can also be displayed in the Reports Runtime ... e **Preview**. Report Runtime is displayed as shown

Diagram 12.15 : Report Runtime Window

9. Close Report Runtime Previewer by clicking on ☒ icon. Click on **View..Data Model** to open the Data Model editor. Data model editor displays a query object named *Q_1*, a group object named as *G_description* (i.e. **G_** followed by the first data column) and data column selected by using an SQL Select statement. The query object and the group object must be renamed appropriately.

Right click on query object and select Property Palette from the pop up menu. Set the **Name** property to *Q_psales*. Similarly right click on group object and select Property Palette from the pop up menu. Set the **Name** property of the group object to *G_psales*. The completed data model editor is shown in diagram 12.16.

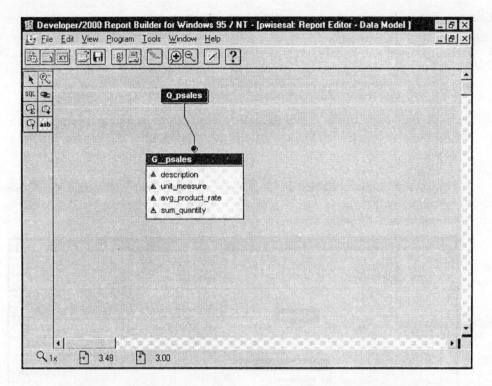

Diagram 12.16 : Objects displayed in the Data Model Editor

10. Click on **File..Save** to save the report. Specify the report name as *pwisesal.rdf*. Specify the path for the report file and click on **OK**. The report file will be saved with the specified named.

CREATING COMPUTED COLUMNS

Computed columns calculate values based either on PL/SQL expressions or on data provided by database columns. There are two types of computed columns that can added to a report:

Formula Columns:
Formula columns compute their values using PL/SQL expressions. Formulas can operate on multiple values per record (e.g. :avg_price * :quantity).

Summaries Columns:
Summary columns compute their values using built in functions of Oracle Reports. Summaries operate on one value over multiple records (e.g. *sum of sales amount*).

Create a Formula using the Formula Column Tool:

1. A formula column can be created in the data model editor. Click on **View..Data Model** to open the data model editor. The Data model editor displays a query object and a group object that encloses a number of columns.

2. Increase the height of the group to make place for the formulae column. Select the *formula column* tool in the tool palette and place it after the last field in the group *G_psales*.

   A new column initially named as CF_1 is created as shown in diagram 12.17. Since a new column within the *G_psales* group is created, it will be displayed as often as the other columns in the same group.

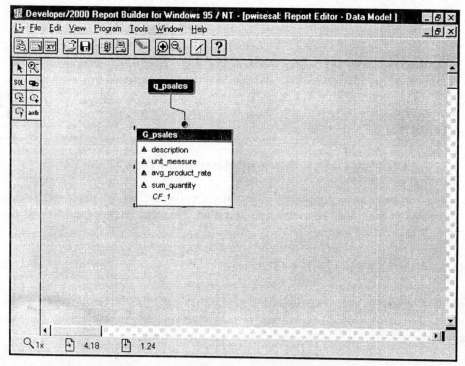

Diagram 12.17: Creating a Formula Column for Sales Value

3. Set the following properties for the formulae column.

   Name   : CF_sales_value

4. Click on the property PL/SQL formulae property. The Program Unit editor is invoked as shown in diagram 12.18.

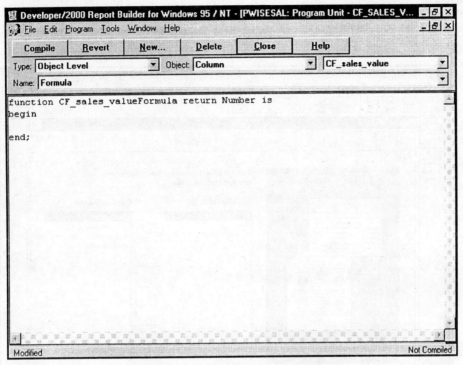

Diagram 12.18: Program Unit Editor

5. Enter the complete formula for the sale value for each product :

> **function** CF_sales_valueFormula **return** Number **is**
> **begin**
> > **return** :avg_product_rate * :sum_quantity ;
> **end;**

The colons appear before *avg_product_rate* and *sum_quantity* because it functions as a bind variable reference; i.e. the values of *sum_quantity* are substituted into the formula at runtime.

6. Click on **Compile**. If the function is correctly typed in, the status line reports, "*Successfully Compiled.*" Otherwise, the status line reports "*Compiled with Errors,*" and the Program Unit editor points out the errors in the Compilation Messages field. (*If this occurs, correct the mistake in the Source Text field and select Compile again.*)

7. Click on **Close** to close the Program Unit editor, then close the property sheet. *cf_sales_value* is now listed as a column belonging to *G_Psales*. The column name appears in italic, indicating that it is a user-created column.

8. Right click on the data model editor and select Report Wizard to invoke the report wizard.

9. Select Fields tab. The newly created field is shown in the available fields list item as shown in diagram 12.19.

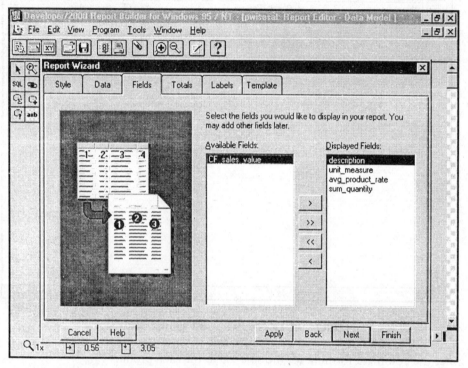

Diagram 12.19 : Formulae Field displayed in the available Fields List

10. Select this field as shown in diagram 12.20 and click on Next.

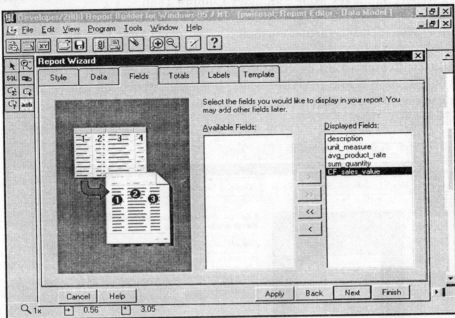

Diagram 12.20 : Selected Formulae Field

11. Select Label tab and change the label of the formula field to *Sales Value*. Click on Finish. New column will now be displayed in the Live Previewer as shown in diagram 12.21.

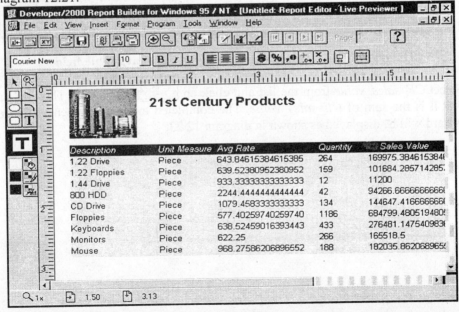

Diagram 12.21 : New Column displayed in Live Previewer

Create a Report Summary using Summary Column Tool:

To create a summary that computes the total sale i.e. *sum of sales value* for each product:

1. Invoke the Report wizard by clicking on **Tools..Report Wizard**. Select the **Totals** tab. A List of available fields for which summary information can be specified is displayed as shown in diagram 12.22.

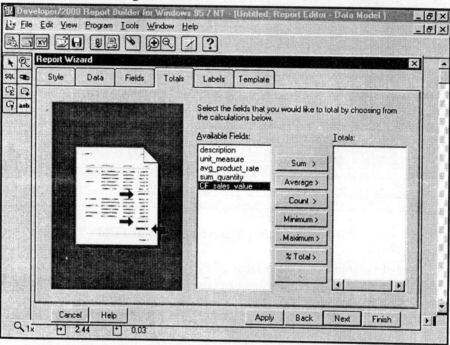

Diagram 12.22 : Totals Tab displaying list of available fields

2. Select *CF_sales_value* from the list and click on Sum > icon. Thus indicating that it is the sum of *CF_sales_value*. The completed totals tab screen in the report wizard will be displayed as shown in diagram 12.23.

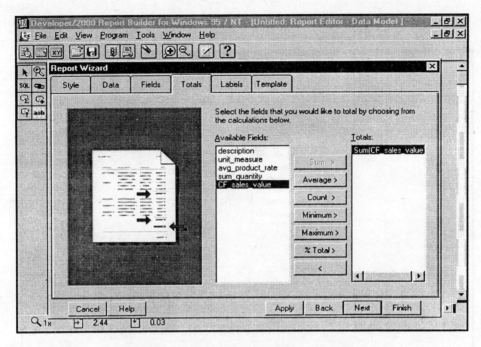

Diagram 12.23 : Completed Totals Tab

3. Click on Finish. The output will be as displayed in diagram 12.24.

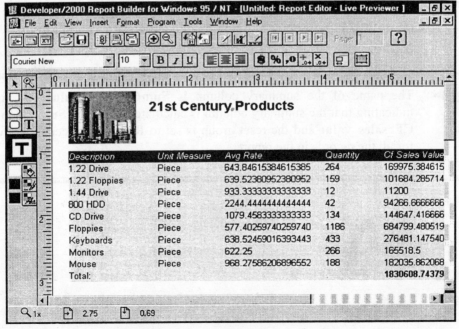

Diagram 12.24: Output of the report

4. Open the Data model editor by clicking on **View..Data Model**. The summary column with a default name will be displayed as shown in diagram 12.25.

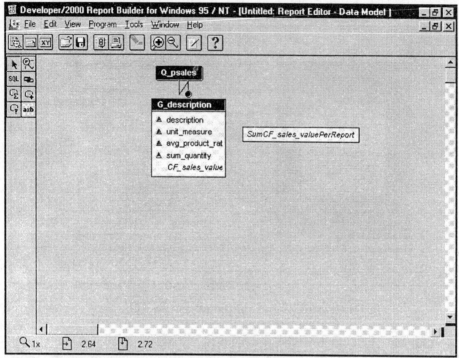

Diagram 12.25 : Summary Column displayed in Data Model Editor

Note

The name of the summary column is **SumCF_sales_value_Per_Report** indicating that the summary column is calculated using the **Sum** function on **CF_sales_value** and the reset group is set to **Report** i.e. accumulate values for all the records in the report.

CUSTOMIZING REPORT LAYOUT

Customizing a report includes changing the default layout to improve the overall appearance and readability of the report.

Some of the useful tools available for achieving this are:

Change Layout Settings:

Oracle Reports offers a variety of options for displaying text and graphics. Any font (e.g. Courier), weight (e.g., bold), and style (e.g., italic) available on the system can be used to create fields, boilerplate text etc.

- Select the item to be changed and click on **Format..Font**. Oracle Reports displays a standard *Font Setting* dialog box. Specify a font name as *Courier New*, size as *10*, *bold*.
- Similarly text for a report can be inserted by creating a new boiler text and entering required *Text*. Specifying the required text. Arranging the fields and texts inside the corresponding group frame, changing the format of the field, aligning the fields with respect to each other etc. can also be done.
- Notice the Fill Color, Line Color and Text Color tools located near the bottom of the Tool palette. The **Line Color Tool** is used to customize borders around layout objects. The **Fill Color tool**, is used to fill layout objects with colors and patterns and, **Text Color tool**, enables you to change the default text color.

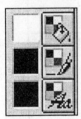

The *Fill/Line/Text Display* shows the currently selected fill, border, and text.

The default fill and border for objects created by Oracle Reports are *transparent*, while the default for objects you create is a black, one-point line around a white fill.

 Note

Since the changing the text defaults, when the layout is re-built, all objects are created with white backgrounds and black borders. To prevent this, set the Fill and Border Color to transparent.

Deleting Default Header and Inserting Report Header:

1. Select the text marked as '21st Century Products' and press the <Delete> Key. The default header will be deleted. Similarly select 'Report Run on' and 'Date' items and press <Delete> key.

2. Click on Text item on the vertical tool bar i.e. button on it and place it in the header. Enter the name of the company and the address as follows :

Shining Star Pvt. Ltd.
H. O. : 215, Mittal Towers,
Nariman Point, Mumbai 400 026.

3. Click on tne alignment tool and change the text alignment to *Left*. Similarly change the font to Times New Roman and font Size as 10.

4. Select all the fields and labels by using <Shift> <Click> and use the down arrow key to move the report data lower down on the page.

5. Place another text item and enter the text as '**Productwise Sales Report**'. Change the font to Times New Roman and font Size as 14. The completed report will be as shown in diagram 12.26.

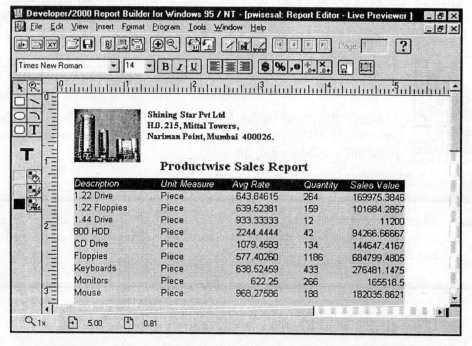

Diagram 12.26 : Report Formatted with appropriate Header

6. Right click on Avg_Rate column and select Property Palette. Set the format Mask property to NNN,NN0.00 as shown in diagram 12.27. Similarly set the format mask for *sales_Value* and *Total*.

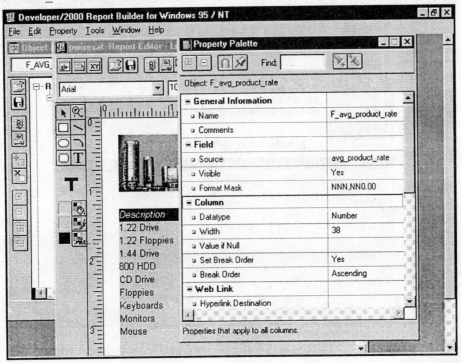

Diagram 12.27 : Specifying Format Mask

7. The completed report format will be displayed as shown in diagram 12.28.

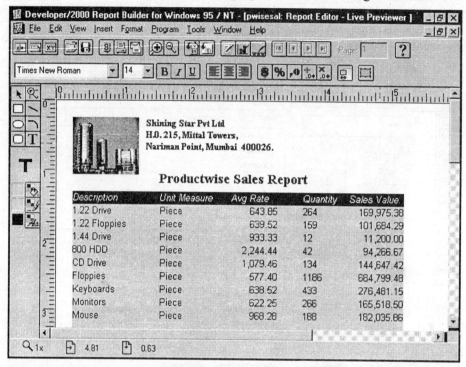

Diagram 12.28 : Report format after Specifying Format Mask

SELF REVIEW QUESTIONS

TRUE AND FALSE

1. Reports with 8 different presentation styles can be created in Reports Builder tool.

     A) True   B) False

2. A report summary object is always placed in a group.

     A) True   B) False

FILL IN THE BLANKS

1. Reports Design file has an extension of _____.

2. Report Runtime file has an extension of _____.

3. BoilerText placed outside the report frame are printed _____ per report.

4. _____ is used to display system date in reports.

5. Fields are enclosed within _____ frame.

6. User parameters are included in _____ model.

7. Report Totals can be created using _____.

8. The two types of computation objects on a report are :

    • _____

    • _____

9. The sub tools for report creation are:

    • _____

    • _____

    • _____

    • _____

10. Two types of parameters are available in the report tool. These are:

   • _____

   • _____

11. Objects used for grouping header and footer information are called _____.

Features of Report Tool

Define a Data Model for a Report
- Queries
- Groups
- Data Links

Specify the Layout for a Report
- Report Layout Formats
- Frames
- Repeating Frames
- Fields
- Boilerplate

Specify runtime parameters for a report
- Parameters
- Parameter Form

Using Oracle Report Interface
- Property Sheet
- Object Navigator
- Report Editor
- Tool Palettes and Toolbar

Creating a Default Tabular Report
- Creating a new Report Definition
- Connecting to the Database
- Specifying Data and Layout for the Report
- Creating Formula Columns
- Creating Summary Columns
- Customizing Report Layout

CHAPTER THIRTEEN

Creating a Break Report

IN THIS CHAPTER

- ➤ Creating a New Definition for Break Report

- ➤ Group Left Presentation Style

- ➤ Specifying Break Field

- ➤ Customizing Break Report Layout

13. CREATING A BREAK REPORT

Break report is created when repeating values for a column have to be printed only once. Thus the break reports are effective only when the select statement includes a column, called a break column containing at least one value which repeats over multiple records.

Focus:

Creating a control break 'Order Backlog Report' from Sales_order, Sales_order_details and Product_master tables that displays all the pending orders along with the products that have not been delivered. The completed report is as shown in diagram 13.1.

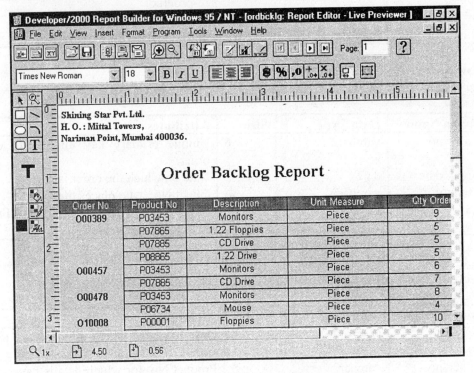

Diagram 13.1 : Control Break Report

The definitions of the tables used are as mentioned below:

Table Name : product_master
Description : stores information about products supplied by the company.

Column Name	Data Type	Size	Column Description
product_no	varchar2	6	Unique Primary key allotted to each product
description	varchar2	25	Description of the product
unit_measure	varchar2	10	Unit by which the product is measured.
qty_on_hand	number	8	Quantity which is available in the stock.
reorder_lvl	number	8	Quantity level when the stock should be re-ordered.
cost_price	number	8,2	Cost price of the product.
selling_price	number	8,2	Selling price of the product.

Table Name : sales_order (Master)
Description : Use to store information about orders placed by the clients.

Column Name	Data Type	Size	Attributes
s_order_no	varchar2	6	Unique primary key allotted to each order.
s_order_date	date		Date on which the order is placed.
client_no	varchar2	6	Client No., who places the order.
status	varchar2	2	Order Status (In Process IP, FullFilled FP, Not Processed NP)

Table Name : sales_order_details
Description : Use to store information about order details.

Column Name	Data Type	Size	Attributes
s_order_no	varchar2	6	Order No. for which details have to be stored.
product_no	varchar2	6	Product No. for which details have to be stored.
product_rate	number	8,2	The rate agreed upon.
qty_ordered	number	8	Quantity of goods ordered.
qty_disp	number	8	Quantity of goods dispatched.

To create the report shown in the diagram 13.1, we will follow following steps:
- Create a new report definition.
- Define the data.
- Create a break group
- Create summary column
- Specify a default report layout.
- Save and run the report.
- Arrange the layout and run the report.

CREATING A NEW REPORT DEFINITION

1. Invoke Oracle Reports Builder and connect to Oracle. Click on **Tools..Report Wizard...** to create new report.

2. Select **Group Left** as a presentation Style as shown in diagram 13.2. Click on Next.

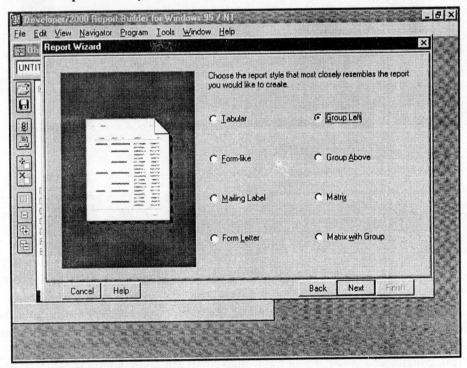

Diagram 13.2 : Specifying Group Left as the Presentation Style

3. Enter the SQL statement as in the Data Tab. The SQL statement is as follows:

select   sales_order.s_order_no,
         sales_order_details.product_no, description,
         unit_measure, qty_ordered
from   sales_order, sales_order_details, product_master
where   sales_order.s_order_no = sales_order_details.s_order_no and
         sales_order_details.product_no = product_master.product_no and
         sales_order.order_status <> 'FP'

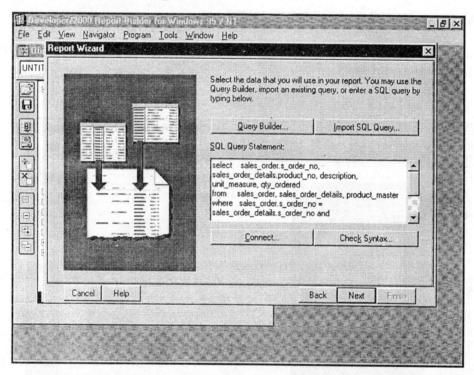

Diagram 13.3 : Completed SQL statement in the Data Tab

4. Group Left report requires the name of the column that must be used as a break column. In the current example, the *s_order_no* is repeating as the multiple items are selected for every order. Thus the break column must be set to *s_order_no*. Select the break column as *s_order_no* in the displayed screen and click on [>] icon.

5. *s_order_no* is displayed in the group field list as shown in diagram 13.4

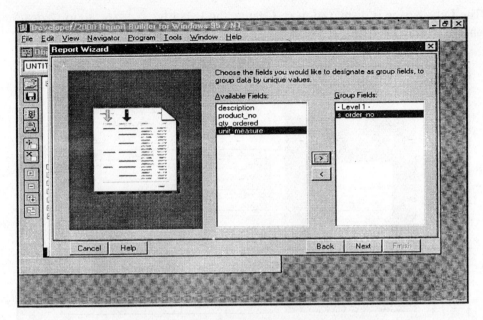

Diagram 13.4 : Selected Group / Break Field

6. The list of columns that must be displayed on the report is asked for. Click on ▶▶ to select all the columns. The completed screen will be displayed as shown in diagram 13.5.

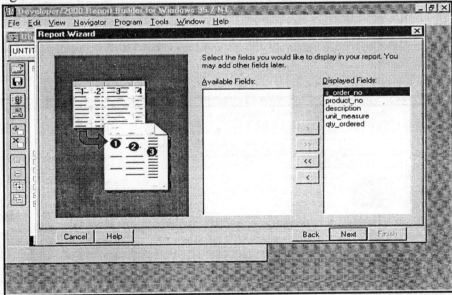

Diagram 13.5 : Selecting columns that must be displayed on the report

7. The Totals and calculation page is displayed next. Since the totals are not required for the selected columns, click on next.

8. The Labels page is displayed next. Change the Label for *s_order_no* to *Order No* as shown in diagram 13.6.

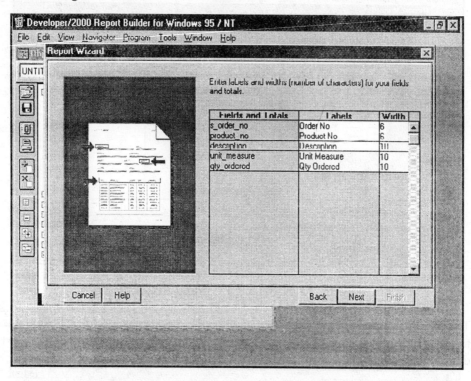

Diagram 13.6 : Changing Column Labels

9. The Templates screen is then displayed. Select 'Cyan Grid' presentation style and click on Finish. A default tabular report with a group break on *s_order_no* is displayed as shown in diagram 13.7.

About Repeating Frames:

Repeating frames hold data owned by their corresponding groups. Repeating frames are called so because repeating frames are repeated as many times as necessary to display all the records.

The report layout contains two repeating frames. The first repeating frame includes column *s_order_no*. All other columns are included in the in the second repeating frame.

4. Save the report as "ordbcklg.rdf" and run the report by clicking on **View..Runtime Preview**. The Report Runtime preview will be displayed in the diagram 13.8.

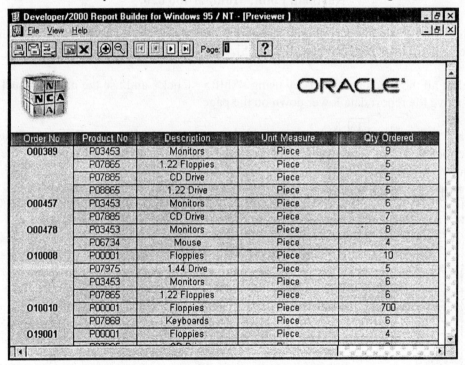

Diagram 13.8 : Report output at Run Time

ARRANGING THE LAYOUT

Deleting Default Header and Inserting Report Header:

1. Select the images displayed on the report and press <Delete> Key. The default header objects will be deleted.

2. Click on Text ⊤ item on the vertical tool bar i.e. button on it and place it in the header. Enter the name of the company and the address as follows :

Shining Star Pvt. Ltd.
H. O. : 215, Mittal Towers,
Nariman Point, Mumbai 400 026.

3. Click on the alignment tool and change the text alignment to *Left*. Similarly change the font to Times New Roman and font Size as 10.

4. Select all the fields and labels by using <Shift> <Click> and use the down arrow key to move the report data lower down on the page.

5. Place another text ⊤ item and enter the text as **'Order Backlog Report'**. Change the font to Times New Roman and font Size as 14. The completed report will be as shown in diagram 13.9.

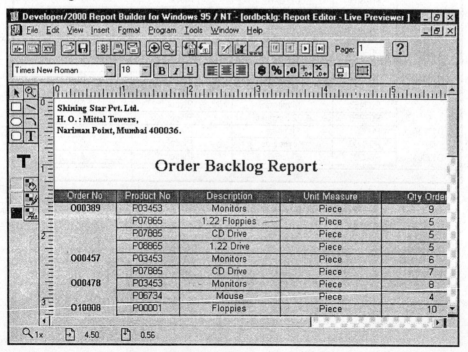

Diagram 13.9 : Final Report Output

SELF REVIEW QUESTIONS

FILL IN THE BLANKS

1. _____ reports are created when repeating values are to be printed only once.

2. _____ and _____ presentation styles are used for break reports.

3. Graph can be displayed on the form using _____ function in the _____ PL/SQL library.

4. A Break Report consists of atleast _____ groups.

A QUICK REVIEW

Specifying Report Definition for a Break Report

Group Left Presentation Style

Selecting Break Fields for a Break Report

Arranging Break Report Layout

CHAPTER FOURTEEN

Master / Detail Report

IN THIS CHAPTER

> Working of a Master / Detail Report

> Differences between Break Report and Master / Detail Report

> Creating a Master / Detail Report

> Creating Group Summary Columns

> Master / Detail Report Layout

> Parameter Passing in Reports

14. MASTER/DETAIL REPORT

A simple master / detail report contains two groups of data i.e. *master group* and *detail group*. For each master record fetched, only the related detail records are fetched.

Master / detail reports are similar to break reports in the way data is fetched. For every master *or break group*, related detail records are fetched.

In addition, if the default **Group Above** layout style is used to format a break report, the output will look like a master / detail report as defined by Oracle Reports. The master record will be displayed in **Form-Like** format (labels on the left) and the detail records will be displayed in **Tabular** format (labels on the top).

CONCEPTS

Break reports and master / detail reports can result in similar outputs but they require different data model objects. A break report uses <u>one</u> query and <u>two or more</u> groups, while a master / detail report uses <u>two</u> queries, each of which has one group.

Relationship between the two queries must be established in a master / detail report. This relation is set by a **Data Link**.

Data Link Object:

Data link object is a data model object, which joins multiple queries. For a simple master / detail report, two queries will be linked using primary and foreign keys of the tables from which data is selected. The Query with the primary key column i.e. *the source for the master records* is called the **Parent Query** and the Query with the foreign key column i.e. *the source for the detail records* is called the **Child Query**.

Linking two tables via primary and foreign keys is similar to specifying a join condition. Information in the data link object is used to join two queries. The **where** clause for the join is added to the child query's SELECT statement at run time.

Note

> Join defined by a data link object is an **Outer Join** i.e. in addition to returning all rows that satisfy the link's condition, an outer join returns all rows for the parent query that do not match a row from the child query.

Layout:

Master / detail report uses **Group Above** layout style in which master records display across the page with the labels to the left of their fields and the detail records appear below the master records in tabular format.

 Tip

A maximum of 1 record per page can be specified to ensure that only one master record and its associated detail records are displayed per page of report output.

CREATING A MASTER/DETAIL REPORT

Focus:

Create a Master / Detail '*Sales Order Form Report*' as shown in diagram 14.1 from '*Sales_order*', '*Sales_order_details*', '*Client_master*', '*Salesman_master*' and '*Product_master*' tables.

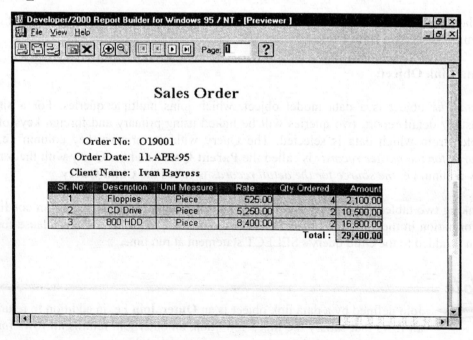

Diagram : 14.1 : Master / Detail Report

The definitions of the tables used are as mentioned below:

Table Name   : sales_order (Master)
Description   : Use to store information about orders placed by the clients.

Column Name	Data Type	Size	Attributes
s_order_no	varchar2	6	Unique primary key allotted to each order.
s_order_date	date		Date on which the order is placed.
client_no	varchar2	6	Client No., who places the order.
status	varchar2	2	Order Status (In Process IP, fulfilled FP, Not Processed NP)

Table Name : sales_order_details (Detail)
Description : Use to store information about order details.

Column Name	Data Type	Size	Attributes
s_order_no	varchar2	6	Order No. for which details have to be stored.
product_no	varchar2	6	Product No. for which details have to be stored.
product_rate	number	8,2	The rate agreed upon.
qty_ordered	number	8	Quantity of goods ordered.

Table Name : product_master
Description : stores information about products supplied by the company.

Column Name	Data Type	Size	Column Description
product_no	varchar2	6	Unique primary key allotted to each product.
description	varchar2	25	Description of the product
unit_measure	varchar2	10	Unit by which the product is measured.
qty_on_hand	number	8	Quantity which is available in the stock.
reorder_lvl	number	8	Quantity level when the stock should be re-ordered.
cost_price	number	8,2	Cost price of the product.
selling_price	number	8,2	Selling price of the product.

Table Name : client_master

Description : Use to store information about clients.

Column Name	Data Type	Size	Column Description
client_no	varchar2	6	Unique primary key allotted to each client.
name	varchar2	20	client's name
address1	varchar2	30	First line in the client's address.
address2	varchar2	30	Second line in the client's address.
city	varchar2	15	City in which the client is located.
state	varchar2	15	State in which the client is located.
pincode	number	6	pin code
bal_due	number	10,2	Balance amount payable by the client.

Report as shown in the Diagram 14.1, is created as follows:

- Create a new report definition by creating 2 queries for master and detail tables and link them.
- Create formula and summary columns.
- Specify a default report layout.
- Arrange the Layout.
- Save and run the report.

CREATING THE REPORT DEFINITION

Master / detail report can be created using multiple queries and selecting 'Group Above' presentation style.

Creating a Master Detail Report using Multiple Queries:

A master detail report can be created using two queries. The first query is used to extract data for the master section and the second query is used to extract data for the detail section.

1. Right click on the Data Model and select Report Editor. Data Model editor is displayed as shown in diagram 14.2.

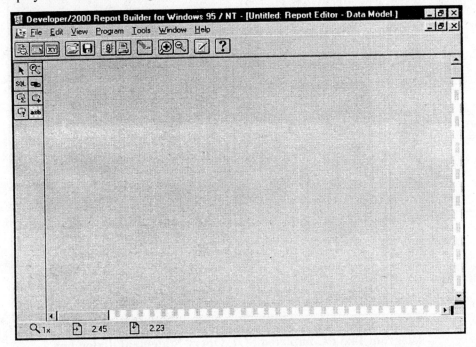

Diagram 14.2 : Report Data Model Editor

2. Select   Query $\boxed{\text{SQL}}$ object from the toolbox and place it on the report work area.

3. *SQL Query Statement* dialog box is displayed. Enter the SQL statement used to extract data for the master section. The completed screen will be displayed as shown in diagram 14.3.

```
select   s_order_no, s_order_date,
         client_master.name "Client Name"
from     sales_order, client_master
where    sales_order.client_no = client_master.client_no;
```

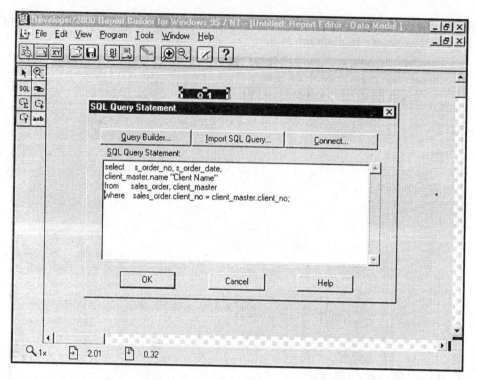

Diagram 14.3 : Completed SQL Query Statement dialog box

4. Click on OK. For every query created, a group object that encompasses the data columns is created and displayed in the data model editor along with the query object as shown in diagram 14.4.

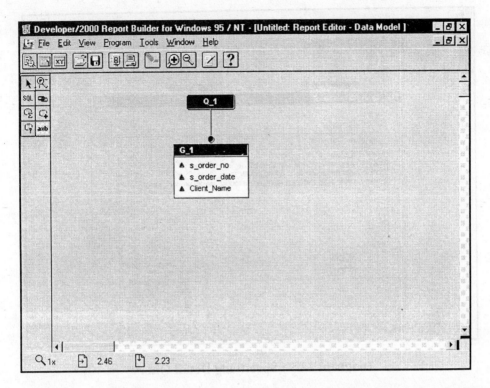

Diagram 14.4 : Query, Group and Data Columns created in Data Model editor

By default the name of the query object is Q_1, the name of the group object is G_1 and the names of the database columns are the same as defined in the SQL query.

5. Open the property palette and change the name of the query object to *Q_master* and the name of the group to *G_master*.

6. Place another query object approximately two inches to the right of the *Q_master* and enter the select statement as shown below:

```
select    s_order_no, description,
          unit_measure, product_rate, qty_ordered
from      sales_order_details, product_master
where     sales_order_details.product_no = product_master.product_no
```

The completed SQL Query Statement dialog box is as shown in diagram 14.5

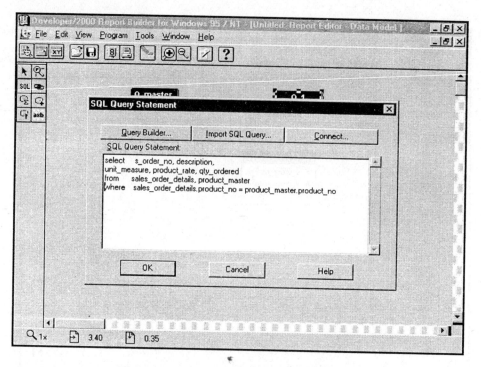

Diagram 14.5 : Specifying Detail Query

7. The completed data model editor will be as shown in diagram 14.6

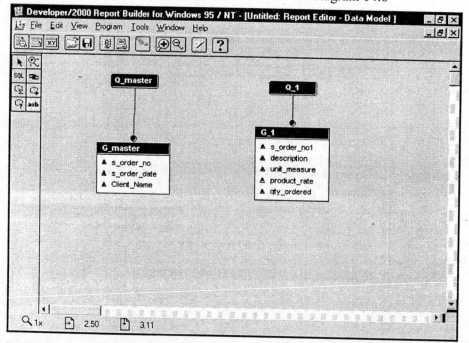

Diagram 14.6 : Completed Data Model Editor

8. Change the name of the detail query to *Q*_details and the name of the group to G_details.

If data columns with the same name are included in the report groups, the data columns will be renamed by using columnname followed by an integer value starting with 1. For example, *s_order_no* is a common data field in *G_master* and *G_details*. *S_order_no* is renamed to *s_order_no1* in the *G_details* group.

Data Link Object:

3. Select the *Data Link* tool i.e. *icon with sign of two intersecting ellipses* and **click and hold on** the *s_order_no* column of the *G_master* group. Drag the mouse pointer to the *s_order_no* column of the *G_details* group and release. A data link (arrow) will appear in the editor as shown in diagram 14.7.

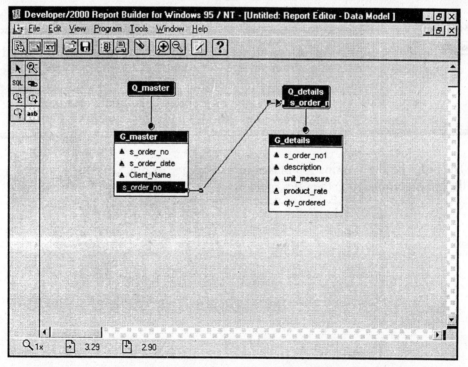

Diagram : 14.7 : Linking Queries using a Data Link Object

Note

The data link object creates a copy of the *s_order_no* column at the bottom of the master group, and the copy of the *s_order_no* column in the detail query.

4. Open the Data Link property sheet by double clicking on the data link. Examine the settings in the property sheet as shown in diagram 14.8. *G_master* is identified as the **Parent Group** and *s_order_no* is identified as **Parent Column**.

   Similarly *Q_details* is listed as the **Child Query** and *G_master* is identified as the **Child Group**.

   The link / join is on the *s_order_no* column. This link is established by using a *where* clause and an *equality* sign. Notice that where appears in the **SQL Clause field**. *'Where'* is the default clause used in master / detail relationship. *'Where'* clause can be replaced with other SQL clauses such as *having* or *start with*.

Note

Finally, notice that an *equal* sign (=) appears in the **Condition field**. An equality i.e., table1.columnname = table2.columnname) is the default condition for master / detail relationships defined via a data link. The equal sign can be replaced with any other supported conditional operator.

The order header information makes up the master record, which is printed once for the products ordered in the sales order.

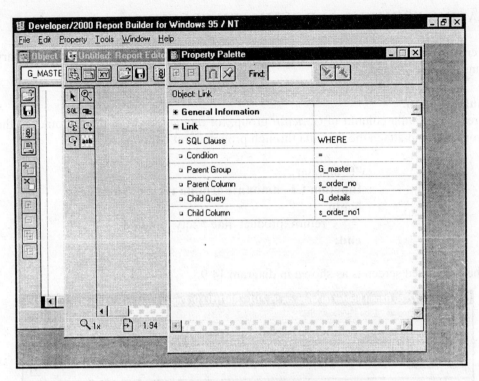

Diagram 14.8 : Data Link Properties

Linking the group G_*master* and the query Q_*details* via the s_*order_no* columns in both the queries is analogous to writing both queries as the single query shown below:

```
select    sales_order.s_order_no, s_order_date,
          client_master.name "Client Name", description,
          unit_measure, product_rate, qty_ordered
from      sales_order, client_master,
          sales_order_details, product_master
where     sales_order.s_order_no = sales_order_details.s_order_no and
          sales_order.client_no = client_master.client_no and
          sales_order_details.product_no = product_master.product_no (+)
```

CREATING FORMULA AND SUMMARY COLUMNS

After creating the required queries and linking them, the necessary formula and summary columns must be created.

Formula Column:
1. Create a formula column in *G_detail* group, for *amount*, right at the bottom. Set the properties and attach the formula through program unit editor as follows :

> Name : CF_amount
>
> Formula : **function CF_amountFormula return Number is**
> **begin**
>   return :product_rate * :qty_ordered ;
> **end;**

The completed screen is as shown in diagram 14.9.

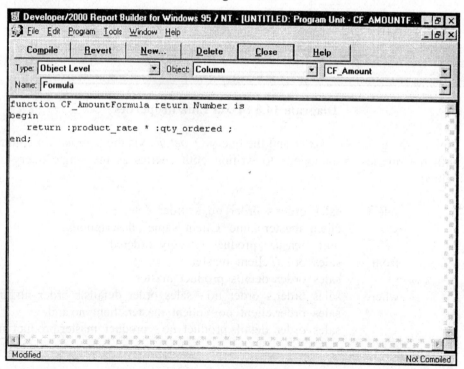

Diagram 14.9 : PL/SQL Code that defines Formula Column

2. Create a summary column in the *G_details* group for serial nos. The summary column must be the first column in that group. Change its properties as mentioned below:

Name   : CS_srno
Function   : Count
Source   : Description
Reset At   : G_master
Data type : Number
Width   : 3
Reset At   : G_Master

The completed property palette will be as displayed in diagram 14.10.

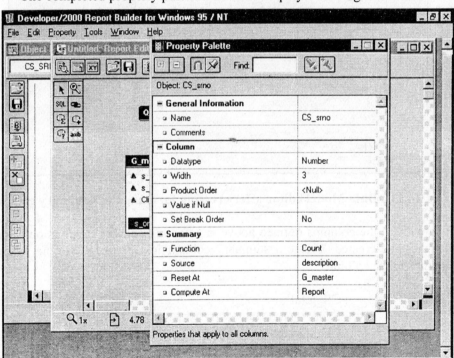

Diagram 14.10 : Properties for the serial number summary column

Note

The serial number value must restart from one for every order. **Reset At** property is set to *G_master* as the value of *CS_srno* should be reset to zero for every new order i.e. for every new value of *G_master*.

The data model editor after defining the formula column and the summary column will be as displayed in diagram 14.11.

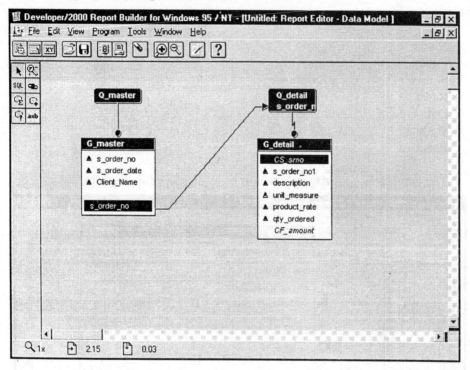

Diagram 14.11 : Data Model editor after creating formula and summary columns

3. Along with all the columns defined above, a column displaying total amount for the order must be created. Create a summary column in *G_master*. Set the following properties to the column.

Name	: CS_total
Function	: Sum
Source	: CF_amount
Reset At	: G_master
Data type	: Number
Width	: 10

The completed property sheet for the summary column will be as shown in diagram 14.12.

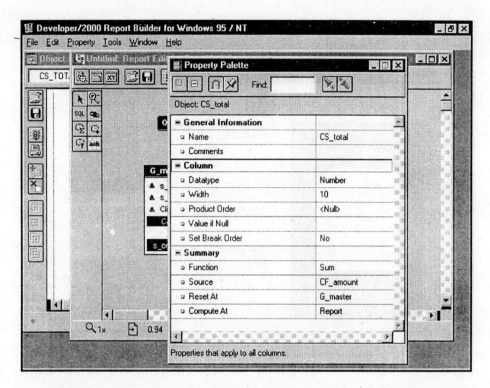

Diagram 14.12 : Property Palette for the Total Amount Column

DEFAULT LAYOUT

1. Select **Tools..Report Wizard** to define the report format. Select presentation style as **Group Above** as shown in diagram 14.13.

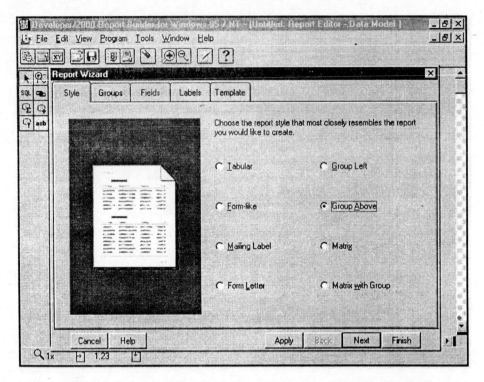

Diagram 14.13 : Specifying Report Style as 'Group Above'

9. Click on Next. The Groups tab displays a list of available group. Both the master and the detail groups must be displayed with the repeating direction as down. Thus select each group one at a time and click on push button labeled '**Down**'. [Down >]

The completed screen will be as shown in **diagram 14.14.**

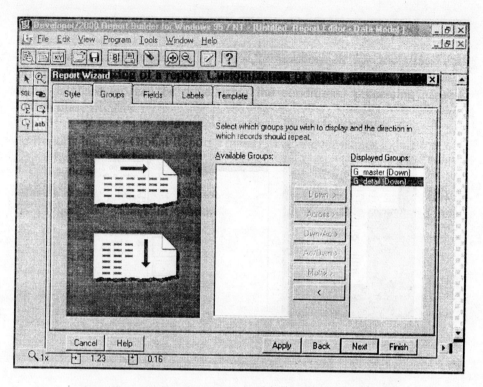

Diagram 14.14 : Selecting Master and Detail Groups

10. Click on Next. The Fields tab is displayed next. Select all the fields other than *s_order_no1* since *s_order_no1* must not be displayed on the report. The completed fields tab is as shown in diagram 14.15.

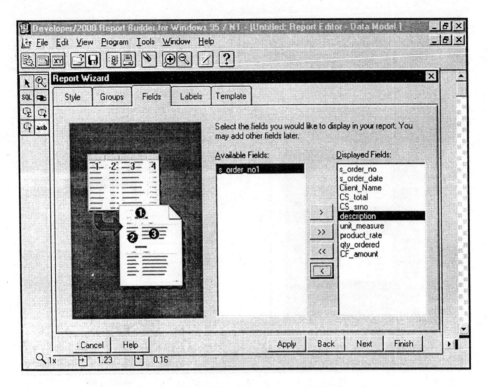

Diagram 14.15 : Selecting fields that must be displayed on the report

11. Change the labels of the fields as follows:

Column	Label
s_order_no	Order No:
s_order_date	Order Date:
cs_total	Total:
cs_srno	Sr. No.
product_rate	Rate
qty_ordered	Quantity
cf_amount	Amount

The completed label tab is displayed as shown in diagram 14.16.

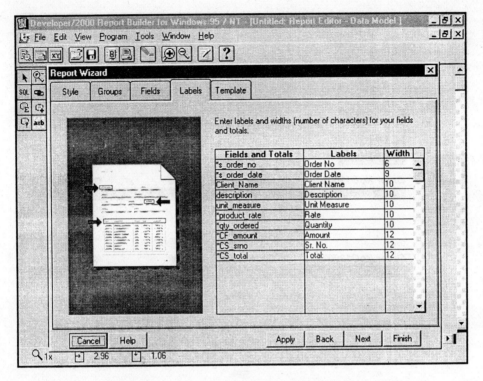

Diagram 14.16 : Changing Column Labels

12. Click on Next. Select **Cyan Grid** pre-defined template in the Template tab and click on Finish.

The completed master detail report will be as displayed in diagram 14.17.

Note

The master/detail default layout creates master records across the page with the labels to the left of their fields, and the detail records below the master records in standard tabular format.

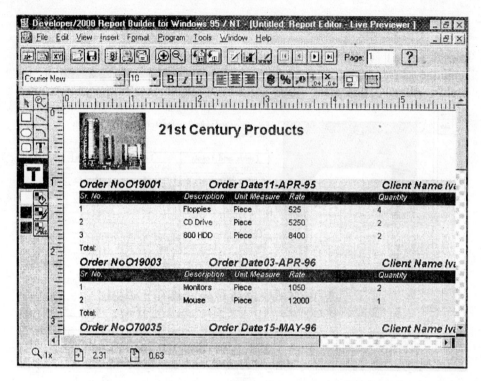

Diagram 14.17 : Report Displayed in Live Previewer

13. Reduce the size of *Sr_No*, *Rate*, *Qty_Ordered* and *Amount* columns. Change the alignment of each of these columns to right. Move the Total label just under the *Qty_Ordered* column.

14. The sales order detail information is displayed on the extreme left. Move the columns that display sales order detail information at the center of the page.

15. Change the fonts of all the fields and labels in the master section to Times New Roman size 12.

16. Select the default pictures displayed in the report header and press <Delete> key to delete these pictures.

17. Place a Text Item in the header. Enter the header text as 'Sales Order'. Change the font of the header text to 'Times New Roman' Size 18.

The completed report format will be displayed as shown in diagram 14.18.

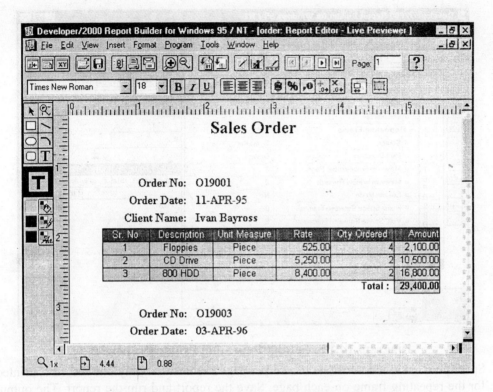

Diagram 14.18 : Formatted Sales Order Report

18. Save the report as *saleord.rdf*.

19. As seen in the Live Previewer, multiple sales orders are displayed on the same page. The system requires that only one sales order must be printed per page. The following properties must be set to ensure that only one order is displayed per page.

    Click on **View..Layout** Model to invoke Layout Editor. Select the repeating frame for the master section and invoke the property sheet by clicking on **Tools..Property Palette**. Set the property **Maximum number of Records Per page** to **1**.

    The completed Property Palette window will be displayed as shown in diagram 14.19.

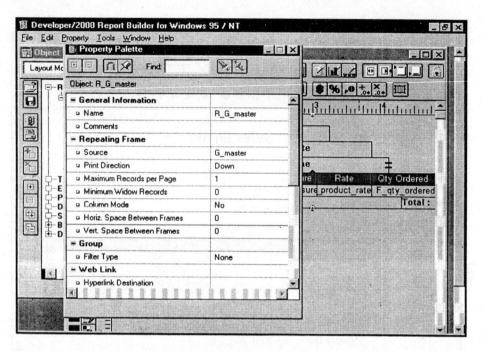

Diagram 14.19 : Setting Repeating Frame Properties

Specifying a maximum of one record per page ensures that only one record is printed for the repeating frame on each page. Save the report and run the report. The output will be as shown in the diagram 14.20.

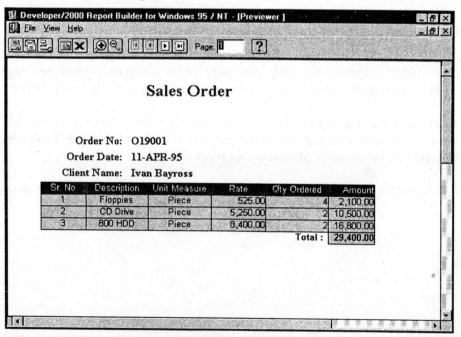

Diagram 14.20 : Final Report Output

Accepting Parameter Values:

Sales Order is displayed based on the sales order number entered. Thus *s_order_no* must be accepted as the parameter and sales order data must be retrieved based on the entered *s_order_no*. The steps are as follows:

1. Expand the *Data Model* node in the object navigator. One of the nodes under the *Data Model* node will be **User Parameters** node.

2. Select User Parameters node and click on the **Create** button on the vertical toolbar to create a user parameter for passing *s_order_no*. A default parameter with name P_1 will be created.

3. Double-click on the icon next to the parameter P_1 to open up its property Palette. Specify the *Parameter Name* as *P_s_order_no*. Set the *Data Type* of the parameter as *Char* and *Size* as *6*. Close the property Palette.

4. The parameter field must be used in the query such that data is retrieved based on the value entered. Thus the SQL Query Statement must be changed to include a where clause. Invoke Data Model Editor. Right click on *Q_master* object and select SQL Query dialog. The query definition screen is invoked.

5. Add the clause **and sales_order.s_order_no like :p_s_order_no** to current select statement. The completed SQL Query Statement dialog will be displayed as shown in diagram 14.21.

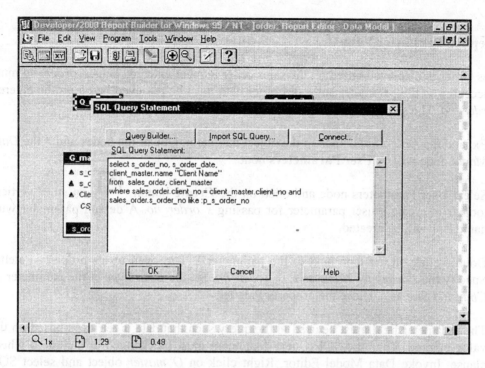

Diagram 14.21 : Adding a Where Clause to the SQL statement

6. Close SQL Query Statement dialog and run the report. A Parameter form is displayed with one parameter i.e. *P_s_order_no* as shown in diagram 14.22.

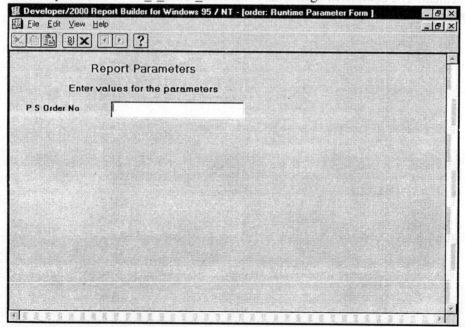

Diagram 14.22 : Parameter Form that accepts Order Number

The values of the parameter *P_s_order_no* are dependent on the value of *s_order_no* in the *sales_order* table. Thus the parameter form can be made more user friendly by providing list of values for the parameter. The steps in creating a list of values for the parameters are as follows:

1. Go to the Object Navigator and open the Property Palette of parameter *P_s_order_no*. Click on the **List of Values** property. Click on **More...** It displays the screen as shown in diagram 14.23.

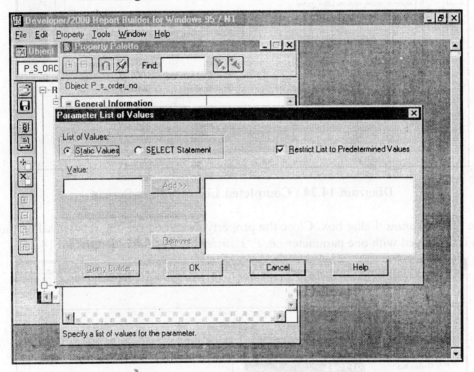

Diagram 14.23 : The Data / Selection tab of the Parameter

2. The list of values can either be :

   • **Static Values** i.e. values that are hard coded in the report.
   • Values from a **SELECT statement**.

   Since the list of values in the current example are based on column values click on **Select Statement** radio button.

3. Enter the select statement as follows:

   select s_order_no from sales_order

The completed *List of values* screen is as displayed in diagram 14.24.

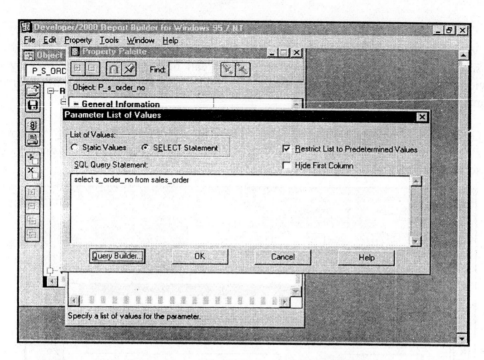

Diagram 14.24 : Completed List of Values Screen

Close *List of values* dialog box. Close the property sheet and run the report. A Parameter form is displayed with one parameter i.e. *P_s_order_no* as shown in diagram 14.25.

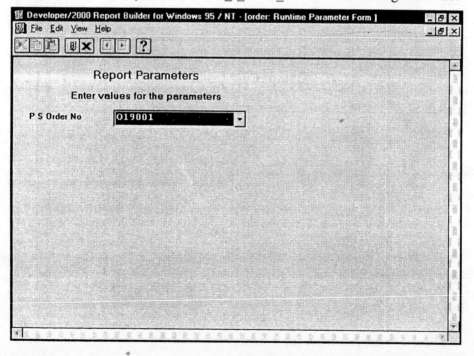

Diagram 14.25 : p_s_order_no List Item displayed in the parameter form

SELF REVIEW QUESTIONS

TRUE AND FALSE

1. Reports with 8 different presentation styles can be created in Reports Builder tool.

    A) True   B) False

2. The RESET AT property for a summary column that must be displayed for every master record is set to the master group name.

    A) True   B) False

3. If columns of the same name are included in the master and detail query, Reports Builder automatically renames the columns.

    A) True   B) False

4. Maximum window lines is a property that determines the number of records that must be displayed in a repeating frame.

    A) True   B) False

FILL IN THE BLANKS

1. Relation Ship between queries is established using a _____ Object.

2. The master query with a primary key defined is also called as _____ query.

3. The detail query with a foreign key defined is also called as _____ query.

4. Joins defined by a data link object is an _____ join.

5. Master / Details report uses _____ presentation style.

6. The Master / Detail link is established using _____ and _____.

7. A List of values for report parameters can be defined as:

   • _____

   • _____

Working of a Master / Detail Report

- *Creating a Master / Parent Query*
- *Creating Detail / Child Query*
- *Connecting a Master Detail Query using a Data Link Object*
- *Displaying Master / Detail Report using Group Above Presentation Style*

Creating a Master / Detail Report

- *Creating a Master / Detail Report Using Multiple Queries*
- *Creating a Data Link Object*
- *Creating formula Columns*
- *Creating Group Summary Columns*

Parameter Passing in Reports

- *Creating a User Parameter*
- *Setting User Parameters Properties*
- *Creating a List of Values for User Parameters*
  - *Static List Of Values*
  - *Values from the Select Statement*

Creating a Matrix Report

IN THIS CHAPTER

15. CREATING A MATRIX REPORT

INTRODUCTION TO MATRIX REPORT

A matrix report is a summary report that presents the desired data with headings across the top and the left side. Matrix report data is displayed at the intersection of the top and left heading. The totals are displayed across the bottom and right side. A matrix report is also referred to as "**CROSS-TAB**" report.

What is a Matrix Report?

A matrix report is a cross-tabulation of four sets of data:
1. One set of data is displayed *across the page* i.e. values are placed one besides the other.

2. One set of data is displayed *down the page* i.e. values are placed one below the other.

3. One set of data is the cross-product, which creates data cells at the intersection of the across and down data

4. One set of data is displayed as the **"filler"** of the cells i.e. the values are used to fill the cells created in step 3.

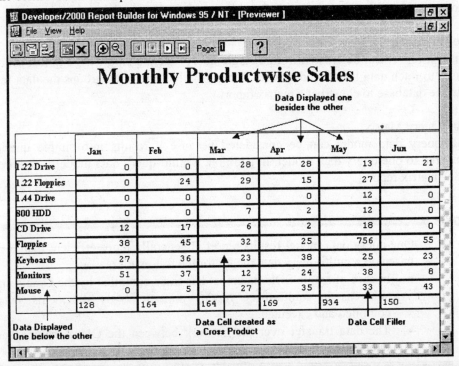

Diagram 15.1 : Sets of data used in Matrix Report

TYPES OF MATRIX REPORTS

Different types of matrix reports can be created using Oracle Reports. The four general types of matrix reports are

- Simple matrix
- Nested matrix
- Matrix Break
- Multi-Query matrix with break

Before discussing the particulars of matrix building, the objects required in the data model editor and the objects required in the layout editor must be known.

Objects in Data Model:

In building matrix data model, the following must be taken into consideration:

1. Number of queries
2. Group structure
3. Summary settings

Number of Queries:

Two types of query structures can be used for a matrix data model.

<u>One-Query Matrix:</u>
A matrix report can be created from a single query where a single SQL Select statement is used to fetch data from the database. Reports Builder tool then groups the data fetched from the database to construct a matrix report.

<u>Multi-Query Matrix:</u>
Multi-query data model can be considered because it results into simple queries as compared to one-query data model. In addition, a multi-query data model is required for nested matrix reports.

Note

One-query data model results report is generally more efficient than a report based on a multi-query data model for the following reasons:
- In case of single SQL statement has to be compiled by the Oracle engine. Whereas in multi-query report, multiple SQL statements must be compiled and executed.
- The data transfer over the network between the Oracle engine and the Oracle Reports tool is less in a single query report.

Group Structure:

Matrix reports are built with four or more groups:

<u>Two or more dimension groups:</u>
In the layout, the information in at least one group goes across the page, and the information in at least one group goes down the page, forming a grid. The groups that provide the data to be displayed across or down the page are called **Dimension Groups**.

The information in Dimension groups is sometimes referred to as "*Matrix Labels*", as they provide column and row labels for the matrix. Dimension groups are contained within the cross product group.

<u>One or more cross product groups:</u>
In the layout, a **Cross Product Group** is represented by the intersection of the across and down dimension groups. Thus the cross product group shows all possible combinations of the values of the across and down dimension groups.

When the report is run, it expands, and each instance of data intersection becomes a separate cell.

<u>One cell or filler group:</u>
The **Cell Group** contains data that is used to fill the cells created by the cross product group. When the report is run, these values appear in the appropriate cells.

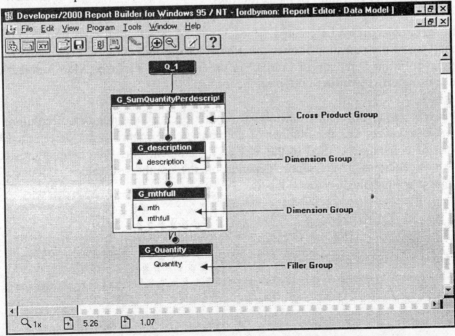

Diagram 15.2 : Groups used in Matrix Report

Matrix Layout:

A matrix layout model must consist of the following layout objects:

1. At least two repeating frames, one with a Print Direction set as 'Down' and one with a Print Direction set to 'Across'.

2. Several group, header, and footer (if summaries are included) frames.

3. A matrix object created for the cross product group that includes cells of the matrix.

4. Boilerplate for each column and row of values, as well as for summaries

Note
 Displaying the boilerplate is optional, but Oracle Reports will generate it by default.

Matrix / Cross Product Object:

Matrix object defines the intersection of at least two repeating frames. The repeating frames are the dimensions of the matrix and the matrix object contains at least one field that holds the **filler** or values of the cell group.

One matrix object must be created for each pair of intersecting repeating frames in the layout. One of the repeating frames must have a Print Direction of 'Down' and the other must have a Print Direction of 'Across' in order to form a matrix. Matrix object can be created using **cross product** button on the toolbar.

Matrix reports are different from tabular reports because the number of columns is not known in advance; i.e., the number of columns in the report is not determined by the number of columns specified in the SELECT statement plus the columns created. The number of columns in the report depends on the number of values contained in the columns providing the horizontal labels.

Focus:

Create a simple single-query matrix report of *Monthly Productwise Sales Report as* shown in the diagram 15.3. The report should show the data based on the year entered.

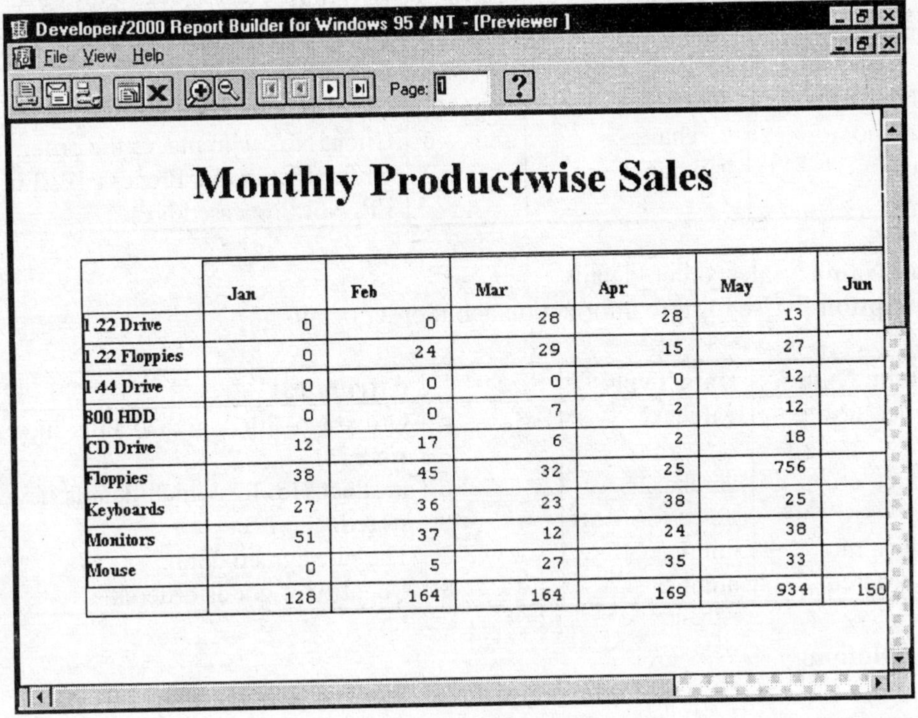

	Jan	Feb	Mar	Apr	May	Jun
1.22 Drive	0	0	28	28	13	
1.22 Floppies	0	24	29	15	27	
1.44 Drive	0	0	0	0	12	
800 HDD	0	0	7	2	12	
CD Drive	12	17	6	2	18	
Floppies	38	45	32	25	756	
Keyboards	27	36	23	38	25	
Monitors	51	37	12	24	38	
Mouse	0	5	27	35	33	
	128	164	164	169	934	150

Diagram 15.3 : Matrix Report

The definitions of the tables used are as mentioned below:

Table Name : product_master
Description : stores information about products supplied by the company.

Column Name	Data Type	Size	Column Description
product_no	varchar2	6	Unique Primary key allotted to each product.
description	varchar2	25	Description of the product
unit_measure	varchar2	10	Unit by which the product is measured.
qty_on_hand	number	8	Quantity which is available in the stock.
reorder_lvl	number	8	Quantity level when the stock should be re-ordered.
cost_price	number	8,2	Cost price of the product.
selling_price	number	8,2	Selling price of the product.

Table Name : sales_order (Master)
Description : Use to store information about orders placed by the clients.

Column Name	Data Type	Size	Attributes
s_order_no	varchar2	6	Unique primary key allotted to each order.
s_order_date	date		Date on which the order is placed.
client_no	varchar2	6	Client No., who places the order.
status	varchar2	2	Order Status (In Process IP, FullFilled FP, Not Processed NP)

Table Name : sales_order_details
Description : Use to store information about order details.

Column Name	Data Type	Size	Attributes
s_order_no	varchar2	6	Order No. for which details have to be stored.
product_no	varchar2	6	Product No. for which details have to be stored.
product_rate	number	8,2	The rate agreed upon.
qty_ordered	number	8	Quantity of goods ordered.

The Solution:

Steps to create the report shown in the Diagram 15.3 are summarized below:
- Create a new report.
- Create a query.
- Create Groups.
- Create Default Layout.
- Create Summary columns.
- Add zeroes in place of non-existent values.
- Add grid lines.
- Create user parameter.

Creating a new report:

1. Open Oracle Report Builder. A New untitled report is created by default.

Creating Query:

2. Click on **Tools..Report Wizard...** to start the report wizard for the new report. Report Wizard shows a number of Tab pages that to enter information required for report creation. The different tab pages are:
    *   Style
    *   Data
    *   Rows
    *   Columns
    *   Cell
    *   Totals
    *   Labels
    *   Template

2. Select **Matrix** as the report style as shown in diagram 15. 4 and click on Next.

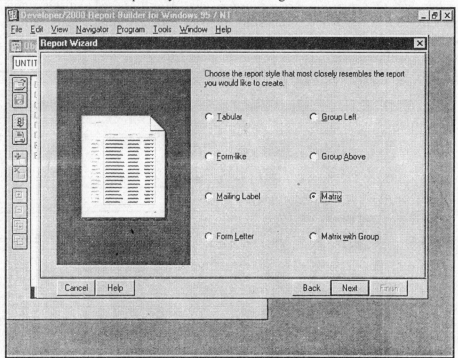

Diagram 15.4 : Specifying Report Style

3. Any report created using Report Builder requires a query using which data will be retrieved for the report. The **Data** Tab allows creation of an SQL statement using Query Builder. The SQL statement can also be entered in the multi line edit box provided in the data tab.

3. Create a query with a select statement as follows :

```
select    product_master.description,
          sum( sales_order_details.qty_ordered) "Quantity",
          to_char(sales_order.s_order_date,'mm') mth,
          to_char(sales_order.s_order_date,'Mon') mthfull
from      sales_order_details, product_master, sales_order
where     ( sales_order_details.s_order_no = sales_order.s_order_no) and
          ( sales_order_details.product_no = product_master.product_no)
group by  to_char(sales_order.s_order_date,'mm'),
          product_master.description,
          to_char( sales_order.s_order_date,'Mon')
order by  to_char(sales_order.s_order_date,'mm') asc
```

'to_char(sales_order.s_order_date ,'mm') mth' is used to order by months i.e. month numbers and *'to_char(sales_order.s_order_date ,'Mon')'* is used to display months in character format. Both the formats are used here data sorting cannot be done on month names (in characters) as it will give *'Apr'* before *'Jan'*. The completed SQL statement will be displayed as shown in diagram 15.5.

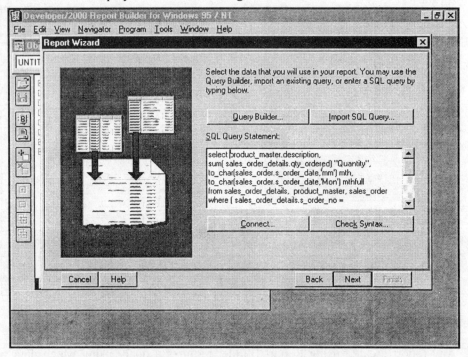

Diagram 15.5 : Query and Group for the Matrix Report

4. Click on **Check Syntax** to ensure that there are no syntax errors in the SQL statement.

5. A matrix report consists of data that must be displayed as labels for the rows. Thus a list of columns are displayed to select the column that acts as row labels.

   Since *description* is used as row labels, select *description* and click on [>] to   set row label to description. The completed screen will be as shown in diagram 15.6. Click on Next.

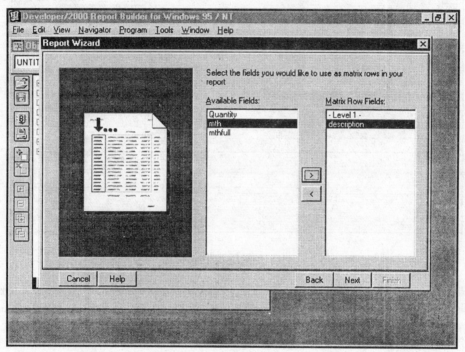

Diagram 15.6 : Selecting Description as Row Labels

6. *Month in character* format must be displayed as Column Labels and these column labels must be sorted on *mm* column. The Column Tab is used to specify Columns that will be used as Column Labels and the column on which these column labels must be sorted. Select *mm* and *MthFull* one at a time.

Note

 When multiple columns are selected as Column Labels, the columns are displayed at different levels by default. In the current example, mm and *mthfull* must be displayed at the same level. To change the level, select *mthfull* and drag it to Level 1.

The completed screen will be displayed as shown in diagram 15.7. Click on Next.

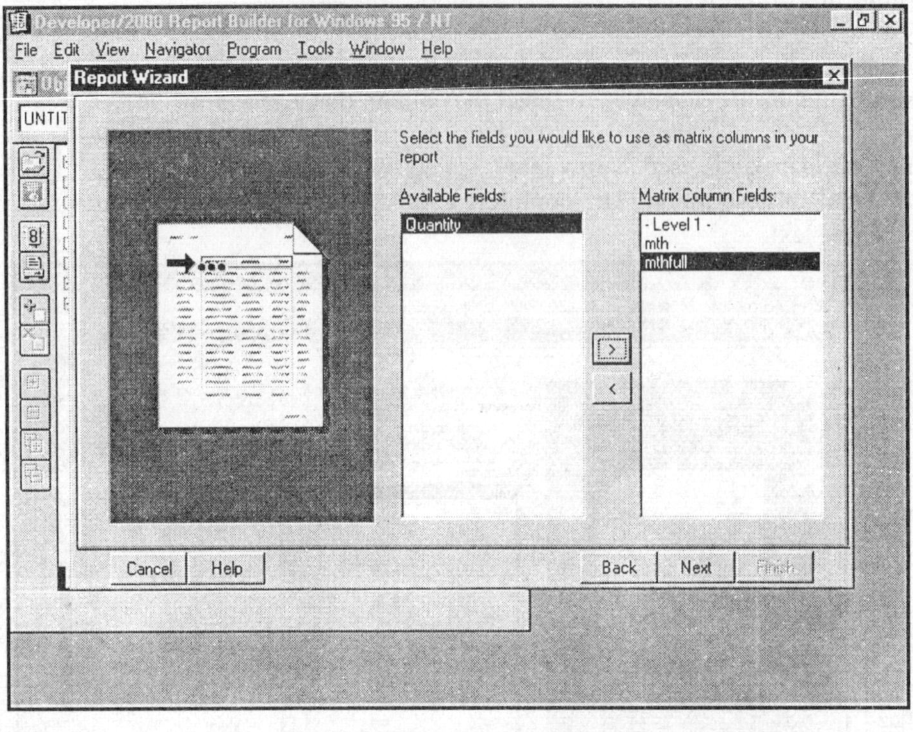

Diagram 15.7 : Selecting MthFull as Column Label

7. *Quantity* for each sales order for a month and a specific description must be displayed at the intersection of the Row Label and the Column Label. The Cell tab is used to specify the column that acts as an intersection column. Select *Quantity* and click on [>] to include *Quantity* as the cell column.

The completed screen will be as shown in diagram 15.8. Click on Next.

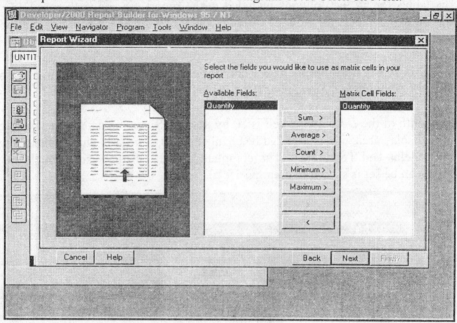

Diagram 15.8 : Selecting Quantity as the Cell Column

8. The Matrix report must display the totals of the cell column for both the Row as well as Column labels. Select *Quantity* and click on `Sum >` to create the required totals as shown in diagram 15.9.

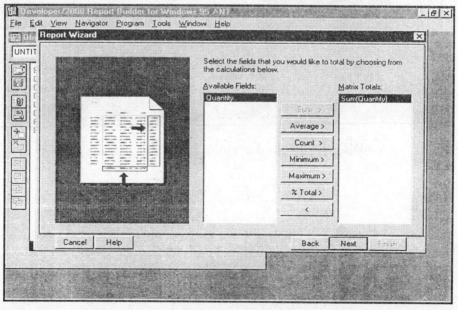

Diagram 15.9 : Layout Style for Matrix Report

9. The labels for all the columns included in the report are shown. Since *Description, Mthfull* act as labels for Row or Column, the labels for these columns will be set to Null.

A Matrix report does not include labels for cell columns and report totals. Thus the label for *Quantity* and *SumQuantityPerReport* must also be set to Null.

The width of the *Description* cell is 10 by default. Since the data in the field requires more display area, the width must be changed to 20. Similarly change the width of all other Fields and Totals to 4. The completed Label tab that using which the report labels can be set is shown in diagram 15.10.

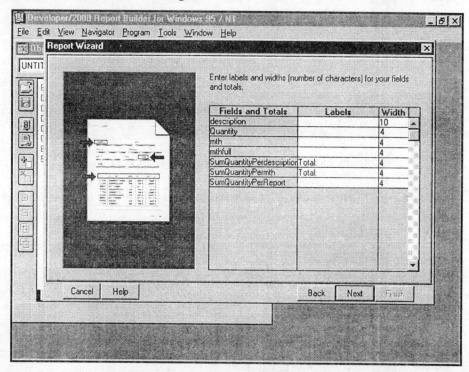

Diagram 15.10 : Layout of the Matrix Report

10. The Template Tab is then displayed. Since the report must be created without using a template, select **No Template** as shown in diagram 15.11and then click on 'Finish'.

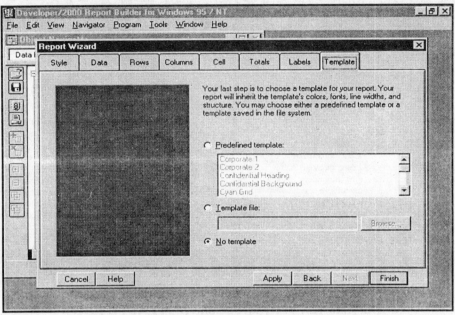

Diagram 15.11 : Report Template Tab Page

11. Report Builder includes a *Live Previewer*, using which the newly created report will be executed and displayed in the *Live Previewer* as shown in diagram 15.12.

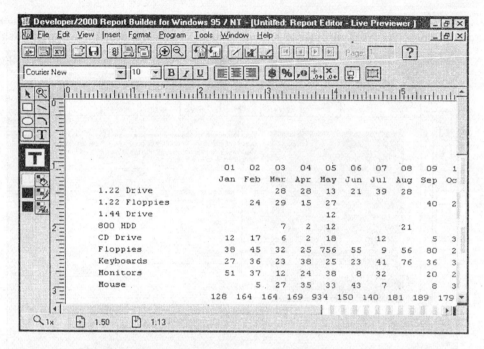

Diagram 15.12 : Report displayed in Live Previewer

12. Save the report as *'ordbymon.rdf'*. As seen in 15.12, month in number format and month in character format are displayed as column labels. Since the month in number format need not be displayed, select the value of month in number format and press the on <Delete> key.

13. Select month in character format and make the font bold-faced. Similarly, select description and make the font bold-faced.

Adding zeroes in place of non-existent values:

The matrix report displays sales of item with blank spaces where no values exist and no summaries included.

Click on **View..Layout Editor** to open the Layout editor. Use the Magnify tool so that the layout can be magnified to twice or thrice its normal size..

The quantity field is the same size as the repeating frame that encloses the quantity field. Select field quantity and decrease the size such that all the four sides are completely enclosed in the repeating frame. The resized quantity field and the enclosing repeating frame are selected in diagram 15.13.

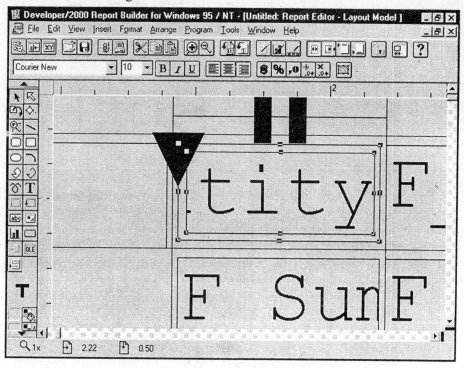

Diagram 15.13 : Resized Quantity field

Select the Text tool and place it just outside the repeating frame that encloses quantity field as shown in diagram 15.14. Type **'0'** (zero).

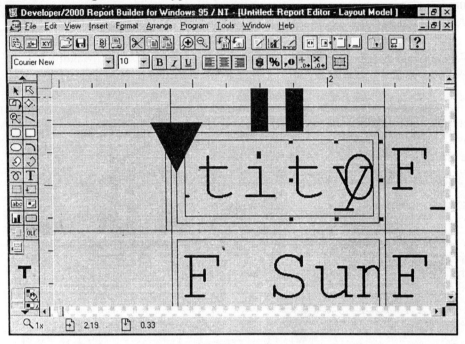

Diagram 15.14 : Text tool placed just outside the repeating frame

Since the text tool is placed outside repeating frame, the text tool with a default name B_1 will not be enclosed in the repeating frame, but will be enclosed in a frame outside the repeating frame i.e. *Frequency R_G_Description:R_G_mth*. Click on **Tools..Object Navigator** to check that the object is placed properly.

The Object Navigator will be displayed as shown in diagram 15.15.

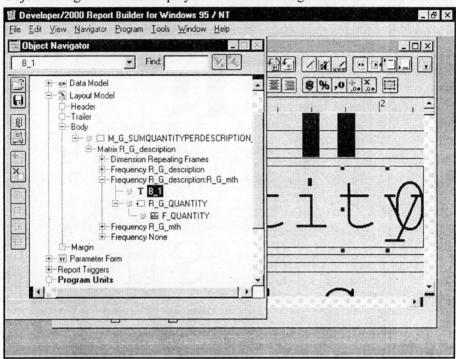

Diagram 15.15 : Text Tool displayed in the Object Navigator

18. Click on the title bar of Layout Editor window to go to the Layout Editor. Click once in an empty area of the Layout editor to deselect the boilerplate. Select *R_G_Quantity* repeating frame by clicking on the repeating frame and then select *F_Quantity* by using <Shift> and <left click>. Click on **Arrange..Move Forward**. This will move both the objects in front of the text tool B_1.

 Tip

 Use the Magnify tool shown above to enlarge hard-to-see objects. The frames can also be selected in the Object Navigator.

19. Examine the layout objects carefully. Since the default fill for Oracle Reports created objects is transparent the zero is still visible behind both the *F_Quantity* field and the *R_G_Quantity* repeating frame as shown in diagram 15.16.

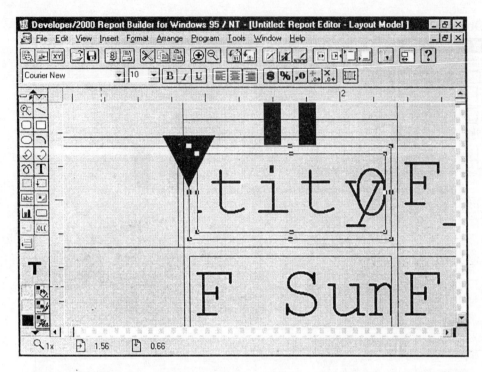

Diagram 15.16 : B_1, F_Quantity R_G_Quantity displayed in Layout Editor

10. The repeating frame *R_G_Quantity* and F_quantity can be made opaque by specifying fill color. Since the report background is white the fill color must also be set to white. Select the *R_G_Quantity* repeating frame. Select the Fill Color tool to display the color palette, then select the white color. A white fill color will hide the boilerplate behind the repeating frame.

The completed screen will be as displayed in diagram 15.17.

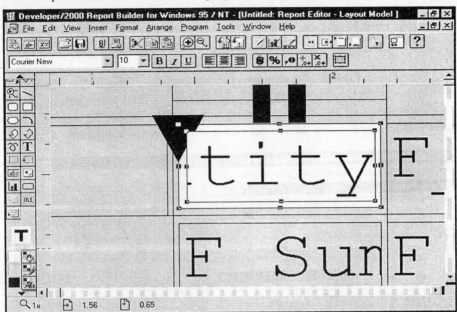

Diagram 15. 17 : Layout Editor after Adding Zeros for no values

11. Save the report and run. Zero will be placed in every empty cell. In the squares where *F_Quantity* is displayed, the zeroes are hidden beneath an instance of the *R_G_Quantity* repeating frame. Where the zeroes appear, no values for *F_Quantity* exist, and thus no instance of the *R_G_Quantity* repeating frame has been created.

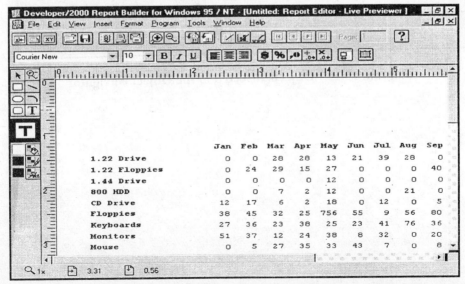

	Jan	Feb	Mar	Apr	May	Jun	Jul	Aug	Sep
1.22 Drive	0	0	28	28	13	21	39	28	0
1.22 Floppies	0	24	29	15	27	0	0	0	40
1.44 Drive	0	0	0	0	12	0	0	0	0
800 HDD	0	0	7	2	12	0	0	21	0
CD Drive	12	17	6	2	18	0	12	0	5
Floppies	38	45	32	25	756	55	9	56	80
Keyboards	27	36	23	38	25	23	41	76	36
Monitors	51	37	12	24	38	8	32	0	20
Mouse	0	5	27	35	33	43	7	0	8

Diagram 15.18 : Report Output after adding Boiler Text for 0.

Grid for the Matrix Report:

A Matrix Report must be displayed in grid format. The steps for creating a grid matrix report is follows:

1. Click on **Tools..Object Navigator** to go to the Object Navigator. Select *M_G_SumQuantityPerdescription_*. Using <Control> and <left click> select the *R_G_Description* and *R_G_Mth* repeating frames in the Object Navigator. The select objects will be displayed in the Object Navigator as shown in diagram 15.19.

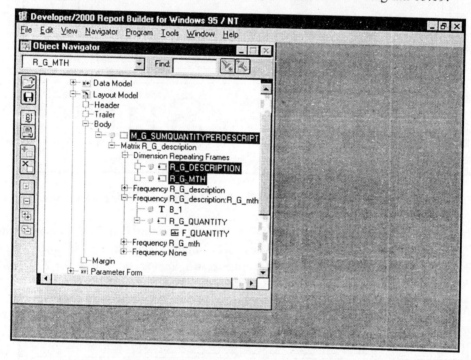

Diagram 15.19 : Objects Selected in the Object Navigator

2. Click on the icon next to the Layout Model to invoke the layout editor. The select objects will be displayed in the Layout Editor as shown in diagram 15.20.

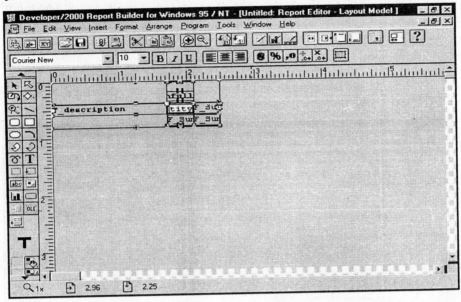

Diagram 15.20 : Object Selected in the Layout Editor

3. From the tool palette select the line tool and select Blank color. Click on View..Live Previewer to view the report as shown in diagram 15.21

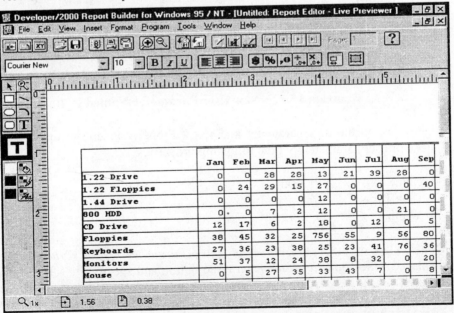

	Jan	Feb	Mar	Apr	May	Jun	Jul	Aug	Sep
1.22 Drive	0	0	28	28	13	21	39	28	0
1.22 Floppies	0	24	29	15	27	0	0	0	40
1.44 Drive	0	0	0	0	12	0	0	0	0
800 HDD	0	0	7	2	12	0	0	21	0
CD Drive	12	17	6	2	18	0	12	0	5
Floppies	38	45	32	25	756	55	9	56	80
Keyboards	27	36	23	38	25	23	41	76	36
Monitors	51	37	12	24	38	8	32	0	20
Mouse	0	5	27	35	43	43	7	0	8

Diagram 15.21 : Matrix Report displayed in Live Previewer

Creating User Parameters:

The current report displays *Monthly Productwise Sales* for all the years. The report must accept year as a parameter and sales for the specified year must be displayed. The steps for creating a user parameter that accepts year are as follows:

1. Click on **Tools..Object Navigator** to go to the object Navigator. Click ⊞ on icon next to *Data Model* to expand Data Model. Double click on *User Parameters* node. A new parameter with a default name is created as shown in diagram 15.22.

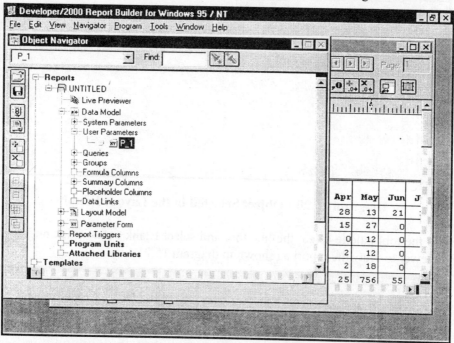

Diagram 15.22 : New User Parameter Named P_1

2. Right click on the user parameter and select Property Palette to open the property Palette of user parameter. Set the following properties.

    Name   : P_Year
    Data Type   : Character
    Width   : 4

3. Double click on the *List of Values* property. *Parameter List of Values* Dialog box is displayed. Click on *Select Statement* radio button and specify the select statement as follows:

    select distinct to_char(s_order_date, 'yyyy') from sales_order

The completed screen will be displayed as shown in diagram 2.23. Close the Property Palette.

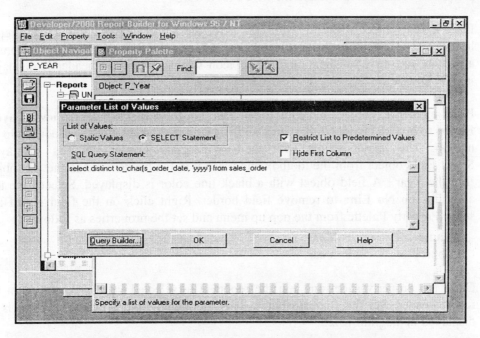

Diagram 15.23 : Specifying SQL statement for List of Values.

4. Click on **Program..Run Report** to run the report. The parameter form will be displayed as shown in diagram 15.24.

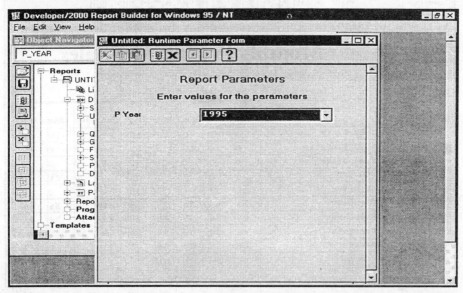

Diagram 15.24 : Runtime Parameter Form

5. Select year and click on ⊞ icon to display the report. Report based on the parameter value is displayed in the Live Previewer.

6. Place a Text object in the Live Previewer for the report header and enter the report header text as 'Monthly Productwise Sales'. Change the font to 'Times New Roman' and font size to 24. Click on the **B** icon so that the report header is displayed in BOLD style.

7. Place another text object and enter the text as 'For the Year'. Click on **View.. Layout Editor** to invoke layout editor. Click on ▣ icon i.e. icon with balloon help as margin. The layout editor with the ▣ margins, headers etc is displayed. Select Field object from the toolbox and place it in the header next to the text object 'For the Year'. A field object with a black line color is displayed. Select Line tool and click on **No Line** to remove field border. Right click on the field object and select Property Palette from the pop up menu and set the properties as follows:

     Name   : F_Year
     Source   : P_Year

8. Close the property sheet and run the report. The selected year is displayed in the report header. Set the font attributes. The completed Live previewer screen is as displayed in diagram 15.25.

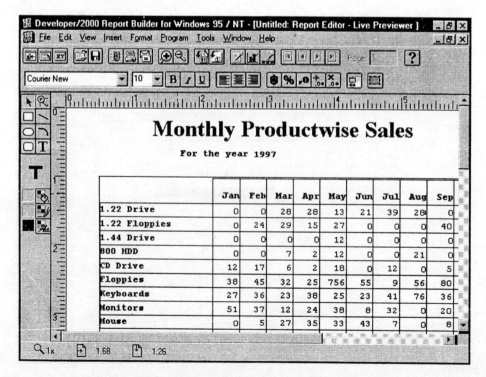

Diagram 15.25 : Report Displayed in Live Previewer.

SELF REVIEW QUESTIONS

TRUE AND FALSE

1. Matrix Reports are also called Cross Tab Reports.

    A) True   B) False

2. Cross Product object is used with a matrix report.

    A) True   B) False

3. A Matrix report is a cross tabulation of data from five groups

    A) True   B) False

FILL IN THE BLANKS

1. The groups included in a matrix report are called:

    *   _____

    *   _____

    *   _____

2. Grid lines are displayed by setting _____ color.

3. Intersection of two or more groups is defined using _____ group.

4. A Matrix report requires atleast two groups as _____ and _____.

5. The data displays that the intersection is called _____ column.

A QUICK REVIEW

What is a Matrix Report

Types of Matrix Reports
- Single Query Matrix Report
- Multi Query Matrix Report

Matrix Group Structure
- Dimension Groups
- Cross Product Groups
- Filler Groups

Matrix / Cross Product Object

Creating a Matrix Report
- Specifying Report Query
- Specify Row and Column Data
- Specifying Cell Data
- Adding Matrix Summary Columns to print 'Down' and 'Across' totals and 'Report' Totals
- Adding Zeros in place of non-existent values
- Creating a Grid for the Matrix Report

Creating User Parameter for Matrix Reports

CHAPTER SIXTEEN

Using PL/SQL With Reports

IN THIS CHAPTER

➢ Types Of Report Triggers

➢ Format Triggers

➢ Action Triggers

➢ Validation Triggers

➢ Group Filter Triggers

➢ Drill Down Reports

➢ Report Audit Trail

16. USING PL/SQL WITH REPORTS

To extend report-writing capabilities, Oracle Reports Builder enables the use of PL/SQL code blocks. If conditional logic in required in a report, PL/SQL constructs can be used to perform the job.

Example:
If a sales value is below the specified target, then such sales values can be displayed with a different text color. This helps to draw attention to these values.

PL/SQL code blocks can be used in different types of triggers available in Oracle Reports:
1. Formula Triggers
2. Format Triggers
3. Action Triggers
4. Validation Triggers
5. Report triggers
6. Group Filters

Each of them are explained below:

Formula Triggers:

Formula Triggers are PL/SQL functions that populate columns of type *Formula*. A PL/SQL function is required for any column of Type Formula. The Data Type of the Formula column determines the return data type for the formula trigger. An example of a formula trigger is as follows:

> **Function** CF_sales_valueFormula **Return** Number **is**
> **Begin**
> > **Return** :avg_product_rate * :sum_quantity ;
> **End;**

Formula triggers are created as the name of the formula column followed by the reserve word formula. The value returned by the formula trigger is displayed in the report field connected to the formula column.

Format Triggers:

Format Triggers are PL/SQL functions executed before the object is formatted. These triggers can be used to dynamically change the formatting attributes (e.g. font, font weight etc.) of any object on the report. They are also used to conditionally print or not print a report column value.

Format triggers return Boolean values TRUE or FALSE. If the return value for the format trigger is FALSE, the value is not displayed in the report. SRW report package can be used to create and format a report.

Action Triggers:

Action Triggers are PL/SQL procedures executed when a button is selected in the Previewer. This trigger can be used to dynamically call another report (drill down) or execute any other PL/SQL. It can also be used to execute a Multimedia file.

Action triggers are used to perform user-defined action and these triggers do not return any value.

Validation Triggers:

Validation Triggers are PL/SQL functions that are executed when a parameter value is entered and the cursor moves to the next parameter. These triggers are used to validate parameter values.

Validation Triggers return boolean value TRUE or FALSE. If the return value is TRUE, the parameter is treated as validated. If the return value is FALSE then a default error message is displayed and an exception is raised.

Rules for the Validation Triggers:
Restrictions defined for Validation Triggers. These are:

1. The PL/SQL code in a Validation Trigger can be a maximum of **32K** characters.

2. In a Validation Trigger, the values of Oracle Reports *parameters* can be read or values can be assigned to them. Report *column* values **cannot** be read **nor** can values be assigned to report columns in a Validation Trigger.

Report Triggers:

Report triggers enable execution of PL/SQL functions at specific times during the execution and formatting of a report. Customization of report formats, initialization tasks, accessing database etc can be done using the conditional processing capabilities of PL/SQL in these triggers.

Oracle Reports has *five* Global Report Triggers. The trigger names indicate at what point the trigger fires:

1. **Before Parameter Form** fires before the Runtime Parameter Form is displayed. From this trigger, the values of parameters, PL/SQL global variables and report-level columns can be accessed and manipulated if required.

Note

> This trigger will fire irrespective of whether the runtime parameter form is displayed or not. This trigger can be used to for validating command line parameter values as well.

2. **After Parameter Form** fires after the Runtime Parameter Form is displayed. From this trigger, parameter values can be accessed and their values can be validated. This trigger can also be used to change parameter values or, if an error occurs, return to the Runtime Parameter Form.

Note

> The After Parameter Form trigger will fire irrespective of whether the runtime parameter form is displayed or not. Consequently, this trigger can be used for validating command line parameters. Columns from the data model are not accessible from this trigger.

3. **Before Report** fires **before** the report is executed but **after** queries are parsed and data is fetched.

4. **Between Pages** fires before each page of the report is formatted, *except the very first page*. This trigger can be used for customized page formatting.

Note

In the Previewer, this trigger only fires the first time the page is formatted. If the user subsequently returns to the page, the trigger does not fire again.

5. **After Report** fires after the Report Previewer is exited, or after report output is sent to a specified destination, such as a file or a printer. This trigger can be used to clean up any initial processing that was done. For example if temporary tables are created during report execution, such tables can be deleted in the *After Report Trigger*.

Note

This trigger always fires, whether or not your report completed successfully.

Which Trigger To Use:
As a general rule, any processing that will effect the data retrieved by the report should be performed in the Before Parameter Form or After Parameter Form triggers. These are the two report triggers that fire before any SQL statement is parsed or data is fetched.

Any processing that will not effect the data retrieved by the report can be performed in the other triggers.

Return values for the report triggers:
Report triggers return boolean value TRUE or FALSE. The impact of the return value varies based on the type of report trigger.

Report Trigger Type	Impact of the Return Value
Before Parameter Form	If the return value is FALSE, an error message is displayed and then the focus returns to the place from where the report was executed.
After Parameter Form	If the return value is FALSE, the focus returns to the Runtime Parameter Form. If the parameter form is not displayed then the focus returns to place from where the report was executed.
Before Report	If the return value is FALSE, an error message is displayed and then returns to the place from which the report was executed.

Report Trigger Type	Impact of the Return Value
Between Pages	If the return value is FALSE, an error message is displayed and then the focus returns to the place from where the report was executed. *If the trigger returns FALSE on the last page,* **nothing happens** *because the report formatting is complete.* The Between Page trigger does not fire before the first page. If the trigger returns FALSE on the first page, the first page is displayed. An error message is displayed when the focus moves to the second page if the report consists of two or more pages.
After Report	If the return value is FALSE, it does not affect the report. A message can be displayed to indicate that the report displayed is probably incorrect.

The Order of report trigger execution is as follows:

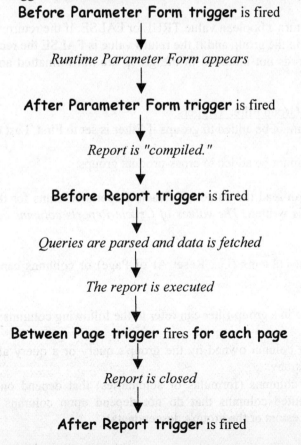

Before Parameter Form trigger is fired

Runtime Parameter Form appears

After Parameter Form trigger is fired

Report is "compiled."

Before Report trigger is fired

Queries are parsed and data is fetched

The report is executed

Between Page trigger fires **for each page**

Report is closed

After Report trigger is fired

Group Filter Triggers:

Filtering records in the group:

Data displayed on the report can be filtered by using WHERE clause. From the data fetched from the database, further record filtration can be done by setting group properties.

Records in a group can be filtered and not displayed in the report by setting the group to:
- **No Filter** i.e. "display all the records fetched from the database"
- **First n** records where n is a user-defined numeric value i.e. "display first n records fetched from the database"
- **Last n** records where n is a user-defined numeric value i.e. "display last n records fetched from the database"
- **Condition** i.e. display records that satisfy the condition specified in the Group Filter Triggers.

Group filters are PL/SQL functions that determine the records that will be included in the group and thus displayed by the Live Previewer tool.

These functions return a boolean value TRUE or FALSE. If the return value is TRUE, the record is included in the group and if the return value is FALSE the record is not included in the group. Records not included in the group are not formatted and displayed in the Live Previewer.

Rules for creating Group Filter Triggers:
1. Group filters cannot be added to groups if Filter is set to First, Last or No Filter.

2. Group filters cannot be added to cross-product groups.

3. Group filters can read the values of Oracle Reports columns for the group on which PL/SQL code is written. *The values of Oracle Reports columns cannot be set in the Group Filter*.

4. Page-dependent columns (i.e., Reset At of Page) or columns can also be read in a Group Filter.

5. A function used in a group filter can refer to the following columns:

   - A database column owned by the group's query or a query above it in the data model hierarchy.
   - Computed columns (formulas or summaries) that depend on unrelated queries (i.e., computed columns that do not depend upon columns in the group, the group's ancestors or the group's descendants)

FOCUS - FORMAT TRIGGERS

Modify the matrix report 'Productwise Monthly Sales Matrix' to include PL/SQL code to change the format of all values of item sales greater than 30 as shown in diagram 16.1. The formatting features that must be applied are:

Weight	: Bold
Type Face	: 'helvetica'
Border Width	: 0
Global Text Color	: 'DARKBLUE'
Border Pattern	: Solid

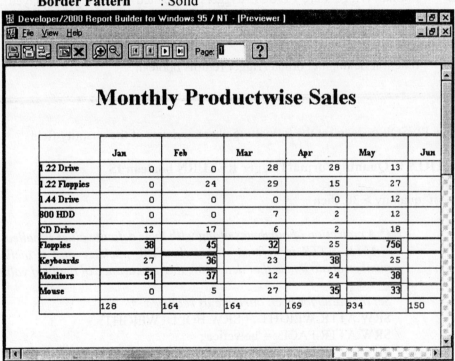

Diagram 16.1 : Matrix Report using Library and Format Trigger

THE SOLUTION

1. Open the 'Productwise Monthly Sales' matrix report in the Reports Builder. The login dialog is displayed.

2. Enter user-id, password and connect string and click on *Connect*. Report Live Previewer is displayed after retrieving records from the database. The text color for the quantity field is set to *black by default*.

3. Right click on the quantity field in the Live Previewer. Select PL/SQL Editor from the pop up menu. A new format triggers is created as follows:

    FUNCTION F_QuantityFormatTrigger **RETURN** boolean **IS**
    BEGIN

    END;

Note

Format Triggers are PL/SQL triggers associated with fields displayed in the Layout Editor or Live Previewer. Thus when PL/SQL editor is opened after selecting quantity field, *a default format trigger is created* as

function fieldnameFormatTrigger returns boolean

4. Write PL/SQL code to set the formatting characteristics of the quantity field.

```
FUNCTION F_QuantityFormatTrigger RETURN boolean IS
BEGIN
        if :quantity > 30  then
```

        /* A collection of attributes along with their default values is called
         ATTR. ATTR is defined within the SRW package and it includes a
        number of attributes that determine the appearance of the field values.

        Set the value for each attribute as required. */

```
        SRW.ATTR.WEIGHT := SRW.BOLD_WEIGHT;
        SRW.ATTR.FACE := 'helvetica';
        SRW.ATTR.BORDERWIDTH := 0;
        SRW.ATTR.GCOLOR := 'DARKBLUE';
        SRW.ATTR.BORDPATT := 'SOLID';
```

        /* The changed attribute values can be applied to the field values by
         placing a Mask on the existing ATTR object. Thus the changed
        attributes must first be added to the Mask. The ATTR object with the
        new mask must then be set for the current object. */

```
        SRW.ATTR.MASK := SRW.WEIGHT_ATTR + SRW.FACE_ATTR
                + SRW.BORDERWIDTH_ATTR + SRW.GCOLOR_ATTR
                + SRW.BORDPATT_ATTR;
```

> */*Apply the mask to the object. Here 0 indicates current object on which*
> *PL/SQL code is written. */*
> SRW.SET_ATTR(0, SRW.ATTR);

    End if;
    RETURN (TRUE);
END;

5. Compile the PL/SQL code by clicking on Compile push button in the PL/SQL editor. Close the PL/SQL editor. The Live Previewer displays the quantity field formatted after executing PL/SQL code as shown in diagram 16.2.

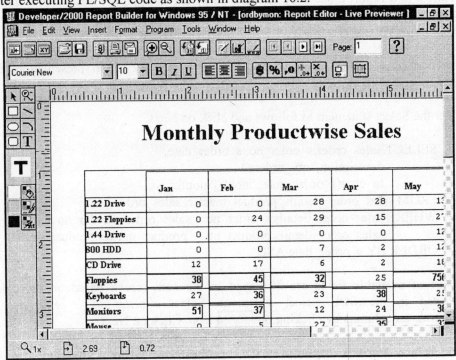

Diagram 16.2 : Formatted Quantity field displayed in Live Previewer

FOCUS - ACTION TRIGGERS

Place a button next to the quantity field. When the user clicks on the button, the corresponding product description and month must be must be passed as parameters to the *Order Details* report that display Order Id, Order Date and Quantity ordered for supplied Month and Product Description.

THE SOLUTION

1. Create a new report module by clicking on **File..New..Report** menu items. The *New Report* dialog box is displayed. Select *Use Report Wizard* radio button and click on OK. Report Wizard is started.

2. The first page in the report wizard is used to specify report presentation. Select *Tabular* and click on Next.

3. Enter the Select statement as follows and click on Next.

```
SELECT sales_order.s_order_no, s_order_date,
       description, qty_ordered ,
       to_char(s_order_date, 'mon') "month"
FROM sales_order_details, product_master, sales_order
WHERE sales_order_details.s_order_no = sales_order.s_order_no and
       sales_order_details.product_no = product_master.product_no
ORDER BY s_order_date ASC
```

4. A list of available fields are displayed in the next screen based on the columns selected in the SQL Select statement. Select *s_order_no, s_order_date* and *qty_ordered* columns by clicking on ⬚ icon. Click on Next.

5. The Totals screen is displayed next. The report must display the sum of quantity ordered. Select *qty_ordered* column and click on icon ⬚ Sum > to include a summary column that adds the values of the *qty_ordered* field. Click on Next.

6. The Labels screen is displayed. Change the label for *s_order_no* to 'Order No' and *s_order_date* to 'Order Date'. Click on Next.

7. The Templates screen is displayed next. Select 'Corporate2' template from the list provided and click on Finish.

8. Live Previewer is displayed. Delete the text header in the Live Previewer. Move the fields to center of the page. The completed screen will be displayed as shown in diagram 16.3.

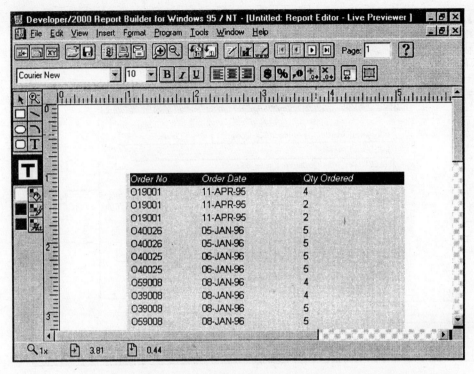

Diagram 16.3 : New Report displayed in Live Previewer

9. Click on **Tools..Object Navigator** to open the Object Navigator window. Create a **User Parameter** and change their properties as listed below:

Name	: P_description
Data Type	: Character
Width	: 20

10. Similarly create another user parameters and set the properties as follows:

Name	: P_month
Data Type	: Character
Width	: 3

11. Double click on query object in the Object Navigator. The property sheet is displayed. Double click on *SQL Query Statement* property and add the where clause as follows:

and upper(description) = :p_description) and
to_char(s_order_date,'mon') = :p_month

The completed query screen is as displayed in diagram 16.4.

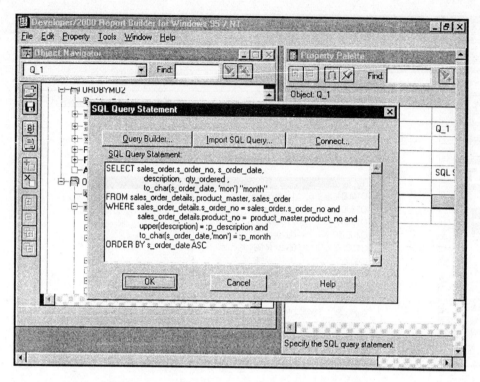

Diagram 16.4 : Query Screen after adding Where clause

12. Open the Layout editor by double clicking on Layout Model in the Object Navigator. Click on 🔲 icon to display the margins reports area.

13. Place a field object in the margin and set properties as follows:

Name	: F_description
Source	: P_description

14. Place two text objects in the header and set the text as 'Order Info for Product' and 'For' respectively. Arrange the fields and labels as shown in diagram 16.5.

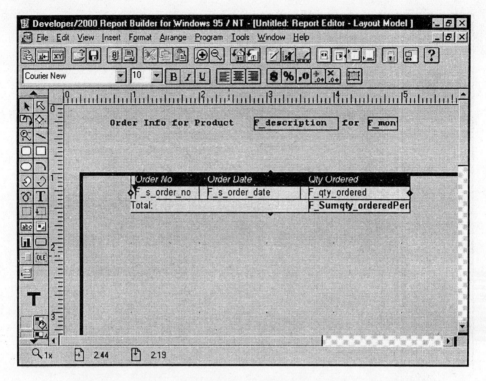

Diagram 16.5 : Labels and Fields arranged in Layout editor

15. Save the report as *ord_det.rdf*. Close the report.

16. Open the **ordbymon.rdf** report and save it as **ordbymo2.rdf** using **File**, **Save As** option in the menu and open its Layout Editor.

17. Reduce the size of the quantity field and place a button next to the quantity field as shown in diagram 16.6.

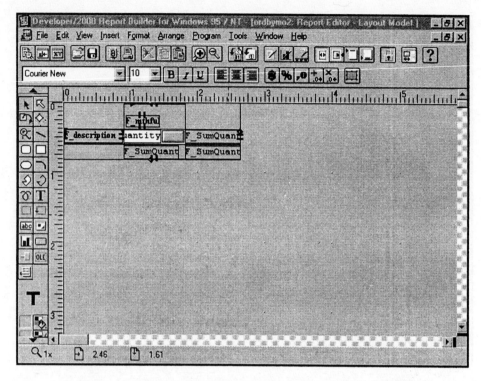

Diagram 16.6 : Button placed next to the quantity field

18. Open the property sheet of the button created and set the following properties:

    Name   : U_order
    Text   : ...
    Type   : PL/SQL

19. The action for the button must then be defined. Right click on the button object and select PL/SQL Editor from the pop up menu. An action trigger is created by default as follows:

```
PROCEDURE U_orderButtonAction IS
BEGIN

END;
```

20. Write PL/SQL code to open order details report and pass description and month as a parameter.

PROCEDURE U_orderButtonAction **IS**
BEGIN

/*Open the ord_det.rdf report with current month and current product description as arguments. Setting paramform=no will not display the parameter form. */

SRW.RUN_REPORT('c:\student\ord_det.rdf paramform = no P_description = ' ||
  '"' || upper(:description) || '"' || 'P_month = ' || '"' || :mthfull || '"');

END;

Tip

ord_det.rdf report is being saved in a directory named '*Student*' in Drive 'C'. Please specify a sub-directory and / or path in which the report was saved as a file appropriate to the computer being worked on.

Note

Values passed as user defined parameters to another report using RUN_REPORT function must be enclosed in double quotes. Thus double quote becomes a part of the string used to pass parameter values.

Example:
When running the report the Report runtime tool expects the report string as follows:

RUN_REPORT(c:\student\ord_det.rdf paramform=no
        P_description="FLOPPIES" P_month="May"

As seen in the above example, except for the values of user defined parameters the string then passed to the report runtime does not require any quotes. The user-defined parameter values must be enclosed in double quotes.

Use of quotes can be explained by using a set of variables and the syntax for assignment as follows:

Syntax Used for assignment	Contents of the variables
Var1 := 'c:\student\ord_det.rdf paramform=no P_description = ;	c:\student\ord_det.rdf paramform=no P_description =
Var2 := '"' /* double quote enclosed inside single quotes. */	" /* Output is a double quote */
Var3 := 'FLOPPIES '	FLOPPIES
Var4 := 'P_month='	P_month=
Var5 := '"'	" /* output is a double quote */
Var6 := 'May'	May
Var5 := '"'	" /* Output is a double quote */
Concatenation of all above variables	c:\student\ord_det.rdf paramform=no P_description="FLOPPIES" P_month="May"

Note

It is assumed that variables used in the above example are defined of type varchar2. *Any assignments to a varchar2 variable must be done using single quotes.*

Caution

Parameters passed to the reports is passed as parametername=value. **Note that there must be no spaces between the parametername, equal to operator and the value. If spaces are available it displays a runtime error.**

21. Compile the PL/SQL code by clicking on Compile push button and close the PL/SQL editor.

22. Save the report and click on **View..Runtime Previewer** to run the report. The runtime report is displayed as shown in diagram 16.7.

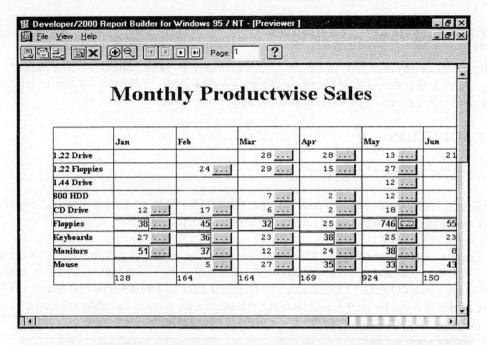

Diagram 16.7 : Productwise Monthly Sales report

23. Click on the button next to *Quantity* value for the month of May and product description as Floppies. The order details report is displayed as shown in diagram 16.8.

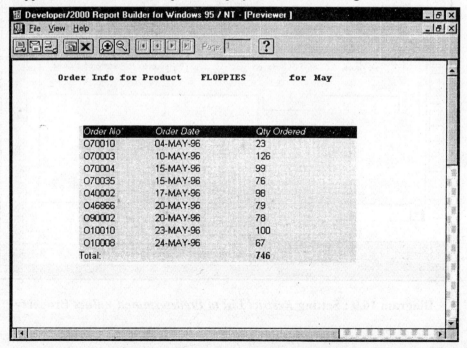

Diagram 16.8 : Order Details Report

FOCUS - VALIDATION TRIGGERS

In the report **ordbymo2.rdf**, make the User Parameter **P_year** editable. Using validation trigger check that the year entered by the user exists in the table (i.e. in the order date field) and stop execution of the report if the year is not found.

THE SOLUTION

1. Open the **ordbymo2.rdf** report.

2. Select User Parameter *P_year* in the Object Navigator. Select **Tools..Property Palette** to open the property palette for user parameter *p_year*.

3. Double click on the *List of Values* property in the property palette. The *Parameter List of Values* dialog box is displayed. This dialog box displays a check box with which can be checked / unchecked to **Restrict List to Predetermined Values**. This Checkbox must be unchecked to make the parameter *p_year* editable as shown in the diagram 16.9. Click on OK to accept the changes.

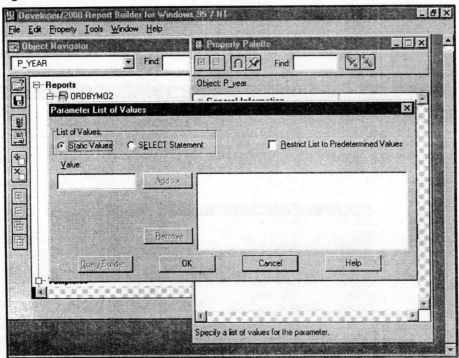

Diagram 16.9 : Setting *Restrict List to Predetermined Values* Property

4. The Property sheet for User Parameter *p_year* is displayed. Double click on *Validation Trigger* property to define a validation trigger. PL/SQL editor with defined Validation Trigger is as displayed in diagram 16.10.

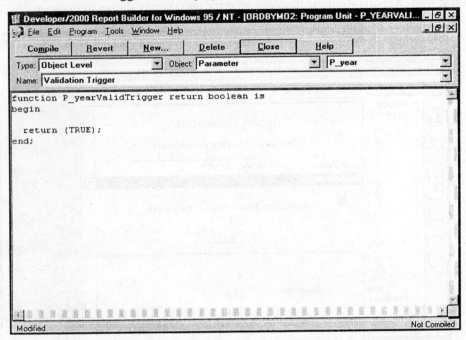

Diagram 16.10 : PL/SQL Editor displaying Validation Trigger

5. Write appropriate validation code to validate user parameter *p_year*.

FUNCTION P_yearValidTrigger **RETURN** boolean **IS**
      str_year Varchar2(4);
BEGIN
      / Check if data for the entered year is available in sales_order table. If available return a boolean value true which indicates normal report execution else display an error message and Terminate report execution. */*
      SELECT distinct to_char(s_order_date, 'yyyy')
          INTO str_year
          FROM sales_order
          WHERE to_char(s_order_date,'yyyy') = :P_year ;
      RETURN (TRUE);
EXCEPTION
      when no_data_found then
          / Message function in SRW package accepts two parameters. These are User defined error number and user defined error message */*
          SRW.message (0001,' There is no data for the year ' || :P_year || '.') ;
          RETURN (FALSE);
END;

6. Compile the code and close the PL/SQL Editor. Run the report. Since user parameter *p_year* is defined, a parameter form is displayed. Enter an invalid value in the *p_year* text item. Reports Runtime displays an error message as shown in diagram 16.11.

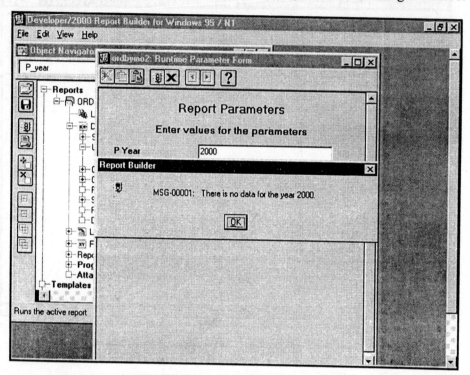

Diagram 16.11 : Validation Error Message Displayed at runtime

FOCUS - REPORT TRIGGERS

Create a simple tabular group report of *Productwise Sales Information* as shown in the diagram 16.12. Use report triggers to store the name of the user who executed the report, the date on which the report was executed.

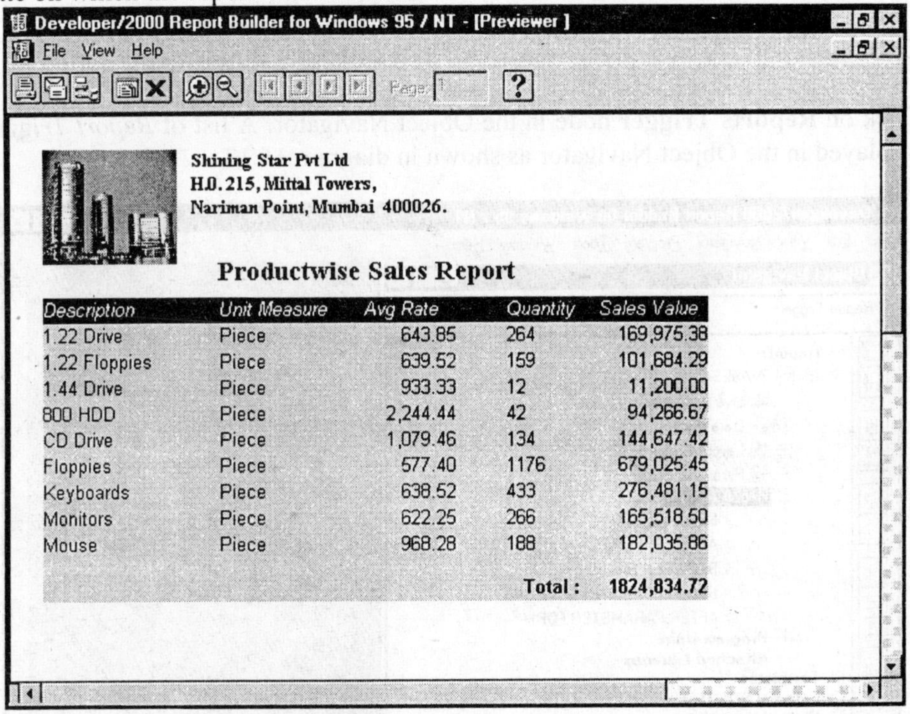

Description	Unit Measure	Avg Rate	Quantity	Sales Value
1.22 Drive	Piece	643.85	264	169,975.38
1.22 Floppies	Piece	639.52	159	101,684.29
1.44 Drive	Piece	933.33	12	11,200.00
800 HDD	Piece	2,244.44	42	94,266.67
CD Drive	Piece	1,079.46	134	144,647.42
Floppies	Piece	577.40	1176	679,025.45
Keyboards	Piece	638.52	433	276,481.15
Monitors	Piece	622.25	266	165,518.50
Mouse	Piece	968.28	188	182,035.86
			Total :	1824,834.72

Diagram 16.12 : Productwise Sales Report

THE SOLUTION

The steps in creating *Productwise Sales Report* with in-built auditing features are as follows:

1. Create a new table named *audit_psales* with the following definition.

Table Name : audit_psales
Description : Holds User Name and Report Execution Date if the produtwise sales report is executed.

Column Name	Data Type	Attributes
User_Name	Varchar2(40)	Name of the user who executes the reports
Report_Date	Date	Date of Report Execution

The syntax for creating the table will be:

> **CREATE TABLE** *audit_psales*
> *(user_name varchar2(40),*
> *report_date date);*

2. Open the report file named *pwisesales.rdf* in the Reports Builder tool.

3. Click on **Reports Trigger** node in the Object Navigator. A list of *Report Triggers* is displayed in the Object Navigator as shown in diagram 16.13.

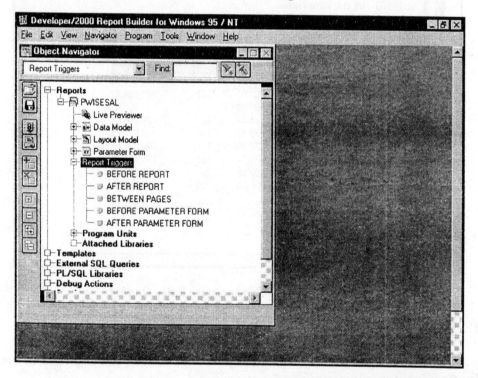

Diagram 16.13 : Report Triggers displayed in Object Navigator

4. Click on the icon next to the AFTER REPORT trigger. PL/SQL editor with defined AFTER REPORT trigger is displayed as shown in diagram 16.14.

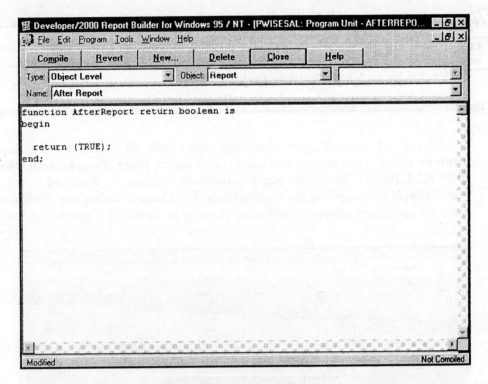

Diagram 16.14 : PL/SQL editor displaying AFTER REPORT trigger

5. Write appropriate PL/SQL code to retrieve the name of the user who has logged in. Insert the user name and the system date into the *audit_psales* table.

```
FUNCTION AfterReport RETURN boolean IS
    str_user Varchar(30);
BEGIN
    /*Get name of the user who has logged in. */
    SELECT user INTO str_user FROM dual ;

    /*Insert the data into the audit_psales table. */
    INSERT INTO audit_psales
        VALUES (str_user, sysdate) ;
    RETURN (TRUE) ;
END ;
```

6. Click on Compile to compile the AFTER REPORT trigger. Save the report by clicking on **File..Save**.

Tip

Report Triggers do not fire when the report is executed in Live Previewer Tool. Similarly, Report Triggers are also not executed if the report runtime is viewed by clicking on **View..Runtime Preview**.

7. To check if the report triggers work, the report must be executed using **Report Runtime** utility. Start reports runtime by clicking on **Start..Programs..Developer 2000 R2.0..Report Runtime**. Reports Runtime window is displayed. Click on **File..Connect** to connect to the required database. *Connect* dialog box is displayed. Enter the user name, password and connect string as shown in diagram 16.15. Click on OK.

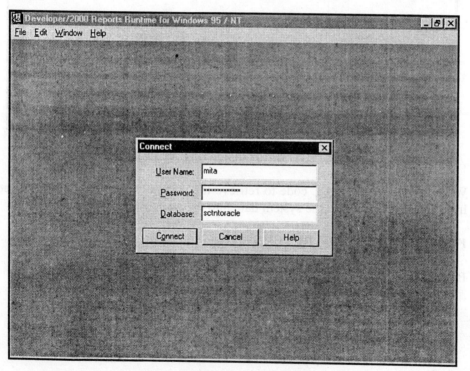

Diagram 16.15 : Report Runtime Tool

8. Click on **File..Run** to execute report *pwise_sales.rdf*. The *Open* dialog box is displayed. Choose the directory where report *pwise_sales.rdf* is saved. Reports Runtime tool allows execution of report definition file (filename.rdf) or runtime file (filename.rep). Since the runtime file used for deploying the software is not created, the report can be run using the .RDF file. To do so select *Type of File* as **Report Definition(*.RDF)**. A list of .RDF files will be displayed. Select *pwise_sales.rdf* file. The completed *Open* dialog is displayed in diagram 16.16.

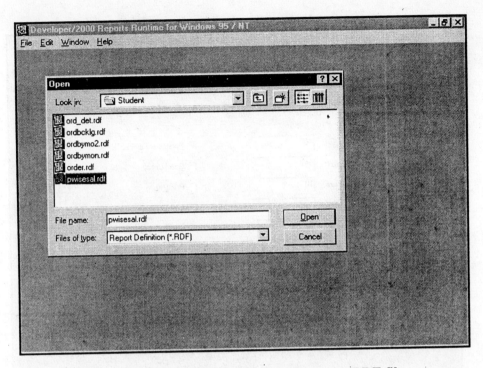

Diagram 16.16 : Open dialog box to open the RDF file

9. Click on Open. The Report Runtime window will be displayed. Start the SQL*Plus utility and execute a global select on table *audit_psales*. No records are displayed in SQL*Plus. Close the report. Since an AFTER REPORT trigger is written to insert data into the table, if the same select statement is executed again, the output will be:

```
USER_NAME            REPORT_DA
--------------------  ------------------
MITA                 22-FEB-99
```

Tip

The AFTER REPORT trigger does not include any commit statement, yet data is inserted into the table and can be viewed by another session i.e. SQL*Plus session. This functionality is achieved since the Report Runtime Settings are set by default as follows:.

On Success : Commit
On Failure : Rollback

The Report Runtime Settings can be viewed by clicking on **Tools..Preferences** and selecting **Runtime Settings** tab in the Report Builder tool. The Runtime Setting screen is displayed as shown in diagram 16.17.

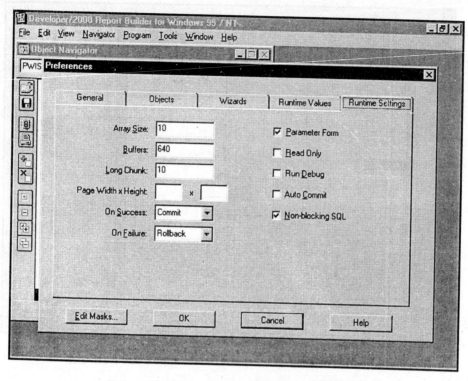

Diagram 16.17 : Report Runtime Settings

FOCUS - REPORT TRIGGERS

The *Productwise Sales Report* currently displays information on all products. Provide a parameter named *p_cutoff_cnt* as shown in diagram 16.18. The number of records displayed on the report must not be more than the value entered in the *p_cutoff_cnt* as shown in diagram 16.18. If no value is entered in *p_cutoff_cnt*, the entire product listing must be displayed. The records must be displayed in the descending order of *qty_ordered*.

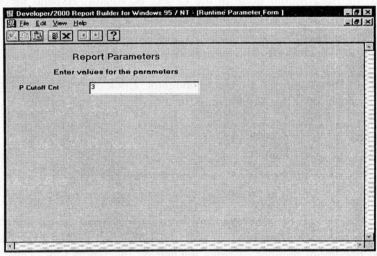

Diagram 16.18 : Parameter Form for the Productwise Sales Report

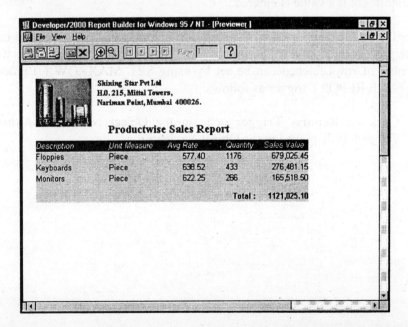

Diagram 16.19 : Productwise Sales Report displayed with Filtered Data

THE SOLUTION

1. Open the *Productwise Sales Report* (pwise_sales.rdf file) in Report Builder.

2. Since the data must be in the *descending* order i.e. highest to the lowest value of *qty_ordered*, an order by clause must be added to the query used in the report.

    Expand the Data Model node in the Object Navigator. Expand the Queries node. Query *Q_psales* is displayed. Change the ORDER BY clause in *Q_psales* as follows:

    ORDER BY Sum(qty_ordered) DESC

3. Select User Parameter in the Object Navigator. Click on **Navigator..Create** to create a new parameter. Set the properties of the user Parameter as follows:

Name	: p_cutoff_cnt
Data Type	: Number
Width	: 3
Initial Value	: 3

4. The number of records displayed on the report is based on the number of records fetched by the query. Reports tool provides a function named SET_MAXROW that sets the maximum number of rows fetched by the report tool. Thus PL/SQL code must be written that to set the maximum rows fetched to the contents of parameter p_cutoff_cnt if a value is entered.

    The PL/SQL code in such a case must fire before executing the report query. Report Query is executed after triggering the BEFORE REPORT trigger. Thus the maximum number of rows fetched can be set by using SET_MAXROW ( ) procedure in the BEFORE REPORT trigger as follows:

    a) Click on **Reports Trigger** node in the Object Navigator. A list of *Report Triggers* is displayed in the Object Navigator.

b) Click on the icon next to the BEFORE REPORT trigger. PL/SQL editor with defined AFTER REPORT trigger is displayed as shown in diagram 16.20.

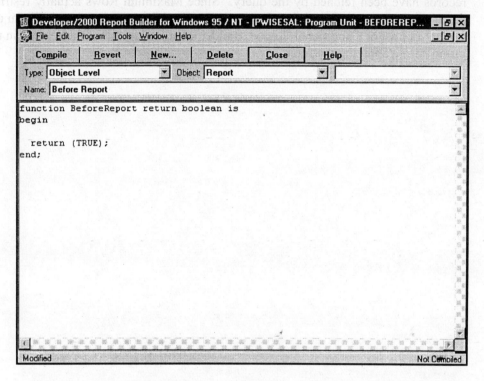

Diagram 16.20 : PL/SQL editor displaying BEFORE REPORT trigger

c) Write appropriate PL/SQL code to set the number of records fetched by the report tools.

```
FUNCTION BeforeReport RETURN boolean IS
BEGIN
        if :p_cutoff_cnt is not null then
                /* Set maximum rows fetched for a specific query */
                srw.set_maxrow ('Q_psales', :p_cutoff_cnt);
        end if;
        RETURN (TRUE);
END;
```

The Maximum Rows property restricts the actual number of records fetched by the query. A group filter determines which records to include or exclude, after all the records have been fetched by the query. Since Maximum Rows actually restricts the amount of data retrieved, it is faster than a group filter in most cases. If you use a Filter of Last or Conditional, Report Builder must retrieve all of the records in the group before applying the filter.

SELF REVIEW QUESTIONS

TRUE AND FALSE

1. Oracle Reports has five Global Report Triggers.

    A) True   B) False

2. Between Page Report fires for every report page.

    A) True   B) False

3. Report parameters passing using run_report( ) procedures are enclosed in single quotes.

FILL IN THE BLANKS

1. _____ are PL/SQL functions that populate columns of type *Formula*.

2. _____ are PL/SQL functions executed before the object is formatted.

3. If the return value for the trigger used for formatting is _____, the value is not displayed in the report.

4. _____ are PL/SQL procedures executed when a button is selected.

5. _____ reports are implemented using action triggers.

6. _____ are PL/SQL functions are used to verify the contents of the parameters.

7. _____ fires before the Runtime Parameter Form is displayed.

8. _____ fires before each page of the report is formatted.

9. Data can be filtered by the reports tool using _____.

10. _____ package includes a number of functions are procedures used that call be executed by reports tool.

11. _____ function is used to display error messages in reports.

12. _____ function is used to restrict the number of records fetched by reports tool.

Types of Report Triggers
- *Before Parameter Form*
- *After Parameter Form*
- *Before Report*
- *Between Pages*
- *After Report*
- *Controlling Number of records retrieved for a report*
- *Report Audit Trail*

Format Triggers
- *Using Format Trigger to Format Report Fields conditionally*

Action Triggers
- *Drill Down Reports*

Validation Triggers
- *Validating User Parameters*

Group Filter Triggers

CHAPTER SEVENTEEN

Working with Graphs

IN THIS CHAPTER

➤ Creating a Display Module

➤ Graph Presentation Styles

➤ Chart Template

➤ Passing Parameters to a Display Module

➤ Calling Display Module from Forms

➤ OG.PLL PL/SQL Library

17. WORKING WITH GRAPHS

INTRODUCTION

Corporations today are flooded with valuable information. The challenge is to interpret this flood of information in a format, which is easily understood.

A graph is a form of information representation, which can visually display a lot of information in a compact form. A graph is a mechanism that allows organization staff to visually analyze information on-line. Using graphs data can be retrieved from a variety of sources and displayed, using charts, line drawing, bit-mapped images etc. An example of the use of a graph for sales report is as shown in the diagram 17.1.

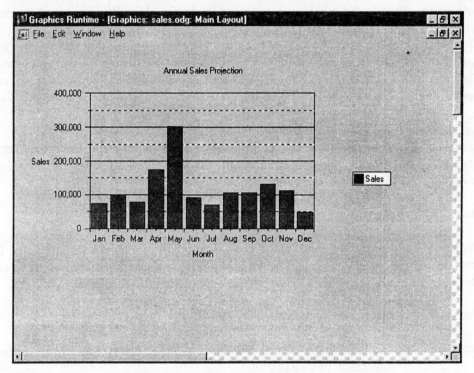

Diagram 17.1 : Annual Sales Graph

Working with Charts:

Graphs comprise of the following components:
- Displays
- Layout
- Queries
- Chart Properties
- Templates

Display:
The primary object of *Graphics Builder* is the *Display*. A display module is nothing but a collection of objects such as *Layout, Template, Queries* and *Triggers*.

Layout:
The Layout editor is the main work area in Oracle Graphics Builder. It is where the layout of a display is designed, by creating and modifying graphical objects (lines, polygons, rectangles, text, etc.). Every display contains exactly one layout, and every layout belongs to exactly one display. The contents of the layout are shown when the *Display* is executed. The information presented can be viewed or the display can be manipulated by using a mouse or keyboard.

Queries:
Query is a SQL SELECT statement or file that Oracle Graphics needs in order to retrieve data for a chart. A chart can be associated with only one query at a time. When a chart is drawn, the data from the current query is used.

Chart Properties:

Chart properties define options for the chart as a whole, including its associated chart template and query. Chart properties are accessible through the **Chart property sheet**, which is a multi tab page object. The tab pages are organized as follows:

Chart   : Includes the chart's *Name, Title, Chart Type* and *Template*.

Data   : Includes query related properties such as a *Query Filter Function* and the range of data to plot.

Categories   : Includes the chart categories and any sub-categories to plot in the chart. Category (independent) data is plotted at fixed intervals. Category data is not considered to be mathematically related and is usually plotted along what is called the *Discrete* axis (i. e. X axis).

Values   : Includes the chart values. Value dependent data generally starts at one value and continues until another value. Value data is considered to be mathematically related and is usually plotted along what is called the *Continuous* axis (i. e. Y axis).

PL/SQL   : Includes any mouse events and associated procedures for the chart.

Chart Types:

The following list describes the types of charts available that can be created along with their usage:

Column

Column Charts type is used to compare sets of data ranges vertically. For example, a Column Chart can be used to show the quarterly sales revenue generated by each sales representative.

Bar

Bar Chart type is used to compare sets of data ranges horizontally. For example, a bar chart can be used to compare monthly sales.

Line

Line chart type is used to show vertical changes for a specific set of data. For example, a line chart can be used to gauge daily or weekly changes in a stock's value.

Mixed

Mixed chart combines multiple plot types such as column and line. For example, a mixed chart can be used to show daily sales revenue, with a line plot type to provide a summary view of the data.

Double-Y

Double Y chart type provides two independent Y-axes on which to plot data. Each Y-axis can show a different range of values. For example, one axis can be used to represent revenue and the second axis can be used to represent income, for a specific month or year.

Pie

Pie Charts type is used to compare the ratios or percentages of parts of a whole. For example, a pie chart can be used to compare annual revenue by department or quarter.

Table

Table Chart type is used to show data in a table format. For example, a table chart can be used to show an Employee Organization Chart.

Scatter

Scatter chart type is used to show data along two-value axis. Scatter charts are well suited for showing standard deviation. For example, a scatter chart can be used to plot the target and the actual sales for each salesmen. If there is a correlation between the two sets of data, the points will be grouped together closely. One or more points well outside the group could indicate a disparity.

High-low

HighLow chart type is used to show fields that correspond to high, low, and close (i.e. stock prices). For each row in a query, a high-low range is plotted on the chart.

Gantt

Gantt chart type is used to show sets of project data over a given amount of time. Gantt charts are generally used to show project milestone timelines.

Chart Templates:

Template is the format of a chart and its properties. A chart can be associated with only one chart template at a time. Each chart template can be associated with one or more field templates, which define the properties of the individual fields, such as bars, columns, pie slices, or lines.

Using a single chart template, multiple charts with the same set of basic characteristics such as grid line settings or tick label rotation etc. can be created. For example, instead of specifying the properties for each chart individually, a single chart template can be created and associated it with multiple queries. The *Chart Template* Editor is used to work with chart templates.

USING GRAPHICS BUILDER

Tools Available with the Graphics Builder:

The tools available with the Graphics Builder must be looked at before attempting to create a chart so that chart creation is made simpler. These are:

1. Object Navigator
2. Layout Editor
3. PL/SQL editor

Object Navigator:
Queries and templates are constituent parts of a Display. The Object Navigator allows navigation through the hierarchy of objects.

Layout Editor:
The developed charts will be displayed in the layout editor. The sizing, positioning and alignment of the chart objects on the screen are done through this tool.

PL/SQL Editor:
More often than not, there is a need to perform tasks, which are specific to an application. Such tasks can be handled by writing code to customize application processing and to meet these specific requirements. The *PL/SQL* Editor gives an interface to define code blocks called *Trigger Code* for appropriate trigger events.

CREATING A GRAPH

Focus:

To design a simple Line graph for sales order transactions. The Graph must display the gross earning for the year grouped by month.

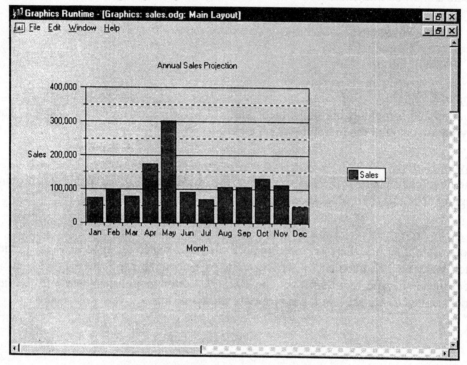

Diagram 17.2 : Annual Sales Graph

The table definitions are as follows:

Table Name : sales_order (Master)
Description : Use to store information about orders placed by the clients.

Column Name	Data Type	Size	Attributes
s_order_no	varchar2	6	Unique primary key allotted to each order.
s_order_date	date		Date on which the order is placed.
client_no	varchar2	6	Client No., who places the order.
status	varchar2	2	In Process - IP, Not Processed - NP and Fully Processed - FP,)

Table Name : sales_order_details
Description : Use to store information about order details.

Column Name	Data Type	Size	Attributes
s_order_no	varchar2	6	Order No. for which details have to be stored.
product_no	varchar2	6	Product No. for which details have to be stored.
product_rate	number	8,2	The rate agreed upon.
qty_ordered	number	8	Quantity of goods ordered.

The Solution:

1. Invoke *Oracle Graphics Builder* Tool. When the *Graphics Builder* Tool is invoked, a new *display* with a default name *disp1* is created and opened in the Object Navigator window as shown in the diagram 17.3.

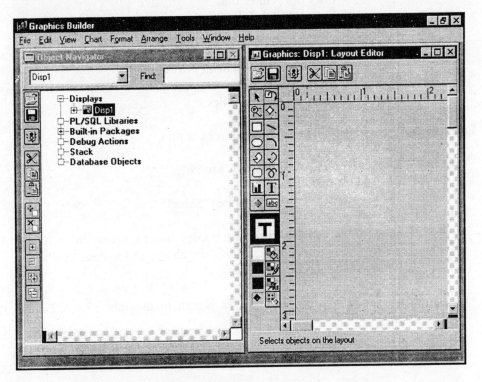

Diagram 17.3 : New Display opened in the Graphics Designer

2. Connect to the database by clicking on **File** and **Connect**.

Creating a Query for the Graph:

1. From the Menu bar select **Chart..Create Chart....** Since a graph is created using a query, a *Chart Genie – New Query* dialog box is displayed

    This dialog box includes two tab pages i.e. **Query** and **Data**. The Query tab includes query properties like Query Name, Query Type.

    Query Name   : The default name given to the newly created query is *query0*.

    Query Type   : The Query Type property determines the data source for a graph. Different options available for the Query Type are:
    *   SQL Statement
    *   SYLK File or a WKS File – These are spreadsheet file formats.
    *   PRN is a printer file.
    *   External SQL File

    The default Query Type is SQL Statement and thus an edit box to enter the SQL statement is available.

2. Change the name of the query object to q_sales.

3. Enter the SQL Statement in the **SQL Statement** option.

    ```
    SELECT to_char(s_order_date, 'Mon') "Month",
           to_char(s_order_date, 'mm'),
           sum(qty_ordered * product_rate) "Sales"
    FROM sales_order, sales_order_details
    WHERE sales_order_details.s_order_no = sales_order.s_order_no
    GROUP BY to_char(s_order_date, 'Mon'), to_char(s_order_date, 'mm')
    ORDER BY to_char(s_order_date, 'mm')
    ```

    The completed screen will be displayed as shown in diagram 17.4. Click on the **Execute** button.

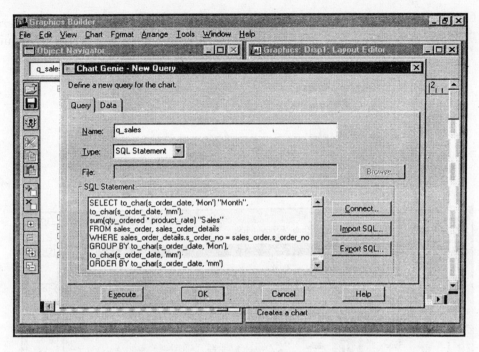

Diagram 17.4 : Query Properties screen

2. A screen comes up displaying the data that resulted from the execution of the select statement as shown in diagram 17.5. Click on the OK button to accept the query.

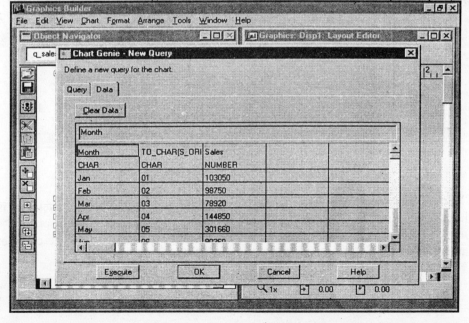

Diagram 17.5 : Data screen in the query properties window

4. Check the data. If the displayed data is correct click on OK. A *Chart Properties* dialog box is displayed. Enter the *Name, Title* for the chart and select the required *Type Of Graph* and its *Subtype* as shown in diagram 17.6.

> Name   : ch_sales
> Title   : Annual Sales Projection
> Type   :
>
> Sub Type   :

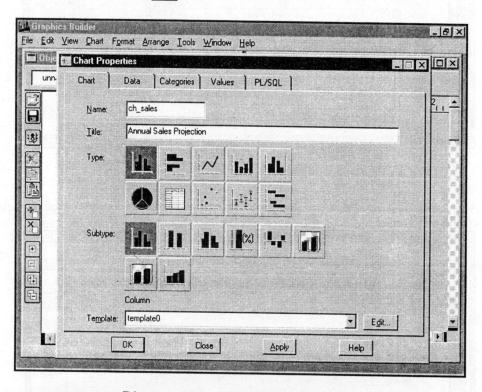

Diagram 17.6 : Chart Properties Screen

3. Click on the **Categories** tab. Since the first column in the SQL statement is a character column, the "Month" column is selected by default. The Insert and the Delete buttons can be used to change the columns for the categories. The completed categories screen will be as shown in diagram 17.7

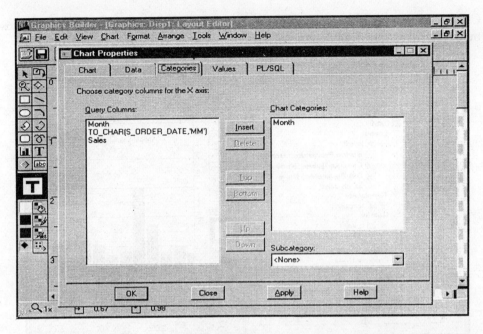

Diagram 17.7 : Specifying the column for the Categories Axis

4. Click on **Values** tab. The first numeric column is selected by default. The first numeric column in the current example is "Sales". The completed screen for the Values axis is as shown in diagram 17.8.

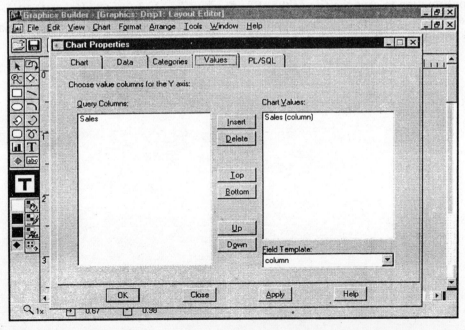

Diagram 17.8 : Specifying the column for Values Axis

5. Click on **Apply** and then OK button to accept the values. The completed graph will be displayed as shown in diagram 17.9.

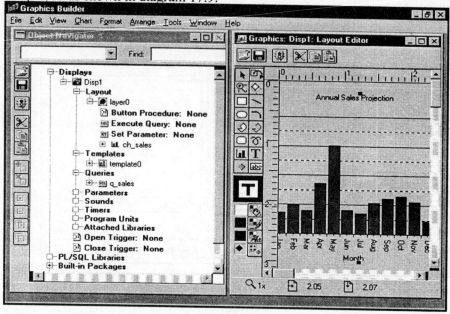

Diagram 17.9 : Graph displayed in the Layout Editor

6. Click on **File..Save**. A display can be saved in the database or as a file. Thus, a confirmation to save the file as the 'File System' is asked for. Click on OK. *Save As* dialog box is displayed. Select appropriate drive and directory and enter the file name as **sales.odg** as shown in diagram 17.10.

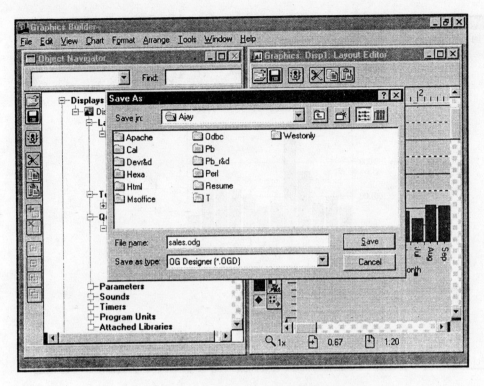

Diagram 17.10 : Save As dialog box

7. Click on **File..Run** to execute the display. The layout editor will be replaced with the Graphics Debugger window. As seen in diagram 17.11, the values displayed for the Categories axis are displayed vertically. Click on **File..Exit Runtime** to return to the layout editor.

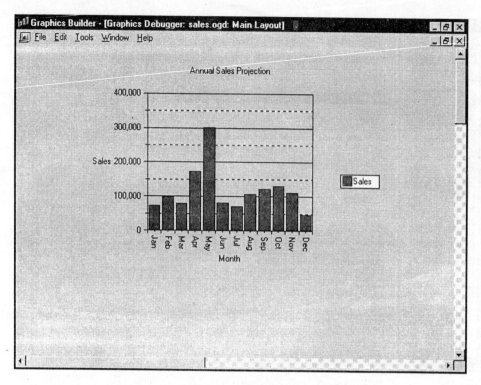

Diagram 17.11 : Chart Displayed at Runtime

To change to horizontal display, double click on the Category values in the layout editor. The *Axis Properties* dialog box is displayed.

Change the **Tick Label Rotation** property to horizontal by clicking on the appropriate radio button.

5. Save and run the graph. Click on the maximize button and resize the graph. The graph runtime output will be displayed.

PASSING PARAMETERS IN ORACLE GRAPHICS

The graph created so far is static. It does not have the ability to accept values and display a graph accordingly. To make graphs dynamic, it would be essential to define parameters that accept input values and pass the values to the graph .

Focus:
Create an Annual Sales Report, which will accept Year as a parameter.

Using the *Annual Sales* graph created in the first exercise, a demonstration on defining a parameter field, which will accept a value for year at runtime, will be given.

1. Open the *Annual Sales* graph and click on the **Parameters** node in the Object Navigator. A default parameter by the name *Param0* will be displayed along with the property sheet as shown in diagram 17.12.

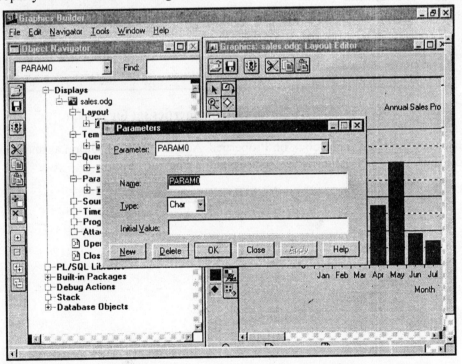

Diagram 17.12 : Creating a New Parameter

2. Enter the *Parameter Name* as *P_year* and *Data Type* as *Char* and Click on **OK**. The completed screen will be as shown in diagram 17.13.

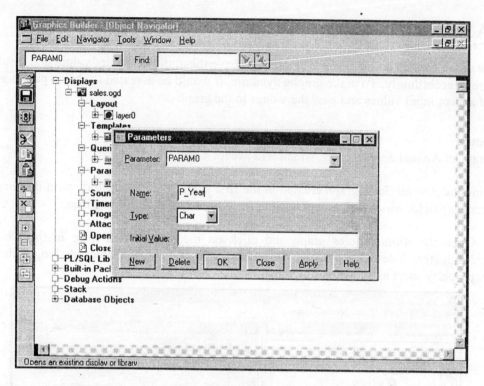

Diagram 17.13 : Parameters Properties set for p_year

3. Right click *Q_Sales* and click on Properties. Add WHERE condition as shown in the diagram 17.14.

    and to_char(s_order_date , 'yyyy') = :p_year

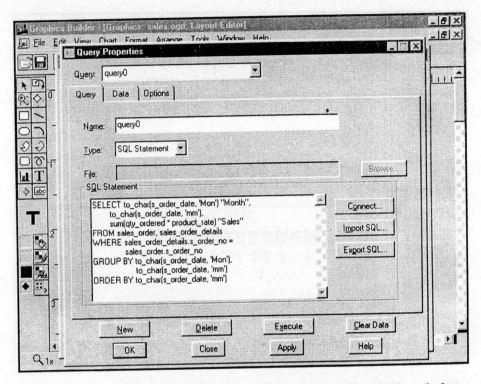

Diagram 17.14 : Adding WHERE clause in the Query Properties window

4. The Oracle Graphics tool does not have its own parameter form. Thus, there is a need to create a form that accepts the parameter value and displays the chart. The forms tool must then call the Oracle Graphics runtime file and display the same in the chart item.

    To create an Oracle Graphics Runtime file click on **File..Administration..Generate**. Oracle Graphics runtime can be stored in a database or it can be stored as a file. To create a runtime file click on **File System** from the popup menu. The Save As dailog box with the Oracle Graphics Runtime file is displayed as shown in diagram 17.15. Click on **Save**.

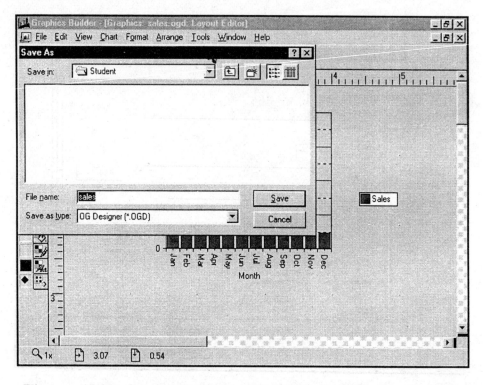

Diagram 17.15 : Creating and Saving an Oracle Graphics Runtime file

Creating a form that accepts parameters and displays the graph based on parameters entered:

1. Create a new form **Chart**. Since the form is used to accept parameters, a block that is not connected to the table must be created. Create a control block named *Chart_Display*.

2. Right click on the block and select *Layout Editor*. Create a text item with the following properties :

Name	: Year
Data Type	: Char
Maximum Length	: 4
Database Item	: No
Prompt	: Year :

3. Place a button item with the following properties.

Name	: pb_Graphopen
Label	: Graph Open

4. Click on the **chart tool** 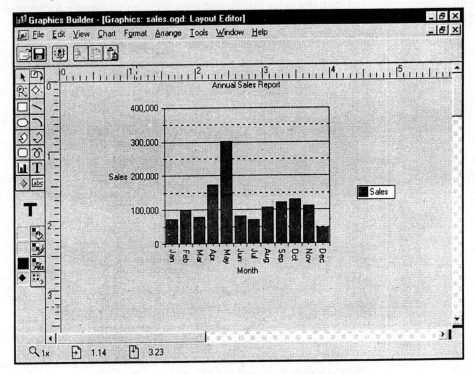 icon and place it on the *Layout* Editor. A *New Chart Object* dialog box asking confirmation to invoke the chart wizard is shown. The chart wizard allows creation of a graph from a data block. Since the graph is already created, select *Build a New Chart Manually* and click on OK.

5. A new chart item is created on the form. Resize the chart item and set the following chart item properties.

    Name   : ch_sales
    File Name   : C:\student\ch_sales.ogr

    The completed layout editor will be as shown in diagram 17.16.

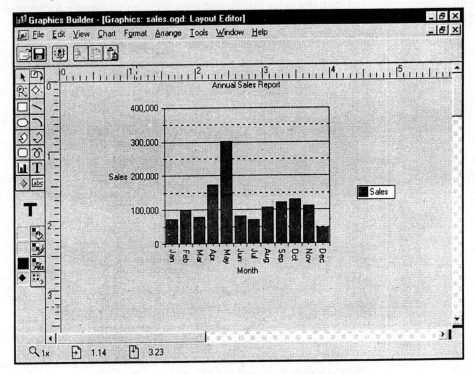

Diagram 17.16 : Layout Editor with a chart tool

6. Create a LOV **Year_LOV** and attach it to the text item **Year**. The select statement for the LOV is as given below.

    select distinct to_char(s_order_date, 'yyyy') into :year from sales_order ;

7. The functions required to call a graph is included in a library named OG.PLL under \orawin95\tools\devdemo20\demo\forms directory. Thus, this library must be attached to the form being created before writing the PL/SQL code to pass parameters to the grap1 and invoke the graph.

Open Object Navigator tool. Click on *Attached libraries* node in the form being created. The *Attach Library* dialog box is displayed. Specify the name of the library as **og.pll** and click on **Attach**. In the command button **Graph_Open**, enter the following PL/SQL code.

Trigger Name	: **WHEN-BUTTON-PRESSED**	Form	: chart
Block	: chart_display	Item	: pb_graphopen
Function	: Open the sales Graph and pass the year parameter to the same.		
Text	: DECLARE		

```
DECLARE
        parmlist   ParamList;
BEGIN
        /* Create a parameter list for data passing */
        parmlist := Create_Parameter_List('plist');


        /* Add a parameter to the parameter list to
        specify the relationship between the named query
        'query0' in the Oracle Graphics display and the named
        record group in the form, 'chart_data'. */

        if not id_null(parmlist) then
                add_parameter(parmlist, 'p_year',
                        text_parameter, :year);

                /* Invoke Oracle Graphics to create the chart */
                og.open('c:\student\sales', 'ch_sales',
                        false, true, parmlist);

        /*Get rid of the parameter list and close the connection with
        the Oracle Graphics file. */

                destroy_parameter_list(parmlist);
                og.close('c:\student\sales', 'ch_sales');
        end if;
END;
```

The runtime screen will be as shown in diagram 17.17.

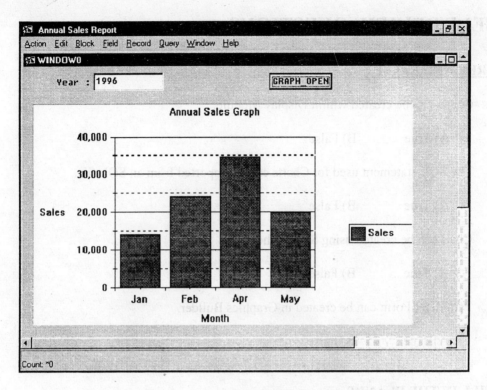

Diagram 17.17 : Oracle Graph displayed at Run Time

SELF REVIEW QUESTIONS

TRUE AND FALSE

1. Charts can be created within Display Module.

    A) True   B) False

2. The SQL statement used for Charts can be imported from an SQL file.

    A) True   B) False

3. Chart can be created using Spread sheet files

    A) True   B) False

4. Parameter Form can be created in Graphics Builder.

    A) True   B) False

FILL IN THE BLANKS

1. X-Axis is also called _____ Axes in Graphics Builder.

2. Y-Axis is also called _____ Axes in Graphics Builder.

3. Graphs can be displayed in a form using _____ form item.

4. Graph can be displayed on the form using _____ function in the _____ PL/SQL library.

A QUICK REVIEW

APPENDIX A

ANSWERS TO SELF REVIEW QUESTIONS

1. Working with Forms

<u>True or False</u>

1. True
2. False
3. True
4. False
5. False
6. True

<u>Fill in the Blanks</u>

1. **G**raphical **U**ser **I**nterface
2. Display
3. PL/SQL
4. Status bar
5.
    - Full Compilation
    - Incremental Compilation
    - Selective Compilation

<u>Pick the Right Option</u>

1. The same
2. None of the above

2. Master Form

<u>True or False</u>

1. True

2. False

3. True

4. True

5. True

6. False

7. False

8. True

9. False

10. True

<u>Fill in the Blanks</u>

1.
   - Tables / View
   - Stored Procedures

2.
   - Form
   - Tabular
   - Form

3. When-New-Record-Instance

4.
- Hint
- Auto Hint

5. Balloon Help

6. Required

7. Initial Value

8. Raise Form_Trigger_Failure

9. Set_Window_Property ( )

10. FORMS_MDI_WINDOW

11. Window_State

12.
- QUERY
- NEW
- CHANGED

13. Default&Smartbar

14.
- Error_Code
- Error_Type
- Error_Text

15. Multiple Document Interface

3. Property Classes and Visual Attributes

<u>True or False</u>

1. False

2. False

3. True

4. True

5. False

6. True

7. False

<u>Fill in the Blanks</u>

1.
    - Aesthetic
    - Functional

2. Inheritance

3. Property Class

4. Add Property

5. Class

6.
    - Iconic
    - Icon Name

7. Tk25_Icon

8. Visual Attribute Name

9.
- Default
- Custom
- Named Visual Attribute

10. Current_Record_Attribute

4. PL/SQL Libraries and Alerts

<u>True or False</u>

1. False

2. False

3. False

<u>Fill in the Blanks</u>

1. Show_Alert( )

2. PL/SQL Library

3. Attached Libraries

4. Name_In ( )

5.
- Get_Block_Property
- First_Item

6.
- Stop
- Caution
- Note

Pick the Right Option

1. Alert_Button1, Alert_Button2, ...

2. is not included in the alert

5. Object Libraries

True or False

1. True

2. False

3. False

Fill in the Blanks

1. Object Library

2. Forms

3. Library Tabs

4. Drag and Drop

5.
   - Subclassed
   - Copied

6. FORMS50_PATH

6. The Master Detail Form

<u>True or False</u>

1. False

2. False

3. False

4. True

5. True

6. True

7. True

8. False

<u>Fill in the Blanks</u>

1. Relation

2. Validate from List

3. Cascading

4. Record_Status

5. Non Isolated

6.
   - LOV
   - Record Group

7.
- pre-insert
- on-insert
- post-insert

8.
- Master Deletes
- Non Isolated
- Isolated
- Cascading

9.
- Automatic Query
- Deferred Query

10. Master

11. Auto Join

12. Copy Value From

13. Item Type

Pick the Right Option

1. CHANGED, NEW, QUERY

2. NEW, INSERT, CHANGED, QUERY

7. Using Multiple Canvases

Fill in the Blanks

1. Stacked

2. Show_View ( )

3. Hide_View ( )

4. Content

5.
- Stacked
- Content
- Tab

6. Label

7. Initial Value

8. Radio Groups

9. Radio

10.
- Label
- Value

8. Using Tab Canvas

<u>True or False</u>

1. True

2. True

<u>Fill in the Blanks</u>

1. Tab

2. New Tab Page

3. List Item

4.
- Data Value
- Display Value

5.
- PopList
- ComboList
- Tlist

6. List Element

7. Record Group

8. Create_Group_From_Query ( )

9. Populate_Group( )

10. Populate_List ( )

11. Object Id

12. Id_Null

13. When-List-Changed

14.
- None
- Formula
- Summary

15. Formula

16.
- Summary Function
- Summary Item
- Summary Block

17. Number of Items Displayed

18. Query All

19. Get_Application_Property ( )

20. Validation

21. Editors

22. Forms50_Editor

23. Mouse Navigable

9. Interlinking related forms and Passing Parameters between forms

True or False

1. False

2. False

3. True

Fill in the Blanks

1.
   - Document
   - Dialog

2. Parent

3. Child

4. Parameter List

5. Id_Null

6.
   - Char
   - 255

7. No_Hide

8. Query_Only

9.
- Data Mode
- Share_Library_Data

10.
- Parameter Name
- Parameter Type
- Parameter Value

11. Default_Where

12. Two

13. When-Create-Record

Pick the Right Option

14. be same

15. :parameter.parametername

10. User Defined Search Form

True or False

1. False

2. True

3. True

Fill in the Blanks

1. Two

2.
- Char
- 255

3. Get_List_Element_Label ( )

4. Get_List_Element_Value ( )

5. Get_List_Element_Count( )

<u>Pick the Right Option</u>

1. a window named window0.

2. Call_form ( ) procedure with parameter value set to NO_HIDE.

11. Working with Menus

<u>True or False</u>

1. False

2. True

<u>Fill in the Blanks</u>

1. Menu Module

2. Set_Menu_Item_Property ( )

3.
    - MMB
    - MMX

4. Menu Bar Items

5. Sub Menu Items

6. Menu Item Type

7.
    - Icon Name
    - Display in Horizontal Toolbar

12. **Working with Reports**

<u>True or False</u>

1. True

2. False

<u>Fill in the Blanks</u>

1. RDF

2. REP

3. Once

4. &Current Date

5. Repeating Frames

6. Data Model

7. Summary Columns

8.
   - Formula Columns
   - Summary Columns

9.
   - Data Model
   - Layout
   - Parameter Form
   - Live Previewer

10.
   - System
   - User

11. Frames

13. Creating Break Report

<u>Fill in the Blanks</u>

1. Break

2.
   - Group Left
   - Group Above

3. Two

14. Master / Detail Report

<u>True or False</u>

1. True

2. True

3. True

4. False

<u>Fill in the Blanks</u>

1. Data Link

2. Parent

3. Child

4. Outer

5. Group Above

6.
   - Where
   - Equal to Operator

7.
- Static Values
- Values from a Select Statement

15. Creating A Matrix Report

True or False

1. True

2. True

3. False

Fill in the Blanks

1.
- Dimension Groups
- Cross Product Groups
- Filler Groups

2. Line

3. Cross Product Group

4.
- Row
- Column

5. Cell

16. Using PL/SQL in Reports

True or False

1. True

2. False

3. False

Fill in the Blanks

1. Formula Triggers

2. Format Triggers

3. False

4. Action Triggers

5. Drill Down Reports

6. Validation Triggers

7. Before Parameter Form Trigger

8. Between Page

9. Group Filter Trigger

10. SRW

11. Message ( )

12. Set_Maxrow ( )

17. Working with Graphs

True or False

1. True

2. True

3. True

4. False

<u>Fill in the Blanks</u>

1. Categories

2. Values

3. Chart

4.
   - Open
   - OG.PLL

INDEX

G